DECISION
OVER
SCHWEINFURT

Also by Thomas M. Coffey

AGONY AT EASTER
IMPERIAL TRAGEDY
LION BY THE TAIL
THE LONG THIRST

Thomas M. Coffey

DECISION OVER SCHWEINFURT

The U.S. 8th Air Force Battle
for
Daylight Bombing

David McKay Company, Inc.
New York

Library of Congress Cataloging in Publication Data

Coffey, Thomas M
  Decision over Schweinfurt.

  Bibliography: p.
  Includes index.
  1. Schweinfurt, Germany—Bombardment, 1943.
2. World War, 1939-1945—Aerial operations, American.
3. United States. Air Force. 8th Air Force. I. Title.
D757.9.S35C63   940.54'49'73   77-1278
ISBN 0-679-50763-9

10 9 8 7 6 5 4 3 2 1
Manufactured in the United States of America

Introduction

When the United States entered World War II in December, 1941, the nation's strategic air power amounted to little more than an unproven concept in the minds of a small group of Army Air Forces officers. They had at their disposal only about 50 heavy bombers that they could certify as battle-worthy, and even these would need modifications before they were actually ready to face the experienced German fighter pilots awaiting them in the skies over Europe.

The most advanced American heavy bomber, the Boeing B-17—known as the Flying Fortress—had been in production since 1935. But a shortage of funds, and other limitations placed upon its development, had prevented the B-17 from approaching its potential as a weapon. Indeed, the British, after trying it out against the Germans, had pronounced it woefully inadequate. This was the plane on which American Air Force strategists depended to prove the validity of their concept of aerial warfare. It was the plane on which they had to depend because there was no other. The newer North American B-24 Liberator was even less advanced in its development.

While the worth of America's best bomber was questionable in December, 1941, the worth of the American Air Forces's strategic concept was considerably more so. The Americans, having equipped the B-17 with as many as ten 50-caliber machine guns, plus the new and remarkably accurate Norden bomb sight, intended to attack precisely defined German military and industrial targets in broad daylight. The British, who had defeated German attempts to bomb England in daylight, and who had failed in their own daylight missions against the continent, were appalled at the American intention to try the same strategy. But they had been unable to persuade the Americans to follow their example and prepare for night bombing of German cities.

The A.A.F. and the R.A.F. were at an impasse over this critically important question of strategy when, on February 22, 1942, Brig. Gen. Ira C. Eaker arrived in England with a pathetically small staff of six to launch the newly created 8th Air Force Bomber Command. Eighteen months later, on August 17, 1943, the question was still undecided when Eaker sent his B-17s to attack the vital German ball-bearing plants at Schweinfurt in what was then the largest operation ever attempted by the American Army Air Forces.

The August 17 mission against Schweinfurt and Regensburg produced what is considered even today one of the two most savage air battles of all time, the second being the October 14, 1943, mission against Schweinfurt, just two months later.

Decision over Schweinfurt is the story of those two crucial missions and the men on both sides who faced each other in those epic battles. But equally important, the book is the story of the birth and growth of the 8th Air Force. It describes day by day the lives and deaths of the men who flew the Fortresses. At the same time, it traces—through hundreds of hitherto unpublished documents—the struggles at command level to maintain and vindicate the American Air Forces's strategic concept at a time when it was under severe attack by such powerful Britons as Prime Minister Winston Churchill and his air advisors and by such influential Americans as the entire Navy high command and many high Army generals. The Schweinfurt missions of August and October, 1943, were climactic chapters in this Air Force struggle for acceptance of its strategy. They were also, without doubt, the most protracted and exciting aerial battles of all time.

The author's two-year task of compiling material for this story leaves him indebted to many people and institutions in England,

Germany, and the United States. Especially helpful were the scores of people who took part in the events the book describes, and who patiently submitted to long interview sessions reviewing those events. The author extends his deep appreciation to the following:

In England: J. H. Adams, Mrs. Joan Billett, Quentin Bland, Mr. and Mrs. Harry Chenery, Squadron Leader Edwin R. Cuff, Ret., Jeffrey Ede, Norman Evans, Dr. Noble Frankland, Roger Freeman, Marshal of the Royal Air Force Sir Arthur T. Harris, Group Capt. E. B. Haslam, Ms. Elizabeth Hook, Mrs. Jeannette Hutchins, Edward Inman, David Irving, Mrs. Harry Klein, Mrs. Anna Knowles, A. W. Mabbs, Kyffin Owen, Mark Phillips, Mrs. Daphne Redgrave, Philip Reed, Basel Thomas Rodwell, Group Capt. Dudley Saward, Col. David Smith, Mr. and Mrs. David Spoll, and Mrs. Frances Thomson. Imperial War Museum, British Museum, London Library, Public Record Office, and R.A.F. Air Historical Branch.

In Germany: Robert C. Ellner, Gen. Adolf Galland, Franz Goger, Dr. Adolf Lauerbach, Dr. Gunther Rubell, Dipl. Ing. Georg Schafer, Jr., Bruce Siemon, Frau Hedwig Singer, Albert Speer, Dr. Med. Gunther Stedtfeld, Wilhelm Stenger, and Leo Wehner. Bundes Archiv, Koblenz; Militair Archiv, Freiburg; City Archive, Schweinfurt; Jagerblatt Magazine, Lutjenburg, and editor Rolf Ole Lehmann (for help in locating German Air Force veterans).

In the United States: Luther E. Adair, Jr., Philip M. Algar, William D. Allen, Maj. Shirley J. Bach, Albert F. Berlin, Arthur H. Blohm, Col. Ray L. Bowers, Hans L. Bringmann, Robert Brooks, Anthony Cave Brown, Lt. Col. Joseph Brown, Ret., Bruce Callander, Col. R. T. Carrington, Jr., Ret., Mrs. Frank A. Celentano, Mrs. Robert Howden Clapp, Dr. Gale Cleven, Col. Bart Cobey, Ret., Lt. Col. William M. Collins, Jr., Ret., Charles Cooney, John Huie de Russy, Gen. Jacob Devers, Ret., William E. Dolan, Edward F. Downs, Lt. Gen. Ira C. Eaker, Ret., Lt. Col. Gerald B. Eakle, Ret., Chet Fish, Robert Fitzgerald, Ellwood H. Ford, James G. Forrest, Douglas Gibson, Mrs. Starr Gregory, Maj. Rob Gruchy, William Wister Haines, Ms. Janet Hargett, Dr. Paul Heffner, Jack Hickerson, Gladwin Hill, Charles S. Hudson, Brig. Gen. Harris Hull, Ret., Edward J. Huntzinger, Maj. Glenn B. Infield, Ret., Edward Jablonski, Delmar Kaech, David Kahn, Frank T. Keneley, Paul Ketelson, Richard E. Kono, Hans J. Langer, Col. Beirne Lay, Jr., Ret., Bruce Lee, Gen. Curtis E. LeMay, Ret., Ben Lyon, Lt. Col. Charles J.

McClain, Ret., Lt. Col. Miles McFann, Ret., T/Sgt. Leroy D. McFarland, Ret., Capt. Marvin W. McFarland, Bruce D. Moore, L. Corwin Miller, Col. Edwin H. Millson, Ret., Gen. Theodore R. Milton, Ret., Col. John R. Mitchell, Ret., Rev. Henry J. Nagorka, Gen. Joseph J. Nazzaro, Ret., Harold Nelson, Ralph H. Nutter, Robert E. O'Hearn, Lt. Gen. Archie Old, Jr., Ret., M/Sgt. George W. Parks, Ret., James Parton, Col. Budd Peaslee, Ret., Horst Petzschler, Gen. Maurice A. Preston, Ret., Leo Rand, Ms. Madeline Rhodes, Max Rosenberg, John F. Schimenek, David Schoem, Col. William R. Smith, Ret., Col. Kermit D. Stevens, Ret., Carlos P. Stewart, Gunther Stuhlmann, Phillip R. Taylor, Alan Tucker, Dominic Ventre, James O. Wade, Frank B. Walls, Ernest E. Warsaw, Ms. Gloria Wheeler, Col. David M. Williams, Ret., Maj. Gen. Robert B. Williams, Ret., Maj. Edward P. Winslow, Ret., Maj. Gen. Stanley Wray, Ret., Robert Wolfe, Ms. Mary Wolfskill, Lt. Col. John H. Woolnough, Ret., and Col. Clemens L. Wurzbach, Ret.

Air University, U.S. Air Force, Maxwell Field, Alabama; Columbia University Oral History Research Office, New York City; Dept. of the Air Force, Office of the Secretary, Washington, D.C.; Library of Congress, Manuscript Division; National Archives, National Records Center, Suitland, Md.; New York Public Library; and Office of Air Force History, Washington, D.C.

DECISION
OVER
SCHWEINFURT

1

The 146 Flying Fortresses of the Fourth Bombardment Wing, emerging from the deep gray mass of clouds that engulfed England, clung to one another in ever-tightening formations as they streaked across the English Channel toward the perilous European continent. From their bright, sunny altitudes of 17,000 to 20,000 feet, the nervous crewmen saw only isolated cloud patches below and over Holland and Belgium in front of them.

Throughout the early hours of the morning at their English bases and as they took off into the dismal gloom, their most immediate worry had been the clouds. But now, in the open sky above the Channel, their chief concern was fighter planes—the two groups of their own that were supposed to be escorting them at least part way to their target, and the many German groups that would be waiting to "escort" them the rest of the way. Among the B-17 crews, a grim joke had been circulating: "Now we have fighters with us all the way. Our P-47s take us as far as Aachen. The Messerschmitts and Focke-Wulfs take us to the target and back. Then the 47s pick us up again when we reach the Channel. If we reach the Channel." An increasing number of Fortresses had failed to do so in recent weeks.

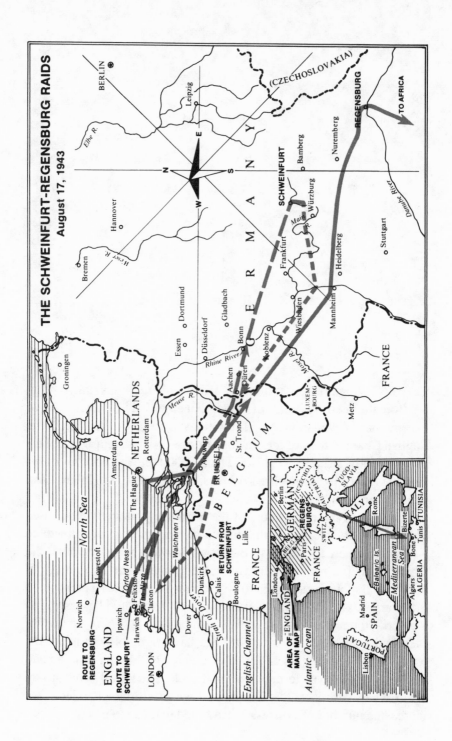

The short range of American fighter planes had become a serious problem since the big bombers began attacking targets inside the German homeland the previous January. Maj. Gen. Ira C. Eaker, the 8th Air Force commander, had been pleading for auxiliary fuel tanks to extend the operating radius of the P-47s.[1] But only a few such tanks had been made available, and they were less than satisfactory.

Today, August 17, 1943, these seven groups of Fortresses, under the command of Col. Curtis E. LeMay, were on their way to attack the Messerschmitt factory at Regensburg, sixty miles southeast of Nuremberg. This mission was part of the biggest bombing operation in the history of the American Army Air Forces and the deepest penetration of Germany since the United States had entered World War II. The Regensburg aspect of this operation was a sizable and significant undertaking in itself. The target was worthy: as a briefing officer had pointed out before takeoff, the Regensburg Messerschmitt plant was then turning out two hundred of the deadly ME-109s each month, nearly 30 percent of Germany's single-engine fighter production. If the mission developed as planned, LeMay's force, after attacking this installation, would not fly directly back to England but south to Africa in a shuttle experiment designed to show Hitler that almost all of his "Fortress Europe" was vulnerable to 8th Air Force bombs.

Perhaps even more significant was the function of LeMay's force today as a decoy. The men who planned this operation hoped that the planes of the Fourth Bombardment Wing would lure most of the German fighters to the Regensburg area so that an even larger force scheduled to take off nine minutes later, 230 B-17s of the First Bombardment Wing, could slip through the German defenses. The objective of the larger force was to attack one of the most crucial targets in Europe: five ball-bearing factories clustered around the railroad yards in the Bavarian town of Schweinfurt, where almost two-thirds of Germany's ball and roller bearings were manufactured. If these plants could be destroyed, most of Germany's war industries would soon be paralyzed because without bearings, no airplanes, trucks, trains, tanks, ships, or submarines, no artillery gun emplacements, no precision machinery of any kind could be produced. Both British and American war planners believed that the destruction of the Schweinfurt factories, if it could be accomplished, would be disastrous to Germany.

3

As LeMay's decoy armada approached the islands of Zeeland on the southwest coast of Holland, he already knew that this Schweinfurt force had been delayed in takeoff by the bad weather, and he was annoyed at its tardiness. His own planes had managed to get off the ground. It was true that the morning fog had been even more dense inland where most of the First Bombardment Wing groups were based than near the coast where LeMay's groups were based, but that explanation did not satisfy him.

Expecting no favors from the English weather, LeMay had made his crews practice instrument takeoffs, and he credited this training for the fact that his wing was en route to its target while the Schweinfurt force might, for all he knew, be still on the ground, as in fact it was. LeMay later declared that if the First Bombardment Wing "had been concentrating on the same sort of bad-weather instrument-takeoff procedure which we had been developing for a solid month, they might have been able to get off the ground as we did."[2] But that morning over the Channel he had other concerns. First of all he wanted to know what had happened to the two groups of P-47s that were supposed to overtake and protect his force, at least for the first hundred miles or so into the continent.

Riding as a copilot in the lead plane of his armada (a 96th Group B-17 piloted by Capt. Thomas F. Kenny), he looked back in vain, and perhaps in some anger, for the Thunderbolts, or "Jugs," that should have been cruising 5,000 or 6,000 feet above and behind him. LeMay was not patient with what he considered inefficient performance. He was such a tough and irascible commander that his men called him "Iron Ass," but discreetly and with respect. While they might fear him, they also believed his methods and demands had saved many of their lives. He was so resourceful that several of his innovations, including the protective box formation in which they were now flying, had become standard operating procedures in the U.S. Air Forces.

The Thunderbolts were actually on their way.[3] The 353rd Fighter Wing, with thirty-two P-47s under the command of Maj. Loren G. McCollom, overflew LeMay's three combat wings at 10:00 A.M., circled leftward, and took up an escort position at 23,000 feet as the bombers crossed the coast at Haamstede. But Colonel LeMay never sighted Major McCollom's formation, possibly because his lead plane was too far forward. The 96th Bomb Group, with which he

4

rode, was about fifteen miles ahead of the 100th Group, which occupied the last and lowest position in his Fourth Bombardment Wing.

Lt. Col. Beirne Lay, Jr., a member of the 8th Air Force Headquarters staff, was an observer that day. Riding as copilot in one of the rearmost planes of the 100th Group, he noticed that the lead planes of the 96th looked like "barely visible specks" when he squinted forward into the bright sun. To Colonel Lay, flying his sixth mission, the "loose-linked column" of B-17s still looked too long, the gaps between groups too wide. He was uncomfortable and he had reasons.[4] As a headquarters representative and one of the six original officers who had accompanied General Eaker when he arrived in England to launch the 8th Air Force Bomber Command a year and a half before, Lay could have flown today with any group he might choose. He had chosen the 100th because its commander, Col. Neil B. Harding, was an old friend. When LeMay tried to convince him he should go with one of the other groups, Lay had insisted on the 100th. Though LeMay had finally agreed, Lay realized now why the Wing commander had been so reluctant. The 100th, flying at the absolute rear of the armada and at the lowest altitude (17,000 feet), would be the most vulnerable both to flak and to fighter attack.

When the twenty-one planes of the 100th Group crossed the Dutch coastline at 10:08, they were "tucked in" as close as possible to the twenty-one planes of the 95th Group (led by Col. John K. Gerhart), which was at the front of the Third Combat Wing. Colonel Lay's B-17, named Piccadilly Lily, led the very last element of the 100th. He found himself remembering "just a little affectionately" the headquarters desk he had forsaken when he applied to General Eaker for combat duty.

Nine minutes into the continent, as the task force passed the small town of Woensdrecht, the first few cloudlike puffs of antiaircraft fire burst harmlessly at some distance from the nearest plane. (Flak bursts looked so much like puff clouds that one rookie bombardier, after his first mission, had said his bomb pattern would have been better were it not for those turbulent little clouds above the target.) About eight minutes later, over Diest, someone on the interplane VHF radio, probably a gunner in one of the lead planes, called out, "Fighters at two o'clock low!" (Under the clock-face system of designating direction, "twelve o'clock" means straight ahead; "six o'clock,"

5

straight behind. "Two o'clock" signifies ahead and sixty degrees to the right.)

When Colonel Lay saw these fighters, two of them, climbing above the horizon, he entertained the momentary hope that they might be from one of the two P-47 groups he had expected but hadn't yet seen. Before he could take much comfort from this hope, the two planes sped through the Second Combat Wing ahead (composed of Col. Elliott Vandevanter's 385th and Col. Frederick Castle's 94th Groups) and nicked two B-17s. Even at the 500-mile-per-hour closure rate between these planes and his, Lay could identify them as Focke-Wulf 190s, the best fighters in the Luftwaffe, the German air force. One of them now had smoke emerging from its nose and bits of metal flying off near its wing root. Smoke was also trailing from the wings of the two stricken B-17s ahead, but they were still in formation.

By this time, the P-47s of the 353rd Fighter Group had climbed to 27,000 feet.[5] At their new altitude, the P-47 pilots were able to see twelve FW-190s diving toward the bombers, but at such a speed and distance they could not be intercepted. After watching one of these German planes go down in smoke (possibly the same one Colonel Lay had seen), Major McCollom checked the fuel consumption of his P-47s and decided, five miles southeast of Diest, just when the bombers were beginning to need help, that he must reluctantly turn and lead his fighters back toward England. Two or three minutes later, flying west away from the bombers, McCollom did catch one stray ME-109, and he personally sent it down in flames. But this victory was small considering the need.

The 56th Fighter Group, forty more Thunderbolts under the command of Col. Hubert Zemke, had now arrived to relieve McCollom's group, but they would be able to escort the bombers only another fifty miles, as far as Eupen, near the German border city of Aachen, before they, too, would have to turn back. Both the 56th and 353rd Groups were carrying extra fuel in belly tanks. (The 56th dropped its tanks in the estuary off Woensdrecht before climbing to 26,000 feet and overtaking the Third Combat Wing ten miles north of Antwerp.) But the tanks they had were new and unsatisfactory. Only five days earlier, on August 12, the 56th had flown its first mission with them. The ground crews as well as the pilots already despised them.[6] The mechanics complained that the fittings were hopelessly awkward and that the tanks themselves, made of pressed paper, were too easily broken. The pilots had an even more serious complaint. They reported that with as little as seventy-five or a hundred extra gallons of fuel in this kind of belly tank, the P-47 couldn't climb above 20,000 feet. A better auxiliary tank would have to be found before American fighters could accompany the B-17s on long-range missions into Germany. Until then, the Flying Fortresses would have to continue going alone, as they were doing today, with only their own machine guns to protect them.

Zemke's group, during its short sojourn with the bombers, spotted fifteen to thirty enemy aircraft and got close enough for an "inconclusive engagement" near Hasselt, ten miles from the Belgian-German border, but could claim no kills. By this time the Germans had already developed the intelligent strategy of waiting until after the American fighters had been forced to turn back before attacking the bombers. Today the pilots in Zemke's group observed that the enemy "appeared unwilling to mix it" with them, staying "either below the bombers or well to the side." Other reports indicate, however, that the Germans were not quite that reticent, and Zemke himself noted that one B-17 was "seen to explode over Diest at 1025 hours with no chutes appearing," Zemke also mentioned that another B-17 was "seen going down over Maastricht at 1030 hours, six chutes appearing." Zemke's P-47s turned right at Eupen. The bombers, already under attack, crossed the German border alone.

The ME-109s and FW-190s were now darting furiously through the Fortress formations, firing 20-mm. nose cannons as well as machine guns. The smell of burned cordite filled the B-17s, especially those in the two rear combat wings, as their gunners spent thousands of rounds of .50-caliber shells. So many fighters were attacking them that few gunners bothered to call out on the interplane radio the position or direction of the "bandits." Over the air now came such bits of advice as "Lead 'em more!," "Short bursts!," "Don't throw rounds away!," "Don't yell. Talk slow."

The German attack soon became more coordinated. Some fighters came in head-on from slightly above while others, from three and nine o'clock, approached at the same level as the B-17s and still more, in the rear, came up from slightly below. The sky was crisscrossed with orange tracer bullets from the B-17 machine guns and dotted with 20-mm.-cannon puffs from German fighters, which

7

sometimes came as close as fifty yards to their bomber targets before peeling off to avoid collisions. Sometimes they turned too late and the air would be filled momentarily with the debris of shattered bombers, fighters, and men.

At 10:41, about ten minutes after the departure of the fighter escort, one squadron of twelve ME-109s and another of eleven FW-190s approached the rear combat wing from six o'clock low, pulled ahead, and then after a 180-degree climbing turn, attacked head-on. As these fighters ripped through the bombers, a few German planes were hit by B-17 machine-gun bullets, but four of the bombers—one in the 95th Group and three in the 100th, the entire second element of Major Gale "Buck" Cleven's 350th Squadron—broke into flames and fell out of formation.

The copilot in one of these planes, apparently dazed by a shell explosion, climbed onto the right wing through a gaping hole the shell had torn in the side of the fuselage. He was not wearing his parachute. As if he were just now realizing this lack, he reached back into the plane, but it was too late. The slip stream swept him off the wing and dashed him against the tail. No one else emerged from the plane, which nosed upward two hundred feet into a stall, then exploded into thousands of scraps of metal and flesh.

Colonel Lay, sitting helplessly in his copilot seat (beside the Piccadilly Lily pilot, Lt. Thomas E. Murphy), was unable to do anything but watch as the great battle continued across the skies of western Germany. He was benumbed by the sight of airplanes plummeting to earth, followed more slowly by clusters of parachutes, German yellow mingled with the American white. He became aware of all the uncomfortable things happening to him. His mouth was going dry; his stomach seemed to be freezing up; he felt as if his buttocks were biting holes in his parachute. And at moments he wasn't sure he was capable of moving. He wished he were flying the plane because he knew that would give him a function on which to concentrate and thus bring him a measure of relief from the horror of watching the guns of the fighters flying straight at him. Murphy, perhaps sensing his discomfort, turned the controls over to him. The fear became more bearable now, even though Lay was certain he would soon be dead.

As the besieged B-17s droned steadily deeper into Germany at their 160-mile-per-hour cruising speed, the enemy strategy became apparent, and the bomber crews abandoned hope that the attacks against them might diminish. The German homeland defenses had recently been reorganized and augmented to meet the growing American daylight threat.[7] In July, two fighter groups had been brought back from the Russian front and several squadrons from the Mediterranean. On any given day now, the German Air Force could pit as many as three hundred fighters against the invading force.

But even more important than the number of fighters was the newly conceived strategy of deploying them in depth rather than in mass. No longer did the Germans concentrate their fighter strength near the English Channel in the hope of repulsing the bombers quickly before they could reach the German border. That strategy, once stubbornly championed by the Luftwaffe's commander in chief, Reichsmarshal Hermann Goering, had failed because only a small fraction of the B-17s could be stopped over France and the Low Countries. The rest, having exhausted the range of the attacking coastal fighters, enjoyed a relatively free run to their targets. To correct this neglect of the invaders, the G.A.F. had now distributed its fighters among a score or more of fields along the 150-mile-wide corridor through which the bombers would have to fly from the continental shores to their most likely German targets. The fighters stationed at each field took off only as the bombers approached; and as each group emptied its guns and exhausted its fuel against the passing invaders, a fresh group from the next field would arrive to replace it. The system was designed to harass the bombers all the way to their target and all the way back. By the time the B-17s turned for home, the fighters that had met them on the way in would be refueled, rearmed, and ready to hit them on the way out.

It was this new strategy that had given rise to the gloomy joke among the bomber crews that they were escorted all the way. Until today, the joke had been an exaggeration. Today it appeared to be an understatement.

At his headquarters in Bushy Park, fifteen miles southwest of London, Gen. Ira Eaker, the square-jawed, tough-looking, but soft-speaking Texan who commanded the 8th Air Force, kept steady communication with his Bomber Command in High Wycombe, thirty miles north, hoping to hear that the First Bombardment Wing would soon be off the ground on its way to Schweinfurt. The fog had begun to lift at Bassingbourn, the base of the 91st Group, nine miles southwest of Cambridge, but would it lift at all the other bases in East Anglia? Eaker fervently hoped so because he knew that this might be the most crucial day in his twenty-five-year military career. He hoped that today he could prove conclusively to the critics of American Army Air Force strategy the feasibility of the concept upon which the Air Force had been developed: daylight precision bombing.

Among these critics were some very important people. Here in England they included Prime Minister Winston Churchill, Air Minister Sir Archibald Sinclair, Chief of the Royal Air Force Staff Air Chief Marshal Sir Charles Portal, and R.A.F. Bomber Commander Air Chief Marshal Sir Arthur Harris. Back home in Washington, critics of the Air Force included almost the entire U.S. Naval Staff, especially the Commander of the Fleet and Chief of Naval Operations, Admiral Ernest J. King, who believed that the national productive energy spent in building a large strategic-bombing force might better be spent building planes for the Navy. Also opposed to the Air Force strategic-bombing policy were many U.S. Army ground-force generals who believed that this same productive capacity might better be spent building tactical-support aircraft for their infantry and artillery units.

In Washington, Gen. Henry H. Arnold, the Air Force Chief of Staff, fought a continuous campaign against other members of the Joint Chiefs of Staff who wanted to limit if not eliminate the slowly growing mass of B-17s operating from English bases. And while Arnold held off the critics at home, Eaker had to contend with the critics in London, at least until he could prove to them the efficacy of the daylight precision strategy.

The British did not support the American admirals and generals who opposed the concept of strategic bombing. On the contrary, the British were strong advocates of the concept. For more than two years they had been sending fleets of R.A.F. bombers against German cities. But they operated only at night, and they gravely doubted that the American B-17s could operate successfully in the daytime, without fighter support, against well-defended targets deep inside Germany. Since the day Eaker and his first 8th Air Force contingent arrived in England a year and a half earlier, Churchill and his air men had been trying courteously but persistently to persuade these inexperienced Americans that they should discard their perilous daylight ambitions and join the R.A.F. in its night raids.

It was now more than a year since B-17 groups began arriving in England to start operations. Today in fact was the anniversary of the 8th Air Force's first mission of the war—a mission on which Eaker himself had flown. But the early missions had been against German targets in France and the Low Countries, not into Germany itself. And while British authorities had been tactful in their public appreciation of these missions, they had been blunt in expressing secretly to each other their private impatience with the first several American efforts. Air Minister Sir Archibald Sinclair, in a September 25, 1942, memo, had asked rhetorically, "What are the Americans doing? What do they intend to do? . . . As far as I know, they have not dropped a single bomb in Germany. . . . Do they contemplate the use of the Flying Fortress at night?"[8]

Air Chief Marshall Sir Charles Portal wrote two days later: "I have . . . serious doubts . . . about whether the Americans will ever achieve their objective. . . . Although it is quite easy to pick off small targets by day when you are not seriously opposed, it is an entirely different matter when you are being harassed all the time by fighters and flak."[9] A month later, Churchill noted: "At present the United States are persevering with the idea of the daylight bombing of Germany . . . in formation without escort. So far they have not gone beyond the limits of strong British fighter escort. They will probably experience a heavy disaster as soon as they do."[10]

While Eaker had not seen these secret memos, he was well acquainted with British thinking, and he was also painfully aware of a growing pressure from General Arnold in Washington for him to prove beyond doubt the capability of the B-17 and the workability of the American Air Force policy. During the past six months, since Eaker's planes had begun to fly shallow missions into western Germany, the British had muted their campaign against the daylight precision strategy, but they were not yet convinced that the 8th Air Force could profitably attack important targets deep inside Germany. Eaker still needed dramatic proof that his B-17s could seriously damage Germany's war machine, and today he hoped to get such proof. But unfortunately, the weather had already compromised the basic strategy. Unless the 230 planes of the Schweinfurt force were to get off the ground very soon, they would be too late for any possible benefit LeMay's force might provide them by diverting German fighters.

As Eaker waited for reports, his impatience at the weather was compounded by frustration at having been forbidden to lead the Schweinfurt mission. He had planned to do so until Lt. Gen. Jacob L. Devers, the American Theater commander in Europe, learned of his intentions. If he went to Schweinfurt, Devers warned him, then his next airplane trip would be back to the United States. General Arnold had made it clear that he didn't want his 8th Air Force commander killed or captured.

While this solicitude on Arnold's part might save Eaker's life, he did not appreciate it. He wanted to go on the Schweinfurt mission even though he believed it would be more perilous than any the 8th had yet experienced. This eagerness did not mean he was indifferent to danger or impervious to fear. He expected the members of his staff to fly missions, and he himself had flown the very first one because, as he explained in a directive on the subject, he felt that the men in command should be "cognizant of the problems facing combat crews and sympathetic with their effort."[11]

Fear was one of those problems. And Eaker, though his whole career had disciplined him never to show it, was well acquainted with it. But the fear he dreaded most was not the physical fear of being killed on a mission. During twenty-five years as a flier, he had often come close to death, and such crises had simply spurred him to action. He might afterward feel shaken momentarily and perhaps even suffer nightmares for a brief period, but the results of physical fear never lasted very long, and the fact that he could take action against its cause was helpful in overcoming it.

What Eaker detested more intensely was a kind of fear against which no physical action would avail, a mental fear arising from awesome responsibility.[12] He was aware of two kinds of mental fear a general had to keep under control. While he had come to terms with a commander's grim necessity to make decisions that would cost men's lives, he had not yet overcome the fear of making a decision that would squander lives. Nor had he overcome the fear of doing something that would contribute to the failure of an important operation. Such fears could keep him awake at night, thinking of alternatives. Had he left anything unlearned or undone that would improve the chances of success? Could he have chosen a better strategy? Were his men well prepared for whatever they might encounter? These were the kinds of fear with which he had to cope today after putting into motion what was conceived as the biggest single mission in the history of the U.S. Army Air Force.

It would be easier for him if he were in the cockpit of one of those bombers ready to take off for Schweinfurt. Then he could do more than sit helplessly at his desk awaiting reports from his bomber commander (Brig. Gen. Fred L. Anderson), wondering if the Regensburg diversionary strategy was doomed by the weather, wondering if LeMay's force should have been recalled instead of being sent on alone, wondering if the Schweinfurt planes would ever get off the ground, if the big mission against Germany's vital ball-bearing factories, planned since the previous autumn and already postponed once, would have to be postponed again. It was now after 11:00 A.M. The Fourth Bombardment Wing had been gone an hour and a half, but no First Bombardment Wing plane was yet off the ground.

As the great air battle between LeMay's Flying Fortresses and the German fighters moved across the skies of west Germany, the odds against the Fortresses seemed to lengthen. The Germans were coming in swarms, concentrating on the already battered Second and Third Combat Wings. More twin-engine ME-110s appeared, and while they were slower and less maneuverable than the ME-109s and FW-190s, they were just as deadly. Groups of five to eleven would arrive from ten o'clock and two o'clock while others would dive out of the sun, to blind the B-17 gunners. Straggling bombers, deprived of the crossfire protection of the tight formations, drew the attention of entire hives of fighters.

Only the leading combat wing, with which Colonel LeMay was riding, remained relatively unscathed, perhaps because, unlike the other two wings which were composed of two groups each, the lead wing had three protecting one another. The 96th was flanked by Col. Edgar Wittan's 390th in the high position on the right and Col. William B. David's 388th in the low position on the left. None of the three groups had yet lost a plane.

The 100th Group in the far rear continued to absorb the most brutal punishment. Near Cologne, Lt. Ernest Warsaw, navigator of a B-17 piloted by Capt. Robert Knox, saw an ME-109 coming up from below.[13] Since the Knox plane was the very last in the armada, it was also the most vulnerable. Warsaw watched in horrible fascination as the Messerschmitt ascended in a steep climb, closer and closer to the Fortress, firing all the while despite the machine-gun bullets the American gunners were sending back at him. Within a few yards of the Fortress, the German plane rolled over and stalled.

Warsaw, looking out the navigator's window, found himself for a moment staring into the cockpit of the enemy fighter. The pilot seemed to be staring back. But his eyes looked vacant. He had obviously been hit by a bullet, perhaps just seconds earlier, and it seemed to Warsaw he was already dead. Yet his finger still squeezed his firing button, and bullets were still pouring from his wing guns.

The plane quickly fell off after its stall, and Warsaw watched it plunge downward. But he had little time to follow the course of the doomed fighter. One of its bullets had struck an oil line in the Fortress. The big bomber's No. 1 engine faltered, sputtered, and died. Though Knox quickly feathered its propeller (a procedure to minimize drag by presenting the edges rather than the faces of the blades to the airstream) and advanced the throttles on the three other engines, the plane lost airspeed so fast that the entire formation was pulling away from it.

Captain Knox called Warsaw on the intercom. "Ernie, what do you think?"

"We have no choice," Warsaw told him. "We can't keep up, and we certainly can't make it to Africa. We've got to turn around and go back."

It would be easier, of course, to head for nearby Switzerland, where, if they landed safely, they would be interned in comfort for the remainder of the war. Knox quickly canvassed the crew. Did they want to try for Switzerland or for Thorpe Abbots, their base in England? The consensus was Thorpe Abbots.

"Okay, Ernie," Knox said. "Give me a heading for home."

Warsaw said, "All right, but first let's get down on the deck." He thought that by flying as close as possible to the ground they would be less noticeable and therefore attract fewer fighters. For Warsaw, the prospect of parachuting and being captured in Nazi Germany was especially chilling because he was Jewish. He had been a first-year law student at DePaul University in Chicago when the United States

14

entered the war and had joined the Air Force the next day. Because of the Nazi persecution of Jews, he considered the war a personal vendetta. And though he did not enjoy flying missions (in addition to all the other hazards and discomforts he was prone to air-sickness), Warsaw did not want this one, his thirteenth, to be his last.

If the crippled Fortress were to have any chance to reach England, he would have to plot a very careful course, avoiding German fighter quadrants and skirting cities, where antiaircraft guns were waiting. As Captain Knox banked the big plane around, Warsaw began studying his maps. After about five minutes of calculation, he looked up and found to his surprise and consternation that the ship was still at 15,000 feet.

Over the intercom he shouted to the pilot, "What the hell are you doing up here?"

Neither Knox nor the copilot answered. The plane was flying straight and level. Warsaw had the eerie feeling that nobody was at the controls, that the plane was flying on automatic pilot.

Moments later, a gunner yelled over the intercom: "A whole squadron coming up at six o'clock!"

When Warsaw looked out the side windows, both left and right, he saw a strange mixture of German planes, twelve or thirteen of them, ME-109s, ME-110s, FW-190s, Junkers 88s, and other types. All were sliding in close, with throttles back, as if they intended to fly formation with the B-17.

Never before had the men in Knox's crew enjoyed such a splendid opportunity. Everyone who could get close to a gun, including Warsaw, opened fire. One after another of the German planes began falling away in flames. It seemed to Warsaw that at least nine of them went down. He was certain that he, personally, had shot down three. He watched them go into the ground.

As he looked out the window he also noticed, but only vaguely, that for some reason the bomber's wheels were down. In the excitement of the moment, however, he gave no thought to the significance of this condition. (It was understood internationally that an airplane crew could signify surrender by lowering the landing gear. This would explain why all those German fighters had felt safe in approaching the Fortress.)

The surviving fighters slid quickly out of range. When they closed

15

in again it was not to fly formation. The stricken B-17 now took salvo after salvo of cannon shells. In less than a minute it was so hopelessly riddled that someone rang the bail-out bell. Warsaw did not know who had rung it. Through all the action, he hadn't heard another word from the pilot or copilot. Perhaps they were both dead.

Giving bombardier Edwin Tobin a bang on the shoulder to make sure he had heard the bell, Warsaw crawled along a little catwalk that led to an escape hatch under the pilot's compartment. He was wearing a small parachute in a chest harness. With a reflex action, he opened the hatch and fell out. As he floated to earth, the plane from which he had escaped was shattered by explosions, yet three more men emerged in parachutes before it plunged toward the ground. Tobin, who was one of them, had been thrown out of the plane by an explosion.

Warsaw, hanging from his parachute, felt a draft from the rear and became aware not only that the seat of his flying suit had been blown away but also that his buttocks were beginning to sting, apparently from shrapnel wounds. He didn't think the wounds could be very serious if it had taken this long to notice them. Anyhow, they didn't constitute his most immediate concern. On the roads below him he could see crowds of Germans, probably angry at the bombing of their cities, awaiting his arrival. Two weeks earlier he himself had dropped a loose bomb on Aachen, not far from here. He hoped no one had dropped any bombs in this area today.

Because Warsaw's parachute was so small, making his descent too rapid for safety, his concern about a possible lynching ended the moment he hit the ground. The hard impact knocked him out. When he regained consciousness a few minutes later, he was surrounded by uniformed Gestapo men. They had kept the angry mob at bay, but when he realized they were members of Hitler's dreaded secret police, he knew that as a Jew he might have more trouble with them than with the crowd. To add to his worries, he suddenly remembered that the letter "H" for Hebrew was stamped on his identification tag. He probably should have had it removed as many other Jewish fliers had done before venturing over Hitler's Europe, but he had wanted the "H" on his dog tag to make sure that if he were killed, whoever came upon his remains would discover his religion. The possibility of his being captured had never occupied his mind as much as the possibility of being killed. If he were to be killed and his body found

16

in Germany, he wanted it registered in the minds of the Germans who found him that this was a Jew who had given his life fighting Hitler and the Nazis. It would not be healthy, however, to have the Gestapo discover while he was a live prisoner that he was a Jew.

When they loaded him into their car, he took advantage of a moment while no one was looking. With a quick yank he pulled the dog tag from around his neck and flung it to the wind.

A few miles west of Aachen, across the Belgian border near Montzen where another of the Fortresses had crashed, hundreds of Belgians gathered at almost precisely the same time, shortly after eleven, but to display quite opposite sympathies.[14] Arriving before the German occupation troops, these Belgians found three American fliers alive in addition to the bodies of several others. They could do little for two of the three survivors who had been injured. These men were captured as soon as German soldiers reached the scene. But the third man, unhurt, was soon lost in the crowd, later to be passed along to the Belgian underground in the hope that he might be smuggled back to England. The Belgians hissed and booed the German soldiers, first when they took personal belongings from the dead Americans in the wreckage, then when they carried away, presumably to a prison hospital, the two injured men.

Colonel LeMay's beleaguered task force, despite its continuing losses, held to its course toward Regensburg. Near Kaiserslautern, the commander's own lead formation sustained its first casualty when a B-17 piloted by Lt. S. W. Tyson of the 390th Group fell out of formation with its left wing in flames.[15]

Back in the Third Combat Wing's 95th and 100th Groups, so many German fighters were swarming through the eviscerated formations that Colonel Lay felt trapped. Since the attacks were continuing without relief even though the bombers were already through what had been considered "the German fighter belt," he was certain that the enemy had brought in several new fighter groups to try out the concept of defense in depth. But how deep could this defense be? How many fighters did they have?

There was no sign yet of a shortage. A dozen ME-109s were coming at him in pairs from twelve to two o'clock. He had to resist an impulse to close his eyes when he looked at the nose cannons pointed at him. A shiny rectangle of metal sailed past the right wing of the Piccadilly Lily. He recognized it as the main-exit door of a Fortress ahead. Then "a black lump" hurtled through the formation "barely missing several propellers." As this lump approached his plane, he could see that it was a man "clasping his knees to his head, revolving like a diver." The man flew past so close that Lay saw a piece of paper blown out of his leather jacket.

Some of the German planes were now shooting rockets, and a few of the slower ones were flying directly above the formations, dropping air-to-air bombs with fuses set to go off at the level of the B-17s. There was so much debris in the air—plane fragments, prematurely opened parachutes, even human bodies—that the whole Third Combat Wing was threatened. Though the target in Regensburg was now only about half an hour away, Lay doubted that any of the 100th Group would get there. They seemed to be facing certain extinction.

Most harried of the surviving pilots in the group was Maj. Gale Cleven, commander of the 350th Squadron below the Piccadilly Lily in which Colonel Lay was flying. Cleven, whose squadron had only three surviving planes after losing all three in his second element, was now receiving the same kind of attention that had sent them down.[16] Just east of Heidelberg, at about 11:30, the plane he was flying, Phartzac (inelegantly named by the crew in honor of their barracks bunks, where all of them might prefer to be at this moment), was hit by five 20-mm. shells, one after another. Several German fighters queued up to come in on the nose of the plane. Others struck at the tail, the sides, and even the belly. Some rolled past so close Cleven could almost read the printing on their undersides. He felt he could reach out and touch them. In the twenty or twenty-one missions he had flown, he had developed great respect for the courage of German pilots. Even when one would come too close and collide with a B-17, the others would continue their head-on tactics.

Today they were as accurate as Cleven had ever seen them. The first shell to hit his plane penetrated the right side of the nose, just beneath the pilot's compartment, where the radio operator, Sgt. Norman Smith, was firing a gun. The shell cut off both of Smith's legs just above the knees. It also damaged the electrical system and radio equipment.

The second shell entered the left side of the nose, injuring the bombardier in the head and shoulder as it shattered a section of plexiglass and ripped away a gun installation.

The third shell hit the right wing, continued into the fuselage and broke the hydraulic system, releasing a flood of fluid into the cockpit. The fourth crashed through the roof and cut rudder cables. The fifth hit the No. 3 engine, which immediately died, then burst into flames.

The crew of the Phartzac needed no more convincing. They were almost unanimously certain that the only place this riddled airplane could now take them was straight into the ground. In their opinion, the time had come to abandon it, and they began offering this opinion to the pilot on the intercom.

Cleven knew these men only casually. They were not his crew. (As squadron commander he didn't have a crew of his own. When he went on a mission, he chose a plane, moved its pilot into the copilot seat and sent the copilot to the navigator's compartment where he could fire one of the guns.) This crew had completed about a dozen missions as a unit and they were considered a good team. But they had never seen anything like what they were seeing today. Even before the shells had begun exploding among them, the action around them had tightened their nerves. Now, their plane was all but torn apart, with gaping holes in the front and sides letting in 35-below-zero air at 160 miles per hour. One engine was on fire. The electrical system was so badly damaged it could go out at any moment. The rudder pedals were useless. And in the radio compartment, one of their men, Smith, who was married just before the group left the States and whose wife expected a baby at Christmas time, had lost so much blood from the stumps of his shorn-off legs that there was no hope of saving his life.

Under these circumstances, the desire of the crew to bail out seemed justified, and one might have expected their pilot to agree. But Cleven was an extraordinary man. He had never been aware of the kind of fear that attacks most men in combat. He claimed no special ability to overcome fear. He simply never consciously experienced it. Being killed, or even shot down, was something that might happen, but he didn't really believe it would happen to him. So he gave it very little thought. In fact, he found the war exciting and rather enjoyed it.

When the Phartzac crew began to plead with Cleven for permission to bail out, he talked to them on the intercom and tried to calm them. The airplane, as he pointed out, was still flying despite its sorry

19

condition. And the fire in the dead No. 3 engine seemed to be burning itself out. On the three good engines, it looked as if they might even manage to keep up with the rest of the formation. Why should they abandon a ship that hadn't yet failed them?

The copilot was not convinced. In the flooded, shattered cockpit, he and Cleven continued the argument about bailing out. It was inconceivable to the copilot that this plane could carry them to the target and then all the way to Africa. It might disintegrate at any moment, and then the whole crew could be killed. Cleven tried to reassure him, but in vain.

Finally, Major Cleven lost his patience. "Listen, you son of a bitch," he said. "You're gonna sit there and take it."

Though he may not have realized it, the key was open on the interplane radio. The whole crew heard his words, and so did some of the men in other planes, including Colonel Lay, just a short distance above.

The effect on Cleven's crew was immediate. They meekly settled down to their jobs. Sergeant Smith, whose bleeding could not be stopped, soon died. But the shell-riddled Phartzac continued precariously toward the target.

By the time LeMay's task force reached the Initial Point from which to begin the bombing run on the Messerschmitt fighter assembly plant in Regensburg, 15 of his Flying Fortresses had fallen to the German guns.[17] But the surviving 131 still held ranks in their formations, the rearward planes moving forward to fill the gap each time one of their companions fell out. LeMay's own First Combat Wing was relatively intact, having lost so far just two of its 62 planes. The German fighters had largely left it alone, concentrating their fury on the smaller Second and Third Combat Wings. Many planes in the Second Wing, and almost all in the Third were now damaged. The most fortunate had simply been ventilated by bullet and shrapnel holes. Several were flying on two or three engines. Some suffered shell holes as big as doors. Others had leaking fuel or hydraulic lines, runaway propellers, battered oxygen or electrical systems, inoperative radios.

LeMay himself, at the head of the fifteen-mile-long column of bombers, did not realize the extent of the carnage behind him. His job had been to lead these planes to the target, and he had done it. The sky was now so clear over south-central Germany that he could see twenty-five miles in all directions.[18] And as LeMay's plane began its straight-and-level bomb run from the Initial Point a few miles northwest of Regensburg, he had the satisfaction of seeing distinctly before him the mile-square complex of factory buildings that comprised the Messerschmitt plant.

He was surprised to find no German fighters over Regensburg as he approached the target, and he saw only two antiaircraft bursts, both ineffective. The 96th's lead bombardier, Lt. Dunstan T. Abel, without any opposition to distract him, dropped his load of American high explosives and British incendiaries directly on the factory buildings. The rest of the B-17s in his group, dropping on his cue, were equally accurate. The time was 11:45 A.M.

During the next twenty-two minutes, succeeding groups in LeMay's task force released 303 tons of bombs on the Messerschmitt plant in one of the most accurate bombardments of the war to date. As aerial photos later confirmed,[19] virtually all the bombs fell either on factory buildings or on the adjacent airfield. Nine main workshops were at least partly destroyed. One hangar was "more than half destroyed," while another main store and workshop was "three-fourths destroyed." Nearly every building was damaged.

Despite their severe losses and despite the most savage opposition any of them had yet encountered, the men of Colonel LeMay's Fourth Bombardment Wing were convinced, when they looked down on the flaming rubble at Regensburg, that they had completely fulfilled their mission. But they had little or no time to enjoy this satisfaction. Fifteen German fighters—ME-110s and JU-88s—had arrived to harass the 385th and 94th Groups directly over the target, and these planes continued their attacks as the big bombers flew south toward the Brenner Pass. Within a few miles, LeMay had lost three more B-17s, raising the total so far to a staggering eighteen, with North Africa still far away. Many of the Fortresses were already so badly damaged or so short of fuel that their crews had little expectation of making it. But as they reached the Alps, these surviving men of the Fourth Bombardment Wing had at least one reason to be thankful. The German fighters had finally turned back, leaving them unmolested for the first time since they had crossed the Belgian coastline. The worst of the day's ordeal had apparently ended. They had

21

flown through the thickest storm of bullets and shrapnel in the history of air warfare. With enough luck and enough gasoline, most of them would be in Africa by late afternoon.

For the Schweinfurt-bound men of the First Bombardment Wing, however, the ordeal had not yet begun. And the decoy strategy that had been designed to minimize that ordeal was now beyond hope of fulfillment.

2

Since the early hours of August 17, long before the Regensburg task force got off the ground, tension had been mounting at the 8th Air Force Bomber Command headquarters (code-named Pinetree) near High Wycombe. Through the night the fog had continued to deepen all over eastern England, threatening cancellation of this most ambitious and carefully planned American operation to date.

At Pinetree, the heaviest pressure bore down upon thirty-eight-year-old Brig. Gen. Fred Anderson, who had arrived in England only six months earlier and had been in charge of Bomber Command for only two months. Anderson was an amiable, efficient West Point graduate who had taken flight training and won his pilot's wings at Kelly Field, San Antonio, in the same 1929 class as Curtis LeMay. Later Anderson had contracted tuberculosis after a plane he was flying lost its engine and crashed into the cold waters of San Francisco Bay. For a time he was in danger of being separated from the service, but after a remarkable recovery, he continued his career and became a specialist in aerial bombing.

Anderson, like many other American generals at this stage of the war, had never held an important combat command. He had, however, supervised bombardier instruction at the Air Corps Technical School, and he had been deputy director of bombardment at Air Force headquarters in Washington. Today he was facing the most important and difficult operational decision he had ever been called upon to make.

Since mid-July, General Anderson and his superior, General Eaker, had held this operation in abeyance, waiting for clear weather over central Germany so that the bombardiers could see their targets. On August 10, just one week earlier, the mission had proceeded as far as preflight briefings before the weather in Germany forced its cancellation. Today, with favorable forecasts for Germany, the weather in England was threatening the venture.

When LeMay's groups managed to get in the air, Anderson eventually sent them to the continent alone because he believed he had no choice.[1] If he had recalled them, they would have had a hard time finding their way down through the dense clouds to their bases. And first they would have had to jettison their bombs over the English Channel, where they might have hit British ships. If LeMay's groups were to go, they had to move while they still had enough fuel to reach their North African destinations, preferably before dark since they were unfamiliar with the bases at which they hoped to land.

So Anderson had sent the LeMay force on its way at 9:35 A.M., but in doing so he had complicated his problem. Since the entire First Bombardment Wing was still on the ground, he had therefore lost the advantage of sending it directly after the Fourth Bombardment Wing, and now he had to decide, even if the First Wing did get airborne, whether to send it to Schweinfurt at all. A gap of two or three hours between the two task forces would give the German fighters plenty of time, after attacking the Fourth, to land, reload, and go up against the First.

The commander of the First Bombardment Wing, Brig. Gen. Robert B. Williams, was standing by at the Bassingbourn base of the 91st Bomb Group, with which he intended to fly. A self-disciplined man, not easily perturbed, he remained surprisingly calm during the long wait, giving no evidence that he was worried about the time lag. He conferred only a few times with General Anderson.[2] They had talked often enough in recent days; they both knew what they wanted to do and what it would take to be able to do it.

24

To Williams it was simply a matter of hoping the fog would lift enough for him to see the fence at the end of the runway. His ability to do so would be only slightly diminished by the fact that he had lost one eye while serving as an American observer during the German blitz against London. With his one good eye Williams still saw well enough to fly an airplane. A man of serious purpose and penetrating expression, he was famous among his men for his insistence on military discipline. But they also thought of him, perhaps more fondly, for his courage in overcoming his handicap and for his individual style. He wore a mustache and carried a swagger stick. An Albany, Texas, native and graduate of Texas A. & M., he had won his wings and commission in 1923 when the Air Force was still called the Army Air Service Corps. No one knew more than he about the B-17 bomber. In 1936, at Langley Field, Virginia, he had been the operations officer of the first group to fly it.

The B-17 had grown directly out of the American concept of strategic daylight precision bombing. By the early thirties, Army Air Corps planners realized that, to make such a concept work, they would need the toughest, best armed, longest ranging, and most complicated warplane ever devised. In 1934 they had granted the Boeing Aircraft Company a contract to develop such a plane, and the graceful, four-engine Flying Fortress of 1943 was the direct descendant of the bomber Boeing undertook to design. But in nine years, so many changes had been made in it that only the 104-foot wing span remained the same.

The original length of 68 feet had been stretched to 74, and the original height of 18 feet had been raised to 19 with the addition of a long, gradually rising tail section that included a rear gunner's compartment below the rudder. This sleek, modern, and very distinctive tail, however, was only the most obvious of the changes the Flying Fortress had undergone during its development. The original Boeing Model 299 had four 750-horsepower engines, a speed of 230 miles per hour at 14,000 feet, a ceiling of 28,000 feet, a range of 2,100 miles, an empty weight of 12 tons, and a fully loaded weight of 21 tons. It carried five .30-caliber machine guns. The B-17F, in which General Williams and most of his men were waiting to take off today (a few crews were in B-17Es), had four 1,200-horsepower engines, a speed of 325 miles per hour (maximum) at 25,000 feet, a ceiling of

37,500 feet, a range of 4,420 miles empty (2,000 miles with two tons of bombs), a weight empty of 17^1/$_2$ tons, and fully loaded of 24^1/$_2$ tons.[3] It carried nine .50-caliber machine guns plus one .30-caliber.

By 1943 standards it was a giant of the sky. It was equipped with the recently developed Norden bomb-sight that under ideal conditions, and without harassment, made it possible to lay a bomb precisely on target from 30,000 feet. It also carried the most advanced radar equipment available in 1943. Its fuel tanks were self-sealing, and the gun turrets above and below the fuselage were automatically operated. It was the most powerful, best armed and most formidable fighting machine in the air. In addition, it was one of the most beautiful airplanes ever built and, in the opinion of most of its pilots, one of the easiest to fly. As stable with a full load as it was empty, it would often continue to fly with controls damaged or with great holes in its wings, fuselage, or tail.

Although the plane was large by the standards of the early 1940s, the B-17's ten-man crew did not find it roomy. Designed for maximum speed, it was more slender than an airliner of comparable length. There was, in fact, practically no similarity between it and an airliner. It had no passenger seats and no upholstery. When the men were not busy, they sprawled out on the floor with their parachutes as pillows. Its interior was unfinished, the ribs and skin of the aluminum fuselage exposed. Most of the floor surfaces, and the catwalk between the open bomb-bays, were also aluminum; they produced a dull, metallic sound when the men moved over them in their big, rubber-soled flying boots.

The plane's various compartments, crowded with instruments, wires, cables, oxygen bottles, and machine guns, were so confining that prospective crew members had to be tested for claustrophobia. To live and work for six or eight hours at a time in such small spaces, while further restricted by heavy, cumbersome, leather-and-sheep-wool flying suits, required economy of movement, mastery of intricate procedures, and high tolerance for discomfort. Because of the bitter cold at upper altitudes, the men had to wear their thick gloves even while operating the B-17's complicated machines and guns. This handicap alone required a dexterity far above average. The waist gunners, at their big, rectangular open windows, had to swing their guns forward or backward, upward or downward fast enough to track fighter planes coming on at speeds of four hundred miles an hour or more. When the two waist gunners stood back-to-back at their posts, they were so close they had to be careful to avoid bumping each other's rumps or elbows. Yet they were quite mobile compared to the turret and tail gunners, who fitted into their plexiglass bubbles like pickles in a jar.

The navigator and bombardier shared a snug, glass-windowed nose compartment that also had to accommodate the navigator's work table and stool, the bombardier's Norden bomb-sight, and a pair of machine guns. The pilot and copilot, above and slightly behind them, shared a cockpit so crammed with dials, levers, cranks, instruments, pedals, throttles, compasses, and control yokes that anyone seeing it for the first time would wonder how they could keep track of so many things. The pilot's compartment also had two very pleasant features: it was heated, and its leather seats were as comfortable as a first-class airline chair. The cockpit, and to a lesser extent the entire plane, had a new-automobile aroma of metal, leather, and gasoline. Even the relatively older B-17s in service had come too recently from the assembly line to have lost that factory smell.

The crews who flew these famous bombers were mostly in their late teens or early twenties, from places like Kankakee and Keokuk, Little Rock and Little Falls, New York and New Brunswick, Miami and Seattle, Bangor and San Diego. They knew more about Gary Cooper, Joe DiMaggio, Bing Crosby, and the Dionne quintuplets than they did about Adolf Hitler. But one important thing they did know about Hitler was that he had enslaved Europe and was coldly eliminating everyone who opposed him. Many of these men were only minimally interested in politics. Franklin D. Roosevelt had been their country's President for so long—half their entire lives—that they could scarcely imagine having another one. When they read, most of them chose comic books or paperback novels, the sexier the better. They considered *Forever Amber* just about as sexy as a book could get, but the letters they wrote to their wives and sweethearts were often sexier. Fantasy was rampant in the G.I. mind. Almost all of them had pictures in their wallets of girls back home, but on their walls they had pictures of Rita Hayworth, Betty Grable, or Jane Russell. On the noses of their B-17s they had drawings or paintings of imaginary girls, as naked as their commanders would allow, with names like "Miss Behavin'," "Ima Vailable," or "Any-Time Annie."

Some twenty-three hundred of these young American fliers were waiting at the nine First Bombardment Wing bases as the morning of August 17 dragged on and the fog hung low. Clad in their heavy, sheep-lined leather suits, they sat in their planes or sprawled on grass nearby, smoking, joking, or griping—about the war, about the Air Force, about the British weather. Some were eating—chocolate bars from the Post Exchange or fruits or doughnuts from the mess hall. But appetites were not high on a morning like this. Some crew members went off by themselves for a few minutes to vomit away their breakfasts and at least a bit of their nervousness. If and when the weather lifted and the planes began to take off, some other airmen would wet their pants in fear, but these men, too, would be on the planes when they left the ground. An already bemedaled bombardier in the 91st was known throughout the group for his inability to control his bladder just before a mission; he was equally well known for being one of the calmest and bravest men in the air when the fighting began.

One young man at Bassingbourn, twenty-two-year-old Lt. David Williams (not related to the general), spent the waiting hours carefully studying aeronautical charts and aerial photographs of the Schweinfurt area.[4] He was to be the navigator on the task force's lead ship, the man responsible for directing the whole formation precisely to its target, deep within Germany, four hundred miles away. Born in Chicago, Illinois, and raised in Valparaiso, Indiana, Williams had enlisted the day after the Japanese attack on Pearl Harbor and had graduated first in a class of two hundred at the Mather Field, Sacramento, navigation school. After sixteen missions he had already become group navigator, not only because of his ability but also, as he realized, because he had been fortunate enough to survive while others around him were going down. On his first mission, to Bremen, April 17, six of the nine in his squadron had been lost. Williams's own mathematical likelihood of continuing survival seemed slim.

Another young lieutenant at Bassingbourn, a bombardier named Edward P. "Ted" Winslow from Springfield, Massachusetts, was sitting on the grass with the rest of the crew beside their plane when their squadron commander, Capt. Donald Sheeler, drove up in a jeep.[5] He had good news for one crew member, Sgt. Star A. Tucker, whose promotion to staff sergeant had just been approved.

Sheeler also noted that this crew, ready for its eighth mission, would be flying a substitute plane, named Dame Satan, because the crew's regular plane was still being repaired.

"One good thing about Dame Satan," he remarked. "She always comes back."

Winslow thought to himself, I wish he hadn't said that.

Capt. William R. Smith, a tough, shrewd coal miner's son from Kingston, Pennsylvania, who had been a miner himself before working his way through the University of Pittsburgh, felt a tightness in his stomach as he waited with his 351st Group crew at Polebrook.[6] He had made a bet that there would be a big mission today because it was the anniversary of the first American foray over Europe. Though he now had the satisfaction of winning the bet, he was wishing he had lost it. He figured the German fighters would finish ripping up the Fourth Bombardment Wing just in time to come after the First. He had a premonition that he and his comrades were about to get "the living daylight" beat out of them.

At Molesworth, Col. Kermit D. Stevens from Eugene, Oregon, commander of the 303rd Group and an Air Force pilot since 1936, expected that this would be an especially bad day for himself and his men because they were scheduled to fly in the "Tail-end Charley" or "Coffin Corner" position—the low group in the last combat wing.[7] Nobody would be behind to protect their rear. Though Stevens was a new commander (this was only his sixth mission), he had learned quickly that for a bomber formation, one flying rule was more important than any other.

"If you want to live," he told his men, "keep the formation tight. It's the straggling, raunchy groups they go after."

The 379th Group at Kimbolton was to lead the rear combat wing (of which Stevens's 303rd was the low element), and the 379th's commander, Col. Maurice A. Preston, a Californian from Los Angeles, had some serious concerns as he prepared for the flight. After twenty missions, his group had lost about 75 percent of its original crews, thus earning an unfortunate distinction as the biggest loser in the 8th Air Force. This situation so distressed Preston that he was developing a program of innovations that would one day earn for the 379th the lowest loss rate.[8] Like Colonel Stevens, Preston was devoted to tight formations. In this respect he agreed with Colonel LeMay, who had devised the combat wing formation now in use. But he was beginning to question the size of the LeMay formation, which ideally was composed of three twenty-one-plane groups, stacked in altitude with the left group below the leader and the right group above.

Preston believed this sixty-three-plane formation was too big and too loose. Planes at the outer edges and lower altitudes had to make extreme adjustments in speed and direction to compensate for small adjustments by planes in the center. The outside bombers often had to strain their engines, simply to keep pace. Preston thought this stress might explain the great number of stragglers and dead engines in the outer groups. Today he didn't have to worry about this problem personally. His group would be in the center, or lead position, of a combat wing. But six of his group's extra planes would be part of a composite group on the outside to his right, and he was worried about them. He did not enjoy being number one in the loss column.

In Preston's plane as a crew member was the group bombardier for the 379th, Capt. Joseph Brown, a man whose achievements were remarkable in light of a childhood accident that had threatened to disable him. The son of a coal miner in the southern-Illinois town of Gillespie, he had fallen from a tree when he was seven years old, shattering his elbow so severely that the doctor decided to amputate his arm. His father adamantly withheld permission.

"But he'll be a cripple," the doctor said.

"Just strap it up," Brown's father insisted, "and I'll take him home."

Reluctantly the doctor complied. In the months that followed, Brown's father massaged, twisted, straightened, and healed the boy's arm so skillfully that when Brown grew up and went to the University of Illinois, he was able to play football under the school's famous coach Bob Zuppke, becoming the regular fullback in 1936 and 1937, Zuppke's last two teams. Though the use of Brown's arm was limited, he managed to pass the Air Force physical examination and qualify as a bombardier. Preston had appointed him group bombardier shortly after the 379th was formed in the fall of 1942.[9] Preston, Brown, and the rest of their crew sat quietly in their plane near the end of the runway on the rise above Kimbolton awaiting word from the tower. Several times, operations officers came out in jeeps with status reports. This crew had a special interest in the Schweinfurt mission because they had received special preparation for it, and had been waiting two months for it to happen. Once in June and three times since then, each heavy-bombardment group had sent a select crew to General Williams's headquarters for secret briefings about the ball-bearing factories. Preston had taken this crew to represent the 379th, so they knew better than most of the others what they had to anticipate.

Lt. Philip Algar, a University of California graduate from Modesto, was one of the eighteen pilots of the 384th Group waiting to take off from Grafton-Underwood, but he knew very little about the target of the day.[10] His crew had received no special training for the Schweinfurt project, and until the aborted mission a week earlier, he had scarcely been aware that Schweinfurt was a ball-bearing center. What had impressed him at this morning's briefing was the distance they were expected to fly today, plus the news that he was scheduled to fly in his group's "Tail-end Charley" position—low plane, low squadron. He sensed his blood pressure rising at the realization that they would be penetrating so far into Germany without fighter support, but when the man said go, you went. So Algar had performed all his preflight preparations with outward calm, acting, in front of his crew, as if this were just another mission.

At the same time, he was determined to minimize his vulnerability, and the only way he could do that was by making sure the planes in front of him stayed close together, offering him a tight nest on which to affix himself. If the rest of his squadron were to string itself out, he would be virtually alone at the extreme edge of the "wheel," racing his engine to hold position each time the combat wing made a turn of two or three degrees. In the hope of preventing this problem, he decided to put his fellow pilots on notice. At the end of their briefing, he had warned them, "If you don't stay in formation, I'll go around you."

Staff Sergeants L. Corwin Miller of Stockton, California, and John F. Schimenek of Superior, Wisconsin, Algar's waist gunners, spent much of their waiting time arranging their ammunition and checking their machine guns.[11] They were pals as well as partners, and today they were switching positions because Miller found it easier to fire from the right side than from the left. Like everyone else, they had been astonished at the briefing to learn how far into Germany they were going, but they couldn't imagine that this mission would be worse than some of the others. After eleven missions, Miller had few illusions about his chances of surviving the required twenty-five. In a letter to his bride of three months he had written: "It isn't so terrible over here in England. Fact is, it's rather pleasant. The only terrible part is on the other side of the Channel." He had written that August 13. Now, four days later, he was sitting in a damp, cold B-17, ready to make his twelfth perilous journey to "the other side of the Channel."

By 10:30 the fog at Bassingbourn and at some of the other bases had begun to clear, bringing General Anderson at Pinetree to his moment of ultimate decision. Was it too late to send the Schweinfurt force? He had to take into account that right now, with the English fog clearing, "weather conditions over the entire route and at the target areas were the best which had been forecast for a period of over two weeks."

Another consideration bore down upon him as he later explained: "Inasmuch as the importance of these targets increased almost daily, the risk involved in dispatching the two bomb divisions individually was felt to be commensurate with the results which the destruction of these two targets would achieve."[12]

He gave the order to go. His staff transmitted it to Williams at Bassingbourn, and at 10:40 the crews there were in their planes. At 10:45 the battery booster cart was plugged into the lead plane of the 91st, to be flown by the group commander, Lt. Col. Clemens L. Wurzbach; a minute later the B-17's first four-bladed propeller began to turn slowly, its engine sputtered, coughed, blew a puff of smoke to the rear, then burst into a roar. A smooth roar, loud but not deafening. Even with all four engines running, the Flying Fortress was not an ear-splitting aircraft. The Air Force had several planes that made much more noise, including even one small training plane, the BT-13, whose single engine could drown out the big bomber's four.

As Wurzbach taxied out to the runway, Col. William M. Gross, air commander of the first two combat wings, settled into the copilot's seat beside him, studying the revised schedule for the rendezvous of the 91st with his five other groups.

Gross and Wurzbach were off the ground at 11:20. Col. Howard

M. "Slim" Turner, air commander of the two rear combat wings, flying with Maj. William S. Raper in the lead plane of the 306th Group, got off at 11:55. It was another hour and a half before the tedious and exasperating task of assembling the four combat wings had been completed. At 1:26 P.M., the 230 Flying Fortresses of General Williams's armada crossed the English coast between Clacton and Orfordness, heading toward Antwerp, Eupen, Aachen, Weisbaden, Darmstadt, and Schweinfurt.

At 8th Air Force headquarters (code-named Widewing), General Eaker, who did not interfere with the decisions of General Anderson at Bomber Command, couldn't help feeling some uneasiness when he learned that the Schweinfurt mission, despite the long delay, was on. He didn't, however, question Anderson's judgment in sending the two armadas. He understood Anderson's dilemma because he had once been Bomber Commander himself and had faced similar problems.

Eaker had found that it damaged morale to cancel a mission at the last minute when you had a force of men and planes all ready to go.[13] It was easier for the men to go through with a mission, however difficult, than to return to their barracks with nothing accomplished after such emotional and psychological as well as mechanical preparation. Since only the completed missions counted toward the twenty-five required in a combat tour, the crews were eager to complete them and have done with their perilous assignment.

For a commander in Eaker's position, there were also other considerations. The weather in central Germany was one of them. For two weeks it had been foul. Today, according to all reports, it would be clear over Regensburg and Schweinfurt. With the end of summer approaching, the weather in general wasn't likely to get any better, so there was no time for delay in fulfilling his most immediate responsibility: to prove the effectiveness of daylight precision bombardment by destroying some important and difficult German targets. The pressure upon Eaker to accomplish this objective, and quickly, came not only from his British allies but also from his Air Force superior in Washington, General Arnold, who was up against the same pressure from his U.S. Army and Navy colleagues.

Arnold had expressed his impatience sharply in recent correspondence with Eaker. He had sent two cables in early June complaining that too few of the bombers at Eaker's disposal were being used in combat. And in a June 15 letter, he had enlarged on that theme:

I realize full well the necessity for having a period of time to acclimate the crews and to get them ready for operations. I also realize that there are certain modifications that we on this side will never be able to put in to meet your desires, so there must always be a delay if your planes are to have all the changes made. On the other hand, I am not sure that all of these changes are absolutely necessary and in certain instances somebody may be leaning over backwards trying to get 100% perfect planes when 90% perfect would do the trick.

Eaker was aware of the conditions in Washington that made Arnold impatient—especially the Navy's campaign to get more planes and matériel assigned to the Pacific War and to cut back B-17 production in favor of carrier planes. But he did not think Arnold was sufficiently aware of conditions in England. Since the 8th Air Force had begun bombing targets inside the German border the previous January, battle damage to its B-17s had been so extensive that there weren't enough depots to keep pace with the necessary repair work. Until this situation could be corrected, many planes that Arnold considered available would be unfliable. Eaker pointed out to him that a B-17's ability to return from a mission today did not necessarily mean it could safely carry a crew and a bomb load on another mission tomorrow. Some B-17s came back so thoroughly riddled it seemed miraculous that they could come back at all.

Eaker had found an apt illustration of this point during an inspection of one of his groups. A B-17 had returned the previous day with such a huge hole in its wing that he was able to stand up on a ladder with his head and shoulders through the hole. Someone took a picture, which he then sent to Arnold with the notation, "Here's one of the planes that was not able to go out today."

In fact, Eaker was suffering from a critical shortage of usable planes. The previous April he had given his name to a plan that envisaged the virtual destruction of five groups of military targets—submarine yards, aircraft plants, oil facilities, military transport, and ball-bearing factories—but which depended for execution upon his getting about 950 heavy bombers by July and about 1,200 by October.[14] He believed that with enough planes he could knock out nine-tenths of Germany's submarine construction, for instance, and three-fourths of its ball-bearing production. But because of demands for aircraft in other American theaters of operation, Eaker had received in mid-August fewer than 800 B-17s. He had been stripped of four of his groups because they were needed to support the invasion of North Africa, and he had just recently avoided having others taken from him. At the same time, his losses over Germany continued to mount. By the end of July 1943, he had an effective force of only 275 heavy bombers.

Though the rate of replacement arrivals was increasing daily, the losses were severe enough to seemingly dictate a curtailment of operations, at least until the range of his fighters could be increased. Eaker could ill afford a hiatus, however, because in so many important quarters it would be interpreted as a proof of failure. On the other hand, if his B-17s could paralyze the ball-bearing plants at Schweinfurt today, the strike would have to be interpreted as a proof of success. He wished these planes had been able to get off on schedule, and he wished he'd had more of them to send. But in a three-square-mile target area, he was confident that 230 B-17s would be enough to do the job.

In the underground Combat Control Center of Germany's Twelfth Air Corps at Zeist, Holland (near Utrecht), and at other western fighter-defense bases, operations staffs had been working nervously, speedily, and without relief since early morning when coastal radar indicated widespread activity above the American airfields in East Anglia.[15] This activity was, of course, the assembly of the 8th Air Force's Fourth Bombardment Wing on its way to Regensburg. Since those early warnings, fighters from defense-corridor bases in Holland, France, and Germany had engaged the Regensburg force in a relentless battle all the way to its target and had inflicted severe losses. But they had failed to turn back Colonel LeMay's armada, and so the Regensburg Messerschmitt plant was now more than half destroyed and still in flames, having absorbed the fury of 303 tons of bombs.

35

The German fighters, after harassing LeMay, had landed to refuel and rearm with the intention of harassing him again on his way home to England. When his force turned south from Regensburg toward Africa, the German defenders had little time to exercise their amazement. Now their radar monitors were registering an even greater force of aircraft over England than they had observed in the early morning. The Americans evidently had a second operation in progress today, even bigger than the first, which meant that the German defense system had better prepare an even fiercer reception for this afternoon than the one it had offered this morning. Adolf Hitler was disappointed in his homeland air defenders as a result of the damage already done by the Americans to German industry and the far greater damage done by the British to German cities, especially Hamburg, which British bombers had more than half destroyed in night raids during the last week of July. Whatever the Americans might be planning now, it must be stopped.

As the concentration of air traffic over England increased, and the German radar sets began to indicate just how large this second force must be, activity intensified at the several German combat control centers. Teletypes chattered. Phones rang. Messengers ran from desk to desk, distributing dispatches. Girls in uniform tried to keep track of current aircraft locations on vast grid maps. Generals and colonels at hurried staff meetings discussed possibilities and issued orders. Another American raid as damaging as the one at Regensburg, and on the same day, would be intolerable. The situation called for extraordinary measures.

Gen. Adolf Galland, commander of Germany's day fighters, had tried to meet the growing American bombing threat by having several ME-109 and FW-190 groups returned from the Russian front and the Mediterranean, but even with almost three hundred planes operational, he still did not think he had enough.[16] So he had arranged, in recent days, to use some night fighters—larger, slower, twin-engine ME-110s—against the Flying Fortresses. Until today, these reserves had not been called into action. Now, however, the decision was made to alert some of the night-fighting groups. Among them was *2 Gruppe Nachtjagdgeschwader 5* (Group 2, Night-fighter Wing 5) stationed at Stendal, sixty miles west of Berlin. It's crews had been informed three or four days earlier that they might be called upon for daylight action.

One member of this group was a twenty-two-year-old navigator and radio operator, Sgt. Hans Bringmann. Born and raised in Berlin, he had entered the Luftwaffe after two years at the university, and since early 1942 had been flying night missions against British bombers.[17] He understood why his group's ME-110s were to be tried against the Flying Fortresses. The ME-110s now carried four 21-cm. rockets (two under each wing) with electric fuses. These rockets had an effective range of about eight hundred yards (which was the outside limit of the B-17 machine-gun range) and they had the explosive power of small artillery shells. When the B-17s were escorted by fast American fighter planes, it might be suicidal for the ME-110s to go near them, but Galland and his staff had calculated that after the B-17s had penetrated beyond the range of their escorts, it would be reasonably safe for the ME-110s to come within rocket range of their machine guns.

Bringmann and many of his companions were not yet convinced. Their planes were rigged for night operations, and all of their combat experience had been at night. They were accustomed to flying singly "as lone wolves,"[18] using radar to seek out the slow, poorly armed British bombers, which were virtually helpless when they were found. In the daytime, the ME-110s would have to maintain tight formations, to which they were unaccustomed. And if they wanted their rockets to be at all effective, they would have to come closer to the B-17s than eight hundred yards. Bringmann had never had to face the combined firepower of a B-17 formation, but he had heard a lot about it. Like most of his comrades, he was not happy at the prospect.

Galland also had at his disposal, in addition to the regular divisions stationed within the daylight defense corridor, several "schwarmes" (four-plane units of ME-109s or FW-190s) piloted by instructors at Luftwaffe flying schools and several industrial "schwarmes" of aircraft-company test pilots.[19] But such pilots had little combat experience. Their casualty rate was high, and their successes were unimpressive. More reliable reserves for an emergency like today's were the fighter groups stationed in southern Germany, outside the limits of what might be considered the American bombing theater. One such group was *2 Gruppe Jagdgeschwader 51* (Group 2, Fighter Wing 51), stationed in Neubiberg, forty miles northwest of Munich.

Lt. Hans Langer was a veteran pilot in this group. Though his career in fighters had spanned only a year and a half, he had already shot down forty-five enemy planes and had been shot down six times himself, each time without sustaining any personal injuries.[20] Like all fighter pilots who managed to survive a year or more of action, he knew when to leave a stricken plane. German pilots were instructed to jump the moment a plane developed serious problems, especially if they were over their own territory. It took longer to replace a trained man than a machine. If, as in Langer's case, a man flew an ME-109, it was dangerous to wait very long before jumping because once the damaged plane went into a dive, it soon built up so much speed that bailing out was impossible.

Langer had learned all this quickly in an aviation career that began with the Heinkel Aircraft Company in 1940. The son of an East Prussian landowner and newspaper publisher, he had left the University of Breslau at age eighteen to work for Heinkel because he wanted to become an aerodynamics engineer. After a year with Heinkel, during which he found time to qualify as a pilot with a commercial rating, he was advised by the company that he should enter the Luftwaffe, and he had gladly done so. He believed in Germany's war aims and had always been enthusiastic about Adolf Hitler's leadership. Early in the summer of 1943, he had been decorated personally by Hitler for his air victories, and he considered his country's dictator ''a great person, the greatest I had ever seen.''

Langer's early days as a fighter pilot had been unpromising. He had thought at first he would never master the skill, partly because it took awhile ''to overcome the fear of having something so foreign in your hands,'' and partly because fighter action was so fast it took awhile to learn to see it clearly and comprehend it. On his third or fourth day of combat, at El Alamein in Africa, he had been shot down for the first time, by an American P-38. Thereafter he had caught on to the necessary techniques rapidly enough not only to survive but also to compile an impressive record in the most dangerous of occupations. His group was alerted at eleven o'clock on the morning of August 17. The Twelfth Air Corps headquarters was guessing that the second American attack might be against Frankfurt. Langer and the eleven other pilots in his squadron stood by their ME-109s.

At 1:15 P.M., German radar indicated that the second American task force had gathered and was crossing the English coast. The First, Second, Third, Fourth, and Fifth German Air Divisions at Deelen, Stade, Metz, Döberitz, and Schleissheim were soon notified, and more than three hundred pilots, already standing by their planes at a score of bases, received takeoff orders. Since the Americans were headed southeast toward Antwerp, Frankfurt still seemed to be the probable target. Ready to intercept the Americans was the largest force Hitler's homeland defense had ever assembled.

3

The two large American task forces, each almost ten miles long, one with 116 Flying Fortresses, the other with 114, droned through the clear air of the North Sea. Looking to the rear, beyond the white vapor trails, the B-17 crews could still see the deep blanket of clouds covering England, clouds they had distrusted as they climbed blindly through them, but from which they had nevertheless emerged with trepidation, envisioning the brutal hostility they expected to encounter in bright sunshine over the continent ahead.

Most of these men were veterans. They had made the trip before out of England's protective gloom into Europe's dangerous daylight. They had learned to cope with the experience, but they would never become accustomed to it. The very thought of it was fearsome enough to make them love clouds and hate the sun. Whenever they flew, they assumed the sun would be shining over Europe because they would not be sent if clouds were expected. They needed clear skies for their pinpoint bombing. But on some days the forecasters were wrong, and as they approached Walcheren Island off the coast of Holland, it began to look as if this might be one of those days. Below them were only a few soft puffs of cumulus, and ahead they still had several miles of sunshine. Over the Dutch coast, however, was a surprising bank of clouds. It would not turn them back. They still expected sunshine above their Bavarian target. But these clouds ahead might be high enough to force a dangerous alteration of their flight plan.

Colonel Gross, commander of the first task force, had a difficult decision to make as his lead plane approached these clouds and he could see that their base was between 17,000 and 21,000 feet. The field order for the mission had specified that it be flown between 23,000 and 26,500 feet. General Anderson was so emphatic about this order he had sent one of his aides, Col. Stanley Wray, a combat veteran and the original 91st Group commander, to make sure each group understood its importance.[1] R.A.F. experts had found, after flying captured ME-109s, that this airplane operated best at 17,000 feet and worst between 21,000 and 23,000. The B-17 operated best at 23,000, hence the stipulated 23,000-foot floor in the flight plan. But as Colonel Gross looked at the cloud layers ahead, he estimated his planes would have to fly higher than 26,500 feet to get above them. If so, they would have to navigate on instruments and might not be able to see their target. He decided, therefore, that despite the advantage it would give the German fighters, he would keep his task force under the clouds unless the ceiling descended further and drove him down into the flak fields below 17,000 feet.

This was a fateful decision for which Gross would later be criticized, but with no enemy aircraft yet visible, with eight squadrons of British Spitfires (ninety-six planes) pulling up alongside to escort his bombers almost to Antwerp, and with two American fighter groups scheduled to escort them as far as Aachen, he apparently felt the risk at 17,000 feet was acceptable. With the task force approaching the clouded coastline, the descent to 17,000 began.

When the lead group, the 91st, crossed the Dutch coast, no enemy aircraft had arrived. The 384th Group, the lowest and rearmost element in Colonel Gross's task force, was not so fortunate. Maj. Thomas P. Beckett, air commander of the 384th, found that as soon as the task force descended to 17,000 feet, "the fighters got to us. Although we had fighter escort (the Spitfires), enemy fighters kept hitting us anyhow."[2]

Lt. Philip Algar's plane, Lucky Thirteen, in the low squadron's tail-end position, was already taking frontal attacks as the 384th flew over the waterways of Holland; and the bombardier, Lt. James McClanahan, at his machine gun in the plexiglass nose, was announcing the German arrivals over the intercom as they approached. Though McClanahan was brave in combat he was also excitable. By listening to his voice, the whole crew could tell how close the Germans were; the closer the enemy came, the higher his vocal register. When they were bearing in upon him, he would be screaming at them as he fired.[3]

One of the German fighters, approaching from eleven o'clock high, released a 20-mm. cannon shell that ripped into the plane just behind pilot Algar on the left side. It plowed through the radio compartment, past the head of S. Sgt. Francis Gerow, and exploded amidship, knocking the top off the oxygen bottle of S. Sgt. Kenneth McKay, the ball-turret gunner. It also drilled a shrapnel sliver into the arm of S. Sgt. John Schimenek, the left waist gunner. But the force of the explosion centered upon the right waist gunner, S. Sgt. L. Corwin Miller, who was already firing from his open window in the side of the fuselage.[4] Miller heard a ''whoomph,'' felt a blow from behind as if someone were hitting him across the back with a board, and was knocked against a bulkhead. Picking himself up, he glanced momentarily at Schimenek, who was staring at him. Both returned to their guns. Schimenek's arm was now stinging ''as if someone had poured battery acid on it,'' but Miller was apparently unhurt. He continued firing at the German planes speeding past his window until his strength began to fade and he realized he had been hit.

Over the intercom he said to Schimenek, ''I think I've had it.'' Though he still felt no pain, he sensed that he was passing out. Locking his knees, he clung desperately to his gun handle.

Schimenek called to Algar, ''Hey, Miller's been hit. He's trying to stay at his gun.''

''Lay him down,'' Algar said. ''Get him down and make him as comfortable as you can. Keep his oxygen mask on.''

McKay, in the ball turret below, offered to come up and help.

''No. You stay where you are,'' Algar ordered. With one gunner wounded and a second one caring for him, he couldn't afford to lose the firepower of a third.

Schimenek, coming to Miller's aid, clipped him on the backs of his knees to make him fall, then laid him out on the catwalk above the bomb bays. To prevent Miller from freezing in the twenty-below-zero atmosphere at 17,000 feet, Schimenek also wrapped eight or nine English blankets around him. Then Schimenek returned to his gun. He did not know how badly Miller had been injured until he looked down to see blood emerging from the man's oxygen mask and freezing as it hit the air.

Miller had now regained consciousness and was in pain. Schimenek scraped the frozen blood from the oxygen mask, exposed Miller's wrist, and jabbed a Syrette of morphine into it. To Miller it felt as if he had been punctured by a railroad spike. Gradually he lapsed back into a coma as Schimenek resumed firing, first his own gun, then Miller's, depending on which side of the plane offered more German targets.

Algar, at the news that Miller was hit, felt fear hit the pit of his stomach for the first time in his seven missions. Never before had anyone in his crew been hit, and the reality jolted him severely when he realized that with more than three hundred miles to go before reaching the target, he had on his hands a man who might die unless he received medical care quickly. But only fleetingly did Algar think of leaving the formation and turning back to England. As aircraft commander, he was responsible for not just this one man but also nine others including himself. If he were to leave the formation, he couldn't hope to get to England alone. The air was full of German fighters. On his own, he would have twenty of them after him. He glanced at his copilot, Lt. Richard V. Wolf, and shrugged. They had no choice but to continue.

The British Spitfires, weaving around the B-17 formations, trying to sort out the German fighters from the American bombers, had managed to engage several enemy planes. But ten miles north of Antwerp, their short operating range forced them to turn for home. Before departing, they claimed victories over four ME-109s and four or five FW-190s, without suffering any losses themselves.

The 92nd Bomb Group led by Maj. James J. Griffith, was the first to encounter the German rockets.[5] Shortly after crossing the coast, the 92nd encountered seven FW-190s firing tracers and 20-mm. cannons. When they were 750 yards behind the group's low squadron, "a very large flash emanated from the center of each enemy aircraft, obliterating it from view." When these planes came back into view they were diving beneath the bombers, but the American fliers scarcely gave them a second glance. By now they were staring apprehensively at several projectiles, each about three inches thick, which were flying into their formation at a high speed but slowly enough to be followed by the human eye. A second or two later, several "large black bursts," half again as big as ordinary flak bursts, appeared among the bombers. These explosions occurred in midair, without benefit of impact. But their effect was so powerful they caused extensive damage to two Fortresses, one flown by Capt. Roland L. Sargent and the other by Lt. J. D. Stewart. Both pilots, however, managed to keep their aircraft in formation.

Between Antwerp and Eupen, more German fighters arrived on the scene, and these began concentrating on the lead formations of the First Task Force—the 91st and the 381st Groups. Lt. Ted Winslow, bombardier in Dame Satan, the "always returning" substitute plane to which his crew was assigned that day, noticed that most of the enemy planes attacking his 91st Group were FW-190s, and he had to admire the courage of some of their pilots as he watched them "rolling, banking, and twisting through our formations with their guns blazing all the time." The B-17 gunners were hitting some of them, but not without cost. Winslow saw the Fortress on his wing, then another and another, catch fire and begin to fall behind.

Near Herstal, sixty-five miles southeast of Antwerp, the 381st suffered its first casualty of the day when one of its planes went down under heavy fighter attack. Crew members of other planes thought they saw seven chutes as this plane began its descent, but two of these chutes failed to open.[6]

In the lead plane of the First Task Force, Lt. David Williams, who had been busy with his calculations as chief navigator for the entire mission, dropped his pencil and slid behind one of the nose machine guns. His group, the 91st, was now over Eupen. FW-190s and ME-109s were streaking in from eleven, twelve, and one o'clock for frontal attacks.[7] Within a short time, Williams and Lt. Sam Slayton, the bombardier, were up to their ankles in spent .50-caliber casings as both fired at top speed. They paused for only a moment when the B-17 on their left wing, piloted by Lt. William Munger, exploded and disintegrated before any of its crew could bail out. Shortly thereafter, Williams and Slayton saw one 20-mm. shell rip a chunk out of the left wing of their own plane and another 20-mm. shell plow into the fuel tank of the same wing. Recognizing death just a few feet away, they awaited with a mixture of resignation and fear the explosion or fire

44

that seemed certain. But moments, then minutes passed, and nothing happened. Their plane, Oklahoma Okie, with Colonel Wurzbach at the controls, continued smoothly to lead the armada despite the cannon shell lodged in its fuel tank.

The armada's air commander, General Williams, in another plane about one hundred feet away, observed the battle with outward composure but inner restlessness.[8] Though he couldn't see what was happening in the rear, he was well aware of the mounting losses in the lead formations and increasingly frustrated at his inability to prevent further losses. Once the action began in an air battle, there was little a commander could do. He could, of course, order his planes to turn around and retreat, but that notion didn't even occur to Williams. He could and did go on the air occasionally to tell his pilots to tighten up their formations. They would do so, then begin to tire under the strain of constant attack and gradually loosen up again, whereupon he would have to pick up his microphone and chew them out once more. But to harangue them too frequently would produce a diminishing effect. Besides, the air waves were already clogged with gunners warning each other of new German arrivals.

As the battle intensified, Williams lost his patience with his limited part in it. He decided he had to get into it with his hands as well as his head. Finding the bombardier's machine gun unused in the nose of the plane, he settled into position and began squeezing out bursts of bullets at the oncoming German planes. The general did not at any time see friendly fighter planes arrive to protect his two beleaguered task forces. Perhaps he was too busy firing his machine gun, or perhaps the sky is so big around such an armada that it is impossible to see everything. Williams may have failed to see the friendly fighters simply because they were not with him very long. But two groups of them, in addition to the Spitfires, did appear, and within the limits imposed by their fuel capacity, they tried to help.

Lt. Col. Donald Blakeslee's Fourth U.S. Fighter Group, with forty-one P-47s that had been scheduled to escort the two task forces from Deist to Eupen, finally caught up to them in the vicinity of Duren, ten miles east of Aachen, which was considered the outside limit of the P-47 range with the paper belly tanks they were using.[9] So these U.S. fighter planes were arriving just about in time for their departure. As they approached, eight or ten enemy aircraft were attacking the lead formation. At sight of the P-47s, the German pilots very sensibly pulled away, realizing these interlopers would be on the scene for no more than two or three minutes, after which the bombers would again be unprotected. Blakeslee's group, having made its pathetically inadequate gesture, was forced to turn to starboard and head back to England. On the homeward flight, the P-47 pilots saw nine German fighters shadowing one of the rear bomber formations but were unable to do anything about it.

Forty P-47s of the 78th Fighter Group, scheduled to escort the B-17s from Antwerp to Eupen, arrived eight minutes late for their rendezvous after seven of their number aborted because of defective belly tanks. These planes, led by Lt. Col. James F. Stone, accompanied one formation of the bombers for a few miles east of Eupen without seeing any German fighters, then circled to return home. Moments later they encountered "small gaggles of FW-190s and ME-109s," which "scattered at [the] approach of [the] group," plus eight twin-engine ME-210s, painted white, perhaps because they had been used in winter on the Russian front. Flight Officer Pete E. Pompetti dived after one of them, raked it with bullets, and last saw it in flames, "tumbling down, nose over tail."

Maj. Eugene Roberts then spotted an ME-110, also painted white. With Flight Officer Glenn H. Koontz on his wing, Roberts gave chase and opened fire when he was about a hundred yards behind the slower German plane. The ME-110 quickly caught fire and went out of control. Roberts pulled up sharply to avoid hitting it, but his wing man, Koontz, blinded by the smoke, hit the German plane's tail with his own left stabilizer. As the ME-110 went down in flames, Koontz's P-47 flew on toward home, suffering no observable handicap despite the loss of half its stabilizer.

Capt. William Smith of the 351st Bomb Group, which led the Second Combat Wing of the First Task Force, watched the departing P-47s with apprehension because in the distance he could see the "little enemies" approaching to replace the "little friends."[10] The German fighters arrived to harass the 351st as soon as the Thunderbolts left, and this time instead of attacking singly or in pairs, the Messerschmitts and Focke-Wulfs were in phalanxes eleven or twelve abreast.

As the cannons popped and the machine guns began to stutter, Smith turned uncomfortably to his copilot, Lt. George Nicolescu, and said, "I've always wondered when they were going to do this."

It had seemed to him the only sensible way for fighters to attack, but he wished the Germans hadn't come to agree with him. The intensity of an assault by a dozen fighters, wing-tip to wing-tip, firing all at once, was so unnerving that Smith could see the entire bomber formation go sloppy. He could feel the sweat inside his sheep-lined flying suit as more German fighters arrived to repeat the new phalanx tactics. Time after time Smith heard the ping of bullets and the bang of shrapnel perforating his plane, and he realized he might hear on the intercom any second that someone in his crew had been hit. But the minutes passed, and though the attacks intensified, sending other Fortresses earthward in flames, his plane flew steadily onward, as if it thrived on bullets.

Several groups of German ME-110 night fighters now joined the battle, launching their 21-cm. rockets into the B-17 formations. One of these was *2 Gruppe Nachtjagdgeschwader 5*, of which navigator-radio operator Hans Bringmann was a member. When his formation approached the American bombers near the German border, he stared in awe at the size of the enemy armada.[11] Flying Fortresses seemed to fill the sky. And darting among them were scores of ME-109s and FW-190s. The slower ME-110 night fighters would have to adopt different tactics. The thirty-six planes of Bringmann's group, each with its four rockets under wing, approached the leading B-17 formations from the front. At about 750 yards, each plane fired all four rockets, then plunged immediately under the American bombers to escape the fury of their machine guns. Having made their single thrusts, the ME-110s quickly turned for home.

Bringmann, looking back at the tight formations of American planes, saw dozens of rockets explode among them. Several B-17s caught fire and began to fall. Though he did not know it, some of these planes belonged to the 381st Group (the low element in the lead combat wing), which was absorbing an assault ferocious and persistent enough to threaten its extinction. Having already lost one plane near Herstal, the 381st lost its second B-17 near Vogelsand, about twenty-five miles east of Eupen.[12] That plane, with one engine dead and another on fire, plummeted to earth at 2:15 P.M. At least nine and perhaps all ten of its crew managed to bail out.

Five minutes later, at 2:20, near the Vogelsand airport, the 381st lost its third B-17 when the plane's right wing caught fire. All ten men bailed out, but only nine chutes opened.

Five minutes after that, at 2:25, the group lost two simultaneously. One had an engine feathered and seemed to be under control except that the nose window was broken, indicating that the pilot and copilot might have been killed by a cannon shell. When this plane fell, only one chute was seen. The other plane that fell at the same time had lost its No. 4 engine, and its right wing was on fire.

Within another five minutes, the group suffered its sixth casualty when one of its planes took two direct hits in the cockpit. Still under attack, the B-17 went into a slow roll, then a spin. One chute appeared.

Ten minutes later, at 2:40, a plane that had been flying for about seventy-five miles with its No. 2 engine afire, suddenly went into a steep dive. Three chutes appeared, after which the entire ship caught fire. But just when all seven men still inside seemed doomed, the tail section snapped off, throwing several of them free. Reports differed on whether four or five more chutes opened.

At 2:45, between Koblenz and Frankfurt, the group lost its eighth Fortress. This one had salvoed its bombs and its No. 2 engine was smoking when it dropped out of formation. The 381st had taken off with twenty-six planes. Now, with only eighteen left, and most of them badly battered, the stricken group had still to go the rest of the way to the target, then all the way back to England.

Just as the 381st Group was losing its eighth plane, the 92nd Group, several miles to the rear near Aachen, was losing its first. Two of its B-17s, those piloted by Capt. Roland Sargeant and Lt. J. D. Stewart, had been struggling to stay in formation since they sustained rocket damage near the Dutch coast. Both pilots had done well to keep their planes in the air, but Stewart's luck now ran out. His Fortress began falling. He gave the bail-out order and the whole crew escaped. Ten chutes opened before the plane crashed.

Near Koblenz, Lt. Philip Algar, pilot of the last plane in the 384th Group's low squadron, heard his left waist gunner, S. Sgt. John Schimenek, call out a warning that a German fighter was on their tail, firing his 20-mm. cannon. (Schimenek was now dividing his time between his own machine gun and that of the wounded right waist gunner, S. Sgt. L. Corwin Miller, who needed frequent attention.) A moment after hearing Schimenek's warning, Algar looked out his side window in time to see a string of cannon shells from the rear, flying past his face at a distance of less than six feet. These shells, set to go off either on contact or after a fixed time, exploded in quick succession—pomp! pomp! pomp!—close enough to put holes in the side of the plane but just far enough from Algar to leave him unscathed.

The 384th, in the coffin corner of the Second Combat Wing, had fighters coming at it from all directions. Algar, looking around, saw an engine catch fire on the lead Fortress of the group's high squadron. The plane's pilot, experienced enough to be a squadron leader, pulled away from the formation, apparently trying to spare the other planes in case he exploded, and also trying to get away from the lower squadrons so that if his men had to bail out, they would not be chewed up by propellers. Unfortunately, this squadron had several new, inexperienced pilots. When their leader pulled out of formation, they followed. Algar, aware of the confusion, told the squadron on the radio to get back in formation and let their leader go. Then he pushed his own throttles forward and moved up to the squadron leader's position. When the errant planes came back to the formation, they fell in on Algar's wing. Though this was only his seventh mission, he suddenly found himself leading a squadron.

Despite the carnage, one combat wing still had not lost a plane. Ironically, it was the most vulnerable rear wing, led by Col. Maurice Preston and his 379th Group. But so many of the fifty-three planes in this wing were already shot full of holes that Preston did not expect their luck to hold. He was especially concerned about the high group on his right; too much distance separated it from his group. Unless this composite high group were to close in, his own top element could not possibly give it the protection it needed on its flank. Since the high group was not under his command, he couldn't order it to come in tighter, but he was especially concerned about it because it included six planes from his own 379th. His group had already suffered such heavy losses during its less-than-three months of combat that he was determined to reverse the trend. He didn't want to see any 379th planes go down needlessly, and he feared the worst if this composite high group remained too far out.

Preston's fears soon proved to be justified. At 2:45, a B-17 in the high squadron of the composite group was hit by a German fighter from the rear. The big bomber went into a steep dive and exploded when it hit the ground. No parachutes appeared.

Five minutes later, a second plane from the same high squadron went into a plunge after an attack by several fighters. On the way to the ground it broke apart. Four crewmen emerged, but not in time to get their chutes opened.

Ten minutes later, at 3:00 P.M., a third ship from the same squadron fell out of formation with one engine on fire and fighters surrounding it. All three of these planes and their crews had been furnished to the composite group by Preston's 379th.

It was apparent now that the decision to fly the mission at 17,000 feet would be costly. Silhouetted against the cloud layer just above them, the B-17s had become sharply defined targets not only for the German fighters but also for the antiaircraft guns on the ground. The antiaircraft fire had been sporadic and may not by itself have brought down any of the bombers, but it had punctured many of them with shrapnel. Some of the German fighters were using the clouds as cover, darting out for sudden attacks, then back in before the B-17 gunners had time to react. The German guns were so accurate and the assault so persistent that the men in the Flying Fortresses began to realize they were in the most critical situation they had ever faced. They hadn't even penetrated as far as Frankfurt and their planes were falling in such numbers that they had left a trail of wreckage across western Europe. On some previous missions they had taken severe losses but never at this rate. Most important, never had the German fighters and antiaircraft guns been able to turn them back short of the target. Never before, however, had they attacked so ferociously. With the battle continuing at this intensity, the B-17 crews could no longer ignore the possibility of total annihilation.

The lead group, the 91st, had suffered only a few rocket attacks, but it was bearing the brunt of the mass attacks by ME-109s and FW-190s. They approached in line astern, sometimes twenty-five strong, from twelve o'clock high or level, while smaller packs of three to eight kept pecking from the rear or from below.

One plane in the 91st, Eagle's Wrath, piloted by Lt. Anthony Arcaro of Brooklyn, had been under constant attack from Antwerp to Frankfurt. As soon as the bomber showed signs of damage, ME-109s singled it out and besieged it four at a time from such close range that on one occasion Arcaro expected a collision. An exceptionally daring German pilot went into a roll after emptying his guns and crossed the nose of the B-17 upside down, so close that Arcaro could stare into his face.

By this time, Eagle's Wrath was shredded with holes and its crew members did not expect it to fly much farther. Yet they continued firing at the onrushing Germans. The radio operator-gunner, Sgt. Delmar Kaech, who was on his fifth mission since transferring in June from the Canadian to the U.S. Air Force, had brought a double supply of ammunition aboard this morning when he learned that the day's target was Schweinfurt.[13] He now had plenty of time to use it because the plane's entire communications system had been shot out, leaving him no radio to operate. He was firing his gun when he noticed that Sgt. H. K. Michaud, the ball-turret gunner, had been killed. As Kaech was trying to get Michaud's body out of the turret, word came back from Arcaro that the plane was no longer fliable. By the time Kaech groped his way back to the radio compartment where he had left his parachute, the plane was in a dive. He put on the chute as best he could, went out the hatch, and pulled his rip-cord as soon as he had fallen clear of the plunging bomber. Unfortunately, he'd had only enough time to get one leg into the harness, part of which was also still unhooked. When the chute opened, the jolt twisted and dislocated one of his vertebrae, sending him to earth with his back in pain, but he had little time to think about that. He was holding on for dear life to his unfastened harness.

When Lt. Hans Langer and his comrades in *2 Gruppe Jagdgeschwader 51* caught up to the Fortresses, the bombers were already east of Frankfurt. Langer's group, after taking off from Neubiberg near Munich, had been vectored toward Frankfurt, which German Homeland Defense officials considered the probable target right up to the moment the bombers began passing it. They now expected Schweinfurt to be the target.

Langer, like most German pilots, knew enough about the Schweinfurt plants to realize their importance; and when he saw the masses of American bombers heading eastward, he felt certain they were going there. He and his group, deciding on a twelve o'clock attack, sped around to the front of the American air fleet. The Germans had settled on the frontal approach as the best tactic against the B-17 because of the effectiveness of the American .50-caliber machine gun.[14] German armaments experts had concluded from early experience that this weapon had one compelling advantage over their own 20-mm. cannon. The machine gun, because of its greater initial velocity, had a longer range. And from the rear or from either side of a Fortress,

51

seven of these guns could fire at once, whereas from the front, a German fighter faced only two, or at most, four.

The first assault by Langer and his comrades was a coordinated effort. In formation they passed through one of the lead Fortress groups, firing their cannons and machine guns. Looking back, Langer saw two B-17s trailing smoke though neither was going down. The ME-109s circled tightly, broke up into pairs, and attacked from the rear, a tactic that gave them more time to aim at the Fortresses even though it did expose them to a greater concentration of machine-gun fire. After this attack, Langer saw four or five more bombers trailing smoke. When he came around to make his third pass, he decided to slip in from the side, thus avoiding the heavy B-17 firepower focused on his comrades in the rear. To slip a plane, a pilot must turn his rudder control one way and his aileron control the other. The effect is to glide sideways while keeping the wings fairly level and the nose pointing forward. For an experienced pilot it is not a difficult maneuver.

Langer slipped just beneath the bombers and pulled up in their midst with one on each side of him and a third only fifty feet in front of him. His ME-109 was now flying formation with the B-17s. Both on his right and on his left he could look American gunners in the eye, confident that they wouldn't fire at him for fear they might hit each other. He had, of course, to contend with the rear gunner in the plane ahead of him, but he also had that plane in his cannon sight. He pushed his button and a moment later saw the plane's No. 2 engine pull away from the wing as if it had been torn off. Then the whole right wing collapsed and flopped over onto the left. The stricken bomber, completely out of control, flipped onto its back and hit another B-17, causing a massive detonation. A huge fireball appeared and was followed by such a powerful concussion it could only have resulted from the explosion of bombs in one or both of the B-17s. Langer, caught in this concussion, either blacked out momentarily or lost his orientation. He felt as if his small fighter plane were being hurled backward. The next thing he knew he was some distance behind the B-17 formation and below it, but still flying, apparently undamaged. The Fortress he had hit and the one with which it collided were plunging to earth.

Langer noticed now that his fuel warning light was on. Turning back to Frankfurt, he landed to refuel and rearm, but by this time the

American armada was too far east for him to catch it. He would have to wait for its return from the target.

As the Americans approached Schweinfurt, they had already lost twenty-one bombers and the German fighters were still swarming around them like wasps, but the surviving Fortresses continued their relentless path toward the target. The 91st Group, still in the lead, was about twenty-five miles from the Initial Point (the spot at which the bombardier takes over for the straight-and-level run to the target) when another of its planes, piloted by Lt. Eugene M. Lockhart, faced a crisis.[15] This Fortress had already sustained damage to its left wing-tip and right horizontal stabilizer. Now it developed a malfunction of the supercharger on the No. 3 engine. Unable to keep pace with a full bomb load, and watching the formation pull slowly away to leave him at the mercy of the attacking fighters, Lockhart ordered his bombardier, Lt. Robert Sherwin, to salvo the bombs, and he ordered the rest of the crew to throw out any equipment they didn't think they would need. Thus lightened, the plane again moved gradually forward on its three good engines to resume its place in the formation.

As the 91st neared the Initial Point, the plane with the reputation for always coming back, Dame Satan, began to look as if it wouldn't. Dame Satan's bombardier, Lt. Ted Winslow, was ready to assume control of the ship when an FW-190 flew directly at him from twelve o'clock level.[16] At the last possible moment the German pilot fired his cannon and swerved from his collision course. One shell hit the supercharger on Dame Satan's No. 2 engine. Another shell or bullet hit one of the bomber's fuel tanks. Within moments, Dame Satan began losing speed and altitude, falling back despite the fact that the pilot, Lt. Jack Hargis, had now pushed all three working throttles full forward. Heavily loaded as it was, Dame Satan couldn't possibly catch up to the formation. Hargis quickly made the same decision Lockhart had made, ordering Winslow to salvo all the bombs. But even after the plane was relieved of this weight, it continued to fall back. Alone with only three engines operating and fuel leaking from one tank, Hargis had no choice but to turn for home and hope for good fortune.

It seemed a bleak hope, especially when the vulnerable Dame Satan began to attract fighters. The damaged Fortress still had its guns, however, and its crew continued to return the German fire. The rear gunner, Sgt. Leland Judy, buoyed everyone's hopes when he announced that he had set one German fighter afire. Shortly thereafter, the remaining fighters retired, perhaps running short of fuel, and Hargis headed toward Belgium, carefully avoiding cities with their unfriendly flak batteries. A sense of hopeless loneliness settled over Dame Satan's crew.

It was about 2:50 P.M. when General Williams, in the second-lead plane of the task force under his command, got his first view of Schweinfurt, about fifteen miles dead ahead.[17] The city was small and flat against a green-gold background, exactly as it had looked on the Top Secret plaster mockup at Williams's headquarters. In the foreground was the meandering Main River, and on all sides the gentle Franconian slopes. The railroad track from Würzburg (twenty-seven miles southwest) curved its way around these hills, then pointed directly at the ball-bearing center and the cluster of five factories that were today's target. Williams could be certain now that though his force had been brutally assaulted and drastically reduced, it would not be stopped.

As the first bombers approached Schweinfurt, a high cirrus layer covered half the sky and the air was clear. At the southwest edge of the city, where the railroad tracks converged into a large marshaling yard, Williams could see the passenger station and freight depots, two "half-moon" locomotive roundhouses, and around all these rail facilities, the five factories so precious to the Germans. There was no doubt now that these factories would be bombed. Williams's lead groups were so close they couldn't possibly be turned back. Despite the fiercest defense any bomber force had ever faced, the Fortresses had once again prevailed.

In the lead plane just ahead of Williams, Colonel Wurzbach and Lieutenant Williams, his navigator, could take satisfaction in the jobs they had done so far. Wurzbach had held his front position despite constant attacks that had taken a chunk out of his left wing and lodged an unexploded shell in his left wing fuel tank. Williams, on this deepest American penetration of Germany to date, had guided the armada precisely to the target. Now, at the Initial Point, it was time for the bombardier, Lt. Sam Slayton, to take over for the bomb run.

Five miles southwest of the city, a fairly intense flak barrage came up to jolt them, but Slayton held a steady course and with a clear view of the target, dropped his bombs. On his signal all the other planes in the 91st Group did likewise. As the group banked westward toward home, its crews could see the first cluster of explosions among the factories.

For the groups behind the 91st, precision would be more difficult. By the time they arrived, smoke and fire would be spreading a cover over the target. If the first bombers had missed, then all the others, guided by their explosions, might also miss, thereby rendering the entire mission useless. Lieutenant Slayton, aware of this possibility, was relieved to know that his bombs had landed where he aimed them.

Only eighteen B-17s remained in the shattered 381st when it approached the target, and as if the group had not suffered enough, one of these was hit, probably by flak, on the bomb run. With its No. 3 and No. 4 engines silenced, it fell out of formation and went into a long glide. The seventeen surviving planes of the 381st dropped their bombs and followed the 91st westward.

In the Second Combat Wing, the 384th, flying the low, coffin-corner position, was absorbing the heaviest punishment. As Maj. Thomas Beckett led his battered group toward the target, only eleven of its original eighteen planes remained in the formation. Two had turned back because of mechanical failures after dropping their bombs on targets of opportunity, and five had been shot down. Several of the planes still plodding onward were carrying wounded crewmen.

In Lt. Philip Algar's Lucky Thirteen, S. Sgt. Corwin Miller, gravely wounded over Holland more than an hour and a half earlier, still lay bundled in blankets on the bomb-bay catwalk. Lapsing into and out of consciousness, he would stare at the ceiling when he was awake and listen to the gunfire around him. He could see the bursts and feel the whoomph as flak exploded beneath the plane, tossing it upward and lifting him off the floor. S. Sgt. Kenneth McKay, whose ball-turret gun had been disabled, was now at Miller's gun, and the air above Miller's head was filled with .50-caliber casings as McKay and S. Sgt. John Schimenek fired back at the Germans.

During one of Miller's conscious periods he tried to stand up but couldn't make it. Whenever there was a lull in the fighting, Schimenek would bend over him, chipping the frozen blood and saliva from his oxygen mask. Though Miller was getting all the oxygen the rest of the crew could spare, he kept motioning for more. He couldn't seem to get enough air. Neither he nor Schimenek realized that the blood coming out of his mouth was only a fraction of what he was losing. His lungs were gradually filling up with it, and so was the inside of his leather flight suit as the wounds in his back continued to bleed.

In the 384th's lead plane, Major Beckett turned control over to the bombardier, Lt. Joseph W. Baggs, when the group reached the Initial Point.[18] They were strangely unmolested by fighters now, but flak barrages were exploding uncomfortably close. As they started down the bomb run, Baggs could distinguish the general target area ahead by the rising smoke clouds. He could see, however, that it would be difficult to pinpoint the factories for which he was aiming. "I picked out what I thought was the target and synchronized on it," he said later. "It was the only thing I could see that resembled the target as described." When the group was almost over the target area, Baggs, peering down through the smoke and flame, could see enough to convince him unhappily that he was to the left of the factory complex, and that if he continued on this course he would probably bomb an open field, thus wasting all the effort spent in getting here. With only a short distance in which to correct his course, he made a maximum adjustment to the right. But was it too late? As his plane brought him to the point of decision, it seemed to him he was "not completely over the target" and "probably would not hit it." He hesitated a fraction of a second, then dropped his bombs. He did not see them descend or explode. Because of the thick smoke, he could see neither the target nor the city just beyond. If any of his bombs had hit the target, they would have had to hit the northeast edge of it, where the ball-bearing factories met the rest of the city. But he wasn't sure. And this uncertainty was disturbing because the entire group had bombed on his signal.

When the Third and Fourth Combat Wings, under the command of Col. Howard M. "Slim" Turner, arrived over Schweinfurt, the target area was a mass of smoke and fire. The bombs of the Third Wing, led by Maj. William S. Raper and his 306th Group, added so much more smoke and flames to the scene that when Col. Maurice Preston arrived with his Fourth (and last) Combat Wing, what he saw looked like the bed of a gigantic furnace.[19] He had no idea where his bombs would do the most good. All he could do was turn the plane over to his group bombardier, Capt. Joseph Brown, and hope for the best.

The outstanding landmarks Brown could see were a white water tower and the railroad yard. With these check points, both familiar to him from the plaster mockup, he felt he needed no others. Ignoring a new swarm of fighters, he picked out his aiming point and dropped his bombs, all incendiaries, with reasonable confidence. On the intercom he asked the ball-turret gunner, "How did they look?"

"On target," the gunner assured him.

"Okay, we're fighting for us now," Brown shouted into the microphone. "Let's get out of here."

They cleared the target without mishap, but some of the men behind them were less fortunate. Lt. Elton "Pete" Hoyt and his crew, flying a plane called Battling Bobbie, were hit by flak over Schweinfurt and forced out of formation. No chutes appeared as the plane descended, but there was no crash either. When Hoyt's comrades in the 379th got their last glimpse at Battling Bobbie, it was on the deck, alone, still flying, westward toward home.[20]

By the time Col. Kermit Stevens approached Schweinfurt with his 303rd Group, the very last in the armada, the city's defenders had launched a massive smoke screen to intensify the black clouds over the already obscure factory area.[21] Though the huge Kugelfischer plant was the 303rd's primary target, neither Stevens nor his pilot, Maj. Kirk Mitchell, could hope to locate it precisely in the inferno ahead. Because they were the low outside group in the Fourth Combat Wing, their wheeling turn into the Initial Point put them off course, and as they passed it, they had to execute a slight "S" to the left to straighten themselves out and establish bombing interval.[22] When the lead bombardier, Lt. Lawrence McCord, took control of the plane, only a minute and a half remained before he would have to release his load. McCord was not destined to have even that much time to sight his target. About a minute before release time, a piece of antiaircraft shrapnel burst through the nose of the plane and into McCord's stomach. The navigator, Lt. R. F. McElwain, and another crewman sprang into action immediately, moving the wounded McCord away from his Norden bomb-sight. But before McElwain could release the bombs, the entire 303rd Group had passed the Kugelfischer plant and was over Schweinfurt. Ironically, the city was now being bombed because its antiaircraft gunners were accurate. If

McCord had not been wounded by flak, these clusters of bombs would have fallen two or three minutes earlier, upon factories rather than houses.

As the last American planes turned west for home, explosions rocked the entire Schweinfurt area and fires were spreading in all directions. Despite the fierce and heroic resistance of 300 German fighters, General Williams's armada had reached its target and 182 Fortresses had dropped about 420 tons of bombs—235 1,000-pound and 719 500-pound high explosives plus more than 1,000 British-made 250-pound incendiaries. An umbrella of smoke covered the city.

A half-hour earlier, Schweinfurt had been one of Germany's most comfortable, peaceful, and attractive towns, an admirable example of how an age-old community, steeped in medieval tradition, could be modernized and industrialized without losing its beauty, style, or architectural integrity. At least eleven centuries old, it had been a free and independent city from the 13th to the 19th century, when it was incorporated into Bavaria. Its town hall had been built in 1570; several buildings around it dated from the 17th and 18th centuries. In 1883, a Schweinfurt mechanic named Friedrich Fischer invented the ball-grinder, a machine that facilitated for the first time the mass production of ball bearings, previously made only by hand. Fischer founded a company that was bought a few years later by another ball-bearing manufacturer, Georg Schafer, who merged it with his own firm to create Kugelfischer & Co. The growth of this company, now Germany's largest ball-bearing producer, had encouraged three competitors to settle in Schweinfurt, making it Europe's most important ball-bearing center. One company, a Swedish-owned firm named Vereingte Kugellager Fabrik (VKF), had two factories here, one just east of Kugelfischer, the other just south of it. Adjoining the south VKF Werke, near the railway yards, were the Fichtel & Sachs Werke and the Deutsche Star Kugelhalter Werke.

Kugelfischer and VKF each employed almost ten thousand workers, while the other two employed at least half that many. Some of the workers were foreigners, French, Belgian, and Polish, conscripted by the German government and housed in labor camps just south of the factories.

Because of war-time needs, all five plants were producing at capacity. The people on the day shift were busy at their benches or machines when the air-raid sirens began to screech shortly after 2:30 P.M. The people of Schweinfurt had only recently begun to consider the possibility that they might actually be bombed. Their town, with fifty-thousand people, was so small and so deep inside Germany that British night bombers were not likely ever to find it, and the American day bombers would have to overcome several hundred German fighters to reach it. Nevertheless, in mid-July, antiaircraft batteries had been set up on the roofs of the plants and on the hills around the city.[23]

The chief of Schweinfurt's Air Defense Police, Wilhelm Weger, now alerted the antiaircraft crews, the fire department, and the brigade of men assigned to ignite smoke pots in an attempt to obscure the ball-bearing factories. Air-raid wardens in the factories and all over town herded people to the less-than-adequate bomb shelters. On their way to the shelters, residents could see the American bombers approaching from the southwest, their silvery fuselages glistening in the bright sunlight.

The flak batteries south of the city began to fire at full speed, filling the skies around the bombers with smoke and shrapnel. These were 88-mm. and 105-mm. guns, easily capable of lofting their shells to the B-17 altitudes of 17,000 to 20,000 feet. The guns on the factory roofs were smaller, 20-mm. cannon, able to fire at the planes only if they dropped lower for their bomb runs.

Leo Wehner, a Kugelfischer employee who was also a reserve lieutenant in charge of the factory's antiaircraft guns, hurried to his command post on the roof of its largest building and inspected the gun crews there.[24] At various locations around the one-square-mile plant he had nine guns, all manned by steel-helmeted Kugelfischer co-workers. When Wehner saw the bombers coming, he ordered his men to prepare to fire, but not to do so unless the Americans came down to the 8,000-foot maximum range of their guns. Through his binoculars he watched the planes approach. It seemed to him they were more than 30,000 feet high.

Soon the B-17s were overhead and the first bombs fell on a large bearing shop. Balls, rings, and sharp chunks of metal began flying through the air. More bombs fell among the buildings, shattering glass, collapsing walls, starting fires, and creating a staccato of booming, painful noise. Wehner realized he and his men on the roof

59

were in immediate danger of death, yet they didn't dare leave it. The ground was a garden of explosions. The men huddled anxiously around their sand-bagged guns while Wehner went into his "command post" hut and dived under the bed.

During the breaks between waves of bombers, Wehner got up and looked out. Dense smoke and dust were rising around all the factories and throughout the northern sections of the city. The southernmost parts of the Kugelfischer plant and the surrounding area seemed to be demolished. Hundreds of bombs had fallen. And though many of them had gone astray, it was astonishing to see how many others had hit the factories, even from such a height. The bombers were still at their original altitudes as they passed overhead and disappeared. Wehner's antiaircraft guns hadn't even been able to take a shot at them.

For twenty-four minutes the attack continued. Throughout the town, people who could not find shelters ran from building to building, trying to dodge the bombs as they looked for a doorway, an archway, or a wall that might afford some protection. Several buildings in the business district were blown apart or set afire, and in the northwest section, more than a hundred bombs, dropped too late by miscalculating bombardiers, destroyed whole blocks of houses.

After the last B-17 passed over Schweinfurt and the explosions ended, a silence descended, broken only by the crackling of fires. When the people were finally convinced that no more planes would come, they slowly emerged from their shelters, stunned, begrimed by smoke and dirt, and in some cases covered with blood. A total of 203 had died—70 men, 77 women, 48 children, and 8 foreign workers. In the factories, about 380 thousand square feet of buildings had been destroyed and more than a million square feet damaged.

At the plants, the workers reappeared and numbly began clearing away debris and searching for possible victims. Destruction was so widespread that none of the factories looked as if it would operate again for a long time. Kugelfischer's Leo Wehner came down from his rooftop gun post and walked through the grounds, inspecting the damage. In one shelter, nineteen people lay dead. A wall had collapsed after a direct hit. In many of the buildings there might be other victims, but if so it would take time to find them. At least twenty bombs had scored direct hits on important structures. Wehner noticed one thing with some satisfaction, however. Fire, which posed the greatest threat to the sensitive ball and bearing machines, had been kept to a minimum.

Dr. Georg Schafer, a stocky, dynamic, quick-moving man who was the principal owner of Kugelfischer and son of its founder, had gone to Bamberg on business and was returning home by train that afternoon when he learned that Schweinfurt was under attack.[25] Because the railway station and yards had been demolished, his train stopped about a mile north of the city. He ran from there to his large, elegant home in the northern suburbs. After finding his family still in their shelter and making certain they were safe, he hurried to his factory, expecting the worst. Schafer had feared for some time that his and the other ball-bearing plants would be attacked. One evening early in the war, he and his family were listening to the radio when German newscaster Hans Fritsche said, "Last night our planes bombed the British ball-bearing center at Chelmsford." Leaping to his feet, Schafer had shouted to the radio, "Shut up, you fool! Don't talk about it!" He had feared the British would get ideas from the Chelmsford raid. His fears had been well grounded. Apparently the British or the Americans or both had remembered Chelmsford all too well.

When Schafer reached his bombed factory, he took one short tour of inspection. It looked even worse than he had expected. Going into the bomb shelter below his battered office, he sat down in utter dejection. He was convinced that all his sensitive machinery had been ruined, that his plant was just a pile of rubble, that the company his father had begun and he himself had built into a huge industry was beyond redemption.

4

All but three of the B-17s in Gen. Robert Williams's Schweinfurt fleet enjoyed a short respite after turning for home. These three succumbed to flak wounds inflicted over the target, bringing the armada's casualties so far to a horrendous total of twenty-five. For the others, the skies ahead looked clear, and some of the more hopeful crew members were beginning to wonder if the German fighters had finally exhausted themselves. They soon found out.

At 3:15 P.M., the first task force under Colonel Gross circled over Meiningen to reassemble and tighten its formations before heading westward. Ten minutes later the second task force under Colonel Turner did likewise. With the smoke and fire of Schweinfurt behind them, the American airmen, deeper inside Germany than they had ever been, could enjoy their first relaxed look at the beautiful German landscape with its wide, winding rivers and green, tree-covered hills. But the respite did not long endure. A few miles west of Meiningen, the ME-109s, ME-110s, ME-210s, and FW-190s began to reappear, first in twos and threes, then in packs of ten and twelve.

The first victim of the renewed attacks was a previously damaged B-17 in the 92nd Group, flown by Capt. Roland L. Sargent. After a concentrated assault, Sargent's plane caught fire, then quickly exploded. Only three parachutes opened among the fragments falling to earth.[1]

As the 91st Group approached the Frankfurt area under sustained attack, one of its pilots, Lt. James D. Judy, who was on his fourth mission, saw a German fighter coming at him "level on the nose." Despite Judy's attempts at evasion, the enemy pilot held his course and in a remarkable display of accuracy, landed at least three 20-mm. shells in the B-17's nose section near the root of the left wing.[2] A large hole opened in the wing, and when Judy tested the controls he found them sluggish. Even more seriously, the shells hit and ignited the plane's batteries, starting a fire just below the pilot's compartment. In moments, the cockpit was full of flames, sparks, and smoke. The plane went into a dive and fell seven thousand feet before Judy and his copilot, Lt. Roger W. Layn, could level it out. Five German fighters that had pursued the bomber in its dive, now proceeded to pump hundreds of machine-gun bullets into it, starting more fires. But the dive had apparently extinguished the worst of the cockpit flames, enabling Judy to keep the plane under precarious control, despite the smoke and fumes, while he sent Layn to the rear to find out how much damage had been done. Layn discovered that the entire plane was riddled; several small fires were burning, and electrical sparks were jumping from the broken ends of the battery cables. When he reported to Judy, they agreed the time had come to abandon ship. Judy had also noticed the rudder and elevator cables were severely damaged and the aileron trim tabs were jammed in the "up" position. With the partial controls left to him, it was doubtful that he could keep the plane in level flight much longer.

Layn again went to the rear to make sure the crew members bailed out safely. Lts. Edward DeCoster and Lewis Allen (the navigator and bombardier) dropped through the nose hatch, and all the enlisted men escaped without difficulty except T. Sgt. Earl Cherry, the engineer, who could not jump for two reasons: he had been badly injured in one foot, and his parachute had burned in one of the fires.

When Layn reported the situation to Judy, the pilot decided there was only one course. Rather than doom Sergeant Cherry to certain death, he would try to get the ship back to England. But there was no need for all three of them to die. Lieutenant Layn, he said, was free to bail out or stay.

Layn decided to stay.

In that case, Judy said, he would try to manage the plane himself while Layn tried to put out the fires and fight off the German attackers.

As Layn returned to the rear, Judy put the ship into a gradual descent, zigzagging to avoid the bullets which were still arriving. At one hundred feet above the ground, he leveled off. He had no navigator, so he simply pointed the plane in the general direction of England.

In the rear, Layn found Sergeant Cherry, despite his pain, hobbling from fire to fire on one foot, beating out the flames with whatever he could find. Cherry couldn't use the fire extinguishers, because their chemicals gave off a noxious gas when they came in contact with battery sparks. Layn went to work at top speed, putting out the flames that continued to erupt, throwing everything movable out of the plane to lighten it, and firing the waist guns at the fighters on their tail. During one lull he went back to the tail gun, which would have given him a better aim at the pursuers, but found it disabled by enemy fire. Returning to the waist guns, Layn fired them alternately as German shells and bullets kept whizzing past.

In the cockpit, Lieutenant Judy was waging a desperate battle with his damaged controls, and it was beginning to look as if he might win. The besieged Fortress continued to fly.

Among the German pilots attacking the B-17s was Lt. Hans Langer of *2 Gruppe Jagdgeschwader 51*, who had brought down two of the big bombers on their way to the target. Langer was not so fortunate this time. Taking off from Frankfurt where he had refueled and rearmed, he attached himself to the first unit he could find in the air since his own unit was scattered. With two other planes he made two passes at the returning Fortresses. He may have scored some hits, but he did not manage to bring any of them down.[3]

Some of his comrades were enjoying greater success. Between Bonn and Aachen, at 4:30 P.M., the 381st Group lost its tenth plane. When this Fortress dropped out of formation, it was surrounded by fighters. It was the seventh to fall since leaving Schweinfurt.

Help for the Americans was on the way. Fifteen miles east of Eupen, forty-six P-47s of the U.S. 56th Fighter Group, led by Col. Hubert Zemke, made contact with the homecoming bombers,[4] but the arrival of the escort was ironically disastrous for one Fortress in the

305th Group. This plane, flown by Lt. Rothery McKeegan, the group's operations officer, was limping along on two engines and holding its place in formation only because the group's flight leader, Maj. J. C. Price, had slowed to 150 miles per hour, the highest speed McKeegan could maintain. Three German planes, an ME-110 and two ME-210s, were circling the 305th and had moved around ahead of it when the first P-47 to appear on the scene dived at them from 27,000 feet.

The Thunderbolt's guns scored such a devastating hit on the ME-110 that it exploded, breaking up into so many metal chunks that the oncoming Fortresses could not avoid all of them. One chunk hit McKeegan's plane, further increasing its damage and decreasing its speed.[5] Though this latest wound may have been enough by itself to doom the Fortress, an FW-190 moved in for the final blow. As the Focke-Wulf sped away, McKeegan's plane burst into flames. It began a gradual descent, still apparently under the pilot's control long enough for eight parachutes to appear. Then, after a gigantic explosion, it simply disintegrated and faded from sight. Of its eight crew members dangling from parachutes, only seven were destined to reach the ground safely. One man's chute, perhaps struck by a piece of burning debris, burst into flames, plunging him to certain death.

The P-47s proved more helpful to their big brothers on the way home than they had been on the route to the target. Zemke's group was effective in diminishing enemy frontal attacks. Flying above the Fortresses where they could see these attacks developing, they simply dived at the German fighters and disrupted their approach. Then they engaged the Germans in dogfights, which kept them busy while many Fortresses escaped. The air battle reached its greatest intensity now over western Germany, then over Belgium, as the American fighters chased the Germans in and out among the bombers, climbing, diving, banking, rolling in desperate acrobatic maneuvers at such high speed that only the men involved in them could make sense of them. Three P-47s were lost in the engagement while Zemke's men claimed the destruction of fifteen German fighters plus four more probables.

Despite the support of Zemke's P-47s, however, bombers continued to fall victims to the German guns. At 4:25 P.M., one went down near Aachen, with all ten men escaping. At 4:40, two were seen going down, with seven parachutes emerging from one but only two from the other. Fifteen minutes later, another fell with only four chutes trailing behind it. Eleven B-17s had now been destroyed on the return voyage, bringing to thirty-three so far the total losses on just the Schweinfurt mission.[6]

And still another Fortress, which had turned back shortly before reaching the target because it had lost an engine and couldn't keep pace, was flying into more trouble as it approached the outskirts of Brussels. This was Dame Satan of the 91st Group, piloted by Lt. Jack Hargis. Unmolested for more than an hour as it plodded slowly across Germany alone, Dame Satan encountered a pair of FW-190s over the little town of Montreuil, between Tournai and Frasnes.[7]

The first of the German fighters made a pass almost head-on from eleven o'clock but did not fire a shot. Lt. Ted Winslow, the B-17's bombardier, was at his nose gun when the second FW-190 approached from one o'clock. He saw the flash of the Focke-Wulf's cannon and pressed his own trigger, but his gun jammed after two rounds. When he looked up, the fighter was "right on top of us." Winslow felt the bomber shudder and vibrate as at least two 20-mm. shells ripped into it.[8]

Over the intercom someone said, "Oh, . . . I'm hit."

"Who's hit?" Hargis asked.

Another voice said, "The radio operator. In the chest."

The plane went into a shallow dive, suffering from such massive damage that Hargis was unable to pull it out and resume level flight. Winslow noticed that his altimeter still registered 16,000 feet, but they were dropping fast.

"Prepare to bail out," Hargis ordered. "Someone help the radio operator."

Winslow and Lt. Richard Martin, the navigator, snapped on their parachutes, tore up and threw out some classified papers, then awaited the next command, which came quickly.

"Bail out when ready. Bail out when ready."

Martin went first through the hatch in the nose. Winslow was about to follow when he heard Hargis's last command. "Hurry up, you guys. I can't hold this thing up all day."

Kneeling at the hatch, Winslow took a deep draught of oxygen, then glanced down at the green and distant earth. He was struck by how small everything looked. Bending forward, he tumbled out head first. A moment later he felt "a terrific jerk and a sensation of being pulled through space at a tremendous speed.'' He could still hear the roar of the plane's engines, and he was certain something had gone wrong. The wind was knocking him about so roughly he couldn't see what had happened, but it felt as if his chute had been caught on the tail. It must have opened too quickly. He envisioned the horrible likelihood that the plunging plane would pull him with it to the ground. But before he had time to reconcile himself to this fate, his chute inexplicably popped open above him ''like a beautiful white umbrella.'' The sound of the falling plane's engines died away.

When Winslow looked around, he saw several chutes below him but none above. Though he couldn't count all of them, members of the Belgian resistance movement, watching from the ground, saw eight open before the plane exploded. A ninth crew member, Sgt. Star Tucker of Athol, Massachusetts, the ball-turret gunner, who had been told of his promotion that morning, got out of the plane safely, but his chute did not open. The Belgians found his body near the debris. Lieutenant Hargis, the pilot, was still in the plane when it exploded.

As Winslow descended, the wind continued to buffet him so severely he feared his parachute might collapse. Approaching the ground, he heard dogs bark, which he supposed were German police dogs, and saw what looked like farm buildings scattered across the countryside. He also noticed with some alarm that the wind was carrying him sideways toward a long row of trees at the edge of one of these farms, and it seemed that even if he missed the trees, he might be impaled on one of several sharp poles sticking up from a hay wagon. To change his course he pulled a shroud line and slipped sharply leftward. This maneuver also took some air from his chute and quickened his descent. He missed the trees and the wagon, landing instead in a beet field. The beets, already dug up, were spread on the ground. Winslow came down hard. His right leg hit one of these beets and twisted sideways with such force he could hear bones snap.

Before he had time even to try standing, a farmer near the haywagon ran over to him. Looking up, Winslow asked, ''Belgian?''

''Oui, oui,'' the man said. ''Et vous?''

''American.''

Motioning for him to stay down, the man warned, ''Cachez! Cachez!''

Understanding enough French to realize he had been told to hide, Winslow hid by gathering bits of foliage around him while the man went away, presumably to get help. A few minutes later a German patrol party passed by, probably looking for the fallen Americans, but Winslow was now sufficiently hidden. Shortly after the Germans disappeared, the Belgian returned with a tan civilian suit and helped Winslow put it on. Several other Belgians gathered around, some of them asking for souvenirs. He gave them his parachute and harness, his Mae West (inflatable vest), and whatever else he didn't think he would need. Suffering the pain of a broken leg (it proved to be fractured in three places), he asked for a doctor, but no one understood him. A small boy gave him cognac, and then the farmer carried him piggy-back to a shed behind his barn.

When Winslow asked about a toilet, someone, understanding only the French meaning of the word, and supposing he wanted to wash himself, went into the house and brought him a face cloth with a basin of water. He finally managed to convey his actual need and they carried him to a pile of straw outside the shed. Then they took him back inside and laid him down on a bed of straw. His rescuer and several other people began to question him in French, but since he could understand little of what they were asking, communication remained minimal.

Again he asked for a doctor. They brought him a country priest who wanted to know whether he was a Catholic or a Protestant.

Winslow, grasping this question, said he was a Protestant.

The priest stayed only a short time before bidding him "au revoir."

Finally a girl arrived who spoke some English. The first question she relayed to him was one the men had been trying to ask. Did he have a gun, and would he give it to them?

The question brought home to Winslow the fact that he wasn't the only person in this little shed who was at war with the Germans. But as he explained through the girl, he wasn't carrying a gun. He asked her if she could get him a doctor. She said she would do what she could but didn't know how long it would take. His leg, dangling from the knee, was twisted grotesquely, but none of these people seemed to grasp the importance of straightening it and trying to set it as quickly as possible. So Winslow asked for some slender boards.

When he got them, he tried to straighten the leg and bind the makeshift splints around it. Then he lay back in the straw hoping the doctor would come soon. The pain was difficult to bear.

Winslow was not the only member of the Dame Satan crew whom the Belgians had been able to reach before the Germans found them. Of the eight who parachuted safely, only one, Sgt. Victor Ciganek, the wounded radio operator, had been captured. He was on his way to a German hospital. The rest, including another injured man, waist gunner Sgt. Gerold Tucker, who had broken an arm and a foot, were now "en sécurité" among members of the Belgian resistance movement. But the German occupation forces and their Belgian collaborators could also count parachutes, and they knew that someplace in the countryside, around the little town of Wannebecq, seven fallen American airmen were being hidden.

Most of the Americans who had parachuted into occupied Europe during the Regensburg and Schweinfurt missions were less fortunate. The majority landed in Germany, where there was no underground organization to help them. Lt. Ernest Warsaw of the 100th Bomb Group, who had been captured by the Gestapo that morning when his plane fell near Aachen on the way to Regensburg, was now confined in a small building a few miles from Aachen, wondering how long he had to live.[9] When he was captured, he had been almost grateful for the presence of the Gestapo because they had saved him from the angry mob of German farmers who had watched his parachute descend. After making him identify two of his comrades (Sgt. Walter Paulsen, radio operator, and Lt. Edwin Tobin, bombardier) who were wrapped in canvas bags and appeared to be dead, the Gestapo men had taken him to the gate house of a nearby country school, which they used for temporary incarcerations.

A short time after Warsaw was brought there, he was astonished at the arrival of Sergeant Paulsen, the radio operator whose "dead" body he had identified. Paulsen had hit the ground so hard he seemed to have no life left in him, but he had quickly regained consciousness. Neither he nor Warsaw (with shrapnel in his backside and a badly twisted neck) was feeling very well, but as the day progressed they began to think that wasn't going to matter very much. A furious crowd had gathered outside the little gate house, and their Gestapo guard was no doubt more sympathetic to the crowd than to the prisoners. Though the guard did try to chase people away, they continued to come back, and only the bars on the windows kept them from getting at the prisoners. The bars did not, however, keep out the various items they brought along to throw through the windows. These included rocks, garbage, and the contents of their outdoor toilets. By late afternoon, Warsaw was wondering if he would survive the first night.

By the time the bullet-riddled Schweinfurt armada reached the continental coast, it had been joined first by forty Thunderbolts from the U.S. 353rd Fighter Group and then by eighty-five British Spitfires of R.A.F. Squadrons 129, 222, 303, 316, 331, 332, 403, and 421, which escorted the B-17s west from Antwerp. The British claimed the destruction of four ME-110s and one FW-190 at the cost of two Spitfires.[10]

Most of the men in the B-17s could feel the relief when the blue water came into view and their German tormenters disappeared. But for some there were still serious hazards to come. In the 384th Group's Lucky Thirteen, piloted by Lt. Philip Algar, the gravely wounded waist gunner, S. Sgt. Corwin Miller, was regaining consciousness less frequently now, and everyone in the plane knew that without medical care he could hardly survive another hour.[11] Whenever he did become conscious, he asked S. Sgt. Schimenek how far they were from home.

"Just a little while longer," Schimenek kept telling him. "Just a little while longer."

As the remnants of the 384th reached the continental coast, Algar, aware of Miller's condition, asked permission to leave the group and hurry home ahead of it. Adopting a course that Lt. Frank Celentano, his navigator, had already determined was the most direct, Algar pushed his throttles forward as far as he dared. Lucky Thirteen headed out across the water alone.

Within a few minutes, Algar saw fighters ahead, and not knowing whether they were friendly, slid under one of the lead groups for protection. But when he spotted the English shore, he ducked the nose of the plane, opened the throttles even further, and raced for the 384th Group's base at Grafton-Underwood, about sixty miles northwest of London. He had to get down out of the rarefied atmosphere as quickly as possible because the plane's oxygen supply was exhausted. Schimenek had administered all of it to Miller.

70

When they reached Grafton-Underwood, Algar flew across the end of the field where he could be seen from the control tower and fired a red flare to indicate he had a wounded man aboard. He then came around to land on the field's shortest runway, firing a second flare during his approach.

The tower acknowledged: "We know you have wounded. We'll have someone to meet you."

By the time Algar brought the plane to a stop at a hardstand near the end of the runway, the group surgeon, Maj. Henry Stroud, was standing by with an ambulance. Miller, who had regained consciousness once more as the plane reached home, experienced an agonizing pain in his chest when his comrades bent his body to get him out of the plane and into the ambulance. As the ambulance sped through the woods to the base dispensary, Miller lapsed again into a coma. Dr. Stroud, who was at his side, could see that the first thing he needed was blood. But was there enough time to find out what type of blood? Even if that information was on Miller's dog tags, would there be time to find a donor?

When Miller was wheeled into the dispensary, Dr. Stroud found that his blood count was down to 41. The man had only a few minutes to live. He was coughing up so much blood his lungs were obviously full of it. Noticing this, Dr. Stroud hit upon a desperate idea. Puncturing Miller's lungs, he pumped the blood out of them into a bottle. Then, as quickly as possible, he pumped this same blood back into Miller's arms. It was one of the most unusual blood transfusions in medical history. All Stroud could do now, after dressing Miller's wounds, was to wait and see if this unorthodox treatment would work.

The two most badly mauled groups, the 91st and 381st, were limping back across the North Sea together, and they were destined to suffer further losses before reaching England. Lt. Eugene Lockhart had managed to keep his crippled B-17 in the 91st formation on three engines all the way from the target. But when he reached the coast, where he could feel relatively safe from enemy fighters, he decided he had better do something about his serious fuel shortage.[12] Leaving the formation at 18,000 feet, he put the plane into a slow glide in the hope that he might have just enough gasoline to reach an air base on the English coast. In case he didn't have quite enough, he also sent out a continuous S.O.S. on a medium frequency for five minutes.

About a third of the way across the North Sea, still fifty miles from England, Lockhart learned that he wasn't going to make it. When his No. 2 engine used up its last drop of fuel and sputtered to a stop, he ordered the crew to prepare to ditch. As all eight men other than the pilot and copilot took their ditching positions in the radio compartment, the No. 4 engine went silent. Lockhart was just above the waves now, flying on only the No. 1 engine at eighty miles an hour, slightly downwind. Moments later, that engine died. The plane, with full flaps down, stalled, then dropped a few feet into the water, tail first. Though the waves proved rougher than they had looked, the plane's nose came up quickly and the crew began scrambling out: Lockhart and his copilot, Lt. Clive Woodbury, from the side windows of the cockpit; the others from the radio hatch. They dragged out their rubber dinghies, inflated them with oxygen bottles, and were scrambling aboard as their plane sank from sight, thirty seconds after touching the water. It was now 5:20 P.M.

Settling into the dinghies, the airmen tried to operate the radio with which one raft was equipped, but they couldn't raise the kite designed to serve as its antenna. Neither could they raise the dinghy's distress balloon nor get its battery-operated flashlight to work. They could only sit and hope they would be rescued, and after two hours that hope would begin to fade because they were nearer the enemy shore than their own. But having come this close to home, they were not fated to drift back into the hands of the Germans. The British Air-Sea Rescue Service had heard Lockhart's S.O.S. At 7:40 P.M., three Spitfires would appear overhead, and by five o'clock the next morning, the ten American airmen, cold and damp, would be landing at Ramsgate. Meanwhile, the loss of Lockhart's plane brought the 91st Group's total casualties to ten out of twenty-four.

While Lockhart's B-17 was flying its last few miles over the North Sea, a Fortress in the 381st Group, piloted by Flight Officer George R. Darrow, was also descending ever closer to the waves.[13] Darrow's battered plane managed to bring its crew to within sight of the English coast, every man safe and sound, before reaching its own final crisis. A few miles off shore, Darrow ordered the crew to begin ditching procedures. After broadcasting a distress signal to the British Air-Sea Rescue Station at Manston, Darrow settled the doomed Fortress for its last landing, on the North Sea. Every member of Darrow's crew got out safely before the plane sank, and all ten were waving from their inflated dinghies when the R.A.F. arrived to rescue them an hour and twenty minutes later. The loss of Darrow's plane made the 381st Group the hardest hit that day, with total casualties of eleven out of twenty-six.

The 91st, however, with ten losses, was still in danger of matching the 381st. When Lt. James Judy's ravaged Fortress reached the continental coast, it was alone with only three men aboard (one injured) and flying on two engines at an altitude of one hundred feet. Judy, his copilot, Lt. Roger Layn, and his engineer, T. Sgt. Earl Cherry, were amazed that it was flying at all. Without a navigator, Judy had groped his way northwest across Germany and Belgium, dodging airfields that might send fighters after him and cities that might send up antiaircraft shells. The hydraulic system was now inoperative as well as the electrical system, which had finally burned itself out. All the controls to the tail surfaces had been shot away, and when Layn tried to splice the broken cables he had found them beyond repair. The electrical system's main inverter had been destroyed, and the aileron trim tab was still jammed. With the ship in this condition, it had taken all of Judy's strength to keep it in control across western Europe. Now that they had reached the coast, he was nearing exhaustion. But Layn couldn't help him, because he still had too many things to do in the rear.

With the threat of German fighters diminished, Layn threw overboard all the remaining boxes of ammunition, any guns he was able to detach from their moorings, and all other articles he hadn't previously jettisoned. Using a hand crank, he tried to close the bomb-bay doors, which had been open since the bombs were salvoed. The doors were hopelessly jammed. As the plane approached the English shore, struggling along slowly just above the waves, Layn realized that without hydraulic power he would have to crank down the wheels by hand. He did so while hanging onto the catwalk above the open bomb-bay doors. He tried to free the ball turret below the plane because its guns were pointing straight down and might drag and cause them to crash when they landed. He found the turret so firmly stuck he couldn't budge it.

Sergeant Cherry couldn't help Layn with any of this because, in addition to his injured foot that was now throbbing with pain, Cherry had severely burned both hands putting out the fires in the electrical system.[14] Layn, fearing that the helpless Cherry might be further injured if the landing proved rough, carried the wounded engineer forward to the cockpit and strapped him into his own copilot's seat. They were over land now and approaching a British airfield, which they later learned was the R.A.F. base at Manston.

Judy, using his last reserves of strength, began landing preparations. He tried the flaps but found they wouldn't go down. He tested the foot brakes and found he didn't have any. The emergency brakes seemed at least partially workable. On his first pass over the field he noticed there was construction work in progress. The only runway that might possibly accommodate a plane as heavy as a B-17 was closed. He would either have to find another airfield or land on grass, which was something the young American bomber pilots had not been trained to do. He didn't have enough fuel left to look for another field, so he decided to try the grass.

Plotting a wide traffic pattern because he had neither the engine power nor the controls for normal turns, Judy, with Layn's help, brought the plane around again. Sergeant Cherry, watching their approach from the copilot's seat, could see sizable holes and ruts on the ground ahead of them and doubted whether Judy would be able to land without crashing. But Judy had no choice. Aiming at what looked like the smoothest possible path down the green field, he settled the plane onto the grass. The wheels held. And if the ball-turret guns scraped the ground, the plane showed no sign of it. Hitting evenly, it sped down the field while Judy applied all his muscle to the brake. Cherry felt certain they would crash at the end of the field, but finally, with only a few feet left, Judy brought the plane to a stop. When he later inspected it, he found approximately five hundred bullet and shell holes in it.

The Schweinfurt mission commander, Gen. Robert Williams, flying in a plane piloted by Capt. Richard Weitzenfeld, had spent much of his time during the flight firing the bombardier's machine gun at German fighters. But eventually the barrel of that gun had burned out and Williams began to brood about a problem that had disturbed him when they were over the target. From what he had seen, he wasn't satisfied that his bombardiers were as accurate as they might be. They weren't bad, but with more training, more practice, they could be better. If a man accepted the American concept of daylight pinpoint bombing of military targets, he had to admit that any bomber which missed its target, by even a few feet, might as well have stayed at home. Williams believed that with proper practice his bombardiers could greatly increase their accuracy. But how, in cloudy England, could the bombardiers get enough practice to make any difference? It was one of the many problems the 8th Air Force had not yet been able to solve.

As for the horrendous casualties his armada had suffered today, Williams did not yet know the extent of the devastation. He could see only the lead groups. He did know that the 91st and the 381st had been badly hit, and he was not surprised. He had expected the mission to be the most hazardous any American air task force had ever attempted. And despite the losses, which he knew were considerable, he was certain it had been a success. The Germans, though they had sent up every plane they could find, had not been able to turn back the B-17s; they had not been able to shield their precious ball-bearing plants from the bombers; and they now knew there was no place in Germany that the Americans could not reach and attack with reasonable accuracy in broad daylight.[15]

As the bomber in which he was flying crossed the North Sea, Williams found out he had a more immediate problem. Captain Weitzenfeld informed him they might not have enough fuel to reach the English coast. Pulling out of formation, Weitzenfeld headed for the nearest point of land and slowed up to get the maximum mileage out of what gas he had. The plane was still flying when they crossed the coast near the mouth of the Deben River, north of Felixstowe, but it had only a few more miles left in it if Weitzenfeld could believe his fuel gauges.

Williams was in the cockpit with the young captain when they spotted a tiny airstrip for fighters, probably an auxiliary field, just outside Martlesham. It had no paved runways, and its short length did not indicate that it ever expected to feel the weight of a B-17.

Williams, having been the operations officer of the first group ever to fly B-17s, was quite experienced at landing them on grass because in those days (1936) there were few paved runways. Knowing that Weitzenfeld had probably never landed a B-17 on grass, the general tapped him on the shoulder and offered to take control.

The young captain, firmly in command of himself and his ship, turned to the general and declined with thanks. He would rather do it himself.

Thereupon he made a perfect approach and a perfect landing. As

75

soon as the plane's fuel tanks were filled, they took off again for the 91st Group's base at Bassingbourn.

At American air bases throughout East Anglia, the B-17s began returning about 5:30 P.M. From then onward, the men awaiting them on the ground began to grasp, with alarm and then anguish, the extent of their losses. One after another the groups limped home, the gaps in their formations immediately apparent to their anxious ground crews. Some of the missing were not actually lost. Several stragglers landed at other bases because they couldn't make it all the way. Some simply came in late, on two or three engines, or, nursing their meager gas supplies, had been forced to leave their formations because they could not keep pace. One pilot, Lt. Elton Hoyt of the 379th, was on his final approach at Kimbolton when his last engine died. He made a perfect "dead stick" landing. Another, Flight Officer Randy Jacobs of the 384th, had to make a crashlanding at Grafton-Underwood because he ran out of gas just a few moments too soon.

Though the 381st Group (11) and the 91st (10) had lost the most, the 384th had lost 5; the 379th, 4; and the 92nd, 305th, and 351st, 2 each. Of the 230 planes that had taken off for Schweinfurt that morning, only 194 had come back. Thirty-six had been destroyed. And 122 of the surviving planes had been damaged, at least 27 of them so badly they would probably never fly again.[16]

The cost in men could not be calculated precisely. Only the Germans knew how many of those shot down had survived to become prisoners. But the 8th Air Force did know that at least 340 of its men (the crews of 34 planes) had fallen into enemy territory. Since the average number of parachutes seen to emerge from falling Fortresses was 5,[17] it was fair to assume that about 170 American airmen had died on the Schweinfurt mission while an equal number had become prisoners of war. And so far the results were not in from that morning's arduous Regensburg battle.

Just as the Schweinfurt armada was returning to England, Col. Curtis LeMay's Regensburg armada was arriving in Africa at two desolate desert bases—Bone and Telergma—about one hundred miles west of Tunis. The first Schweinfurt bomber crossed the English coast near Felixstowe at 5:31 P.M. The first Regensburg bomber, carrying Colonel LeMay himself, touched down at Telergma at 5:28 P.M. It was not LeMay's first landing in North Africa.

A few weeks earlier, General Eaker had sent him to Tunis to brief the former 8th Air Force Commander but now Mediterranean air commander, Lt. Gen. Carl Spaatz, about the plans for shuttle bombing. If the England-Africa shuttle proved practical, it would confuse and spread the German defense system and make a larger part of Hitler's Europe vulnerable to American bombs. Spaatz's chief of staff, Col. Lauris Norstad, had offered a ready suggestion to LeMay on that preparatory visit.

"Telergma is your field," Norstad had said. "It's both a depot and a combat field. There you'll have supplies, extra mechanics— everything you need. That's the place to land. You can get well serviced there. All the parts you need, all the maintenance people and support."[18]

Today, however, when LeMay touched ground and taxied to the cluster of shabby buildings around the operation tower, he found the base virtually abandoned. Only a skeleton crew remained to welcome him. The war in Africa had moved eastward, and with it the mechanics, spare parts, and supplies Norstad had assured him he would find in Telergma.

LeMay was still fuming about this unhappy state of affairs when Col. Beirne Lay, the Eaker staff member who had come on the mission with the 100th Group, arrived at Telergma. Lay was also astonished at the condition of the base, but that was hardly in the forefront of his mind. After the soul-shaking experiences he had just survived, he was so happy to be on the ground that even this forlorn place looked good to him.[19] From his copilot's seat at the rear of the armada he had seen the worst of the day's action, and even though he didn't yet know the precise number of lost or badly damaged planes, he knew that the toll had been dreadful.

When Lay began talking to LeMay about his experience, LeMay seemed flabbergasted. At the front of the task force, the attacks had not been so severe. The 96th Group, which LeMay accompanied, had not lost a single plane. Though he knew the air battle had been fierce and his force had suffered losses, he had no way of realizing their extent because he couldn't see what was happening several miles behind him and also because he had trained his men to maintain radio discipline, to avoid comforting the enemy by broadcasting harmful information. If the damage was as extensive as Lay believed, and if there were no repair facilities available here, their situation was indeed critical, especially since General Eaker was expecting them to bomb another target the next day on their return flight to England.

As one after another of LeMay's groups landed (some at Telergma, some a few miles away at Bone), and the squadron commanders made their preliminary inspections, it became apparent that Colonel Lay's alarming analysis was correct. Though LeMay did not yet have an exact summary of the situation, he sent a message to Eaker indicating that the condition of his force was not good. Then, like his men, he watched hopefully for the arrival of stragglers, ate sparingly at a primitive canteen that had been built by the French when they owned this base, and eventually settled down to sleep, with his parachute as a pillow, under the wing of his plane. By this time he was aware that he had lost 24 of the 146 planes with which he had left England.

When LeMay's message arrived at 8th Air Force headquarters in England, General Eaker already knew it had been the worst day the 8th had ever suffered. He knew he had lost at least fifty planes on the double mission. Now it looked as if he had lost many more than that, depending on the exact situation in Africa. While he had expected heavier casualties than on any previous mission because of the deep penetration of Germany, the lack of fighter cover, and the crucial importance of the targets, he had not envisioned the dire results that were becoming apparent.

If LeMay's force were as badly stricken as indicated, and if it were to attempt another mission on the way home, the already prohibitive losses would continue to mount. LeMay, being as aggressive and determined as he was, might try it anyway. There was only one way, Eaker decided, to assess the situation properly. He would fly to Africa the next day and see for himself.[20]

Albert Speer, the quick-witted, handsome young architect who was now Hitler's Minister for Armaments and War Production, had been at a meeting of the Ship Building Commission in the Berlin suburb of Wannsee, discussing a serious bottleneck in steel-pipe manufacture, when he was informed of the Schweinfurt attack.[21] He had asked one of his deputies to get more information as soon as possible. It was not easy for him to think about a pipe shortage when a ball-bearing shortage was threatened. Ever since he had assumed the enormous responsibilities of his present job eighteen months before, he had been worried about the ball-bearing situation. It seemed to him that ball-bearing production was one of four or five areas of endeavor in which the German war effort was crucially vulnerable. The others were oil production, synthetic rubber, chemicals, and communications. If the allied air attacks were to be concentrated on any one of these industrial sectors, Germany's ability to make war might be decisively curtailed.

The ball-bearing industry was even more vulnerable than the others because so much of it was concentrated in those five factories clustered around the railway yards at Schweinfurt. On September 20, 1942, a month after the Americans began their daylight bombing, Speer had called Hitler's attention to the importance of the Schweinfurt factories, and two days later he had suggested to Hitler that the Schweinfurt antiaircraft defenses be increased. Hitler had agreed, but very little had been done about it.

Speer had subsequently suggested that ball-bearing production be dispersed; Hitler, apparently trusting him and probably not very keenly interested in the subject, had acquiesced without any special reaction. The only move Speer had yet been able to make toward decentralization of the industry was to expand other ball-bearing factories at Steyr, Erkner, and Cannstatt. Would this be enough? He didn't think so.

Speer remained mindful of the possibility that the Americans might attack Schweinfurt. He had watched carefully and with growing concern as they gradually expanded their operations and improved their techniques. He had developed a fearful respect for the devastation either the American or the British bombers could inflict. And after the British destruction of Hamburg July 24 to 27, his respect developed into alarm. At a Central Planning conference July 29, Speer said: "If the air raids continue on the present scale, within three months we shall be relieved of a number of questions we are at present discussing. We shall simply be coasting downhill, smoothly and relatively swiftly. The urgent question is simply, can we produce more single- and twin-engined fighters? And what can we shut down for that purpose? Otherwise, we may as well be holding the final meeting of Central Planning."

Three days later, Speer told Hitler essentially the same thing. If six

79

more cities were attacked as severely as Hamburg, he warned, it would bring German armament production to a total halt.

Hitler, who had refused even to go and look at Hamburg, to comfort the survivors there, showed remarkably little concern at the possibility of other German cities suffering the same fate. In answer to Speer's prediction he had said simply, "You'll straighten all that out again."

Speer was not the only high German official alarmed by the Hamburg catastrophe. At a conference in Speer's office July 27, Field Marshal Erhard Milch, the German Air Force armaments chief, said pessimistically, "We are no longer on the offensive. For the last one and a half or two years we have been on the defensive. . . . For the last three months I have been asking for one month's fighter production to be assigned to home defense."

That very evening, Goering answered Milch's plea by ordering, with Hitler's approval, that home defense be given top priority in the Luftwaffe. This did not stop Hitler and the High Command from insisting on the continued manufacture of heavy bombers with which they hoped to retaliate against England and even the United States, but it did stimulate some increase in fighter production. And more immediately, it brought back to Germany some front-line fighter groups. The result was that the American bombers on August 17 faced many more fighters than they would have faced a month earlier.

While Speer was awaiting more information about the Schweinfurt attack, Hitler, by early evening, had already heard enough about it to fill him full of wrath. If that many American bombers had been able to fly all the way across Germany to attack a city in Bavaria, there must be something wrong with his fighters. It didn't matter how many B-17s had been shot down. The important fact was that almost two hundred of them had survived to drop their bombs. Four days earlier, when the Americans bombed the Focke-Wulf fighter factory at Wiener Neustadt, Hitler had severely scolded the Luftwaffe chief of staff, Gen. Hans Jeschonnek. Now he summoned Jeschonnek once more and intensified his castigation. Though Jeschonnek may have felt that Goering, the Luftwaffe commander in chief, was the man to whom Hitler should be talking, he nevertheless accepted the abuse.[22]

That night, the British struck another heavy blow against Germany and the Luftwaffe in a successful attack against the highly secret

80

rocket laboratory and factory at Peenemünde on the Baltic. At least 750 people were killed, many of them almost indispensable scientists. Because of a mix-up in signals, most of the German night fighters were looking for the British over Berlin while the Peenemünde attack was in progress. When Jeschonnek learned about this fiasco, he decided he wasn't going to face Hitler again the next day. He wrote a note that said, "It is impossible to work with Goering any longer. Long live the Führer." Then he put a bullet in his head.

At Schweinfurt, Kugelfischer owner Georg Schafer was still sitting dejectedly in his bunker at 10 P.M. when Wilhelm Stenger, the comanager of his ball division, returned from a trip to Marienthal and found him there. Schafer was disconsolate. The entire ball plant had been knocked out. It looked as if everything of value had been destroyed. It would be difficult to salvage anything.[23]

"I'll get a lamp," Stenger said, "and take a look around."

He went first to the ball plant that he considered the core of the entire enterprise. Without balls there would be no ball bearings. This plant was a two-story building. The upper floor had collapsed and fallen onto the lower floor. The place was a mess, but fortunately it had not burned. To Stenger, about half the machinery looked as if it could be repaired. He returned to Schafer and said so.

At this heartening assessment, Schafer suddenly shook off his depression and became once more the dynamic German entrepreneur who had made Kugelfischer the large company it was. Leaping to his feet he said, "Well then, let's do it!"

There was still a question of exactly what to do. Even if they were to restore the whole factory completely, it might be bombed again, and more disastrously the next time. The entire plant could not be moved, but certain critical elements, like the ball machines, should be elsewhere. Schafer was already building a branch facility near the town of Eltmann, thirty miles east of Schweinfurt. As many of the ball machines as possible should be taken there. When? Right now. Schafer was not willing to wait even until morning. He ordered the night shift to begin immediately removing the repairable machines by truck to Eltmann.

Albert Speer hadn't yet received all the Schweinfurt details when he learned about the Peenemünde attack. During the night he flew to Peenemünde and talked to his friend, Gen. Walter Dornberger, the rocket base commander. From there he flew directly to Schweinfurt on the morning of the 18th to inspect the damaged factories, gather photographs of them, and talk to the managers. The following day he flew over Regensburg to look at the bombing results there, then on to a meeting with Hitler who was at his East Prussian headquarters near Rastenburg.[24]

When Speer was ushered into Hitler's presence, he did not minimize the seriousness of the ball-bearing situation. The American attack would cause an enormous loss of production. (Though he couldn't yet cite any figures, the Short Statistical Report on War Production, January 1945, indicated the August 17 raid had caused an immediate drop of 34 percent in ball-bearing output.) He showed Hitler the photos of the damaged plants and pointed out that in most of them (Kugelfischer excluded) fires had been disastrous because great quantities of oil were used in the manufacture of ball bearings. It flowed through the machines and drenched the floors around them. When the oil ignited, the machines, delicately calibrated, were damaged beyond salvation.

Much of the other damage to the factories could be overcome, and much of the lost production could be restored unless the Americans kept renewing their attacks. That was the most important question: would the Americans hit Schweinfurt again? If so, when and how often? One consideration comforted Speer. He believed the Americans had made a grave mistake in dividing their forces, sending only slightly more than half their planes to Schweinfurt while the others hit the Messerschmitt plant at Regensburg. This plan indicated to him a flaw in American strategic thinking. If the Americans had attacked only Schweinfurt, he would have been much more concerned because it would have indicated that they really knew what they were doing. But while he understood their desire to knock out German fighter production, it seemed to him that if they had realized the full importance of ball bearings, they would have concentrated their entire force upon Schweinfurt. Since they apparently hadn't considered it worthy of the hardest blow they could strike against it, he concluded that ball bearings were not a top-priority American target.

Hitler was quite calm now about the Schweinfurt matter. He seemed to derive some comfort from Speer's appraisal and also from the great number of American planes shot down. In any future raids, he believed, the Americans would not find it as easy to get through by daylight as the British did at night.

When Speer left the Führer that morning, no drastic measures had been decreed. Even the question of ball-bearing-plant dispersal, though agreed upon, was not completely settled. Speer was certain that various components of the Schweinfurt plants should be dispersed to a number of other communities; but even with Hitler's tacit approval would he be able to disperse them? If he were to dismantle and relocate the currently operating factories he would lose at least three or four months' worth of sorely needed production. And in order to move them, or even parts of them, to other communities, he would have to win the approval of the politically powerful gauleiters (local leaders) of those communities. These men were close to Hitler's heart. Many of them were his cronies. They were the core of his Nazi constituency. And they were not likely to welcome into their towns or cities factories that might attract American bombers. For the present, Speer could only launch a tentative move toward dispersal and try to find some gauleiters who would accept ball-bearing factories. At the same time, he would have to hasten the reconstruction of the damaged plants and hope the Americans, not fully aware of the importance of what they had done, would forgo any attempt to do it again.

5

At the 351st Bomb Group's base on a hill outside Polebrook, about sixty-five miles north of London, Capt. William Smith and his crew, like most of the men who had flown to Schweinfurt the previous day, were sleeping in on the morning of August 18. They had no reason to get up early. A stand-down had been ordered for the entire 351st because, after the Schweinfurt mission, none of the group's planes would be in shape to invade German territory today, even though only two of them had actually been lost. Smith's own B-17, perforated with bullet holes, needed patching. But fortunately, neither he nor any of his men had been wounded.

Smith was "in the sack" at his officers' barracks when a sergeant from group headquarters knocked on the door.[1] "Captain, you've got to get up," he said, speaking with that easy informality that was common in the Air Force between officers and enlisted men. "You're going to Africa."

Still half asleep, Smith said to the sergeant, "No, you've got that wrong. They went to Africa yesterday."

After the men of the First Bombardment Wing returned from Schweinfurt the previous day, they had been told about the Fourth

84

Bombardment Wing's shuttle from Regensburg to Africa. The sergeant said, "This is different, Captain. This is some kind of a special mission. You'd better get dressed and go see the colonel."

Ten minutes later, Smith was in the office of the 351st Group commander, Col. William A. Hatcher, Jr., who said to him, "Read that twix from 8th Air Force headquarters."

The telegram said: "Please select a highly qualified crew to come down to Bovingdon [a base near London] and stand by for General Eaker and party to proceed to Africa."

"That's you," Colonel Hatcher said to Smith.

"But as I recall," Smith said, "our only airplane still usable last night was Spare-ball."

This B-17 had earned its name because it was used only as a spare. Nobody wanted it. One of its engines habitually spewed oil onto the wing, and the mechanics couldn't figure out what was wrong. No one had flown it to Schweinfurt. The group was just able to supply the quota without it.

"That's the plane you've got," Hatcher said to Smith. "We don't have another."

As Captain Smith was walking back from base headquarters to round up his crew and pack his bag, he saw film star Clark Gable, at that time a captain assigned to the 351st Group as a ground officer, pedaling toward him on a bicycle. Smith had gotten to know Gable and liked him. A plain and friendly man, the famous actor was popular with everyone in the outfit. When he saw Smith, he said, "I hear you're going to Africa."

"How did you know that?"

Gable smiled. "The word's gotten around. I'd love to go with you. I've never been in Africa."

Smith thought that sounded like a good idea. Though Gable was not a flier, he had taken the trouble to qualify as a gunner so he could go on missions. He would fit well into the crew. But after giving the idea serious consideration for a moment, Smith decided he'd better forget it. This was not a junket. It was a secret mission. What would the commanding general say if he showed up for the flight with a movie star along just for the ride. Reluctantly, Smith shook his head at Gable and went looking for his regular crew.

Three hours later, Smith and his men, in the despised B-17 called Spare-ball, landed at Bovingdon, which was the 8th Air Force headquarters field even though it was almost an hour's drive from head-quarters. It was mid-afternoon before General Eaker arrived with the two men he had chosen to accompany him—Brig. Gen. James Hodges, commander of the Second Bombardment Wing (a B-24 wing that had not flown the previous day), and Col. Richard D. Hughes, a target-selection specialist on Eaker's staff. Eaker shook hands with every member of Smith's crew, then said, "Let's go."[2]

Due to the German fighters that patrolled the Atlantic off the coast of France, their route would not be direct. Like all Africa-bound planes at that stage of the war, Spare-ball had to fly first to a field near Land's End in Cornwall, at the western tip of England, then, after waiting until dark, along a southwesterly course down the Atlantic, skirting France widely enough to be outside the range of the JU-88s.

Despite Eaker's outward composure, his mind was occupied with some heavy concerns as he took off for Africa. He still didn't have enough information to evaluate fully the results of the Schweinfurt-Regensburg mission, which was without doubt the biggest and most momentous operation he had ever launched. He could take comfort from reports that the bombing had been quite effective at Schweinfurt and very effective at Regensburg. The Regensburg reports were still sketchy, but preliminary analysis of the Schweinfurt bombing indicated that extensive damage was inflicted on all the plants and on the town. While he had no way of knowing how perilously severe Germany's production chief, Albert Speer, considered this damage to be, Eaker had no doubt that Schweinfurt had been hard hit. And according to indications from LeMay, the Messerschmitt plant at Regensburg had been almost destroyed. It was fair to assume that the raids had been highly successful in damaging the German war effort. But that conviction could only partially comfort Eaker. He was now living painfully with the knowledge that he had lost a total of sixty B-17s in the two attacks—a prohibitive 16 percent of those dispatched. In addition, early reports indicated that twenty-seven of the Schweinfurt planes had been so badly damaged they might never fly again, and ninety-five of the surviving planes had sustained lesser damage.

Eaker did not yet know how many of LeMay's planes would have to be junked as a result of the Regensburg raid. This was one of the unpleasant facts he would discover when he reached Telergma.

86

By the time Captain Smith landed Spare-ball at Marrakesh at 7:00 A.M. on the morning of the 19th, the plane's oil-spewing engine had splattered the whole wing behind it. But the engine was still operating. Its condition did not seem to worry Eaker. He asked Smith how quickly they could take off again for Tunis. Smith was worried about the engine, and he knew his crew was as tired as he was. He found that on top of the Schweinfurt mission, this long journey to Africa where he had never before been, the added responsibility of piloting the 8th Air Force commanding general, and the fact that it was now almost twenty-four hours since he had slept had brought him almost to exhaustion. But it seemed obvious that Eaker was in a hurry. Smith asked the mechanics to check his bad engine. Unable to find anything organically wrong with it, they simply filled it with oil and wished him luck. Less than three hours after landing at Marrakesh, Spare-ball took off again, east across the top of the Sahara.

Several times as the plane droned through the sunny sky, Smith felt himself on the verge of falling asleep at the controls. The desert air was so warm, especially for men accustomed to England's chilly climate, that Eaker opened the waist-gun windows to catch the breeze. When they landed near Tunis, at the end of another eight-hour flight, Elliott Roosevelt, the President's son, who had become a brigadier general in command of a reconnaissance unit, was on hand to meet them. In two staff cars, Roosevelt took Eaker and his aides to the headquarters of General Spaatz, Eaker's old friend and one-time 8th Air Force superior, with whom he now wanted to confer. At last, it looked as if Smith and his crew would have time to eat and sleep. But the mess hall at this desert base was closed. A sympathetic sergeant finally took them to a tent where they found a gallon can of marmalade, several loaves of bread, and some fruit juice.

They were still spreading marmalade on big chunks of bread when someone drove up from the flight line and shouted, "Hey, you guys, get back to your plane. They want you to take them to Telergma."

It was well into dusk when Smith and his crew returned to their plane to find General Eaker awaiting them with a sizable party. In addition to his own aides, he had with him General Spaatz, General James Doolittle (commander of the Twelfth Air Force), General Roosevelt, and Colonel Lauris Norstad. As Captain Smith warmed up his engines, carefully testing his bad one, he came to the chilling realization that if this plane failed to hold up for another hundred

87

miles, he might become a famous footnote in the history of the war—the pilot who flew the plane in which three famous generals and a President's son were killed. But Spare-ball, still spewing oil, carried them all safely to the desolate base at Telergma, where Colonel LeMay was waiting to greet them. He had set up a headquarters in a tent. Here the generals and their staffs retired to confer.

Eaker's first question to LeMay was, "Curt, when will you be able to go back?"[3]

"As soon as we can hang some bombs and put some fuel in these crates," LeMay assured him. But it would not be that easy. For the first time, Eaker learned the worst. As for the bombing results, LeMay was convinced, after talking to his men, that the Regensburg Messerschmitt plant had been "totally destroyed." The losses, however, were sobering. Besides the twenty-four B-17s that had failed to reach Africa (six of these had gone down in Italy or the Mediterranean), at least twenty and possibly more would never fly again. And perhaps twice that number were so badly damaged that they needed repairs.

LeMay still lacked precise damage figures because there was no maintenance organization on this desert base. His own crews were doing the work. But LeMay was not discouraged, nor did he spend much time complaining, even though he did wish that Colonel Norstad had been able to let him know about the change in conditions at Telergma. The morning after his arrival LeMay had directed his men to get to work immediately, cannibalizing the derelict planes for parts with which to repair the salvageable ones. Hard-nosed as ever, he still intended to bomb German installations at Bordeaux on his way back to England. The only thing he couldn't say for certain was how long it would take to get ready.

Eaker, at this meeting and during the subsequent inspection of the men and planes, was greatly impressed with LeMay's qualities of leadership, his refusal to surrender to circumstances. But Eaker could also see that this force was no longer in combat condition.

"There will be no mission," he said to LeMay. "Your men will not be subjected to hostilities on the return to England. We'll see to it that you go across North Africa and over the Bay of Biscay at night."

LeMay had not asked for such consideration. He still believed that, given time to repair his planes, he could hit Bordeaux on the way home. And there were strong reasons for hoping he could do so. Eaker did not want to let the Germans think they had reduced LeMay's force to impotence, and neither did he want LeMay's men to feel they had been defeated. It would help their morale if they could return to England proudly in broad daylight, bombing the enemy on the way, rather than sneak home at night around the coast of France. By the time this meeting ended, the Bordeaux mission was on again. But the concept of shuttle missions to Africa was off. Only in England were there maintenance facilities for large bomber forces.

It was the next afternoon (August 20) before Eaker was ready to leave Telergma for the long flight back through Marrakesh to London. Aware that Smith and his crew were now nearing exhaustion, he gave them a day's rest at Marrakesh. But on the second day, even though the weather was threatening, he decided he could no longer delay his return to England. In the wake of the Schweinfurt-Regensburg mission, he had a lot of problems to solve and a lot of replanning to do.

At midday on the 22nd, Captain Smith pulled Spare-ball off the Marrakesh runway and headed north on the reverse of the route that had brought them to Africa. It was virtually the same route General Eaker had flown in a Dutch airliner from Portugal to England just eighteen months earlier when he and six staff members, in civilian clothes and with no airplanes, arrived to begin the organization of the 8th Air Force Bomber Command. The basic problem he had faced then was the same one he faced now, except that today it was more precisely defined and more immediate. He still had to prove to his British colleagues and to a lot of important people back home that the daylight bombing strategy of the American Air Force was both effective and practical against Hitler's Germany. He had hoped to prove his point beyond doubt at Schweinfurt and Regensburg. And he felt he had proven it to the Germans. He had struck mighty blows against the ball-bearing plants and the Messerschmitt factory. But the critics of daylight precision bombing might be less impressed by Germany's losses than by the 8th Air Force losses. Besides the sixty Flying Fortresses that went down during those two missions, Eaker now knew that forty to fifty others would never fly again, and perhaps one hundred more would need significant repairs. Gen. Robert Williams, who led the First Bombardment Wing to Schweinfurt, had reported that four of his groups were so badly depleted he would be able to put only six combat boxes in the air if called upon for an immediate mission. And LeMay's Fourth Bombardment Wing was in an even worse situation due to the lack of repair facilities in Africa.

It was almost catastrophic to lose more than fifty crews and more than one hundred planes in one day. Eaker had not expected to lose so many. Yet he had expected the operation to be the most perilous and most expensive in the history of American air warfare. Why then had he launched it? Why had he felt compelled, without the benefit of long-range fighter support, to attempt such a dangerous mission? In order to understand his reasons it is necessary to go back at least as far as that earlier flight, on February 20, 1942, when he and his six original staff members arrived in England to organize the 8th Air Force Bomber Command.

6

February 20, 1942—eleven weeks after the Japanese attack against Pearl Harbor and the U.S. entry into World War II against Japan, Italy, and Germany. During these eleven weeks since December 7, the war had not gone well either for the Americans or for their British allies.

The Japanese, having battered the U.S. Navy in Hawaii, had then destroyed, in the waters off Malaya, two of Great Britain's finest warships, the Prince of Wales and the Repulse. On February 15, after capturing the Crown Colony of Hong Kong, the Japanese took Singapore, which had been a British possession for more than a century. They were now advancing so rapidly against American forces in the Philippines that at this very moment, Gen. Douglas MacArthur, the U.S. commander, was preparing to evacuate.

In London, Prime Minister Winston Churchill had reorganized his war cabinet the previous day. And in the Atlantic, German submarines were sinking thousands of tons of allied shipping every day.

On the outskirts of Lisbon, in neutral Portugal, at five o'clock the morning of February 20, two taxicabs carrying seven Americans in

91

civilian suits honked their horns in front of the barred gate of Cintro Airport. When no one arrived to open the gate, a man in the second cab got out and opened it himself. He was Ira Eaker, at that time a brigadier general.[1]

Eaker's rapidly rising Air Force career was remarkable. In an organization dominated by West Point graduates, he had begun as an unpromising outsider, a country boy who had never even seen the Military Academy until long after he became an officer. The son of a Texas farmer and the product of small-town schools in such places as Field Creek and Eden, Eaker had joined the aviation section of the Army Signal Corps during World War I. He didn't become a flier on the strength of any special mechanical aptitude or romantic notions about the wild blue yonder. He knew nothing about airplanes at the time and had never even driven an automobile. As a student at Southeastern Teachers' College in Durand, Oklahoma, he had enlisted in the Army, together with the thirty-six other men in his senior class, on April 7, 1917, the day after the United States declared war on Kaiser Wilhelm's Germany. Because these men were college students, they were sent to an officers' training school in Arkansas, where Eaker became a second lieutenant.

He was drilling his platoon at his first station, Fort Bliss in El Paso, one day in October 1917, when a Signal Corps plane landed on the parade field with engine trouble. Though Eaker had never seen an airplane engine, he climbed onto the wing to take a look at it. A spark-plug lead had come loose. Little as he knew, he could see that was wrong. He put the wire back in place and said to the pilot, "Maybe this is your trouble." When the pilot started the engine, it ran perfectly. "You know so much about airplane engines," he said to Eaker, "you should go into flying."

Within a few weeks Eaker did so; and after World War I, when the Signal Corps aviation section became the Army Air Corps, he remained with it and launched a spectacular career. He was one of the pilots on the flight that made the first complete circuit of South America in 1927. He was chief pilot of a plane called Question Mark, which established a record in 1929 by refueling in flight and remaining aloft continuously for more than 150 hours. And in 1936, he was the first pilot ever to make a transcontinental flight entirely on instruments. He had also been at one time or another the personal pilot for the Air Corps commander, the assistant secretary of war, and

General MacArthur when he was Army Chief of Staff. In December 1940, Eaker became commander of the 20th Fighter Group stationed in California. And in August 1941, he made a six-week trip to England as an observer of the Battle of Britain.

Shortly after the U.S. entered the war, Gen. Carl Spaatz had been appointed commander of the new 8th Air Force. When General Arnold called Eaker into his Washington office January 18, 1942, to announce that he was to organize the 8th Bomber Command in England, Eaker was astonished because he was not a bomber man.

"I've been in fighters all my life," he reminded Arnold.

"That's why I chose you," Arnold said. "I want you to put the fighter spirit in our bomber effort."

Arnold also had some advice for Eaker that day about selecting his staff. Because the Air Force was still small a month after Pearl Harbor, and because the war was large, Arnold had very few first-class career officers to spare. He suggested that Eaker seek out some well-qualified civilians who were willing to join the Air Force.

"You can easily take a smart civilian and make him into a smart officer," Arnold observed, "but you can't take a dumb officer and make him a smart officer. So you find yourself some smart civilians and I'll commission them for you."

This advice accounted for the fact that three of the six staff officers taking off from Lisbon with Eaker on the morning of February 20, 1942, had been civilians a few weeks earlier. Maj. Peter Beasley, the oldest man on the staff, had been an airplane manufacturer. Capt. Fred Castle had been working for the Sperry Company on Long Island, New York, though several years earlier he was an Air Corps pilot. And Lt. Harris Hull had been a Washington newsman. The ranking officer on this staff, Lt. Col. Frank Armstrong, was a highly regarded career man who had been under Eaker's command in 1934, when the Army carried the U.S. mail. Lt. William Cowart had been a fighter pilot under Eaker's command in 1940. And Capt. Beirne Lay was a Yale graduate who had joined the Air Corps and won his pilot's wings in 1933, then left the service to launch a very successful writing career. He had resumed active duty in July 1941, when war seemed imminent. And in late January 1942, Lay was walking along a corridor at Air Force headquarters in Washington when he came upon Eaker, whom he had known for three years.

Eaker said, "Beirne, you want to go with me?"

Captain Lay said, "Yes, sir." Before he could ask where they were going or in what capacity, Eaker had hurried down the hall to his next appointment. But Lay was one of the six men with him as he took off in a regularly scheduled KLM airliner from Portugal to England.

The fact that the new 8th Air Force Bomber Commander and staff had to reach England by way of Pan American Clipper to Portugal, then a Dutch airliner to London, was a measure of the U.S. Air Force's shortage of equipment in early 1942. Eaker could have flown himself to England, but there wasn't an airplane to spare. During a two-day layover in neutral Lisbon while awaiting their KLM flight, Eaker and his men had to get accustomed to the strange experience of rubbing elbows with Germans, their enemies, in the Metropole Hotel lobby and restaurant. The night before they left Lisbon, their baggage had been ransacked, convincing them that the Germans knew who they were. This realization added suspense to the flight. Adolf Hitler might not hesitate to have a Dutch airliner shot down if he knew that the newly appointed American bomber commander and staff were aboard.

The Dutch plane, a Douglas DC-3, had been airborne about a half-hour when Eaker noticed that it was turning in a circle. Surprised at this maneuver, he walked forward to the cockpit where the pilot pointed out to him that other planes were following them.

"There's too much activity to suit me," the pilot said. "I'm going to land [at Porto in northern Portugal] and see what's going on, let it die down."

After an hour on the ground, the plane took off again and headed out over the Bay of Biscay. When they were far beyond sight of land, the pilot called Eaker to the cockpit and pointed out in the distance a twin-engine German fighter that was flying toward them at their altitude, on a course calculated to intercept them. Whether it was a JU-88 or an ME-110, a DC-3 could not escape it. Eaker and his companions could do nothing but wait. As they soon observed, the German plane was having troubles of its own. Black smoke began pouring out of its port-side engine. As it came nearer, the engine continued to smoke. Finally, before it was close enough to fire a shot, it turned away from the airliner and headed back toward the coast of France. Eaker felt certain that this German fighter's mission had been to shoot down his plane, and his conviction was strengthened when,

94

shortly after he arrived in London, he was told that the airliner following his on the same route had been shot down.

It was after 5:00 P.M. when Eaker and party reached London, having landed first at Bristol, then transferred for a short flight to Hendon, where they were greeted by Air Vice Marshal J. E. A. Baldwin, representing the R.A.F. Bomber Command. After checking in at the Strand Palace Hotel, Eaker went immediately to the Whitehall headquarters of Maj. Gen. James Chaney, who, a month earlier, had been appointed commander of all U.S. Army forces in the United Kingdom. At Chaney's office, Eaker was told to "be present for a conference" the next morning.[2]

When Eaker introduced his six-man staff to Chaney and his much larger staff the next day, he was expecting only that Chaney would offer him whatever help he might need in procuring a headquarters for Bomber Command and launching his mission. Eaker already knew what that mission was to be and how he was to approach it. General Arnold had spelled it out verbally. And General Spaatz, who would not be arriving in England until summer because he was busy with organizational details at Bolling Field near Washington, had spelled it out even more precisely in a six-page organizational memorandum.

But it was quickly apparent that General Chaney, a senior Air Force officer himself, had some ideas of his own about the development of Bomber Command. He could see no compelling reason why it would need a separate headquarters. He floated the suggestion that Eaker and his small staff would fit nicely into these Whitehall offices he was occupying.

Aside from the danger of Eaker's tiny nucleus being swallowed up by Chaney's already sizable apparatus, the suggested arrangement might also create a situation in which Chaney, who outranked Eaker and was also his titular superior, would soon take over actual if not official control of Bomber Command. This was hardly what Eaker wanted, and it was obviously not what Arnold and Spaatz wanted. Spaatz had written in his organizational memo: "As much as possible of the Theater Commander's functions and responsibilities should be delegated to the commanders of his Air Force, Ground Force, Service of Supply and Naval Forces."[3] Those words could almost have been in specific anticipation of the delicate problem Eaker faced. But

95

Spaatz and Arnold were back home, and Eaker—a brigadier general —could not openly defy a major general who was also the theater commander.

Arnold and Spaatz had warned Eaker that he would have difficulties with the British, but there had been no reason to suppose he would have difficulties with Chaney. They had known each other for many years. Chaney was several years older and militarily more conservative than Eaker, who was then forty-six and full of new ideas about the role of air power in the war. But Eaker considered Chaney a friend, even though the two had never been closely associated. Eaker would have to be carefully diplomatic in the days and weeks to come if he wanted that friendship to endure. Fortunately, he had a natural gift for diplomacy. It was one reason Arnold had put him in charge of what was expected to be the first full-scale American military cooperation with England—the aerial bombardment of Hitler's Europe. Eaker neither embraced nor rejected the opportunity to place himself under Chaney's wing. As quickly as possible, he changed the subject.

Next morning, Sunday, February 22, Eaker met the R.A.F.'s new bomber commander, Air Chief Marshal Sir Arthur Harris, and walked to church with him.[4] By coincidence, the two men were both becoming bomber commanders at exactly the same time. Harris had just been appointed as part of the shakeup that also saw the reorganization of Winston Churchill's war cabinet. Churchill was not satisfied with the R.A.F. bomber offensive against Germany as it had so far developed. He wanted to see Hitler's cities treated the same way London and other British cities had been treated by German bombers during the Battle of Britain, and in Harris he had a man who completely agreed with him.

Harris, the son of a civil servant in India who had always wanted to be a soldier, was born in England in 1892 while his parents were home on leave. Though deafness had deprived the elder Harris of his cherished military career, he could see no reason why his growing son should not become the soldier he himself had wanted to be, except that the boy was stubbornly unwilling. Young Harris was so "dead set against" going into the Army that he went instead, at the age of sixteen, to Rhodesia, where he became, among other things, a coach driver, gold miner, and farmer. It took World War I to fulfill his father's fondest ambition for him.[5] After enlisting in the First

Rhodesian Infantry Regiment, he eventually went to England and got into the Royal Flying Corps (forerunner of the R.A.F.) as a second lieutenant on probation. This began a career that was now reaching its zenith as Harris took command of the R.A.F.'s bombing campaign against German cities, the only military offensive Britain had yet been able to take against Germany during two and a half years of war.

Churchill had every reason to believe that Harris would add punch to the bomber offensive because Harris was dedicated to it as something that, by itself, could destroy Hitler and end the war. He had already won Churchill's heart by talking about his dream of sending a thousand bombers a night against Germany. Harris's determination to repay the Germans for their destruction of British cities, and in the process prove the irresistible power of aerial bombardment, had earned for him a reputation as the toughest, most hard-headed, most committed man in the R.A.F. Positive in his convictions, he was quick to assert them and uncompromising in his resolve to enforce them. Unlike Ira Eaker, he had never been described as a tactful, diplomatic man.

These two generals had met a few times when Harris visited the United States on R.A.F. missions to buy airplanes and matériel, but they were not well acquainted. Eaker, knowing Harris by reputation, could hardly guess what to expect of him. He was aware that like most R.A.F. experts, Harris had a low opinion of America's best bomber, the B-17, which would have to be the mainstay of the 8th Air Force.[6] He also knew Harris was skeptical of the possibilities of daylight precision bombing. Eaker was therefore ready to defend the American position in arguments about these important matters.

But today no arguments developed. Harris was the very model of British cordiality as they walked to church together. Did Eaker need any help in selecting a site for his headquarters or in procuring necessary equipment? Indeed he did. His little staff of six had arrived without so much as a typewriter. Harris would gladly take care of all that. Would Eaker like to inspect the R.A.F. Bomber Command setup and attend operational conferences? He would be welcome anytime. Would he need some office help until his own personnel began to arrive? Harris was shorthanded himself, but he would loan Eaker as many people as he could spare. By the time the two men reached church, Eaker was much more confident about the fulfill-

97

ment of his mission and more relaxed about his relations with the British.

The irony of these two generals walking to church as they discussed plans to drop bombs on thousands of Germans probably did not occur to either man. The moral justification for World War II had already been defined so clearly by 1942, and accepted so universally outside Germany, that people took it for granted. In the minds of most of the British and Americans, whether military or civilian, Adolf Hitler had reduced the ethical considerations of the war to simple terms. It might be argued that Germany had been treated too harshly by the Versailles Treaty after World War I. But all the privations visited upon Germany, even if totally unjustified, could not excuse or mitigate the ghastly captivity and brutality Hitler's men were now imposing upon all of Europe. The two hundred million people Hitler had enslaved, and the souls of the other millions he had eliminated, were crying out for someone to stop him by any possible means. The only morality the Allies could now afford to recognize was the ethical imperative of eliminating the evils Hitler represented.

Some possible methods might be too extreme, but the bombing of cities did not seem so after Germany instituted the practice on a vast scale in Poland, Belgium, Holland, Russia, and England. If the destruction of German cities and industrial centers could foreclose Hitler's ability to make war, that seemed to constitute justification enough, especially since it was evident that Hitler himself recognized no moral restraint in his methods. What would the enslaved people of Europe say if anyone told them they would have to accept their enslavement because it would be inhuman to bomb Germans?

The desperate need to defeat the Nazi machine was accepted by almost everyone in Great Britain and America and by all British and American leaders, including both Eaker and Harris. They were passionately dedicated to the defeat of Hitler, and bombing Germany was the only means at their disposal. For two years to come, bombing would be the only direct offensive action the Allies could launch against Germany proper.

That afternoon, Eaker and his small group took a two-hour drive through London's bombed-out areas, mostly in the East End around the dock and factory districts but also around St. Paul's Cathedral, where scarcely a building remained intact. It was a tour that made them realize immediately what kind of war they were entering. They passed block after block of disorderly brick piles, sheared-off walls, and twisted, broken roofs of what had once been houses. Pieces of charred furniture, soot-marked toilets, and still-standing brick fireplaces arose out of the pitiable debris to demand attention. Londoners, long-since accustomed to the devastation, seemed hardly to notice it as they walked through these streets. Their famous "bobbies" were wearing steel helmets, and every few blocks Eaker's party would see middle-aged men in fire-warden's uniforms.

The London into which these American officers had arrived was suffering all the rigors of a city under siege. The war was felt not only in these vast areas destroyed or damaged by German bombs but in every part of the city, in every family. After two and a half years of war, the English had given up so many of their comforts that very little was left for the government to ration. Coal was so scarce that, despite the winter cold, householders could keep a fire in only one room, and there only in the evenings. They couldn't even augment these tiny flames with waste paper or cardboard because of the desperate paper shortage. Every spare scrap had to be turned in and recycled. Cloth was so scarce that women were wearing short skirts, not to attract men (who incidentally were also scarce because they were in service) but simply to save material. The wheat content of bread had been drastically reduced. The soap ration was down to four three-ounce bars per month. Matches were in such short supply that "a girl could safely beg one from a strange man without being considered fresh." The alcoholic content of beer had been so severely reduced it was almost impossible to get drunk in a pub. And liquor, for the few who could find it, cost the equivalent of seven dollars a bottle, three times what Americans were accustomed to paying in 1942. Canned food was equally hard to find. The British government was down to its last stocks, and women stood in long queues to buy it.

By the time Eaker and his men finished their Sunday-afternoon tour, London's short winter day had ended, and as they returned to the frigid, rather austere apartment building (the Cranmer Court on Sloane Street) to which they had been transferred from their hotel, the heavy darkness had introduced them to another chilling wartime phenomenon—the blackout. There were no street lights, and the dimmed house lights added no illumination to the streets because all windows were covered with blackout curtains. It was a sparse meal

99

to which Eaker and his men sat down at Cranmer Court that night, but they felt guilty eating even the small portions put before them.

During his first week in England, Eaker's most delicate job was to disassociate himself as much as possible, and as subtly as possible, from General Chaney's headquarters. He had an amicable meeting Tuesday with Chaney's staff in which they seemed to accept most of his proposed program for the development of his unit.[7] But the next day he had a more difficult meeting with Chaney's quartermaster, who had agreed to a British plan of feeding standard English rations to American airmen and housing them in tents without heat. Eaker was not surprised that British quartermasters should make such a proposal, but he was astonished that Chaney's staff had accepted it. This winter was especially bitter, with snow and ice on the ground. Eaker feared that after his aircrews spent their first wet, frigid night under canvas, then woke up to find that they had to eat British food, they would soon be fighting him instead of the Germans. The question of tents and British rations, he said, should be held in abeyance until he had time to make a field inspection. Chaney's quartermaster and his British counterparts agreed.

Though Eaker didn't know it, he was destined to get help in this matter from a high source. R.A.F. Commander Air Chief Marshal Sir Charles Portal had addressed himself to this very subject on January 23rd in a secret staff memorandum: "I am sure that the American units, coming bodily from conditions in the U.S.A. to the wartime conditions in this country, will feel the difference very sharply, and that it will therefore be advisable to put at their disposal the best and most completely equipped stations that we can manage to give them. For one thing, they are . . . accustomed to living in very high temperatures, and it would be a very real hardship to put them into stations with poor accommodation and inadequate heating."[8]

As soon as this memorandum was felt at operational levels, the question of unheated tents was settled. The British were ready to build for American airmen the same Nissen huts with pot-bellied stoves in which they housed their own airmen.

Eaker and staff paid their first visit to British Bomber Command headquarters (a cluster of low brick buildings and underground shelters in a wooded dell near High Wycombe) on the afternoon of February 25 and were pleasantly surprised to learn that Air Chief

Marshal Harris, acting upon the earlier conversation with Eaker, had already set aside for them not only a temporary office within his own headquarters but also a nearby house large enough to accommodate all of them until they could make permanent arrangements. It was a well-appointed house, probably built by the R.A.F. for the use of a senior officer, and the invading Americans were delighted to get it. But they would soon find that, because it was heated by only the standard British fuel ration, it was almost too cold for Americans to consider habitable. The temperatures in its big, drafty rooms would be incentive enough to hasten their search for quarters of their own.

Late in the afternoon, Harris invited the Americans to tea at the home of one of his aides. Several members of the Bomber Command staff were there, as was Lady Jill Harris, an arrestingly beautiful young woman the bomber commander had married four years earlier. (Shortly after his marriage, when Harris was expecting to be posted to an active overseas command but was assigned instead to a dull desk job in the Ministry, he had talked himself back into the overseas post by telling the Chief of Air Staff that his bride's trousseau was entirely tropical.) General Eaker found Lady Harris as friendly and concerned as she was attractive. The conversation with her, as with her husband, stuck to general topics—the English weather, which was especially cold and gray that day; wartime food shortages; the blackout in London; and mutual friends in Washington, where the Harrises had become well acquainted during their several visits.

Eaker, who had been in England before, felt quite at ease in this rather formal English social setting, but some of his aides found the scene somewhat strange—their rough-and-ready bomber commander balancing teacups with his big, blunt-featured British counterpart in a handsome drawing room and in the company of several smiling women, while Hitler's armies and air forces were pointed ominously at them only a hundred miles away across the narrow English Channel. What kind of a war was this?

Once more, the arguments Eaker expected between Harris and himself did not materialize. But the next day, in Harris's office, the two men got down to the most important issues in both of their minds. When they began discussing the twenty heavy-bomber groups that General Arnold hoped to send to England in 1942, Eaker wanted to know what stations they would occupy and what facilities would be available. An enormous logistic problem was at hand involving a quarter of a million men, shipping, harbors, railroads, water supplies, communications systems, housing, mess halls, warehouses, operational structures, and runways. For the runways alone, hundreds of thousands of tons of concrete would have to be poured.

Harris had anticipated all these problems, and he had in mind for Eaker's possible use several R.A.F. satellite bases already built at such places as Polebrook, Molesworth, Chelveston, Thurleigh, and Kimbolton. But specific solutions to the problems depended on the exact use of the American heavy bombers when they arrived. Harris was keenly aware of the American desire to launch a daylight precision bombing program against German industrial and military targets, independent of the R.A.F. night bombing program against German cities. In January, less than a month earlier, he had been in Washington talking to Arnold about the general strategies of the R.A.F. and the 8th Air Force and about a British proposal that the first 250 Flying Fortresses to reach England be used for coastal patrol.

Arnold had vehemently, perhaps even angrily, rejected this British proposal and had reiterated the American determination to bomb German targets in the daytime. Arnold had also given Harris a fascinating insight into the American Air Forces's problems with the American Navy. And he had emphasized the possibility that the British might damage themselves if they insisted on diverting B-17s to coastal patrol.[9] Harris's conversation with Arnold prompted an extraordinary cable, marked "MOST SECRET," which Harris sent January 29, to R.A.F. Chief of Air Staff Portal in London:

Arnold asks me to tell you that so far as he can judge at present, he aims to get up to 20 heavy bomber groups into U.K. this year. He hopes to achieve at least 16 but this is likely to be adversely affected by certain tendencies now growing in force e.g. in spite of lip service to the agreed grand strategy [the U.S.-British overall war plan], the Far East looms ever larger and more insistently in the thoughts of the highest ones in the land. Added to this, the Navy has now realized the limitations of the flying boat and covets the heavy bomber in quantity. Recent successes against Jap. ships lend weight to their case and in any event they have always opposed the bomber plan by fair means or foul. They are concerned only with having seas safe for sailors to sail on and do not think as far as winning the war or even making land safe for landlubbers to live or fight on. Our proposal to sidetrack 250 B-17s to Coastal Command has made the airmen here very hot under the collar. "We are thereby flying straight into the Navy's hands."

As to what he wants to do about it, Arnold was not clear, but in general he expressed an urgent desire that you should fight every proposed diversion of H.B.s from the bomber force and from direct action against German territory to the last ditch. I told him he would be preaching not only to the converted but to the very leader of the sect, but that I would nevertheless inform you. He implores your backing in the fight against diversions and that my assurance that he has it will be backed by reiteration on the highest levels that the bomber plan still holds the field as the agreed war winning strategy.

Despite the thorough understanding of the American position that Harris exhibited in this letter, he could only partially agree with it. He completely agreed that the Flying Fortresses should not be used on coastal patrol. He wanted them used against German cities, and the quicker the better. If the 8th Air Force was to operate as a separate unit, in the daytime, it would take several months before it became strong enough to launch a significant campaign. By contrast if the B-17s could be incorporated into the R.A.F. night-bomber stream, they should be able to get into action against Hitler after a very short orientation period. Would it not be best, therefore, to settle the new B-17 groups right into operational R.A.F. bases as they arrived?

Eaker, already concerned about the possibility that Chaney, his American superior, would swallow up his command, now had to worry about the British doing likewise in a different way. If Eaker agreed to any plan of absorbing his B-17s into British bases and into the R.A.F. night-bomber stream, he would be acquiescing to the rapid dissolution of the 8th Bomber Command as a separate American attack unit. It was easy to imagine the reaction back home to daily news stories about R.A.F. raids against Germany that would mention, perhaps down toward the last paragraph, that "American Flying Fortresses also took part." Eaker had no authority, from either General Arnold or General Spaatz, to accept such a plan. If he did accept it in his official capacity as 8th Air Force Bomber Commander, they might then have to go along with it. But they would never forgive him for it. Nor would he forgive himself. He was as committed as they were to the concept of daylight bombing.

American crews wouldn't even be qualified for night raids, because pilot trainees, in the stepped-up wartime program, would receive only a necessary minimum of night flight experience. Eaker could picture with horror the confusion these boys would create, groping their way home to unfamiliar British bases in the dark after raids against Germany. Even the British pilots, with all their experience, had enough trouble. Navigation at night was still so difficult in wartime blackout conditions that the R.A.F. sometimes wasted whole missions because they failed to find big cities and dumped their bombs harmlessly in nearby rural areas.

The B-17 itself presented obstacles to night bombing. Not only was it designed and equipped as a day bomber, but equally important, it left behind it in flight a glow from its engine exhausts that would make it easy for the German night fighters to see and attack. Some kind of device might be developed to dampen this glow, but that would not change the American Air Force commitment to daylight bombing.

The British perhaps could bomb only at night because their planes were lightly armed and did not have the Norden bomb-sight, which would make even the smallest of targets vulnerable to precision attack. But the B-17s would have the Norden, and they would also have as many as ten .50-caliber machine guns with which to defend themselves.

Though neither Harris nor Eaker raised his voice during the discussion, both were aware of its almost global importance. Both believed firmly that the outcome of the war depended on the proper use of air power. Harris received Eaker's arguments sympathetically but could not embrace them. It was essential that the maximum force be brought to bear against Hitler as quickly as possible. The Nazi dictator now controlled the entire European continent, and it was not impossible that he might yet find a way to invade England or to destroy it with rocket bombs. Couldn't the 8th Air Force join the R.A.F. in night raids, Harris wondered, at least temporarily, until it was strong enough to launch its own day raids?

Eaker had anticipated this proposal also, and he was wary of it. He dared not settle his bombers on R.A.F. bases and send them out at night with the R.A.F. Once that was done, it would never be undone. It was his mission to see that the 8th Air Force operated as a unit, and in the daytime against German military and industrial targets. In short, it would have to have its own airdromes, communications system, weather network, and everything else such an organization might need.

Surprisingly, the argument between these two men was not only polite; it was also friendly. They had liked each other from the start, and each understood the national military policies that governed the other. But while they were more than cordial, they were both intense. When they finished, neither had been swayed from his position. Harris was too gracious, however, to leave the matter at an impasse. He gave Eaker the list of eight satellite air bases he had in mind for possible 8th Air Force use and invited him to inspect them. He also reiterated his eagerness to help his American colleague in every possible way despite their differences.

In the days to come, the friendship between Eaker and Harris quickly deepened. Almost every morning, Eaker attended Harris's operations conferences at Bomber Command, where he heard in detail the results of the previous night's R.A.F. raid and the plans for the following night. Both he and his staff were treated by Harris's aides to quick cram courses in everything the R.A.F. Bomber Command had learned during more than two years of war against Germany. Eaker inspected the eight air bases Harris had suggested to him and found them potentially satisfactory. Harris visited General Chaney in London to support Eaker's point of view in selecting several other airdrome sites, which Eaker contended should be as far south and as near the east coast as possible to keep the distances between bases and targets at a minimum. Many damaged B-17s would be coming home to these bases short of fuel in the months and perhaps years ahead. A few miles would often make the difference between getting home and not getting home.

Harris also supported Eaker's insistence that the 8th Bomber Command be allowed to set up headquarters separate from Chaney's Theater headquarters in London, where Chaney believed all U.S. military commands in the United Kingdom should be centered. While Eaker was careful never to criticize Chaney, he was beginning to think the Theater commander, although an Air Force officer himself, had not attuned himself with General Arnold's plans for Air Force expansion.[10] Chaney, who had been in London a year or more, seemed still to be thinking in terms of the peacetime Air Corps with its eighteen hundred officers and eighteen thousand enlisted men. He couldn't seem to visualize the two-million-man U.S. Air Force Arnold was trying to create or even the quarter-of-a-million-man 8th Air Force that Spaatz and Eaker envisioned. Chaney's decision-making processes were too slow and deliberate for a man-on-the-run like Eaker. Chaney knew too many reasons why something could not be done but too few reasons why it could be done. The very size of Eaker's 8th Bomber Command plans seemed to him to put them beyond the realm of possibility. But since Chaney did not forbid Eaker to pursue these plans, the new bomber commander pushed forward as if every day were his last. Indeed, any day could be his last if Arnold should decide he was moving too slowly. Arnold was not a patient man, and Eaker had been associated with him long enough to realize it. After a week in England, Eaker still didn't know where his headquarters would be. It was about time to decide.

Eaker and Harris agreed that their command centers should be as close together as possible, not over five miles apart, to facilitate liaison. They and their staffs would have to have daily conferences to coordinate operations, regardless of whether those operations were to be joint or separate. Harris told Eaker to go ahead and select a site, after which he would do everything possible to help him get it. Eaker then sent his staff out to search the nearby countryside for buildings that might accommodate them. They reported back that they had found an ideal-looking place—a girls' boarding school called Wycombe Abbey, about four miles from R.A.F. Bomber Command headquarters. Wycombe Abbey was a large, white-stone, castlelike building with enough smaller structures to house four hundred men, on an immaculately landscaped knoll a mile and a half south of the town of High Wycombe. Linden trees lined its walks and driveways. Rolling lawns swept down to a pond on which a few swans and countless ducks made thier homes.

When Eaker saw it he decided it would be ideal. But when he told Harris he wanted it, the crusty air marshal didn't think he had much chance of getting it.

"We tried to get it ourselves," he said, "but we failed. The girls in that school are daughters of what I call the port-drinking classes.''

Eaker was not to be dissuaded that easily. His men, after a thorough survey, had reported to him that there was no other place. Wycombe Abbey had the only complex of buildings in the entire area that could possibly house a command center as large as the one he would need. If he wanted to be within a few miles of R.A.F. Bomber Command, he had no choice.

"I'm afraid you'll have difficulty," Harris warned him. "Too many of our ministers' wives are graduates of that school. But you put in for it. We'll make a fight for you, and we'll hope you get it.''

On March 3, Eaker wrote a letter to General Chaney asking him to secure Wycombe Abbey through the Air Ministry, as quickly as possible, for use as 8th Bomber Command headquarters. To speed this letter on its way, he sent his aide, Lt. William Cowart, to deliver it to Chaney by hand. After three days, he had heard nothing. On March 6, he went to London himself to brief Chaney on what he had accomplished so far, but they did not discuss Wycombe Abbey. Eaker learned the next day, which he spent entirely at Chaney's headquarters, that the requisition for the facility hadn't even been forwarded to the Air Ministry.

It was not easy to determine whether Chaney himself had been responsible for sidetracking the request, but it was obvious that several of his staff officers were against it. Perhaps they saw the establishment of a Bomber Command Center in High Wycombe, thirty miles from London, as the decisive step in Eaker's emancipation from them. He could no longer ignore the growing evidence that many of these officers, most of whom came from the Ground Forces, were "unalterably opposed to an Army Air Forces [organization] in Britain." They insisted they were "perfectly able to handle" Air Force command responsibilities, and that the development of Eaker's Bomber Command would make them "merely rubber stamps." Since there were no ground operations in England, they considered Air Force operations their "primary mission" and were "not willing to surrender it.''

For Eaker, the time had come to bang a few heads, whatever the result might be. He insisted that his request for Wycombe Abbey be submitted forthwith to the Air Ministry. Three days later, Chaney's chief of staff, Brig. Gen. Charles L. Bolte, assured him that the requisition had been forwarded. By this time there was an additional urgency to choose a headquarters site because more officers were arriving in England to join Eaker's staff.

On the 13th, an Air Ministry representative came to talk about the Wycombe Abbey application; two days later, two others came. For ten days conversations continued. Finally, the Ministry man announced to Eaker that the property could not be made available. He suggested that Eaker make a survey and find another site.

By this time Eaker was quite tired of the subject but more than ever determined to have the facility. "We've already made a survey," he said, "and those are the only buildings close to R.A.F. Bomber Command that would accommodate us."

"Unfortunately," the Ministry man explained, "a lot of girls from the colonies, Australia and Canada, are in that school. And we have to keep them here. We can't send them home because of the submarine menace."

It seemed to Eaker that there might be places to keep these girls other than Wycombe Abbey. "If you're more interested in educating your daughters than in winning this war," he said, "I'm glad you told us."

In a country where politeness was highly valued, these were strong words, and Eaker knew it. "That's putting it harshly," the man said, "but let me go back and talk to my people again."

A few days later, Eaker learned that Wycombe Abbey would be his headquarters. Though General Chaney may have been displeased, he did not step in. Eaker had now made the move that virtually pulled him out from under the Theater commander.

While Eaker's relations with Chaney were developing strains beneath the surface, his relations with Marshal Harris became ever friendlier. Harris, in pursuit of one of his initial promises, had said to Eaker one day, "I'm going to give you a small [office] staff since you haven't got one yourself yet. I'm going to give you some of our WAAFs [Women's Auxiliary Air Force]. You'll find they are very useful people. They're more dedicated than the men. You'll be surprised to learn that they're the people who keep our Secret files. They don't get drunk at the club on Saturday night and tell all they know."

Harris had temporarily assigned about two dozen of these WAAFs to 8th Bomber Command. Eaker had already accepted them when

Chaney made it clear that he disapproved. Eaker, in desperate need of clerical help, kept the women despite Chaney's opposition.

Eaker's staff, as a gesture of thanks for favors received, held a reception in their quarters for Harris and his staff, providing, through the American Post Exchange in London, a display of liquor the likes of which few of these British officers had seen since 1939. Harris's staff reciprocated by inviting the American officers to dances where there were usually more attractive girls than there were men. Harris, who had cosmopolitan tastes in food and had therefore gone to the trouble of becoming a highly accomplished chef, invited Eaker to his home for a dinner featuring a Virginia ham he had brought back from his latest trip to Washington. Thereafter, Eaker's dinners with the Harrises were frequent.

One day, the Harrises suggested that until the Wycombe Abbey facility was secured and ready for occupation, Eaker should move with them into a new home the R.A.F. was providing for them, a pleasant, three-bedroom country house with stables and garden, three miles from his headquarters.

Lady Harris, to assure Eaker that the invitation had been serious, renewed it one evening. It would give them all a chance to get better acquainted, she explained, but there would also be a practical consideration. Despite her husband's high military rank, she had to do her marketing with the same ration cards as any other British housewife. The more ration cards she had, the more food she could buy, and the better they would be able to dine. She and her husband both made it sound, very graciously, as if Eaker would be doing them a favor by moving in with them.

He was so charmed he happily agreed to do so, even though he knew there might be another motive involved in the offer. Despite the growing personal warmth between Harris and Eaker and despite the generous help Harris had provided, the arguments between the two men about bombing policies and strategies continued, as it did also at lower levels among their staff members. The R.A.F. had not abandoned its desire to remake the American Air Force in its own image.

After Eaker moved into the Harris home April 5, he found himself spending evenings in what the air marshal called his "conversion room," a study where he had set up a stereopticon machine that showed three-dimension aerial photographs of the German cities the R.A.F. had bombed. These were specially processed pictures taken by British reconnaissance planes as soon as the smoke cleared the day after a raid. In some, there were buildings with flames still flickering. An observer of these photos could peer straight down into the empty, gutted shells as if from only a few hundred feet directly above.

It was such an impressive display that people spent hours looking at it. South African Premier Ian Christian Smuts had spent the whole evening at it when he visited the Harrises. The air marshal, usually wearing his favorite plum-colored, velvet smoking jacket and waving one of his favorite Lucky Strike cigarets from the end of a holder, provided a running commentary with the pictures to prove the R.A.F. strategy was the one that would win the war against Hitler. Harris had already "converted" several American war correspondents by treating them to this performance.

In his discussions with Eaker, Harris persuasively stressed the time element. Weeks and months could be saved if the newly arriving American heavy-bomb groups would simply affix themselves to the R.A.F. for night raids. The Americans, after all, were just getting started at this job of fighting Hitler. They didn't realize how clever the Germans were. The British had been at the job for more than two years, and it was only natural that they had learned a few things. They had now got their system working pretty smoothly, and the most effective contribution the American bombers could make toward winning the war would be simply to mesh in with it.

Eaker would point out that they had already agreed on separation of effort. Military airdromes were so close together in England even now that the air space was congested every night the R.A.F. sent out its bombers. It would become perilously crowded if the 8th Air Force were to begin sending its fleets up into the dark skies at the same time. On the other hand, congestion would never become an unmanageable problem if the R.A.F. were to continue its night raids while the A.A.F. limited itself to the daytime.

Harris believed the air-space congestion could be handled in either case. And he spoke eagerly of the possibility that combined British-American armadas of a thousand planes a night, even two thousand, might soon be visiting devastation on the Nazis. When Eaker would remind him again that his B-17 crews were not trained for night operations, he would insist that they could be trained.

But what of the B-17 itself, which was designed and equipped for daytime operations? It would be a waste of all that armament and all that extra equipment to use the plane at night.

On the subject of the Flying Fortress, Harris tried to be tactful. He knew it was going to be the basic heavy bomber of the 8th Air Force, and therefore he couldn't dismiss it as if it had no merit. In fact, he believed it had some very good features. He wished his R.A.F. bombers were armed with its .50-caliber machine guns, for instance, instead of the .30-caliber "pea shooters" with which they had to face the German night fighters. But despite all the B-17's merits, he and most other British air experts had grave reservations about it.

The previous October 30, Air Vice Marshal R. H. Peck, one of Portal's deputies, wrote a letter to Air Vice Marshal Robert Saundby at Bomber Command that illustrated the then-current R.A.F. attitude toward the B-17.

"A pernicious article has appeared in a recent issue of the 'Saturday Evening Post' in America," Peck wrote to Saundby. "It takes the line that the Boeing Fortress is the finest bomber in the world and that the stupid British have refused to take advantage of its qualities, refused to order it and cannot make effective use of it. I have been requested to produce a counter to this mischievous propaganda. . . . Would it be possible for you to get one of your staff to give me some notes on the limitations of the Fortress as we have found them? What has gone wrong with it and why we are not able to make all the use of it which the Americans think we ought to be able to?"

The R.A.F. at that time already had two B-17s but didn't like them well enough to order any more. On November 3, 1941, Saundby sent Peck a Bomber Command memorandum dated November 1 which listed the faults the British had found in these early-model Fortresses.

The plane was so "dependent on suitable weather conditions," this memo stated, that there was a "severe limit" on the frequency with which it could operate. "Even when clear conditions exist, the formation of condensation trails [from its engines] still further limits the occasions when the aircraft can penetrate to their targets without risk of interception." The bomb load was "uneconomical in relation to the crew and technical maintenance required." The armor was inadequate. "An armoured bulkhead is now being fitted but the additional weight will tend still further to reduce the operational height." To fire the plane's heavy waist guns "the large blisters must

111

be opened, with the result that internal temperatures lower to the order of minus 50 degrees centigrade." The plane admittedly had "a ceiling considerably in excess of any other bomber in service," but, the memo contended, "prolonged flights at heights above 30,000 feet impose very considerable physical and mental strain on the crew, with the result that they are incapable of making the fullest use of their equipment."

Since Saundby was now Harris's chief deputy at Bomber Command, the air marshal knew all these arguments and could supply a few others. He had told General Arnold in Washington that the B-17's hand-held guns would not do in combat. The plane would have to be equipped with turrets, and it would also need fighter escorts. Even then, he had insisted, daylight bombing with it would be "very sticky."

In addition, the plane carried too small a bomb load. The ten machine guns plus ammunition needed for daytime combat would add so much weight that the pay load would be limited to about a ton. The bomb-bay doors were too small, Harris told Eaker, and so were the bombs the Americans planned to drop.

Harris was even more emphatic in warning Eaker about climatic factors. The areas in the United States where American fliers trained, mostly California and Texas, were quite different from the areas they would be bombing in Europe. "How many days," he asked rhetorically, "will you be able to see the ground in Europe from 20,000 feet? Damned few."

Eaker had too much faith in the B-17 and in the skill of American pilots to accept these arguments. He knew the plane would need certain modifications, and the crews would need extra transition training when they arrived. But he was convinced that when they got into battle they would do as well in the daytime as the British were doing at night. While the bomb load would be smaller, each bomb dropped on a specific military or industrial target would damage the German war effort much more than a larger bomb dropped at night on the house of one or two German workers. The ten B-17 machine guns were heavy, of course, but if they could hold off German fighters so that the bomber could reach an important target in full daylight when the bombardier could see it, they would be worth their weight. The 8th Air Force B-17s, unlike those the British had tried, would have the remarkable Norden bomb-sight, which would enable them to

112

distinguish and hit even the smallest of targets. Such sophisticated equipment would be wasted if the planes were consigned to night raids in which bombs were dropped indiscriminately on populated areas.

The argument that the 8th Air Force should simply tack itself on behind the R.A.F. was the same argument America's World War I commander, Gen. John J. Pershing, had encountered when he was asked to tack his infantry forces on behind the French and the British. Pershing had held out for establishing a separate American force, and his policy had proven itself by saving thousands of American lives.

With Pershing's successful example behind him, Eaker would be foolish not to follow it, especially since the U.S. Government, including the President and all the senior military men, favored a repetition of it. The U.S. Air Force, in committing itself to the B-17, had bought thousands of planes, thousands of expensive bomb-sights, and hundreds of thousands of machine guns it would not need if it were to opt for a night bombing effort. The course ahead was almost fixed in concrete as far as Eaker could see, and it was a course he personally approved. Yet he could not ignore in Harris's arguments the weight of British experience against the Nazis. It was difficult to answer Harris when he said, in effect, we know what we're talking about because we've been through it. At such times, Eaker would say, "All right, then, if you want me to do it your way, the fellows for you to talk to are the Combined Chiefs of Staff. We get our directives from them."

Harris knew this, but he also knew it was American Air Force pressure that had persuaded the Combined Chiefs to accept the concept of daylight bombing. He conceded that the B-17s would have more and better guns than the British night bombers and would be able to fire from more angles. "You have side guns, for example, which we don't have. We have only tail guns. But all your guns still can't protect you from fighters because fighters are faster, more maneuverable." U.S. bombers, Harris said, would be under continual attack for all the hours into and out of the target, besides which they'd be sitting ducks on their bomb runs when they would have to keep a straight path at a constant elevation.

"I just don't think you can do it," he insisted. "I don't think Americans appreciate the German defensive effort on the so-called West Wall, how much antiaircraft they have, how intense the opposition, and what the rate of loss will be. God knows I hope you can do it. What a wonderful thing it would be if we didn't give those fellows any rest. But we know something about daylight bombing. We tried it, and we couldn't do it. The Germans tried it against us, and they couldn't do it."

As for the B-17, he reminded Eaker of the two that Arnold had sent to the R.A.F. "We sent them across and got the hell shot out of them."

"That doesn't prove anything," Eaker replied. "Bomber losses are always in direct proportion to the size of the force. And we don't intend to send one or two B-17s against the West Wall defenses. We're going to send them in sufficient numbers to overpower the defenses."

Harris listened with respect, but he was not convinced.

7

As if the war were too small a burden for the besieged and impoverished British, the weather during the winter of 1941-1942 continued cold and gloomy until April. General Eaker and his staff had been in England almost two months before they saw a sunny day. But when that day arrived it was glorious. The air was warm and fragrant, the birdsong deafening. A few blossoms were popping out, and the bright sunshine intensified the many shades of green in the rain-soaked English countryside.

Eaker, still living at Air Marshal Harris's home, rode with him as usual to the R.A.F. operations conference that morning. In the car, the two men said nothing for a while, each gazing out at the pleasant sight of spring, each feeling the lift in mood that comes with the reappearance of a long-absent sun.

Finally, Eaker, sitting in the front seat, turned around to his British colleague and said, "Now I see, Bert, why you people fight for this bloody country."[1]

The personal relationship between the two men had progressed to where they were Bert (Harris's family nickname) and Ira to each other. Eaker's ability to get along with people had so far served him well. While he was not as close to any of his other R.A.F. colleagues as he was to Harris, he and his staff had found all their British counterparts cordial. He was not yet certain, however, that this cordiality indicated respect. Some of the British staff officers were known to refer to him and his men as "Eaker's amateurs." This less-than-gallant designation might simply reflect a widespread English view of Americans as rich, brash, and naive. On the other hand, it might have arisen from Eaker's continuing insistence that his 8th Bomber Command would attack the Germans in its own way. It was only natural for the British to look with some amusement, if not outright scorn, upon these presumptuous colonials who thought they knew all about fighting the Germans before they had even flown their first mission over enemy territory.

Eaker knew, of course, that relations between wartime allies were not always smooth, thanks to cultural differences as well as conflicting national interests, but he knew also that a large part of his job was to make certain that he and his men did get along with the British. Before leaving Washington he had briefed his staff on how to behave in England, using as his text his own experiences there, plus a series of instructive letters the American Air Attaché in London had written about things to do and things not to do. He didn't want any of his people to be baited into anger by slighting labels like "Eaker's amateurs." If he was to win the respect of the British, it would have to be not by fighting them but by fighting the Germans.

At any rate, neither Eaker nor his staff had much time to pay attention to what the British were saying about them. After approving and accepting the first eight airdromes the British offered them, they specified the changes they would need and helped supervise the reconstruction. They also surveyed at least one hundred more possible sites and asked for fifty-three more complete airdromes to be built before the end of 1942. They worked out tables of organization not only for their headquarters section but also for such necessary support facilities as hospitals, ordnance and quartermaster depots, engineering and maintenance units, and so on.

They arranged for a continuing flow of food shipments from the United States sufficient to supply independent American mess facilities, and they set up their own rationing system for other provisions arriving from home. On March 25, they issued their first commissary rations—six oranges, six apples, and a dozen eggs per man. They worked out procedures for the arrival of their first two heavy-bomb groups and, using British guidelines, established minimum extra training requirements for all incoming units. They supervised the conversion of the Wycombe Abbey girls' school into a military headquarters and allotted the space there both for offices and living quarters. Each of them made several trips to London to keep General Chaney's staff apprised of what they were doing. And in their spare time, Eaker and the other pilots on his staff—Armstrong, Castle, Lay, and Cowart—flew British Spitfires to maintain flying proficiency.

Lay and Lieutenant Hull, who was already up for promotion, conferred with a group captain (equivalent of colonel) in charge of R.A.F. Bomber Command Intelligence, about plans to establish an 8th Bomber Command G-2 organization. Although the British opposed these plans, the group captain was cooperative, explaining how his section had developed, what methods they had found best, where they got their most reliable information, and what kinds of people made the best intelligence officers. Escapees from the Nazis, he said, were their most useful sources. Newspapermen were no good because they tended to be too dramatic. Women were poor interrogators, but lawyers and school teachers were quite good. As for pilots, they were too blasé. Hull, who had been assigned to build 8th Bomber Command's intelligence section, left for London April 6 to enroll in a special secret British intelligence course.

Eaker, in addition to his other activities, paid a series of courtesy visits to British dignitaries, spent an informative evening with an R.A.F. bomber squadron, kept up his correspondence with his superiors in Washington, welcomed new arrivals for his staff, held informal talks with several war correspondents, planted a garden with the aid of Cowart, had a new pair of jodhpurs made for him by a London bootmaker, and conferred with an ordnance officer about procuring 4,000-pound bombs for his B-17s. Perhaps under the influence of Air Marshal Harris, he told Captain Lay that he now considered a two-ton bomb "just a baby." In the evenings he was ready for poker whenever he could get anyone to play with him. Because he had a reputation as one of the best poker players in the U.S. Air Forces's, quite a few of his associates developed a tendency to disappear whenever they saw him looking around for cards.

His work habits were methodical but quick. He was not an extreme disciplinarian because he considered patience and loyalty more important qualities. He told one of his aides that he thought patience might be the most important quality for a general to develop. With patience, a man could inspire the kind of loyalty that would create its own discipline. Eaker's greatest weakness as an administrator was a tendency to get too involved with details. He took part even in the floor-plan design for the Wycombe Abbey headquarters.

With all of this on his mind, Eaker managed nearly every morning to attend Harris's operations conference. Never having been a bomber commander until now, he was able to learn important lessons about the job ahead of him simply by watching Harris. In addition to the daily decisions about the next night's mission and the problems arising from the previous night's losses, Harris had to deal with a succession of even larger difficulties, some of which he had inherited when he took over the R.A.F. Bomber Command. The Germans had recently set up a new radar box defense system that made it easier for their night fighters to find his bombers. They had also set up a continuous searchlight belt over the Ruhr that exposed the vulnerable bellies of his bombers. He had worked out a method of partially defeating these defenses by concentrating his stream of planes in closer succession so the Germans would have time to catch only a small percentage of them, and this method was quite effective except that it increased the danger of his bombers colliding with each other.

To add to his woes, a structural defect had developed in the wing-tips of some of his four-engine Lancasters, Britain's best heavy bombers, forcing four squadrons of them out of action. It might be several months before he got them back. At the same time, the Admiralty, becoming desperate because of the appalling ship losses to U-boats, was pleading with Prime Minister Churchill to take six more squadrons of Lancasters for submarine patrol in the Bay of Biscay. Still new himself in the position of bomber commander, Harris was beginning to feel a heavy pressure, which he later described very vividly:

I wonder if the frightful mental strain of commanding a large air force in war can ever be realized except by the very few who have ever experienced it? While a naval commander may at the very

118

most be required to conduct a major action once or twice in the whole course of the war, and an army commander is engaged in one battle say once in six months or, in exceptional circumstances, as often as once a month, the commander of a bomber force has to commit the whole of it every twenty-four hours; even on those occasions when the weather forces him to cancel a projected operation, he has to lay on the whole plan for committing the force. . . . Our climate being what it is, I should have been able to justify myself completely if I had left the whole force on the ground, if I had done nothing whatever, on nine occasions out of ten. But this would have led to the defeat of Britain in the air. . . . It is best to leave to the imagination what such a daily strain amounts to when continued over a period of years.[2]

When Harris took charge of Bomber Command, it had only 378 serviceable planes, and only 69 of these were heavy bombers. It was not surprising that he continued his attempts to convert Eaker to his night-bombing gospel. The bomber offensive, he pointed out, was the only allied operation that was helping the desperate Russians, who had already lost nearly half their country to the German army, and who might quickly lose the rest of it if the coming summer's German drive were not stopped. The nightly threat of British bombers was at least forcing Hitler to keep his fighters and most of his antiaircraft artillery at home, where they couldn't add to the Russian burden. But even more important than helping the Russians, the bomber offensive, by disrupting German arms production, was bound to help the British and American soldiers who would one day, perhaps within the year, be invading the continent.

Eaker was not disposed to deny any of this, but he in turn pointed out that if a night bomber offensive was that useful, a day bomber offensive would be even more so because its bombs would fall accurately on the very targets that were most important to destroy. The British, up to now, were sometimes so inaccurate at night that they would bomb the wrong city or would bomb dummy "cities" set up by the Germans to mislead them—the same kind of dummy "cities" the British had used successfully at times, complete with dim blackout lighting patterns and papier-mâché buildings, to divert the German bombers from London and other real cities.

The R.A.F., Harris would remind him, was already adopting very good new radar measures to improve its aim.

But the British would never be as accurate at night, Eaker would insist, as the Americans were going to be in the daytime.

On April 13, the two men interrupted their argument long enough for a joint birthday party, both having been born the same day, Harris in 1892, Eaker in 1896. That afternoon, Eaker's staff surprised him with a party including a cake. That evening, Lady Harris did likewise with a cake for both of them. And the air marshal, lest Eaker forget their argument, had another surprise for him. He gave Eaker a stereopticon machine for looking at bomb-damage photos in three dimensions—exactly like the machine he himself had in his ''conversion room.'' They toasted each other and the assembled company in Old Fashioneds made of prewar bitters, a bottle of whisky Harris had brought back from the States, and oranges from Eaker's first commissary ration.

If Eaker needed any support in maintaining the American viewpoint on the uses of air power, he got it when Gen. George C. Marshall, the U.S. Army Chief of Staff, visited England with President Roosevelt's personal adviser, Harry Hopkins, the week of April 8 to 15, 1942. The primary purpose of Marshall's trip was to convince the British that the Allies could and should invade the continent that very year, in September, rather than waiting until 1943 or 1944. (Marshall presented his plan with typical American assurance that, however difficult a task might be, you could accomplish it if you were determined to do so. And Churchill agreed to the plan with typical British sophistication, just to be polite, even though he considered it totally impractical.)

While Marshall was in England for his talks with Churchill, he took time out on the 12th to drive to Eaker's temporary headquarters at R.A.F. Bomber Command.[3] After a luncheon at Harris's home, attended also by Chief of Air Staff Portal, Marshall accompanied Eaker to his office to meet his fledgling staff. Eaker was delighted to spend this time with him because, like many American military men, he considered Marshall the nation's greatest living general and probably one of the greatest of all time. General Arnold, for instance, had such respect for the Army Chief of Staff that he had once said to Eaker, ''If George Marshall ever took a position contrary to mine, I

120

would know I was wrong." Marshall supported strongly the build-up of the 8th Air Force in England.

After introducing Marshall to his men in the crowded conference room, the only room they had that was large enough to accommodate twenty people, Eaker spent an hour outlining the progress and problems of the 8th Bomber Command during its first seven weeks.

As usual, Marshall listened more than he talked. He was so forbiddingly dignified that he did not prompt light conversation. He didn't encourage familiarity. Few men called him George. Even President Roosevelt, notoriously informal with most people, addressed him as General Marshall. Yet Eaker found him an easy man to talk with because he gave such complete attention to everything that was said. And in turn, he could quiet a room and gain full attention for himself simply by giving some indication he was ready to speak—squaring his shoulders or taking a slightly deeper breath. (Later in the war, Eaker was to notice that at summit conferences between people like Roosevelt, Churchill, Charles DeGaulle, or other dignitaries, whenever Marshall spoke, they all fell quiet to listen.)

Upon hearing what Eaker and his men had to say and the questions they raised, he assured them that the original American war plan, affirming the policy of daylight precision bombing by a separate U.S. force, was still in effect. He then wanted to know when they would be ready to begin operations. Without discussing the major purpose of his visit to England, he said he did not believe that Allied armies would ever be able to invade the continent unless Allied air power managed to defeat the Luftwaffe. (Since Marshall must have realized this could not be done before the coming September, it is possible that his proposal for a continental invasion that fall was as sophisticated as Churchill's acceptance of it. Perhaps Marshall knew that such a project for 1942 was premature but was proposing it because he feared an invasion might never take place unless preparations for it were begun immediately.)

Eaker assured Marshall that he already had the destruction of the Luftwaffe well fixed in his mind, together with the reduction of German weapons manufacture, as the prime purpose of the 8th Air Force mission in Europe.

Marshall was apparently satisfied with this general assurance. He said nothing about getting the job done before September. As for the difficulties of making the British appreciate the American viewpoint, he advised Eaker and his men to swallow their irritations and strive for an understanding of the British viewpoint. "We are laying cornerstones," he said. "Forget yourselves. Rise above your own views." In conclusion, he assured them that what they were doing would evolve into a large-scale air effort against Hitler. But he didn't mention any hope that this might happen quickly enough to facilitate a September invasion of the continent. As he knew, the 8th Bomber Command's first airplanes weren't even scheduled to arrive until July.

In a letter Marshall wrote to Portal a month later (May 8), he included some remarks that illuminate his thinking at the time and help to explain his obviously impractical proposal for a second front in 1942:

Until, and unless, we actually initiate combined offensive operations—ground as well as air—the pressures from other fronts for more matériel, planes, and the shipping involved, will be constantly increasing. Therefore we must accept calculated hazards and accordingly resist the attrition of the forces that must be concentrated as quickly as possible for our major purpose.

You personally have been struggling with this problem for many months, but even so I do not believe you can accurately picture the destructive diversions constantly pressed on me from a number of directions. Unless a determined stand on this issue is taken now, I am convinced that we will bleed ourselves white instead of gathering the strength necessary for the lead-off toward a knock-out blow.

This letter may also help explain Marshall's continuing support for the build-up of the 8th Air Force. Important as the war against Japan might be, Hitler was still the primary enemy. Since England would be the best springboard for the war against Germany, England was the place to concentrate America's military strength, including air power. Any attempt to concentrate it elsewhere was a "destructive diversion."

Eaker and his staff, after moving into the beautiful Wycombe Abbey school April 15, immediately organized a volleyball game, then laid out a softball diamond. Eaker took for himself a ground-floor office that had belonged to the headmistress and also her two-room living suite on the floor above. To protect the school's paintings, its library, and its paneled walls during the American stay, the work rooms had been lined with false walls of beaver-board. During the first evening of the occupation, the main dormitory's electric-bell system rang constantly. The cause was soon obvious. When the officers moved into their new bedrooms, they found at the head of each bed a little printed sign, intended for the schoolgirls who had lived there. These signs read: "Ring for mistress."

Because the school's maintenance, kitchen, and mess hall personnel had remained, the officers were able to dine in their new headquarters on their first night. And two weeks later, they held their first party, to which they invited everyone who had been helpful to them. Three hundred and fifty people came.

Airdrome construction was moving ahead with remarkable speed and efficiency. The British had already built so many fields for their own R.A.F. that they were now able to complete each one within two months. The first eight fields, those that had already been built and needed only to be converted for American requirements, were almost ready, but the 8th Bomber Command still had no planes to land on their runways. Eaker was becoming impatient for the arrival of his first B-17s, and he was not alone. Winston Churchill, in a March 29 letter to President Roosevelt, had pleaded for the arrival of American bombers before July, at which time Arnold expected to be able to send the first groups.

"Can you not manage to expedite this?" Churchill asked Roosevelt. "Never was there so much good work to be done and so few to do it. We must not let our summer air attack on Germany decline into a second-rate affair. Everything is ready for your people here and there are targets of all kinds, from easy to hard. . . . Even a hundred American heavy bombers working from this country before the end of May would list [sic] our air offensive to the proper scale."

Arnold couldn't send the planes and crews, however, until he had them. In a letter to Portal (April 16), he reaffirmed the July shipment schedule with the assertion: "We are bending every effort to provide a powerful air force to collaborate with the R.A.F. in offensive operations this summer and fall. However, it is apparent that the

123

summer will have passed before we can build up a force large enough to carry our share of the burden.''

Arnold used this same letter as an opportunity to reaffirm his determination to practice daylight bombing: ''In addition to night bombardment, which I do not believe can be counted upon alone to wear down German air power, daylight offensive operations must be resumed.''

But however often Arnold, Spaatz, and Eaker reasserted the American intention, it was not often enough to induce the British to accept it. Plans were now underway to send the first American fighter planes to England. The R.A.F., convinced that these planes would do more good in Northern Ireland where they could be assigned to submarine patrol, asked their chief representative in Washington, Air Marshal Douglas C.S. Evill, to try out the idea on Arnold and associates. Evill reported in a May 12 cable that the idea had not got off the ground:

> You are up against a very strong determination on the part of Arnold, Spaatz, and others to concentrate the training and employment of their forces in the U.K. entirely upon proving that the daylight bombing offensive can be made a success. . . . Under these circumstances Americans are inclined to regard any suggestion that they should use their pursuits [fighters] for air defence purposes or be located in Northern Ireland as something that deliberately or otherwise will have the effect of diverting them from their main purpose. . . . They will not easily be turned from their determination to use their pursuits primarily as escorts to their bombers.

Not yet discouraged, the British, at the same time, were at work on another approach to American intractability, which they naturally perceived as a critical problem in view of their own very limited resources and Hitler's growing strength. What they most fervently wanted the Americans to do was to build Lancaster bombers instead of Flying Fortresses. They considered the Lancaster the world's best bomber because it could carry the heaviest load. (In a modified version, it was eventually able to carry a six-ton bomb.) Equally important, the American adoption of the Lancaster would be the simplest possible way to settle the day-night bombing controversy. The Lancaster could not take as much punishment as the B-17 and therefore had to be used at night.

While Arnold was countering the Lancaster campaign in Washington, Eaker was doing likewise in London. Eaker was hearing it not so much from Harris, however, as from Portal and other members of the Air Staff. He finally said one day, with a smile on his face but with his exasperation beginning to show, "You fellows keep this up and we [Americans] will all be in the Pacific." This was one possibility that frightened the British, who were well aware of the desire, widespread in America, to finish the Japanese first and let Hitler wait his turn. Gradually the R.A.F. made a slight shift in position. They had more experienced aircrews than they had planes, whereas the Americans were only in the process of training the bulk of their crews, none of whom had seen battle against the Germans. Until the American crews were ready, would it not be sensible to send over every available plane immediately and let the British crews fly them?

This was a difficult plea to ignore because at the Washington Conference in December, right after the American entry into the war, General Arnold had agreed with Portal that the R.A.F. should receive ten thousand American airplanes (of all types) in 1942. But that quota, because of the alarming Japanese advances in the Pacific, now seemed impossible of fulfillment, especially if the 8th Air Force was to receive the planes it would need. Churchill's apparent approval of Marshall's 1942 (or 1943 at the latest) second-front plans gave Arnold an opportunity to slide out with a modicum of grace from a commitment he was physically unable to keep. Every possible plane would now have to be saved in preparation for the invasion. Arnold's April 16 letter to Portal, regretting that the British would have to "carry most of the fight to the enemy until the fall," was a preparation for this bad news and a hint of more to come.

On May 26, Arnold himself arrived in London (accompanied by Rear Adm. John H. Towers, the U.S. Navy air chief, and Maj. Gen. Dwight D. Eisenhower, newly appointed chief of the U.S. Army operations section) to acquaint the British with the aircraft allocation quotas they would have to accept. The fact that Arnold's nickname was "Hap" or "Happy" and that almost all of his photographs showed him with a wonderously open, pleasant smile on his face did not mean he was an easy man to get around or even an easy man with whom to get along. Undeniably engaging as well as intelligent, he often used a combination of personal magnetism and warm persuasion to get what he wanted. And his powers of persuasion had been proven by the fact that since assuming direction of the Army Air Corps in 1939, he had raised its status to that of Army Air Forces, with virtual independence from the rest of the Army. He had also managed in that time to wheedle billions of dollars in Air Force appropriations from Congress. Under his command, the slow-moving, impoverished, eighteen-thousand-man peacetime Air Corps was in the process of becoming the largest air force the world had ever seen.

But Arnold hadn't accomplished all of this merely by using his persuasive charm. Despite a condition that resulted in high blood pressure and required him to hold down his rate of heartbeat by use of a special medicine, he was energetic, restless, quick, impatient, hard-driving, and, in the words of one associate, "tough as an old boot." His demands upon his staff members and his frequent habit of circumventing them to avoid paperwork and get quick action made it a constant and often harrowing adventure to work for him. One Sunday morning a few weeks before his trip to England, one of his staff colonels had fallen dead on the carpet in front of his desk while Arnold was berating him about the possible inaccuracy of some airplane production statistics the unfortunate man had put before him.[4]

Arnold was not likely to be afraid even of a personage as impressive as Winston Churchill. On his arrival in London the dreary morning of the 26th, he told first Portal and then Churchill the bad news—the R.A.F. in 1942 would be receiving five hundred fewer heavy bombers and fifteen hundred fewer medium bombers than he had hoped to send them. This unhappy revelation began four days of strenuous conversations the British did not enjoy.

American factories were scheduled to produce sixty thousand aircraft in 1942. Churchill said he couldn't understand why, with that many planes, the United States should raise an issue over allocating "a mere five thousand" to the British. He wanted to hit the enemy, and he wanted to do it right away. The greatest possible number of bombs must be dropped, and he meant within the next few months not a year in the future. What did Arnold think of those sentiments?

Arnold realized that American planes could bomb the enemy right away only if he gave to the British the B-17s intended for Ira Eaker's 8th Bomber Command. He quickly made his views clear to Churchill.[5] The American Air Force, he said, had exceptional young men available to it, "the cream of the crop," and they could fly American planes better than the youngsters of any other country.

Churchill assured him that in general he looked with favor upon the idea of American pilots flying American planes, but that at this moment there was a necessity for maximum impact against the enemy.

Arnold reminded him of one of the key arguments that had sold the U.S. Congress on providing lend-lease aid for besieged countries like Britain and Russia. Congress had been persuaded partly by the assurance that lend-lease arrangements, while furnishing planes to other countries, would be building production capacity against the time when the United States would also need military aircraft. That time had come, and the American people wanted an American Air Force now. They wanted quick action in Europe just as much as Mr. Churchill wanted it. But how could the American Air Force be built up if at the same time American production had to meet all the current needs of Australia, China, Russia, Great Britain, and the U.S. Navy?

In subsequent conversations at staff level, when specific aircraft quotas were under discussion, Admiral Towers, speaking for the U.S. Navy, declared that too few transport planes were being built. The Navy, he pointed out, was sacrificing production of some capital ships because the need for cargo ships and planes was so great. He suggested it would be in the best interests of both nations if the Boeing plant in Long Beach, California, which was producing sixty Flying Fortresses a month, were converted to the production of large transports. Some combat planes, he said, were being overproduced at the expense of cargo planes.

Arnold was not enchanted by this proposal. Speaking in his usual rapid-fire style and calling upon his amazing ability to quote statistics, he said 8,320 cargo planes were now under order in the United States, including 5,600 large ones. The U.S. airlines had another 200 of them if they were needed, and if an acute shortage developed, combat planes could be used for transport whereas transport planes could never be used as bombers.

What he did not say to the assembled British and American military men, but did say to himself, was that it annoyed him to have to keep defending the U.S. Air Force against the U.S. Navy, especially at a time when he was hard-pressed to defend the Air Force and its potential airplanes against the British. As he later wrote:

When asked what solution they might have for getting greater production and making more planes available to the British, or for securing more air transports, the answer of the Navy representatives was, "Stop manufacturing B-17s at the Long Beach plant, and build cargo planes." . . . When [Air Marshal Sir W. R.] Freeman asked what the Navy was able to give up to help, if the Army Air Forces stopped manufacturing B-17s, our Naval officers said, "Nothing—there is nothing the Navy could give that would help any." . . . The Army Air Forces was expected to give everything to everybody. . . . Naturally, from then on, I had to take a much more hard-boiled attitude.[6]

Arnold never did come to an agreement with Admiral Towers on this matter, but eventually he worked out an aircraft quota agreement with Churchill and Portal, which they didn't like but had to accept because he was giving and they were receiving. It promised them 480 fighter planes, 100 heavy bombers for the Near East, 108 medium bombers for North Africa, and large consignments of other planes that were being phased out of the American Air Force. The British would receive no other heavy bombers except for a few to be used by the Coastal Command. Most important in Arnold's mind, it officially settled the issue as to who would fly American bombers from English bases. Only Americans would fly them.

Unable to prevail against Arnold in the matter of aircraft allocation, the British accepted this defeat with good grace and prepared for one more battle in what had now become a six-month campaign. They were still determined to convert Arnold to night bombing, and this was their first opportunity to meet him on their home ground since the war began. They wanted to put on a show that would impress him.

On the night of May 30, Churchill invited him, with Tower, Eaker, and American Ambassador John G. Winant, to a dinner at Chequers, the Prime Minister's official country residence thirty miles northwest of London. Also present were Portal and Harris. Tonight Harris, who had already subjected Arnold to a session in his "conversion room," was staging something even more persuasive—the R.A.F.'s first 1,000-plane mission against Germany. In the largest raid ever launched, 1,046 aircraft (376 of them snatched temporarily from operational training units) were taking off to drop 1,455 tons of bombs on Cologne as Churchill and his guests sat down to dinner. Since Churchill's social evenings always lasted far into the following morning, Harris was able to announce before the guests retired that the raid had been smashingly successful.

Though the details were fragmentary, Arnold was indeed impressed. However, he was not converted. On the issue of day versus night bombing, the evening was a standoff. As Arnold later wrote, "Of all the moments in history when I might have tried to sell Mr. Churchill and his R.A.F. advisers on the future of American precision bombardment by daylight, I had picked the night when they were selling their own kind of bombardment to the world."

During his London stay, Arnold also visited Eaker's stately new headquarters at Wycombe Abbey, where he found most of the staff playing touch football on the lawn. When Eaker showed him through the building, Arnold noticed some of the British WAAFs who were doing the typing, telegraphing and general office work, and even keeping the "Secret" files. Eaker explained that Harris had very generously loaned these girls to him.

"How are you getting along with them?" Arnold wanted to know.

"No problem at all," Eaker assured him, "but you know, these people are right out of Bert Harris's hide, and he'd like to get them back. I think you ought to ask Hobby [Col. Oveta Culp Hobby, commander of the U.S. Women's Army Corps] to get us a company of our own WACs."

That evening, when Eaker joined Arnold in London for dinner, the Air Force commander had already spoken to the European Theater commander, General Chaney, about the matter. With a wry smile, Arnold said to Eaker, "Chaney won't have any WACs in this theater. He thinks it will create a morals problem."

Eaker said, "General, if I were you, I'd get some anyway."[7]

This incident may have helped settle some questions already in

Arnold's mind about Chaney. Late that same night in his hotel room, he discussed with General Eisenhower and Major General Mark Clark, who had also accompanied him, "the need for a theater commander who could meet the British senior officers on even terms." Eisenhower and Clark both agreed that a change was advisable. When Eisenhower left, Arnold and Clark agreed that Eisenhower would be the ideal man for the job. Arnold decided he would speak to General Marshall about it when he returned to Washington.

After Arnold's departure, Eaker and his men settled down once more to the painstaking task of getting ready for the arrival of their first bomb groups. They had been in England for more than three months now trying to bring about the birth of a bombing force, but they hadn't yet dropped a bomb. They didn't even have an airplane. It seemed at times as if the planes would never arrive; yet mountains of work still had to be done in preparation for them.

In the midst of this frantic preparation, Eaker received a phone call from the mayor of the neighboring town of High Wycombe, who wanted the general to attend a dinner, June 5, with him and the town council.

Eaker, swamped with work, begged to be excused.

A short time later, the mayor called again to press the invitation. "It won't take long," he said, "because we don't have much food. You'll be able to get away very shortly and return to your work. But I think since we're your neighbors, it would help both sides if you came over and met my council and had dinner with us."

Eaker finally said, "All right, but with the understanding there'll be no speeches."

As the mayor had promised, the dinner took only an hour. But after it was finished he said to Eaker, "It just happens that a lot of our serving men and women are having a dance across the street. The member of Parliament from this district will be there, so I think we ought to go over."

Eaker, taking a poor view of this development, said, "I hope you're aware, that's breaking our agreement." But he did accompany the mayor, and when they entered the huge community hall across the street, he was faced with a crowd of two thousand British service men and women in uniform. During an intermission in the dancing, the mayor got up on a platform and spoke for fifteen minutes, welcoming the first increment of American airmen to arrive in England. When he ended his speech by introducing Eaker, the general could not, in good grace, refuse to open his mouth. But if he had to speak, he decided he would make it short.

"We won't do much talking," he said to the crowd of British soldiers and sailors, "until we've done more fighting. We hope that when we leave, you'll be glad we came."

8

It was with some relief that Brig. Gen. Ira Eaker learned in mid-June 1942 of the appointment of Dwight Eisenhower, now a new three-star general, as the U.S. Army's European Theater commander. Though not well acquainted with Eisenhower, Eaker knew that if Arnold had suggested him the man must be, unlike some ground-force generals, a solid supporter of air power.

At the same time, Eaker was happy to greet his immediate superior, Maj. Gen. Carl Spaatz, the 8th Air Force commander, on Spaatz's arrival in England. Spaatz, who had remained in the States almost four months longer than Eaker to arrange and expedite the flow of men and matériel across the Atlantic, was now ready to occupy the headquarters prepared for him—code-named Widewing —at Bushy Park. On June 19, Spaatz held a "hello" press conference in London, during which he asserted once more the American determination to bomb Germany in the daytime.

Eaker now had with him an ally upon whom he felt he could always depend. "Tooey" Spaatz was one of his closest friends, the two men having first met in early 1919 when Eaker, as a first lieutenant, was assigned to Rockwell Field in San Diego. Major Spaatz was the executive officer there at the time and Colonel "Hap" Arnold was the commandant. Arnold had been in France only a few months during the war, but Spaatz had been there for a year and a half, as commander of a flying school. Near the end of the war he joined a fighter group and shot down three German planes.

Because of the general demobilization at the end of World War I, the most important job Arnold, Spaatz, and Eaker had to do at Rockwell Field was to reduce the garrison from about four thousand to four hundred men. Eaker was ready to get on with the job immediately in the most direct possible way, by resigning his own commission, but the other two talked him out of it. The friendship among the three men, which began at Rockwell, had continued through the years. Eaker, after two years of study under Air Corps auspices at Columbia University Law School, served under Arnold in 1924, when Arnold was Air Corps Chief of Information. Eaker served with Spaatz on the Air Staff from 1925 to 1927, and in 1929, when Eaker was chief pilot on the Question Mark endurance flight, Spaatz, who was five years his senior, commanded the project. In 1919, when Eaker ended his service at Rockwell Field to take a temporary assignment in the Philippines, he had said to Spaatz and Arnold just before leaving, "Bear in mind, if I stay in the service, I want to come back and join you." During the two decades between the wars, there never was a year when the three did not get together someplace. Arnold, being older than the others, was usually in a command position, and whenever possible he would ask to have them assigned to him.

Spaatz had forever endeared himself to Arnold as a result of an incident in 1920. When the Army stripped its officers of their temporary war ranking and returned them to their permanent ranks, Arnold, a colonel, became a captain overnight, but Spaatz, a major, kept his rank because he had earned it in battle. The following morning, Arnold acknowledged the fact that Spaatz was now his superior by switching desks with him. When Spaatz came into their office, he was horrified at this sudden reversal of roles. Rather than assume command over his former superior, he immediately arranged to have himself transferred to another base.

Arnold, Spaatz, and Eaker had all been members of the young and zealous Air Corps officer group that idolized Col. William "Billy" Mitchell and supported his campaign for the rapid development of

American air power in the years directly after World War I. At Mitchell's celebrated 1925 court-martial, in which he was convicted of insubordination for accusing his superiors of incompetence in their refusal to emphasize air power, Arnold acted as his liaison man, Spaatz testified for him, and Eaker was an aide on his defense staff. All three championed the views not only of Mitchell but also of other early air advocates such as Gen. Guilio Douhet in France and Gen. Sir Hugh Trenchard in England.

One reason Eaker got on so well personally with Harris and Portal in England was that as young R.A.F. officers they had championed these same men, especially Trenchard, who insisted even during World War I that air power would dominate any future wars. Harris still believed this so passionately that on June 17, 1942, he sent Prime Minister Churchill a letter that began like a trumpet blast with the words: "Victory, speedy and complete, awaits the side which first employs air power as it should be employed." Germany, he contended, had made a disastrous mistake by getting bogged down in land campaigns, but England, not presently engaged on land, could "knock Germany out of the war in a matter of months" by devoting its full strength to his bomber offensive.

"Involvement in land campaigns," he wrote, "serves but to reduce us to the level of the Horde. We are not a Horde. We are a highly industrialized, underpopulated, physically small nation. Our lead is in science, not spawn; in brains, not brawn. To enter upon a continental land campaign, other than on a mopping up police basis, is to play right into Germany's hands. . . . It is imperative, if we hope to win the war, . . . to concentrate our air power against the enemy's weakest spots."

Harris asked the Prime Minister to give him command of all the British bombers now in the Coastal Command and in the Middle East and to get "every possible bomber from the United States" for a campaign of devastation against all important German cities.

Spaatz and Eaker would go a long way toward sharing Harris's views, but with the modification that such a campaign would be more successful in the daytime against crucial targets. Spaatz was so confident about day bombing that when he was in England as an observer during the Battle of Britain, he had told newsman Drew Middleton, "The British are winning. They forced them [the Germans] to bomb at night. The Germans won't beat them that way."[1]

Eaker, who had talked to Harris about the letter before it was sent, appreciated the spirit of Harris's argument. He too believed that air power, well used, could win the war, but he had told Harris that as far as the United States was concerned, it was daydreaming to think the Army and Navy would be willing to sit back and let the fledgling Air Force win the war. Harris had said the same was true in England, but he was going to tell them what he thought anyway.

The arrival of Spaatz in England presaged finally the beginning of 8th Air Force operations, but on a very modest scale. Though no planes had yet arrived, several crews from the American 15th Light Bomber (A-20) Squadron had come to study R.A.F. methods. On July 4, six of these crews were invited to join six British crews in a twelve-plane mission using American-made but British-owned A-20s. The attack was against four German airfields in the Low Countries, and two of the six American-manned planes failed to return. A third, piloted by Capt. Charles C. Kegelman, came back on one engine. General Eisenhower, aware that this mission was the first American air action against German-held territory, awarded the Distinguished Service Cross to Kegelman and Distinguished Flying Crosses to his three crewmen. As Spaatz and Eaker personally presented these awards at Molesworth July 11, they could take some satisfaction in the fact that they had finally begun to fight, but their minds were on bigger deeds. The Flying Fortresses of the 97th Bomb Group had begun arriving at their Polebrook base July 6, and serious preparation was in progress for the first U.S. heavy-bomber mission against the Germans.

As Eaker greeted the crews of these B-17s and flew with them to watch them work, he developed a sinking awareness that they weren't quite ready. However well they may have been trained, they now had to cope with conditions they had never before encountered.[2] The weather alone was a serious factor. The British Isles were so often covered with thick, low clouds that for fliers of limited experience it could be difficult just to get off and back onto the ground. They also had to learn a whole new set of procedures for use of the crowded airspace over England. And the pilots had to be drilled in the absolute importance of flying tight formations for mutual protection.

Eaker quickly became concerned about the qualifications of the gunners. They were much less accurate on their first practice missions than they would have to be. On July 6, he directed one of his aides, Col. Claude Duncan, to make certain the 97th Group intensified its gunnery practice.

Eaker was now so busy making final preparations for the debut of his 8th Bomber Command that he no longer had much time to spend with Air Marshal Harris. On July 14, he moved all his belongings from the Harris home to his quarters at Wycombe Abbey, leaving Lady Jill Harris a note that indicated the depth of his feelings for her and her husband: "Very few abodes have I left during my 25 years of military service," he wrote, "with the lump in my throat I had this morning as I carried my effects from that comfortable room. . . . If I spent the rest of my life, I could not repay you and Bert for your many kindnesses to me."

On July 16, Eaker learned that General Eisenhower would like to visit the first B-17 base at Polebrook. Two weeks passed before the new theater commander had time to do so. But when he arrived, with a party including General Spaatz, a practice gunnery mission had been arranged for his observation.[3] Eaker was apprehensive as soon as he escorted Eisenhower and Spaatz onto the base. He believed in the Army doctrine that a disorderly camp was a symptom of sloppy discipline among the men, and in his view, the grounds of this camp were not orderly. The 97th Group had been here almost a month. There was no excuse for the place to be untidy. At the same time, he had a more important reason to be apprehensive. He was not yet confident of the group's gunnery skill.

The one-and-one-half-hour practice flight confirmed his doubts. The mission was a dismal failure. The gunners were so inadequately trained they seldom hit even the easy targets. What would they do against veteran German fighter pilots? Eisenhower and Spaatz were polite, but Eaker was embarrassed and angry. He reprimanded the wing commander and group commander on the spot and arranged for one of his six original staff officers, Col. Frank Armstrong, to come to Polebrook and take charge of the group.

As soon as Armstrong arrived the next day, the 97th's practice flight program was increased and the English country people around Polebrook were subjected to the constant din of B-17 formations overhead from dawn to dusk. With R.A.F. fighter planes acting as mock enemies, the American gunners got an idea what it was going to be like when they had to fire their .50-caliber machine-gun bullets into the mouths of 20-mm. cannons. Eaker was beginning to realize that he might have to establish gunnery ranges, perhaps off the coast of Northern Ireland, where all new crews could be sent for extra training. But that wouldn't help the crews of the 97th Group. They would have to learn to shoot the hard way—against the Germans.

From Eisenhower, Spaatz and Eaker now found out about an important new high-command development that also concerned them.[4] The Combined Chiefs of Staff, on July 24, had officially scrapped General Marshall's plans for a massive military build-up in England (code-named ROUNDUP) and the earliest possible invasion of the Continent. Instead of this operation, the Chiefs, at the insistence of Churchill and his advisers, had decided upon an invasion of North Africa (code-named TORCH) during the autumn of 1942. Though General Eisenhower had been selected to command this operation, he, being a Marshall disciple, did not favor it. He once referred to the day it was decided, July 24, as "the blackest day in history." Eaker tended to agree because he could see the probability that planes earmarked for the 8th Air Force might now be sent to Africa. Within a few days he heard from Arnold that the reality would be worse than that. Arnold informed Spaatz and Eaker not only that they would be deprived of two of the next three B-17 groups they expected but also that they would lose the 97th Group with which they were expecting to begin operations.

As a result of the TORCH decision, the 8th Air Force lost its "first priority" rank among American air forces around the world, and all of its bombers were classified as "available" for the North African invasion. This reevaluation did not mean the 8th was to be completely dismantled. The Combined Chiefs had stipulated that both the R.A.F. and the A.A.F. would continue to receive enough airplanes for a "constantly increasing intensity of air attack" against Germany. But it was difficult to imagine how this attack could constantly increase if most of the planes went to Africa.

While Eaker protested in vain against the African invasion, which he considered an unfortunate diversion from the main campaign against Hitler, he decided at the same time to get his planes into action as quickly as possible and make the maximum use of them before he lost them. He ordered Colonel Armstrong to prepare the 97th Group for its first mission August 10, 1942.

On August 5, Eaker and Spaatz went to Eisenhower's London headquarters and presented their plan for this mission, which he approved. Eaker was "tremendously impressed" by the Theater commander's "keenness for air operations and his evident interest in our personnel." Eisenhower said he wanted to be notified when the planes would be returning from their first mission so he could be at the airdrome to meet them.

Spaatz and Eaker then asked his authorization for each of them to go on missions. Three days earlier, Spaatz had spoiled Eaker's dream of flying the first mission by announcing that he himself wished to do so. He did agree that as far as he was concerned, Eaker could go on the second one and also on certain R.A.F. missions that promised to be instructive. But this arrangement needed Eisenhower's ratification.

Eisenhower approved, though he stipulated that they could not go out together. He then asked Spaatz who should succeed him if anything should happen to him. Spaatz immediately named Eaker. When Eisenhower asked Eaker the same question, he named Col. Newton Longfellow, who had arrived in England only nine days earlier to become his chief of staff. Eaker had known Longfellow since his two years in the Philippines (1919-21), where they had served together. At the end of that tour of duty, the two had taken leaves and spent five months together, coming home the long way around the world, stopping wherever they could find airplanes to fly. In Saigon they flew with the French Air Force, and in Cairo with the British.

When British senior officers learned that Spaatz and Eaker intended to fly missions, they expressed strong disapproval. They said in effect, we've gone to a lot of trouble to help you chaps prepare for your roles. We've given you all the secret information we have. If you go out and get killed, we'll have to start over again with somebody else.

Harris was particularly critical. He once told Eaker, "It has taken me many years to get to know the things I should know to be bomber commander. Portal and the Secretary for Air [Sir Archibald Sinclair] would relieve me if they knew I contemplated it."

Spaatz was persuaded by these arguments. Eaker, though he might agree with them, felt a strong obligation to go because he was bomber commander. He said to film star Ben Lyon who was planning to join the Air Force to become a member of his staff, "I don't want any American mothers to think I'd send their boys someplace where I'd be afraid to go myself.''[5] When Spaatz announced he would not be flying the first mission after all, Eaker decided to fly it himself. It was at this time (August 8, 1942) that he issued his directive suggesting his staff officers fly "sufficient operational missions in order to be cognizant of the problems facing combat crews."

The 8th Air Force by now had its first sample of one kind of combat-crew problem. On July 25, a gunnery sergeant who had flown the A-20 mission July 4 against German airfields committed suicide, possibly because he could not face the strain of continued combat. As if in anticipation of such battle-induced psychological crises, the previous day, Spaatz had ordered the establishment of a facility called the 8th Air Force Provisional Medical Field Service School, designed to teach medical officers as much as possible about the problems peculiar to fliers in combat.

Eaker was also taking an important step to safeguard the mental health of his bomber crews. At the suggestion of Air Marshal Harris, he directed that no one be required or even allowed to fly more than twenty-five missions. Harris had said to him, "We made a mistake under the emergency pressures of the Battle of Britain. We let crews go until they were killed. We have found out you must give a combat crew a chance for survival. We learned in the long run that you must set a [fixed] number of missions."

On August 8, after arranging for his own participation in the debut of his bombers, scheduled for two days later, Eaker sent a three-page letter to Arnold in Washington reaffirming his faith in American air strategy. "The tempo is stepping up as we approach the zero hour," he wrote. "Tooey's and my theory that day bombardment is feasible is about to be tested where men's lives are put at stake. . . . Amid all the discouragements—slow arrival of equipment; small numbers available; bad weather and necessity for more training—one thing stands out brightly. Our combat crews have the heart and stamina, the keenness, the will to fight and the enthusiasm which will make them the toughest air fighters . . . in this theater."

Perhaps because of the intensive extra training to which Colonel Armstrong was now subjecting these combat crews, Eaker was feeling much more optimistic even about their gunnery skills. "The other day I flew with one of our B-17E crews on a gunnery and bombing mission," he told Arnold, "and I wished many times that you had been aboard. Every time the tow-target came within 1,000 yards, the gunners opened up and cut it to shreds. I would never have believed it was possible to hit a sleeve in quantity a thousand yards away if I had not seen it."

He was feeling equally pleased with the development of the rest of his organization. "We not only have the best collection of officers ever assembled in one place," he wrote, "but they are all working like one congenial happy family." If Eaker's assessment was accurate, the 8th Air Force Bomber Command was ready for action.

The British press, which until recently had been discouraged by censorship from mentioning American air activity in England (Eaker's name did not appear in the London *Times* until July 13), now began to take notice of it. The *Times* aeronautical correspondent, Peter Masefield, was invited to tour U.S. bases, including Polebrook, in early August and wrote a short article that amusingly described the British view of the invasion of East Anglia:

> Visiting the aerodromes in this country which have been taken over by the United States Army Air Force, as I have been doing during the last few days, one gets the impression of having made an impossibly fast journey to America. At one moment one is driving along a typically English country road, and the next, as if by magic, one is transported . . . to an aerodrome which is as typically American as Randolph Field, Texas, the equivalent of our Cranwell.
>
> All trace of British occupation has disappeared. . . . The aircraft are American, and so are the petrol trailers, lorries, mobile workshops, bomb trolleys, Jeeps, salvage vehicles, etc. . . .
>
> The Americans are not relying on this country for even the smallest items; they have actually brought with them their own dust-bins—garbage cans, they call them.[6]

On the evening of August 9, the 97th Heavy Bomb Group at Polebrook was alerted for its first combat mission the next day. But by the morning of the 10th, the clouds over East Anglia were so low and so thick the operation had to be canceled. On the 11th, the weather remained bad, but late in the day prospects improved and the big event was rescheduled for the 12th. That morning, however, the base was "socked in" once more, and it remained that way for five days.

On the 14th, General Spaatz received an impatient cable from General Arnold. Why were Eaker's bombers still on the ground? There was pressure in Washington for the 8th Air Force to get going. It would be easier for him to win appropriations from Congress, easier to gain acceptance for Air Force policies if Spaatz and Eaker would hurry up and begin successful operations.

While Arnold fretted in Washington and Eaker anxiously watched for a change in the weather, Sir Charles Portal in London was quite calm about the coming American air offensive. The brilliantly analytical but ascetic and undemonstrative R.A.F. Chief of Air Staff wrote an internal policy memorandum (August 13) in which he said about the coordination between Harris and Eaker:

> Fortunately they are located close together and are firm friends and I do not think there will be the slightest difficulty in fitting in their programmes. Spaatz may tend to interfere with Eaker to start with but I think he will soon discover that it is unprofitable to do so and Eaker will then be left with the same freedom as Harris already enjoys.

In this same memo, however, Portal made it plain that he still had little faith in daylight bombing when he referred to "those night operations which they [the Americans] will undertake with their medium bombers, and possibly later with their heavies if they find that day bombing is too expensive."

Harris still firmly believed that day bombing would be too expensive, but he had virtually given up arguing with Eaker about it. He told one of his aides, Group Capt. Dudley Saward, that he thought the Americans were about to suffer some bad casualties, but that they might as well try it because they knew more about day bombing than they would be able to learn about night bombing in several years.[7]

At 11:00 A.M. on the morning of August 17, with the weather clearing rapidly, Brigadier General Eaker began his first operations conference and ordered the 8th Air Force Bomber Command's first combat mission that afternoon. The operations conference didn't take long. The mission would be against the railroad marshaling yards at Rouen, France, sixty-five miles northwest of Paris and thirty-five miles inland from the English Channel. Eaker and staff had planned it so minutely and had discussed it so many times during the last week while waiting for the weather to clear that there wasn't much to say now except, "Do it."

After the conference, Eaker himself flew to Polebrook where twelve crews of the 97th Bomb Group had been on alert for a week. Their morale, according to the 8th Bomber Command diary for the day, was "wearing thin from repeated 'dry runs,' bad weather and impatience to get at the Hun." Eaker, however, was impressed by "the nonchalance of the crews" when he arrived in early afternoon and announced that he would accompany them. He found "evident enthusiasm" and "could detect no nervousness or anxiety—they seemed quite like veterans."

At 3:14 P.M., the first engine of Col. Frank Armstrong's B-17 kicked over, emitting a puff of blue smoke, and twelve minutes later, at 3:26, the Group commander got off the ground followed by the five other planes in his flight. Eaker, riding as an observer, took off in the seventh plane, named Yankee Doodle, which was to lead the second flight of six. The twelve planes assembled over the field, climbed to 22,500 feet, and turned toward France. They did not constitute a very impressive armada, but they were the first American Flying Fortresses to attack Hitler's Europe. After eight months of war, a lot of people back home were thinking it was about time they got around to it. Eaker was sharply aware of this attitude as he took a position in the radio operator's compartment of his plane. If today's small operation were to fail, it might be a fatal blow to the concept of daylight bombing. And the fact that the operation was so small increased the possibility of failure. Daylight bombing strategy was based on plans to send out large formations of bombers with so many guns defending one another that fighter planes would court quick destruction by coming close to them. Since a twelve-plane formation could hardly be called large, and since none of the men in these twelve planes, including Eaker, had ever before faced combat, it was quite possible that today the German fighters would be able to come as close as they pleased.

There was little danger that the Germans would appear immediately. At the English coast, four squadrons of British Spitfires fell in beside the B-17s to escort them as far as the coast of France.[8] For the round trip from there to the target, in the little town of Sotteville, three miles north of Rouen, the big bombers would be alone. About halfway across the Channel, in sunny skies, Eaker saw ahead of him the coast of France. As they crossed the coast and lost their short-range fighter escort, he was pleased at the good order of this rookie group's formation although he felt it could be even tighter. Having taken special training to qualify as a gunner (one of his directives ordered that no one could go on a mission unless he could fire a machine gun), he took his turn at the radio operator's topside emplacement, but no German fighters had yet appeared.

When the bomb-bay doors opened as the B-17s approached the target, Eaker went to the bomb compartment where he found out what it was like to ride in the body of a B-17 under combat conditions. With the big square waist-gunners' windows open on both sides as well as the bomb-bay doors and the radio operator's top gun hole, and with the air temperature around thirty-five degrees below zero, it felt as if "a howling gale" were rushing through the plane.

From the bomb-bay opening he looked down to see a bend in the Seine and then the village of Sotteville. The Americans had still seen no fighters, and no flak had come up to greet them. Directly over the rail yards, Eaker watched the B-17's five 600-pound bombs drop, one after another. But he had to go to a side window to see them land because some sensible crew-member closed the bomb-bay doors the moment the load was gone. As the formation turned right after the bomb run, the burst of the bombs was visible. It seemed that from each plane's string, a long, mushroomlike pall of smoke and dirt arose. Two such bomb clouds flanked the roundhouse while four more were well spaced along the marshaling yard. Two bursts were short of the target; two more were to the right of it, but within the complex of railroad buildings.

Shortly after the B-17s turned for home, German fighters—three FW-190s—arrived to harass them. As the first of these pulled up sharply from below, it seemed to be aiming its guns at Eaker's plane, but its bullets came closer to the plane just astern. The two other Focke-Wulfs, also approaching from below, attacked the last B-17 in the formation, and Eaker could see the bottom turret gunner in that plane return their fire. But when the German fighters retired, neither side appeared to have been damaged. From the radio operator's gun opening, Eaker looked out and counted his planes. All twelve were still in formation, though one seemed to lag slightly as black smoke trailed from its left outboard engine.

An hour and a half later, all twelve were safely back home on the ground and the 8th Bomber Command had survived its first combat action without a loss. In his report to Spaatz, Eaker mentioned the need for tighter formations and more gunnery training. The crews, he said, were alert and vigilant. As for the Flying Fortress, he was convinced it had "excellent defensive firepower." He didn't think it should be used extensively above 25,000 feet "due to extreme crew discomfort" from the cold. But he considered it a great credit to the aircraft that pilots "less than six months out of flying school" could handle it so satisfactorily.

"I think it is a great airplane," he concluded. "It is too early in our experiments in actual operations to say that it can definitely make deep penetrations without fighter escort and without excessive losses. I can say definitely now, however, that it is my view that the German fighters are going to attack it very gingerly."

The following day, Air Chief Marshal Harris, taking cognizance of the fact that Eaker had ridden in a plane called Yankee Doodle, sent him a congratulatory telegram which read: "Yankee Doodle certainly went to town, and can stick yet another well-deserved feather in his cap."

Two days after the Rouen mission, on the 19th, a formation of twenty-four Flying Fortresses, escorted partway by Spitfires, attacked a German airdrome at Abbeville in support of the costly British commando landings at Dieppe. The Fortresses again returned without a loss, and General Eisenhower was at Polebrook with Eaker to welcome them home.

On August 20, twelve Fortresses hit the marshaling yard at Amiens/Longueau and all came back. On the 21st, the Fortresses got off the ground sixteen minutes late for their rendezvous with the Spitfires. As a result, they were without escort when a flight of FW-190s attacked them near the Dutch coast. Though one B-17 copilot was killed and his pilot wounded, all the planes returned to base. On August 24, 27, 28, and 29, the Fortresses of the 97th Group invaded the continent without even meeting a challenge from German fighters.[9]

On August 25, Eaker wrote a report to Spaatz about the lessons learned as a result of the first five missions. Crew training, which he called "the essence of success," should stress general alertness and, in pilots, the ability to hold a tight formation. "Enemy fighters," he

144

said, "will concentrate on any airplane which falls back in the formation." Crew comfort, he believed, would have to be improved. At 23,000 feet, the temperature was sometimes as low as forty-four degrees below zero, cold enough to freeze the oxygen masks and to cut the efficiency of the men by 50 percent.

The oxygen supply system was not entirely satisfactory, because the hose connections were too short to allow the gunners full freedom of movement. Turret guns were definitely more accurate than any of the others. And a flexible gun in the nose would be desirable.

These were comparatively small problems, however, and most of them were correctible. Events so far had done nothing to diminish his enthusiasm for the B-17, especially in bombardment results. The accuracy of the bombing, he said, made it safe to infer that even with "young inexperienced crews such as those we have had to use, small point targets can be hit with precision in daylight bombing from altitudes between twenty-two- and twenty-four-thousand feet."

Two days later, Eaker had received a set of aerial photos taken by British reconnaissance planes (the 8th Air Force didn't yet have a reconnaissance unit) of the first two American targets. These British photos indicated such an astonishing degree of accuracy by the U.S. daylight bombers that they gave Eaker even greater reason to praise his men and planes. In another report to Spaatz August 27, he said:

The 97th Group have demonstrated that their bombing will have the order of the following accuracy: 10% of the bombs dropped will be dead on the aiming point, considering it to be a rectangle 100 yards on the side; 25% of the bombs dropped will be within a circle with a radius of 250 yards from the aiming point; 40% of the bombs will be within an area included in a circle with a radius of 500 yards from the aiming point; 90% of the bombs will be within a circle with a radius of one mile from the aiming point; the additional 10% of the bombs will be strays due largely to defective bomb release mechanism.

Compared to night area bombing, information from the actual plots of British Bomber Command indicates that about 5% of the bombs will be dropped within a circle of a one-mile radius. The best of their bombing has shown 10% of the bombs within a circle with a one-mile radius from aiming point. It is safe and conserva-

145

tive to say, therefore, that high level day bombing will be at least ten times as effective for the destruction of definite point targets as night area bombing.

It had taken the Americans a long time to get started, but their bombing debut had proven so persuasive that the British also praised it. Some of Eaker's R.A.F. colleagues were openly impressed, perhaps because the evidence of the American success had come from their own reconnaissance photos. If the 8th Air Force could maintain this accuracy, they agreed, then daylight bombing might work after all, and the Flying Fortresses might be able to knock out Germany's aircraft factories, thus eliminating at the source the fighter planes that were bedeviling their night bombers. It was an exciting prospect.

Some people in the R.A.F. became so enthusiastic about the potential of the Flying Fortress that they began leaking information to the British press. As a result, aviation writer Colin Bednall wrote a rhapsodic article about the big American bomber for the September 2, 1942, *London Daily Mail*. Bednall seemed to think the Flying Fortress was going to revolutionize the war in the air:

So remarkable has been the success of the new Flying Fortresses operated by the United States Army Air Force from this country that it is likely to lead to a drastic resorting of basic ideas on air warfare. . . . Many experts had grave misgivings when the Americans began operations in Europe with Fortresses, which compared unfavorably with our own heavy bombers. . . .

These calculations, however, made no allowance for two vital factors. First: instead of the 10 .30-calibre machine guns carried by the Lancaster, the new Fortresses are armed with no fewer than 12 [*sic*] .50-calibre machine guns. Second: in daylight it could bomb with extreme accuracy from great heights and therefore avoid much of the ground flak which night bombers have to penetrate because they must come lower to sight their target.

The Flying Fortress . . . had won a fine reputation in the Pacific, but it had to prove itself in the much more highly developed air war of Western Europe. . . . Just how well it has established itself within the short space of a fortnight is now the subject of close study by startled experts on both sides of the English Channel.

146

During its short span of action, the B-17 had now flown more than one hundred sorties against the continent. It had not yet faced full-scale German defenses. While it had attacked German-occupied territory, it hadn't yet penetrated the skies over Germany itself. Yet in the course of some very accurate daylight bombing, it had managed to knock down several of Germany's best fighter planes, the FW-190s. To an increasing number of people, the Flying Fortress was beginning to look like the miracle weapon for which everyone on the Allied side was waiting and hoping.

9

If the men of the 8th Bomber Command believed their early success presaged a smooth, triumphant future, they were soon disillusioned. Difficulties of all kinds arose quickly. The first was perhaps a welcome one—growing pains. After waiting six months for their first airplanes, they now began to get them almost faster than they could absorb them. The 301st Group, with twenty planes, had flown the northern ferry route across the Atlantic (Newfoundland-Greenland-Scotland) to settle into the base at Chelveston in early August, and the 92nd Group, with twenty-three of the newest model B-17Fs, had arrived a short time later to take residence at Bovingdon, but the end of the month came without either group's even approaching operational status.

General Spaatz, possibly expecting General Arnold to get after him for their tardiness, decided to get after General Eaker about it. He pointedly asked Eaker at an 8th Air Force headquarters meeting August 29[1] why these groups weren't yet flying missions and why the 97th Group was putting an average of only twelve planes in the air per mission. As it happened, the 97th and 92nd had just traded airplanes because Eaker had decided the 92nd would not be needing its brand-new B-17Fs. He realized he had to establish a combat-crew replacement and training center, and as soon as the 92nd had flown a few combat missions, he intended to use this group, at Bovingdon, as a nucleus for it. He explained to Spaatz that the 97th was handicapped because its newly acquired, latest model B-17s still had a lot of bugs to be eliminated. During a twelve-plane practice flight, the guns had worked on only three. Several of the planes had now been flown long enough to need one-hundred-hour inspections, which the ground crews were doing as quickly as possible. And there was such an acute shortage of generators and spark plugs that one-fourth of the 97th's planes had been put out of commission.

The 301st and 92nd Groups were also suffering from the spark-plug and generator shortage. They didn't have enough tow-target planes or sleeves for gunnery training. Practice bombs for the 301st had arrived only the previous day; and the crews hadn't even had a chance to learn to fly the close formations Eaker had found necessary in combat.

Spaatz suggested that they invent their own tow-targets, and if they didn't have practice bombs, they should use 100-pound high explosive bombs on the practice ranges. He wanted the two new groups in action as near as possible to immediately.

Though Spaatz may have felt it was his job to hustle Eaker, he was generally sympathetic to Bomber Command's growing problems. He realized that in any new military organization, the maintenance and supply systems could create even more trouble than combat. Anticipating his needs, Eaker had petitioned the British for a parts and repair facility and had been given an already-existing depot at Burtonwood in Lancashire, complete with a staff of technicians accustomed to working on the R.A.F.'s American-made aircraft. But unfortunately, Lancashire soon proved to be too far north and west to be convenient to East Anglia, where all the American operational bases were. Since there was still a shortage of trucks (or lorries) and since all the signposts had been removed from British roads in 1940 (to confuse the Germans in the event of an invasion), drivers had endless difficulties finding the little country towns near which the bases had been built.

The new groups, impatient for parts and supplies, decided not to wait for Service Command deliveries. They sent their own trucks to Burtonwood, driven by Americans who had been in England only a few days (the ground echelons arrived by ship at about the same time as the air echelons) and who therefore lost their way even more frequently than the Service Command drivers. On August 28, Eaker thought of a solution to this problem. He put in a requisition for two C-47 transport planes (the military equivalent of the Douglas DC-3) for each heavy-bomb group. These planes could bring priority parts and supplies from Burtonwood to the bases in less than an hour.

Meanwhile, acting on the experiences of the first few combat operations and the increasing evidence of weather problems ahead, he asked for reconsideration of an earlier proposal to provide blind-landing trucks for the ends of runways at which homecoming planes would be prayerfully aiming. And he sent (through two of Arnold's aides) a set of suggestions for improvements in future model B-17s. He recommended that the entire oxygen system be revamped and better masks installed. He suggested bullet-proof glass for pilot and copilot side windows; 20-mm. cannons in some of the turrets; mechanical means to operate the turrets in the event of electrical or hydraulic failure; and above all, a better heating system for the crews. Since it was not possible to heat the airplane itself, he asked for electrically heated, plug-in flying suits.

One after another, the initial difficulties were worked out and the new groups got ready for their introduction to combat. On September 5, the 301st made its debut by joining the 97th in another mission against the railroad marshaling yards at Rouen. A total of thirty-seven B-17s, still a pathetically small number, hit Rouen that day, and once again all of them returned.

Next day, September 6, another new heavy-bomb group, the 93rd, flying America's other four-engine bomber, the B-24 Liberator, began arriving from the states under the command of Col. Edward J. Timberlake, Jr. While it was settling into a base at Alconbury (four miles northwest of Huntingdon), the 92nd Group was getting its first taste of combat. The 92nd that day sent fourteen B-17s along with twenty-two from the "veteran" 97th on a raid against an aircraft factory at Meaulte. Six of the 92nd's planes had to abort.

The thirty planes that droppped their bombs were on their way home when they met a flight of FW-190s. The German pilots had now been encountering the heavily armed American bomber for three weeks and perhaps had been working out some strategies against it.

150

Today they attacked more ferociously and persistently than ever before. Within a few minutes, the Flying Fortress had finally lost its unblemished record. One of the 97th planes went down near Flasseslles, and another, from the 92nd, fell into the English Channel.

General Eaker, who had worried about his virtually unscathed crews becoming overconfident, could now concentrate on other worries. The men of the 8th Bomber Command gained valuable respect that day for the skills of German pilots.

Three days later, Eaker had a new problem so serious it threatened to make academic the question of the B-17's merits against German fighters. On September 9, General Eisenhower, calculating the needs of the North African invasion, informed Spaatz that the 8th Army bomber offensive against Germany would have to be not just curtailed as anticipated but completely stopped, at least for the near future. Two days later, General Arnold in Washington, undoubtedly alerted by Spaatz, sent a cable to Eisenhower arguing against any such intentions. Though Arnold understood the need for planes in Africa, he didn't want the 8th Bomber Command forced out of business after all the work it had done to get into business. He listed for Eisenhower some of the benefits of keeping the 8th in operation. Besides reducing the German war effort by attacking important targets, it was attracting the attention of the German Air Force and drawing German fighters away from other fronts. (The implication was that one of those other fronts might be North Africa.) Arnold fell short, however, of asking or demanding that Eisenhower abandon his plan of shutting down the 8th. He asked only that Eaker's bomber operation be continued until the last possible moment. Arnold knew that Eisenhower's decisions came from George Marshall, with whom Arnold had once said he would consider himself wrong to disagree.

To Eaker, who had repeatedly declared that he considered the North African invasion an unfortunate diversion from the main task of attacking Germany directly, Arnold's less-than-defiant cable to Eisenhower looked like an open surrender of the 8th. The fact that it might be a reluctant or even necessary surrender by Arnold was no consolation. Eaker talked heatedly to Spaatz about the matter, but Spaatz was at a disadvantage. He had just been chosen as Eisenhower's air commander in Africa. While Spaatz agreed with Eaker that it would be tragic to dissipate the bomber effort against Germany just

151

when it was developing enough force to make an impression, he was also aware that any planes he helped Eaker keep would have to come out of the force he himself was going to need in Africa. Eaker was beginning to feel lonely in his campaign to hold his 8th Bomber Command together. And he had been so outspoken in his arguments he sensed that Eisenhower was becoming annoyed at him.[2] Despite all this difficulty, one consolation came his way. On September 17, 1942, he was promoted to major general.

Winston Churchill, who had originated the threat to foreclose the 8th Air Force when he insisted on the African invasion, now came unexpectedly to Eaker's aid, perhaps because he had second thoughts about the possible long-term results of an 8th Air Force hiatus. The increasing pressure from certain elements in the United States to concentrate the American war effort in the Pacific made it uncertain that the 8th Air Force, once removed from England, would ever return. It may have been with this prospect in mind that Churchill wrote to President Roosevelt on September 16. After observing politely that "the results of the first operations by your Flying Fortresses have been most encouraging," he set out, without mentioning Eisenhower, to undermine Eisenhower's plans:

> In spite of the fact that we cannot make up more than 32 squadrons of bombers, instead of 42 last year, we know our night bomber offensive is having a devastating effect. . . . If we can add continuity and precision to the attack by your bombers' striking deep into the heart of Germany by day the effect would be redoubled. To do this effectively and without prohibitive loss they must have numbers to saturate and disperse the defences. . . . I hope you may consider it wise to build up General Spaatz's strength. . . . We must make TORCH [the North African invasion] a success. But I am sure we would be missing a great opportunity if we did not concentrate every available Fortress and long-range escort fighter as quickly as possible for the attack on our primary enemy.

> I cannot help feeling some concern at the extent to which the programme for the build-up of American air forces in this country is falling behind expectations.

Churchill's belief that day bombing was a mad ambition did not prevent him from seeming to support it in this letter when such support was convenient to his purpose. At the moment his purpose was to make certain that large numbers of American planes would keep coming to England. After the planes arrived he could get back to his debate with the Americans on how they should be used.

Among Churchill's top air advisers, that debate was sharpening. What could be done with the Americans to make them see their errors, to persuade them to redirect and refocus their contribution to the bomber offensive against Germany? Sir Archibald Sinclair, the Liberal Party leader who had been Churchill's second in command with the Royal Scots Fusiliers in World War I and was now his Secretary of State for Air, was growing impatient with the Americans. Unlike some people in England, he was not even slightly impressed by the 8th Bomber Command's early efforts against the Continent. By late September he was so dissatisfied with what he had seen of the Americans so far that on the 25th he decided he couldn't keep still any longer. That day he wrote a letter to Air Marshal John Slessor, the Assistant Chief of Air Staff:

What are the Americans doing? What do they intend to do? I know the number of American aircraft in this country. How many officers and men of the United States Air Corps are here? As far as I know they have not dropped a single bomb in Germany. Is it true that they have not dropped a single bomb outside the range of our single seater fighter cover? . . .

What is their operational policy? . . . When do you think they will drop their first bomb on Germany? Will they start next month?

Is there any possibility that they will join in the night bombing of Germany? Is there any possibility that they will be able to damp the flames of the Flying Fortress sufficiently to bomb Germany? Do they contemplate the use of the Flying Fortress at night? If so, will it be sufficiently modified before the end of this year?

Air Marshal Slessor, to whom Sinclair addressed this letter, was more sympathetic toward American policies than any other high officer in the R.A.F. He had spent time in Washington, and he had spent time at 8th Air Force headquarters in Bushy Park, talking to Spaatz and Eaker about their hopes, problems, and methods. His reply (September 26) to Sinclair's impatient letter was painstakingly patient. There were, he told Sinclair, six American heavy-bomber squadrons (B-17s) operational. (The British squadron was roughly equivalent to the American group. Actually seven U.S. groups were now in England, but only three had seen combat.) Some of these groups, Slessor pointed out, were being prepared for what he called "a certain operation" that severely restricted their use. This "certain operation" was the planned North African invasion, still so secret he didn't want to mention it on paper. He was very understanding, however, about the problems it had already created for the 8th Air Force:

> General Spaatz has suffered a setback by having to set aside his first units operational for the certain operation. He has now to start again at the beginning breaking in new units as they arrive. He is wisely doing this gradually. . . . His crews arrive without adequate operational training, and in particular his gunners need more firing. We are now going into the difficult but important problem of getting them adequate range facilities.

Slessor still held out hope of an enormous U.S. air effort in Europe, but he could lend no comfort to Sinclair's hope that the 8th Air Force would eventually convert to night bombing:

> They intend to do precision bombing of Germany by daylight. . . . They believe that with their good defensive armament they can do it when they get sufficient numbers. Their early operations lend some support to this belief—the B-17 has shown that it can defend itself and take an enormous amount of punishment. It has yet to be proved whether it is possible to carry the war deep into Germany by day. But they believe they will, and I personally am inclined to agree with them once they get really adequate numbers. . . . No, they have not yet bombed outside our fighter cover because they have not yet passed through Phase 1. But they have had several notable fights without fighter escort, in which they have given a good account of themselves. . . . Their bombing has been extremely accurate as a rule. And I think we have seen enough of their performance in this and other theaters to be sure that their air crews are fine material. . . . General Spaatz intends to get into

Germany before the end of this year, and I think as good a guess as any would be . . . sometime in the first half of December.

Slessor also included an almost naked warning in this letter to Sinclair. There was a significant danger, he pointed out, in pushing the Americans too far away from their cherished policies. He was not certain that if their day bombing failed, they would then wholeheartedly embrace night bombing:

> I think that those Heavy groups already in this country when that situation arose would probably be modified and trained for night work. Whether they would attempt to build up the force I think is doubtful. . . . It would involve a fundamental readjustment of American air policy, with all its consequential repercussions on equipment and training. And I think it might well involve a sharp swing away from this theatre towards the PACIFIC.

Slessor's immediate superior, Chief of Air Staff Portal, was not so sanguine about American prospects for success. By coincidence he asked for Slessor's comments the same day (September 26) on a note he had prepared about the U.S. bomber force. In this note, Portal began by acknowledging that to him the great question was still "DAY" or "NIGHT." He believed a good night bombing force could be quickly turned into a day bombing force, but it would be difficult to turn a day force into a night force because it would involve production as well as training. The hope that America might yet switch from the B-17 to the Lancaster was still with him:

> The Americans will not get a night bomber force by the beginning of 1944 unless they start now. Are they going to start or are they going to persist in an attempt at 100% day effort?
>
> The danger seems to be that if they suffer heavy casualties with 5 or 6 groups they will merely say that the job requires 15 or 20 groups and by the time they have 20 groups they will probably be committed to 40 or 50. In the end they may find themselves no more successful with 50 groups than the Germans were with the same numbers in the Battle of Britain.
>
> Is it not therefore essential to persuade the Americans to lay the

foundations in aircraft production and in training for at least a substantial part of their offensive to be by night bombing?

On the production side, neither the B-17 nor the B-24 appear to be ideal night bombers and the obvious course of action would seem to be that they should build a very large number of Lancasters.

Slessor's reaction to Portal's note came within hours, and it was entirely negative. Always an outspoken man, Slessor was as vigorous in disagreeing with the Chief of Air Staff as with the Secretary of State for Air. He attached a copy of his reply to Sinclair, then enlarged upon it in his response to Portal:

Perhaps I am unduly optimistic, but I have always felt that when we get large numbers of bombers we shall be able to go in by day. I think if the Germans in the Battle of Britain, even with the same number, had had aircraft with the performance, armour, armament and precision bomb-sights of the B-17, the answer might have been very different. . . .

I have talked about this a great deal to Spaatz and to others of my American friends. They are, I think, a bit unwarrantably cockahoop as a result of their limited experience to date. But they are setting about it in a realistic and business-like way . . . And making all allowances for their natural optimism, I have a feeling they will do it.

I think it can be said with certainty that no large scale training for night bombing is contemplated and they have not really thought out what they would do if they find the day policy is not practicable. They have hung their hats on the day bomber policy and are convinced they can do it. And I think to cast doubts on it just at present would only cause irritation and make them very obstinate.

Slessor's pro-American attitude, instead of convincing Portal, appalled him. And the fact that Slessor had written a long letter impressing this attitude upon Sinclair (their official channel to Churchill) was so alarming that on the following day (September 27) Portal himself wrote a letter to Sinclair embracing an opposite viewpoint and showing only in isolated instances an effort to accommodate Slessor's ideas:

I entirely agree that a force of 3,000 heavy and medium bombers able to pick off small targets with precision in any part of Germany by day would enable us to win the war, but I have even more serious doubts than A.C.A.S. (P) [Slessor] appears to have about whether the Americans will ever achieve their objective. I am particularly dubious on two points.

First, although it is quite easy to pick off small targets by day when you are not seriously opposed, it is an entirely different matter when you are being harassed all the time by fighters and flak. . . .

Secondly, there is the question of their "ammunition range" when unescorted. The Ruhr is 300 miles away, and assuming that the American fighters can go in 200 miles the Fortresses would have 200 miles to fly unescorted. Berlin is 550 miles and would involve 700 miles' unescorted flying. . . . I do not believe that with uncontrolled wobble-guns they can shoot well enough to defend themselves for nearly three hours against fighter attack with the ammunition that the Fortress can carry. . . .

My own prophecy . . . is this? The Americans will eventually be able to get as far as the Ruhr, suffering very much heavier casualties than we now suffer by night, and going much more rarely. They will in effect do area bombing. . . . I do not think that they will ever be able regularly to penetrate further than the Ruhr and perhaps Hamburg without absolutely prohibitive losses. . . .

On the other hand, I have no doubt that if by the end of 1943 we had a force of 3,000 American heavy and medium bombers properly trained for night flying to our standards, we and they together could pulverize almost the whole of the industrial and economic power of Germany within a year, besides utterly destroying the morale of the German people.

In a slight concession to Slessor's view, Portal went on to tell Sinclair he agreed that there was some danger of the Americans' "confining themselves to bombing of Occupied Territory or even going off to other areas" (i.e., the Pacific) if their daylight bombing failed. But he stuck to his contention that they should be persuaded to alter their course:

I think it is essential that they should be induced to insure to some extent against this [probable daylight failure] if only to the extent of 20% of their force. To do this they would have to develop an efficient night bombing aircraft and to study on a relatively small scale the problem of night training. . . . I am prepared to wait until the end of the year before taking this matter up, as I realize that it would be difficult to get the Americans to listen at the present time. . . . I thought, nevertheless, that I should let you know that my doubts about the feasibility of the day bombing of Germany are a good deal stronger than those held by A.C.A.S. (P) [Slessor].

Portal's concluding lines made it evident that the whole purpose of his letter to Sinclair was to counteract Slessor's letter to Sinclair the previous day, which Portal had not read before it was dispatched. While the Chief of Air Staff carefully avoided rebuking his prestigious assistant chief, he wanted to make it clear that Slessor's sympathy for the American viewpoint did not represent the ruling attitude in the R.A.F. He was also making it clear that the Americans had not yet seen the end of the British resistance to daylight bombing.

Spaatz and Eaker were aware that some high British authorities were less enchanted by the early successes of the 8th Bomber Command than the press and public seemed to be, but the two American commanders knew nothing about this ominous exchange of views between Sinclair, Slessor, and Portal. Indeed, Spaatz and Eaker had begun to think British opposition to American policy was softening because of the apparent success of the Flying Fortress. They knew, however, that the British would not be fully convinced until Fortresses in significant numbers could penetrate Germany's West Wall defenses, drop bombs on important targets, and return home without prohibitive losses.

Though Eaker was destined within less than three months to lose three groups (97th, 301st, and 93rd) to the African invasion, plus a fourth scheduled for England but diverted directly to Africa, he was at the same time receiving four other groups from the States. The ground echelon of the 306th reached its base at Thurleigh, six miles north of Bedford, September 6, and the air echelon flew in a week later.

Construction of barracks and other facilities was not yet completed when the 306th arrived at Thurleigh under the command of Col. Charles B. "Chips" Overacker. The place was in such a mess that one man named it, with apologies to Winston Churchill, "Mud, Sweat and Tears."[3] For a short time some of the men had to sleep in tents, and the officers' mess was so small it had to operate in three shifts, but few of the officers complained. Until American rations arrived, no one was very eager to eat the food.

Operations, flight-control, and intelligence personnel were sent immediately to training schools and R.A.F. stations for indoctrination. Pilots and navigators learned the air-traffic system over the British Isles, and then the operational training and practice missions began.

The 303rd Group, under Col. James H. Wallace, began moving into Molesworth (ten miles west of Huntingdon) September 12, and the ground echelon of the 305th arrived at Grafton-Underwood, sixty miles northwest of London, the next day. The 305th Group commander, Col. Curtis LeMay, and his planes were being held in Syracuse, New York, pending some required modifications.

Between the first and 17th of October, the planes of the 91st Group arrived at Kimbolton (six miles north of Thurleigh), and virtually destroyed the runways there simply by landing on them. These runways, hastily built for fighter planes during the Battle of Britain, had not yet been reinforced for bomber use. The heavy B-17s tore ruinous holes in them.

The town of Kimbolton was the site of one of England's most stately castles, which had been for three centuries the country seat of the Dukes of Manchester. In this castle, Catherine of Aragon, Henry VIII's first wife, spent the last two years of her life. It was now occupied by the Kimbolton Boys' School. When the newly arrived "Yanks" began coming down the hill from the air base to look at the town, they soon found that their British hosts were happy to see them. Especially the girls, many of whom had lost their British boyfriends to the war, but not only the girls. A history teacher at the school, Mr. Kyffin Owen, recalled later his own reaction to the first sight of U.S. airmen in town: "I shall never forget, I stood by the pub, the Jones, and I looked around the corner and saw the first Americans walking down the street. And wasn't I glad. We were all alone here until the Americans came."[4]

These first Americans to arrive were not destined to stay very long. Having ruined their runways, they needed another base; when their commanding officer, Col. Stanley Wray, appealed to 8th Bomber

159

Command to find one for them, he was told to fly to Bassingbourn, nine miles southwest of Cambridge, and inspect the base there. As soon as he saw it, he decided to look no further. Built as an R.A.F. base with permanent buildings, it was one of the more attractive airdromes in England. Wray was so eager to grab it before some other group arrived to take it that he hurried back to Kimbolton, gathered his airplanes, and, in deliberate haste, led them to their new home October 10, not even waiting for his ground echelon, which arrived four days later.

Colonel LeMay and the thirty-five brand-new B-17s of his 305th Group were still in Syracuse at this time, waiting for some changes to be made in the planes' ball-turret guns.[5] Meanwhile he was conducting navigational training flights, taking care of last-minute details, and even scrounging winter equipment for his men, who had just come with him from Tucson, Arizona, and were still wearing summer uniforms.

While LeMay was in Syracuse, he received a visit from Fred Anderson, then a colonel in General Arnold's office. Anderson had come to offer, in a friendly way, a piece of disturbing information. Gen. George C. Kenney, Air Force commander in the Pacific, was pleading desperately for more bomb groups, and since LeMay's unit was almost ready to go, Arnold's headquarters was thinking of sending them west rather than east to England.

LeMay protested. "Fred, they can't do this to us!" His ground echelon was already in England with the whole group's baggage and equipment. "This will be one screwed up mess if they try to send us to the Pacific."

"Couldn't agree with you more," Anderson said, "but this is what they're talking about."

"For God's sake," LeMay pleaded. "Stall them as much as you can, will you?"

Anderson, who had known LeMay since they were cadets together at Kelly Field, agreed to do so, undoubtedly aware of what LeMay intended to do in the meantime. The moment Anderson left, LeMay called his staff together and announced that they had better finish, post haste, everything they had left to do because he was determined to head for England before Air Force headquarters had time to change their orders and send them west. LeMay and his thirty-five planes arrived at Grafton-Underwood October 27 without interception.

160

General Eaker, enmeshed in all the necessary details of getting his new groups into operation and at the same time planning daily missions despite one weather postponement after another, could no longer spend as much time as he would have liked with Air Chief Marshal Harris, whose advice he still found valuable. But he did continue to see Harris on occasion. The British bomber commander and Lady Harris came to a luncheon at Pinetree September 26 with Lady Nancy Astor, the formidable American-born member of Parliament. Though Eaker didn't realize it, she was a devout prohibitionist. When he asked her if she would like something to drink, she said with some heat, "Certainly not! You people will lose the war if you don't stop drinking." After lunch, when she went to High Wycombe to make a speech at the opening of the local Boys' Club, he was able to excuse himself from accompanying her by pleading work and by sending five of his aides instead.

His conversations with Harris now seldom touched upon the day-night bombing argument. Though Harris sensed the Americans were still "feeling their way," and though he remained unconvinced that day bombing could be sustained without prohibitive losses, he genuinely hoped he was wrong. The thought of bombing Germany on a twenty-four-hour schedule pleased him mightily.[6] He and Eaker talked often now about how they could help each other get more planes, and how they could both avoid losing any more of them to the North African "diversion," which they both deplored.

The autumn of 1942 was so dark and rainy in England that on October 7, Spaatz told Eisenhower the weather was the one weakness he could see in the American daylight-bombing program.[7] There was no mission that day because the bases were "socked in," and there hadn't been a mission for five days. The B-17s had flown only one mission since September 7, exactly a month earlier. The weather did not weaken Spaatz's enthusiasm for daylight operations, but he knew it was causing restlessness among other people. Some hitherto strong supporters of the American policy were developing doubts. And some were becoming openly convinced that the 8th Air Force, or whatever was left of it after the African invasion began, should join the R.A.F. on night raids, which did not require precision. In an effort to answer these people and to prove that night bombing suffered from even more serious limitations, Spaatz asked Eaker to prepare a paper on the subject. On October 8, another dismal day that produced another 8th Bomber Command postponement, Eaker relieved his day-bombing frustrations by writing a discourse about the problems of night bombing:

> Only two reasons can exist for bombing at night: one, for greater safety of bombardment aircraft and crews, i.e., economy of force; or two, to bring pressure upon the enemy during the hours of darkness without interruption. These are the only two reasons for night bombing because it is perfectly clear that the efficiency of bombardment during the daylight hours is much greater.[8]

Day bombers, he argued, were more efficient because they could locate targets more easily and identify them more precisely through their bomb-sights, thereby establishing a more accurate bombing pattern. It would take a thousand bombers at night to do as much damage to a specific target as a hundred could do in the daytime.

Inevitably, Eaker's paper on night bombing turned out to be also a dissertation on day bombing, which he was prepared to discuss with greater enthusiasm:

> There was a quite common belief in this country that day bombing was too expensive because of the heavy fighter losses which the enemy could inflict. Our bombing experience to date indicates that the B-17 with its twelve .50-caliber guns can cope with the German day fighter, if flown in close formation. There will be losses, of course, but there is no evidence that the losses will be of such high order as to make day bombing uneconomical. The evidence in this regard will be more impressive as our force is built up. I think it is safe now to say that a large force of day bombers can operate without fighter cover against material objectives anywhere in Germany, without excessive losses.

It was not an unreasoned statement. The 8th Bomber Command had flown only twelve missions, to be sure, but on five of these, the B-17s, in small numbers and beyond Spitfire protection, had encountered German fighters. Only two B-17s had been lost in these confrontations while American gunners claimed twenty-two German fighters shot down, twenty others probably shot down, and more than twenty damaged. This was impressive evidence that the B-17 could take care of itself. The fighters it had faced were the best in the German Air Force—FW-190s and ME-109s.

The day after Eaker wrote that paper, the weather cleared and he sent his largest force to date—108 heavy bombers including some B-24s of the 93rd Group—against the Fives-Lille steel plant in France. The 93rd and 306th Groups were both making their debuts that day, and their performances were not auspicious. Their bombs were so poorly aimed that few hit the target, and several landed in populated areas, causing French civilian casualties. None of the American groups bombed well on this mission. Because of a combination of fierce German-fighter resistance and hopeless confusion caused by the rookie groups, only 69 bombers hit the primary target and only 9 of their bombs fell within 500 yards of the "bull's-eye." The FW-190s and ME-109s, out in great numbers, shot down 4 American bombers—3 B-17s and 1 B-24—but American gunners, when they returned home, claimed 56 German fighters shot down, plus 26 probables and 20 damaged. Despite their 4-plane loss, which was not excessive for a 108-plane mission, the American crews were becoming cocky about their ability to handle the Germans, with or without Spitfire assistance. The Americans now began referring to their B-17 as the P-17 (the letter "P" designating "pursuit" or "fighter") and talked about giving fighter cover to the Spitfires.

British newspapers praised the October 9 raid as an American victory and despite their incredulity were generally polite about the astonishing kill claims of the American gunners.

Prime Minister Churchill was not so polite three days later in a "personal minute" on the subject to Portal. With it he enclosed a Reuters News Agency dispatch from the United States that was printed in the *Yorkshire Evening Post* that day (October 12):

American newspapers are naturally elated today about the unprecedented feat of the United States Flying Fortresses and Liberators in last Friday's daylight raid on Lille in northern France, when the bombers shot down 48 German fighters and probably destroyed 38 others. [These were adjusted figures.] . . .

The New York Mirror says: "The Lille raid established American Flying Fortress and Liberator bombers as veritable battleships of the air, self-sufficient for both offence and defence. The pursuit ship is becoming obsolescent and will be replaced by the many-gunned air cruiser." . . .

The New York Times said: "There are suggestions from England, reluctant at first, but now more enthusiastic, that the big bombers of the United States are all right. They always were. . . . In time, with equal numbers, our large bombers may be able to accomplish just as much destruction with fewer raids at high altitudes as the British have done at low altitudes and lose fewer planes. It is still debatable, but the American big bomber is beginning to prove itself."

Churchill, in his minute to Portal, asked bluntly, "Is there the slightest truth in these American claims? What is the Air Ministry view?" Portal, after assigning aides to investigate, answered the Prime Minister the next day, October 13:

The Air Staff do not believe that anything like the numbers of enemy fighters claimed by the Americans on Friday were actually destroyed by them.

Our opinion is that not more than 60 German fighters were operating between Lille and the coast during the attack.

The British fighters escorting the greater part of the American bombers claim to have destroyed four Germans over Lille. The experts who analyse German R/T [radio transmission] traffic after a battle, have what they consider to be good indications of the shooting down of 10 Germans. They say that since they can only intercept part of the traffic, it is almost certain that more than 10 were shot down and judging by past results they put the probable number at about 20. Subtracting the 4 shot down by fighters, this would leave 16 for the Americans. . . .

If the Americans did in fact shoot down 16 Germans for the loss of 4 bombers, this is a very fine performance which is in no way spoilt by the excessive claim. It is unavoidable that when a German fighter catches fire or its pilot bails out after ten different air gunners have shot at it, three or four may honestly claim it and each obtain confirmation from someone else. . . .

Friday's exploit by no means justifies the optimism in the

164

American press extracts which you sent me and it has little bearing on the ability of the Fortress to bomb targets in Germany with precision. Lille is about 40 miles from the coast, the Ruhr 125 miles and Frankfurt 230 miles. . . . The Germans must be expected to fight with much more determination over Germany than over France. . . .

My own view is that only very large numbers (say 400 or 500) going out at one time will enable the Americans to bomb the Ruhr by daylight with less than 10% casualties, and I doubt whether even then the bombing will be very accurate.

The German submarine campaign in the Atlantic had, by this time, intensified to such alarming proportions that Churchill was becoming desperate. Between January and October of 1942, the number of U-boats in the fearsome Atlantic "wolf-packs" had increased from 90 to 196. In August, 108 Allied ships, more than one-half-million gross tons, were sunk, and the losses continued to increase through September and October. In a telegram to Roosevelt's assistant, Harry Hopkins, October 16, Churchill pleaded for help:

I am . . . oppressed with the heavy U-boat sinkings and the biting need for more long range aircraft to harry the U-boats in their passage out and home from the Biscay ports and Northabout between Iceland and the Faroes, and to strike at the packs collecting round the slow convoys in mid-Atlantic. It would be of the greatest possible help to us if you could give us at least another 50 Liberators . . . to help the direct offensive against U-boats.

The 8th Air Force had already been invited to join the anti-U-boat campaign by attacking the submarine pens along the coast of France. Both Spaatz and Eaker welcomed this operation because the sub-pens seemed to offer very promising, high-priority targets that could be attacked with relatively small forces. Eaker, in his August 27 bombing-accuracy report to Spaatz, had said, "The present submarine menace can be almost entirely eliminated, not by searching for individual submarines in the sea lanes, but by destroying the submarine effort in the factory, in the yards where it is built, and in the bases from which it is launched."

The October weather kept frustrating his attempt to test this theory. Between the 9th and the 20th, eleven missions were initiated then canceled. Finally, on October 21, sixty-six B-17s and twenty-four B-24s set out to attack the submarine shelters at Lorient on the south coast of Brittany, at the top of the Bay of Biscay.

Though the ceiling had risen, the clouds had not dissipated, and only the thirty planes of the 97th Group were able to find an opening through which to bomb. As they descended to 17,500 feet for their bomb run, FW-190s arrived and shot down three of them in quick succession. Despite this untimely interruption, they were able to place twenty-one of their thirty one-ton bombs within a thousand yards of the aiming point. They scored direct hits on five concrete submarine shelters.

When these results were confirmed by R.A.F. reconnaissance photos a few days later, Eaker had to temper his optimism about destroying the submarines in their pens. Despite the five direct hits, the American bombs had not done the slightest damage to the shelters. The concrete protecting the submarines proved to be more than twelve feet thick. When Eaker talked to Spaatz about this discovery, it was with considerable pessimism.[9] Even a two-ton bomb was not likely to penetrate that much concrete. But neither Spaatz nor Eaker could cancel the campaign against the sub-pens now that it had begun. On October 26, they both talked to Eisenhower and found that he was counting on them to continue bombing the pens in support of the African invasion fleets.

Even if Eisenhower had been inclined to excuse them from banging their bombs uselessly against the sub-pens, Churchill would not have tolerated it. The Prime Minister was becoming so excited at the prospect of driving the Germans out of Africa and thereby reopening the Mediterranean to British shipping that he wanted all possible resources devoted to the African campaign. Influenced partly, perhaps, by Portal's slashing arguments September 26 and October 13 against American air strategy, he had now decided that the 8th Air Force as then constituted had little chance of inflicting significant damage within Germany's borders. If the Americans were going to do any good at all in the near future, they would have to be persuaded to devote their full air effort to the support of the North African campaign. On October 22, Churchill read to his Chiefs of Staff an air-policy paper that set down this point of view:

The utmost pressure must be put upon the United States authorities here and in America to utilize their Fortresses and Liberators in support of our sea communications during "TORCH.". . . At present the United States are persevering with the idea of the daylight bombing of Germany by means of Flying Fortresses and Liberators in formation without escort. So far they have not gone beyond the limits of strong British fighter escort. They will probably experience a heavy disaster as soon as they do. We must try to persuade them to divert these energies (a) to sea work, beginning with helping "TORCH" (including bombing the Biscay ports), and (b) to night work. See my telegram to Mr. Hopkins on these delicate subjects.

. . . The Americans have such vast resources of production that they can afford to pick and choose, chop and change, to an extent unpardonable over here. We ought to press them by every means to adopt a highly selective attitude and think less of target numbers than of producing the right designs. Especially we should urge them to take up night bombing on a large scale. . . . We should urge them to build Lancasters for us or, if this is impossible, supply parts on a great scale for a Canadian assembly plant. We should urge the development of the Mustang (P-51 fighter plane) with the right engines.

In Churchill's telegram to Hopkins (October 16) "on these delicate subjects," he was no more delicate than in his address to his Chiefs of Staff. After insisting that the United States should develop night bombers and should produce Mustang fighters powered by advanced Rolls Royce engines, which "in Portal's view would be far ahead of anything in the fighter line you have in hand," he suggested to Hopkins that he should not believe everything he heard about the B-17:

I must also say to you for your eye alone and only to be used by you in your high discretion that the very accurate results so far achieved in the daylight bombing of France by your Fortresses under most numerous Fighter escort mainly British, does not give our experts the same confidence as yours in the power of the day bomber to operate far into Germany. We do not think the claims of fighters shot down by Fortresses are correct though made with

167

complete sincerity, and the dangers of daylight bombing will increase terribly once outside Fighter protection and as the range lengthens.

The shift in Churchill's thinking about what to do with the American Air Force embarrassed Sinclair and Portal because he was now using their own arguments against American air policy in an apparent effort to take the 8th Air Force away from the project which was dearest to them—the bomber offensive against Germany—and devote it instead to a project which had become dear to him—the invasion of North Africa—but which the Air Ministry disapproved. Sinclair and Portal, like Eaker and Harris, regarded the African campaign as an unfortunate diversion from the one campaign they felt could win the war: the bombing of Germany. While Sinclair and Portal might not like the way the Americans intended to go about it, they very much counted on the 8th Air Force to join the R.A.F. in some kind of massive effort against Germany.

When Churchill asked Roosevelt in mid-September for a faster build-up of the 8th Air Force in England, pretending even to support day bombing in his desperation to attract more planes and crews, the men at the Air Ministry could agree completely with his strategy because they presumed the newly arriving planes would be used against Germany. But Portal, in his October 13 minute to Churchill discounting American gunnery claims and deploring pessimistically the American daylight policy, did not take into account Churchill's growing concern about the submarine menace and the grave danger it presented to the African invasion fleet. Portal perhaps unwittingly gave Churchill a whole set of arguments to use in persuading the Americans immediately that they must divert their air energies to TORCH.

Though it was partly under Portal's and Sinclair's influence that Churchill had virtually written off the 8th Air Force as an instrument against Germany, these men were now alarmed because he had gone beyond them and was using their ideas for a purpose they opposed. Their position was delicate, however, because they could not openly proclaim their opposition to TORCH. They had, therefore, to shift their argument carefully. Sinclair, who had impatiently asked Slessor in late September what the Americans were doing and when they

168

intended to prepare for night bombing, wrote a minute to Churchill October 23, 1942, in which he sounded almost like an advocate of American daylight bombing:

American opinion is divided; some want to concentrate on the Pacific; others against Germany; some want an Air Force which would be mainly ancillary to the Army, equipped with Army support aircraft; . . . others want to build up a big bomber force to attack the centre of German power. It is in your power to crystallise American opinion and to unite it behind those schools of thought which want to attack Germany and want to do it by building up an overwhelming force of bombers in this country.

Instead, however, of uniting those schools of thought, . . . you will throw these forces into confusion and impotency if you set yourself against their cherished policy of daylight penetration.

In the opinion of the Air Staff, and in my own inexpert opinion, this policy of daylight penetration has a chance of success, if only they can get the numbers and if only they are not rushed by impatience into taking on heavy opposition with half-trained gunners. . . .

If it succeeds it will be possible in the earliest months of next year for us to send a thousand bombers over Hamburg one night, for the Americans to follow up with 500 or 600 bombers the following day and, if the weather is kind, for us to follow up with a large force of heavy bombers the next night—and then to go on bombing one city after another in Germany on that scale. . . . If it fails, it will at least do a lot of damage to the German fighter force in the process. . . .

The American Air Force in this country are determined to try out this theory. They are not irresolute; they are being hampered by diversions of their best trained crews to "Torch" and by the slow arrival of their bomber squadrons. Already, however, they have got as far as Lorient outside the shelter of our fighter cover, and bombed their target with astonishing accuracy. . . . It is their firm intention to drop bombs on Germany in daylight next month. It would be a tragedy if we were to frustrate them on the eve of this great experiment.

To ally ourselves with the American Navy against General

Spaatz and General Eaker and the United States Air Force in this country, and to force them into diverting their highly trained crews to scaring U-boats instead of to the bombing of Germany would be disastrous. It would weaken and alienate the very forces in the United States on which we depend for support in a European as distinct from a Pacific strategy.

Air Chief Marshal Harris, possibly alerted by Sinclair, Portal, or both, wrote a letter to Churchill the same day on the same subject. The bomber commander, a man who had never been afraid to speak up to anyone, virtually belabored the Prime Minister for some of the things he was "alleged" to have said recently. Like Sinclair, Harris began with some instruction about the military/political situation in the United States:

> My American friends are despondent.
> They foresee the success of efforts by the U.S. Army, and particularly the U.S. Navy, to get them off bombing France and, thereafter, keep them off bombing Germany. . . .
> I am informed, and I know this to be true, that there is now a great and growing weight of high public and official opinion in the United States in support of the bomber plan. . . . But the U.S. Navy and, to a lesser extent, the U.S. Army are almost frantically engaged in doing all they can to scotch this plan. . . .
> To that end [they are] pressing that the whole U.S. Bomber resources now in this country should be switched toward the Atlantic war and the protection of the convoys.
> It is, moreover, alleged that you personally are in favor of this.
> Armed with so formidable a stick wherewith to beat the dog, the U.S. military authorities on this side are alleged to be quoting—or rather misquoting—you in regard to the futility of continuing to bomb French targets, and as to your leaning towards employing all the U.S. Bombers on the Atlantic war rather than on bombing Germany.
> You will please excuse frankness in this matter. My information is that . . . unless you come down personally and most emphatically on the side of throwing every bomb against Germany, subject only to minimum essential diversions elsewhere, the Bomber Plan,

170

insofar as U.S. assistance is concerned, will be hopelessly and fatally prejudiced within the very near future for an unpredictable period if not for keeps.

Some of Harris's information came from Eaker, who would be taking command of the entire 8th Air Force as soon as Spaatz left for Africa, and who had already got wind from Spaatz that if present plans were fulfilled, he would have not much more than a paper air force left to command. Churchill knew, of course, whose voice was behind Harris's pen, but he was not much impressed. In his opinion the 8th even now was little more than a paper air force. He made that opinion clear when he wrote a personal minute October 26 answering Sinclair's detailed defense of the Americans. Churchill declared that he was "not at all convinced of the soundness" of the Air Minister's October 23 minute on the merits of daylight penetration or "the tactics we should pursue toward the Americans," but that in any case he hadn't yet raised the daylight argument with "any American authority." (Though Harry Hopkins was Roosevelt's closest adviser and personal representative, he had no official position and could therefore be excluded in Churchill's mind from recognition as an "American authority.") In the matter of what should be done with the 8th Air Force, Churchill wrote to Sinclair almost contemptuously:

> It is much better at the present time to persuade the Americans to use Flying Fortresses and Liberators to give additional protection to convoys for "TORCH" (assuming of course that they can make the distances), though this may be at the expense of their daylight raiding of France. I hope that, having got them on the trade routes for this purpose, they will remain there and help to control the Bay of Biscay, both against U-boats and enemy blockade runners. The alternative would be to take more Lancaster squadrons from Bomber Command, which I have been trying my best to prevent for a long time past.

This short, offhand note from the Prime Minister left Sinclair very little room for a reply. He and Portal agreed that, in Portal's words, "no reply is called for." But they could not resist answering Churchill two days later, in effect, when they sent him their comments on his week-old Air Policy statement. They assured him that Spaatz was already "providing all we ask for in the way of anti-submarine patrol and bombing of the Biscay ports during the passage of the TORCH convoys," and that Arnold was sending an extra sixteen B-17s and B-24s from America to help protect the TORCH shipping. They then went on to plead that he should not decry the American daylight attack plan:

We are convinced that it would be fatal to suggest to them at this of all times that the great bomber force they are planning to build up is no good except for coastal work and perhaps ultimately for night bombing. They are convinced that they will be able to bomb Germany by day and they are determined to do so. They may be wrong—indeed we think they are unduly optimistic on the subject. . . . We fully agree that we should advise them to address themselves to the difficult problem of night-adapting their bombers and adjusting their training programme in case they find the daylight policy too costly. But if we go any further at this stage we may find ourselves confronted with an abandonment of the policy of an all-out air offensive against GERMANY, and a swing to the PACIFIC where their heavy bombers have already shown themselves capable of taking on the Japanese by day.

We are not sure whether you realize the extent to which General Spaatz has suffered setbacks in fitting his bombers for their true role against Germany. Squadrons [groups] which were scheduled to come to his Command have been diverted to Hawaii and to the South-West PACIFIC; the first squadrons to be operationally fit, on which he was depending to leaven those that came after, are being diverted to TORCH. . . . Are we now to press him to divert them to the anti-submarine work in the ATLANTIC?

Churchill was so deeply involved with the African invasion and so worried about the possibility of the U-boats dooming it to failure that he would not have been able to accept the counsel of his air advisers even if he had completely agreed with them. He did agree with them on the importance of the bomber offensive against Germany. Though Harris was destined to be blamed after the war for bombing German cities excessively, the planes under his command never dropped a bomb that Churchill (and indeed the entire British and American nations) did not approve and applaud. Every mission Bomber Command launched was covered by Churchill orders. Stung by the punishment of British civilians in the Battle of Britain and painfully aware of how close the people in east London came to rebellion as a result of the German bombs they had to absorb at the height of the blitz, Churchill was convinced that the punishment of German workers would greatly diminish their industrial output, eventually paralyze the German war effort, and perhaps even give rise to a rebellion against Hitler. Churchill did not intend ever to suspend this offensive. Under Portal's inadvertent influence, however, he had come to the conclusion that the American contribution to it was likely to be almost worthless. In a letter to Portal (November 2, 1942), he bluntly said so, citing some of Portal's earlier words to strengthen his points:

The number of American Air Force personnel [in England] has risen to about fifty-five thousand. . . . So far the results have been pitifully small. . . . Far from dropping bombs on Germany, the daylight bombers have not ventured beyond Lille. Twenty-one bombing raids have been carried out on France and two on Holland, and in almost every case they have required very strong British Fighter escort. . . . The claims of the Fortresses are probably exaggerated three fold (see minute from C.A.S. [Portal] attached). A reasonable estimate is that they have actually shot down twenty-eight enemy aircraft for the loss of eight Fortresses and one Liberator. Not a bomb has been dropped on Germany.

Meanwhile the American public has been led to believe that a really serious contribution has been made by the American Air Force. It is not for us to undeceive them, but there can be no doubt that they will find out for themselves before very long. . . . Considering the American professional interests and high reputations which are engaged in this scheme, and the shock it would be to the American people and to the Administration if the policy proved a glaring failure, we must expect most obstinate perseverance in this method. . . . [That] leaves us in the position that for many months ahead large numbers of American Air personnel will be here playing very little part in the war and, what is much graver, American Air production will be cast ever more deeply into an unprofitable groove.

The difficulties which confront the American planes are most serious. The first is the danger of running out of ammunition and thus becoming easy prey. . . . What would happen if the Fortress ran out of ammunition would be a massacre. The accuracy of their bombing depends upon their not being harassed while over the target. The days when the weather is suitable for this form of high level bombing are few and far between, especially in the winter. On an average, conditions are likely to be suitable on only six days a month in Germany. . . . they frequently have to wait for ten days before being able to make a sortie. Everyone must admit this is a very grievous situation. What ought we to do?

Churchill's low opinion of the American air effort and its potential now hung like a sword over the 8th Air Force. If he were to write to Roosevelt what he had written to Portal in that November 2 letter, the American President could hardly escape the conclusion that the 8th was no longer welcome in the United Kingdom since the Prime Minister felt it was "playing very little part in the war." And there was no way in which Eaker might counteract Churchill's attitude, because he didn't even know about it. He was completely without knowledge of the extensive secret correspondence between Churchill, Sinclair, Portal, and Slessor about the 8th Air Force and its prospects.

While Eaker remained ignorant of this aspect of his continuing problem with the British, he was aware of enough other problems to keep him busy. The 8th's only experienced bomb group, the 97th, would be leaving for Africa in another week. (The North African invasion was to begin November 8.) Shortly thereafter, two more groups would follow, leaving him nothing but four groups of rookies. And he was beginning to wonder how long these groups would have to wait before getting their chance to become veterans. The weather had kept his entire force on the ground since October 21. In two months, since September 7, his bombers had been able to fly only three missions. (By this time Churchill must have begun to think that even his six-missions-a-month prediction was too optimistic.) Finally, on November 7, Eaker was permitted by the weather to send his planes out again. But even then, at the insistence of Churchill and Eisenhower, he was allowed only to bounce his bombs harmlessly off the concrete submarine pens at Brest. If, as he had told an aide, he considered patience a general's highest virtue, he should now be content because he was getting an apparently endless opportunity to practice it.

10

Only three times in December of 1942 did the weather clear enough for the 8th to fly. On the 12th, two heavy bombers went down in an attack against the Rouen marshaling yards. On the 20th, two were lost at Romilly sur Seine. And on the 30th, three went down on another mission against the Lorient submarine pens. One of these was a 306th Group Fortress that inexplicably pulled out of formation a few moments after the bomb run. A second plane, which followed to protect the first, suffered the same fate, illustrating dramatically the importance of staying in formation.

During four and a half months of operation in 1942, the 8th had flown 1,547 bombing sorties (individual bomber thrusts) with a loss rate of slightly less than 2 percent (thirty-two aircraft), which sounded better than the R.A.F.'s loss of approximately 4 percent,[1] except that the R.A.F. was dropping most of its bombs within German borders.

The 305th Group's commander, Colonel LeMay, had now flown enough missions to convince himself that the traditional one-level formation did not offer maximum protection to the bombers. On practice flights he had worked out the first version of the multilevel box formation, which was soon adopted by the entire 8th Bomber Command. Because his formation demanded for the sake of accuracy a straight bomb run without any evasive action to avoid flak or bullets, it suffered a costly debut when he tried it out on the first mission of 1943—January 3 against St. Nazaire.[2] Gale-force headwinds prolonged the bomb run that day for more than nine minutes. So many planes were hit that nine of them fell before reaching home. LeMay's ideas, however, were not blamed for these heavy losses. His formation was such an obvious improvement over the old one that the only question about it was not whether to continue it but how to refine it.

General Spaatz had gone to Africa with Eisenhower, and General Eaker had taken over as 8th Air Force commander. His replacement as bomber commander, Brig. Gen. Newton Longfellow, soon found an unfortunate situation developing in the 306th Group at Thurleigh. The very popular commander of this unit, Col. Charles "Chip" Overacker, was so solicitous of his men that their discipline began to suffer. Since the group's performance on missions was also below average, the disciplinary shortcomings were looked upon as a probable cause. Unlike some other commanders, Colonel LeMay, for instance, Overacker believed in maintaining a close rapport with his men. He treated them like a father, and they loved him. But like a father, Overacker sometimes let them get around him. LeMay, on the other hand, was the kind of man no one could get around. It was not because he was a nice guy that his men referred to him as "Iron Ass." He was so tough they feared him. Yet many of them later credited him with saving their lives by forcing them to meet his standards.

Longfellow and Eaker, perceiving that the standards of the 306th were falling below those of the other groups, decided a change would have to be made. Again, Eaker called upon Col. Frank Armstrong, one of his six original staff members. The previous August, when troubles developed in the 97th Group, Armstrong had taken charge of it, led it on the 8th Air Force's first mission, and soon made it the Bomber Command's best group. After the 8th had five missions to its credit, Eaker, addressing Spaatz on the importance of leadership, had said, "It is not accidental that the three operations which Colonel Armstrong has led were completely successful, while the two operations led by other officers resulted in one aborted mission and one with serious injuries to two aircraft." Eaker thought so

177

highly of Armstrong he had held him back when the 97th Group left for Africa. Now he sent him to Thurleigh to command the 306th. It might take a while for the men there to get to like him, but in the meantime, they would respect him.[3] (This incident later became famous as the central theme of the novel *Twelve O'clock High*, written by another of Eaker's original six, Capt. Beirne Lay, Jr. and by one of General Spaatz's staff officers, Maj. Sy Bartlett.)

The four intact B-17 groups still with the 8th Bomber Command (91st, 303rd, 305th, and 306th) had now flown an average of eight missions per group, and Eaker had long since decided they were ready for their first trip to Germany. But since mid-December, Germany had been cloudy every day. On the few occasions the Fortresses could get off the ground, they had no choice but to head south for the submarine ports, where there was at least a chance of a break in the clouds.

These raids, frustrating as they were, gave the American crews significant experience against German fighters. The information Eaker's men brought back from encounters with FW-190s and ME-109s heightened in his mind a concern he had felt for some time about the range of the American fighter planes now being sent to his Fighter Command. The P-47 Thunderbolts arriving in January had an expected operating range of only 175 miles, which meant they would be able to escort the bombers no farther than the Spitfires were now going. While Eaker still felt the B-17s could take care of themselves, it was obvious that fighter escorts would make their job easier and cut their losses.

Having been a fighter pilot and commander for most of his career, Eaker placed a high value on fighter protection. In the fall of 1941, he had flown the first P-47 to come off the Republic Aviation Company assembly line on Long Island, New York. And shortly thereafter, when he was repositioning fighter squadrons in California for the Pacific Coast defense, he happened to be at Mines Field, San Diego, the day the first P-51 Mustang came off the North American Aviation Company assembly line there. He took advantage of the opportunity to fly that plane also. He found the Mustang "the best fighter plane I had flown." Though he believed it was "somewhat underpowered," he assumed that weakness could be corrected by the installation of one of the larger aircraft engines then under development.[4]

The Mustang had been created, not for the Americans but for the

British. When Air Marshal Harris was in America with an R.A.F. purchasing commission in April 1940, James H. "Dutch" Kindelberger, president of North American, had said, "Why don't you let us design a new fighter plane for you?" The British said, "Go ahead,"[5] and by the end of the year the Mustang was in production. But when R.A.F. test pilots flew it, they noticed what Eaker had noticed—its Allison engine wasn't powerful enough, especially at high altitudes. The British at first could think of nothing to do with the Mustang except to put it in the R.A.F.'s Army Cooperation Command for use as an infantry support plane. Then they replaced its 1,200-horsepower Allison engine with a 1,620-horsepower Rolls Royce Merlin engine, whereupon the Mustang became an outstanding aircraft, destined eventually to be acknowledged on both sides as the best of the widely used fighter planes in World War II.

It was this plane that Churchill (October 16, 1942) told Harry Hopkins the Americans should hasten into production because Portal had told him it would be "far ahead of anything in the fighter line you have in hand."[6] Unfortunately, the American Air Force Test Facility at Wright Field, Ohio, had already decided the plane was unworthy of development, not only because it was underpowered but also because its liquid-cooled engine would presumably be more susceptible to bullet damage than an air-cooled radial engine. It is difficult to imagine how this conclusion was reached in light of the combat successes of the liquid-cooled German ME-109 and the British Spitfire. The Spitfire used the Rolls Royce Merlin engine. The Wright Field refusal to take the Mustang seriously was a chief reason that radial-engine P-47 Thunderbolts were now arriving in England instead of Mustangs. Eventually this technical assessment by Air Force experts at Wright Field would be recognized as one of the most unfortunate mistakes of the entire war. Reliance on their judgment delayed for at least six months the acknowledgment by high Air Force officials of the need for mass production of the P-51. Had the Merlin-powered Mustang been hastened into production as soon as possible after British tests proved its merits, it might have appeared in the skies over Europe, protecting the American bombers, during the early months of 1943.

Though Eaker knew about the British modification of the Mustang and realized it was a superior plane, he needed fighters so badly he took what he could get. To wait now for P-51s would cause another intolerable delay. And to suggest that American factories convert from Thunderbolts to Mustangs would be to court an even longer delay. It would create an uproar within an already harried American aircraft industry. The Thunderbolt was undoubtedly a good airplane. Eaker therefore welcomed it despite its short range. He had anticipated the range problem the previous October when he asked the British Ministry of Aircraft Production about manufacturing auxiliary fuel tanks for the P-47. He now renewed this inquiry and asked if such tanks could be made in England.[7] He did not receive an immediate answer.

Eaker was less friendly with the people at the Ministry of Aircraft Production than he was with most of his British associates. In a December 6, 1942, letter to Arnold, he had complained that M.A.P. representatives had made disparaging remarks about U.S. airplanes to a group of American manufacturers visiting London.[8] One of these manufacturers had returned home to proclaim that the B-17 was unsuitable for combat in Europe and that the Lancaster was a better bomber. The campaign to convert the Americans to the night-bombing Lancaster was still in progress, and Eaker resented it. "This sounds like Masefield talking," he wrote to Arnold. He was referring to Peter Masefield, the London *Times* aeronautical correspondent who, Eaker said, "represents the M.A.P. view of British aircraft." He accused Masefield and the M.A.P. of misleading the Americans. "Naturally the British manufacturers are thumping the drum for their own products," he concluded. "The British operational people have no such ideas."

As this conclusion proves, Eaker was still unaware of the exchange of views between Churchill, Sinclair, and Portal. He didn't know how deeply they still distrusted the strategy and equipment to which he was committed. But he discovered how highly they regarded his personal integrity and discretion when he received a visit from an R.A.F. officer named Group Capt. Frederick W. Winterbotham. He had come at the behest of the Prime Minister, Winterbotham said, to make Eaker privy to the most closely guarded secret of the war—the Ultra secret.[9] British cryptographers had broken Germany's most confidential communications codes, enabling them to intercept and read all the messages between Hitler and his top commanders. The Prime Minister, aware that information gained by Ultra would be valuable to the 8th Air Force, had decided Eaker should be briefed on the secret, and Winterbotham was here to explain it to him.

Even this early in the war, Ultra had already been immensely valuable to the British. It had helped them evacuate their troops from Dunkirk by keeping them informed of the movements of German units pursuing them. It had guided the R.A.F. in disposing its fighter forces during the Battle of Britain. And it had facilitated the recent landings in North Africa by ascertaining where the least resistance would be found. Eaker knew very little about it, but he had received one warning about it. Spaatz, in a message from Africa, had told him, "Don't let them read you in on it." Spaatz had learned in Africa that because he knew the Ultra details, he was not permitted to go on missions or even go near the front lines for fear he might be captured and compromised. Eaker, not wishing to lose this option, thanked Winterbotham for the Prime Minister's kind offer but suggested that the 8th Air Force Intelligence chief be chosen as his surrogate for Ultra secrets.

Churchill had been cordial to Eaker whenever they met, and this indication of personal trust, even though the American general declined to take advantage of it, was very gratifying to him. He would have been mistaken, however, to suppose it signified an acceptance of American air policy by the Prime Minister. Churchill's dissatisfaction with 8th Air Force operations was intensifying as 1943 began. A terse minute to Sinclair (January 4) demonstrated his feelings: ". . . I note that the Americans have not yet succeeded in dropping a single bomb on Germany."[10]

Sinclair and Portal had been trying for almost three months to convince him that the Americans were doing as well as could be expected under harsh circumstances. After Churchill's brutal condemnation of the American effort in his November 2 letter to the Air Ministry, Portal had replied (November 7) with a stout defense,[11] to which, however, the Prime Minister had paid little attention as his January 4 minute testified. He was now more than dissatisfied. He was angry.

Sinclair and Portal went to work on another attempt to mollify him—an "Air Policy" statement that they handed back and forth to each other for revision before sending it finally to Downing Street January 9, over the Air Minister's signature.[12] It began somewhat

181

timidly with the admission that the Air Ministry did not yet know "the truth about American capacity to bomb Germany in daylight." The U.S. Air Force now had bombers in action on five fronts around the world in addition to the United Kingdom. The 8th Air Force had suffered losses of experienced units and many other vicissitudes. Nevertheless, its crews had often given good accounts of themselves in combat. It was reasonable, therefore, to remain patient and optimistic about their prospects:

The view of the Air Staff is that there is a good chance that the Americans and the R.A.F. will be able to bomb Germany in daylight. *Given sufficient strength to saturate the defences*, they think it quite possible that our losses—though possibly heavy in the initial phase—will in the aggregate be no heavier than by night, and that the results, combined with night attack, should be doubly effective. No one can say for certain until it has been tried—and tried repeatedly. Clearly, however, it would be wrong to try it prematurely, with insufficient numbers and with crews inadequately trained. . . .

Americans are much like other people—they prefer to learn from their own experience. In spite of some admitted defects— including lack of experience—their leadership is of a high order, and the quality of their air crews is magnificent. . . .

They will not turn aside from day bombing till they are convinced that it has failed: they will not be convinced except by their own experience.

Such a note was hardly forceful enough to convince a man as strong-minded as Churchill, especially when he was angry. In a savage reply the next day, he leaped upon Sinclair's conclusion:

I object strongly to paragraph 5. What is meant by "Given sufficient strength to saturate the defences"? This is quite a meaningless condition unless some idea of numbers is attached to it. By "defences" do you mean flak or enemy fighters? Then again, take the statement "No one can say for certain until it has been tried— and tried repeatedly." So far they have not tried at all. Even when they begin, the weather will make the chances of experiment few

General Eaker (left) and George VI, King of England, discuss problems of mutual concern. *Photo Courtesy of Imperial War Museum*

Lt. Colonel Fargo (back to camera) greets (left to right) Maj. General Eaker, Mr. Anthony Eden, Lt. General Devers, and Brig. General Armstrong upon their arrival at 305th Bomb Group Base in England, June 25, 1943. *U.S. Air Force Photo*

R.A.F. Air Chief Marshall Harris (center) talks with General Arnold, CG U.S.A.A.F. (left) and Maj. General Eaker, CG 8th Air Force. *U.S. Air Force Photo*

Germany is the target of planning session in England for mission by 8th Air Force. Top row (left to right): Lt. Gen. Ira C. Eaker, Brig. Gen. Frank O. Hunter, Brig. Gen. Robert C. Candee. Bottom row (left to right): Lt. Gen. Carl Spaatz, Gen. Dwight D. Eisenhower, Maj. Gen. W. H. Frank. *U.S. Air Force Photo*

A familiar sight to crewmen of B-17's flying over Germany was another Flying Fortress in same formation against background of clouds and flak. View is through opening for waist gun. *U.S. Air Force Photo*

Not nearly so familiar a sight as B-17 crews would have preferred were flights of P-51 Mustang fighters. Early decisions to downplay production of P-51's caused them to be in short supply when critically needed as B-17 escorts. *U.S. Air Force Photo*

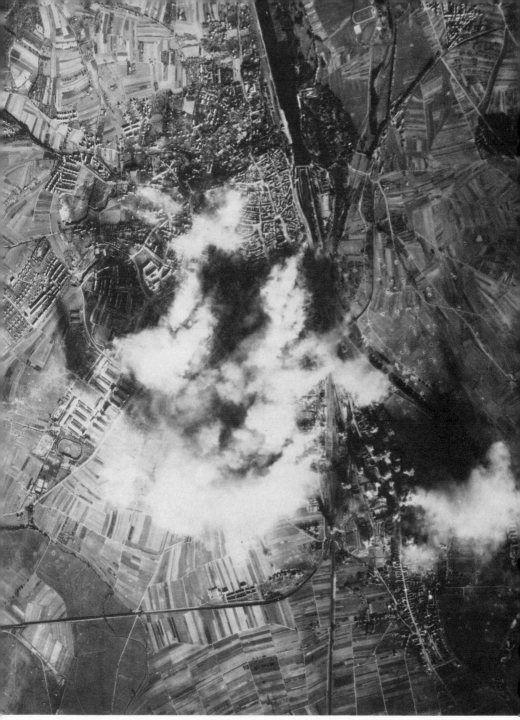

Wing camera of B-17 in which Edwin Millson flew as navigator took this photo during an early stage of second Schweinfurt raid, October 14, 1943. *Photo Courtesy of Colonel Edwin Millson*

View photographed by another plane later in the October 14 raid shows the increase in smoke as fires spread through factory area of Schweinfurt. *U.S. Air Force Photo*

On the ground at Schweinfurt, fires continue to blaze furiously after B-17's had turned homeward to face once again the onslaught of German fighter planes.

After the Flying Fortresses have passed, leaving fires and bomb damage in their wake at Schweinfurt on October 14 raid, workers emerge from Kugelfischer plant to see what can be done.

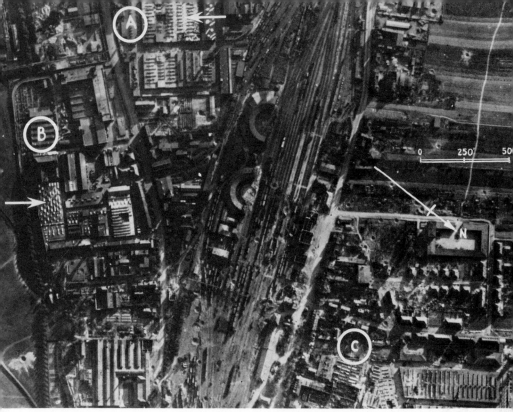

Reconnaissance photo of Schweinfurt, Germany, after raids shows hits on machine shops (A and B) and powerhouse for shops (C). Arrows in left part of photo show where camouflage is used to confuse damage assessors. *U.S. Air Force Photo*

Close-up of battle damage to the nose of a B-17 that nevertheless fought its way back to England and landed safely. *U.S. Air Force Photo*

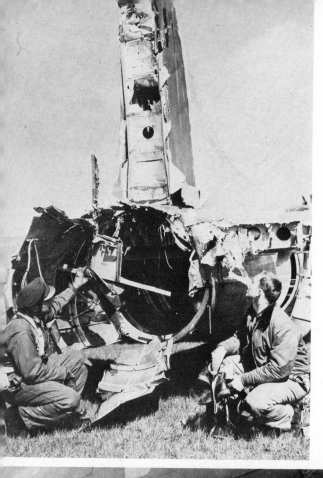

Pilot and co-pilot inspect damage in which tail-gunner's compartment in which gunner was riding was sheared off shortly after bombs were dropped. *U.S. Air Force Photo*

Wounded airman is removed from B-17 after safe landing at base in England.

and far between. Thus it may be four or five months before the Americans are convinced one way or the other.

Meanwhile I have never suggested that they should be "discouraged" by us, that is to say, that we should argue against their policy, but only that they should not be encouraged to persist obstinately and also that they should be actively urged to become capable of night bombing. What I am going to discourage actively is the sending over of large quantities of these daylight bombers and their enormous ground staffs until the matter is settled one way or the other. It is much better for them to work in Africa.

The Air Ministry was now so alarmed about what Churchill might or might not be planning to do that General Eaker was invited the next day (January 11) to visit Sir Archibald Sinclair.[13] They had a pleasant talk in which Sinclair solicited Eaker's arguments supporting American policy. Sinclair got the impression that Eaker was "straining at the leash," but that the loss of so many airplanes to TORCH had frustrated him as much as had the weather. Nevertheless, Eaker assured the British Air Minister that he was ready right now to bomb certain targets in Germany, which he named, and that he could do so with fewer losses than he was sustaining against the submarine bases in the Bay of Biscay.

Eaker was not told how much trouble Sinclair and Portal were having with Churchill over American air policy, but he was shown one of the papers the Air Ministry had prepared in defense of the 8th Air Force.[14] This was enough to make Eaker suspect that something untoward was in the air.

On Wednesday, January 13, Eaker received a cable directing him to report as soon as possible to General Arnold in Casablanca. Casablanca! What was Arnold doing there? Eaker had written to him in Washington just two days earlier. Eaker had received no inkling of the Churchill-Roosevelt conference, which was to begin in Africa January 14.[15]

The British weather, plus the German fighter patrols from France that forced Africa-bound planes to fly a roundabout route into the Atlantic, delayed Eaker's arrival in Africa until late in the evening of the 15th. The next morning, General Arnold's aide, Col. Eugene Beebe, took him to the villa where the U.S. Air Force commander was staying, within the Anfa Hotel compound just outside Casablanca. Arnold was in the bathroom shaving, but he didn't allow that to delay his meeting with Eaker. He still had lather on his face when the two men greeted each other—not enough lather, however, to conceal the grimness of his expression. Eaker, who had often enough seen Arnold when he was angry, had seldom seen him this deeply disturbed. Eaker sensed immediately that some kind of serious trouble was afoot. Arnold wasted no time telling him what it was.

"At lunch yesterday," he said, "I heard the Prime Minister ask our President to discontinue daylight bombing. And he got an agreement from the President that your 8th Air Force will join the R.A.F. in night bombing. What do you think of that?"[16]

Arnold knew very well what Eaker would think of it but apparently wanted to hear him express it. Eaker said: "General, that is absurd. It represents complete disaster. It will permit the Luftwaffe to escape. The cross-Channel operation will then fail. And our planes are not equipped for night bombing. Our crews are not trained for it. We'll lose more planes landing on that fog-shrouded island in darkness than we lose now over German targets. The million men standing on the West Wall can go back to work in the factories or make up another sixty divisions for the Russian front. Every time our bombers show on radar, every workman in the Ruhr takes to the shelters. If our leaders are that stupid, count me out. I don't want any part of such nonsense."

"I hoped that would be your reaction," Arnold said. "Of course I know the reasons you've given as well as you do, but in my judgment, the American Chiefs of Staff will join the British Chiefs in acceding to Churchill's request. And that will settle it because if Roosevelt accedes, it'll finish daylight bombing for the 8th Air Force in England. It occurred to me that the only chance we had to get the Prime Minister to change his view was to have you come down and see him. I've heard him mention you favorably. If you can't convince him that we should continue daylight bombing, I think we're finished with it. I'm going to try to arrange a meeting for you tomorrow."

Though Churchill had not specifically asked Roosevelt for a moratorium on daylight bombing until the previous day (January 15), Arnold had learned of his intentions shortly after arriving in Casablanca on the 13th. Perhaps Portal or Slessor, who arrived with Churchill a half-hour later, gave Arnold a strong hint of what he could

184

expect. He has said he had advance knowledge that he was in for a fight on the issue. "I knew the British had taken the matter up with the Prime Minister and were determined that the Americans should not do daylight bombing." He had also learned that the President and the Prime Minister had already exchanged some preliminary ideas on the subject. The "British" whom Arnold blamed for influencing Churchill were his R.A.F. colleagues, Portal, and possibly Slessor.

It was ironic that Arnold should be holding them responsible after all their recent efforts, in their secret memoranda, to defend the Americans against Churchill. Arnold never learned about these memoranda. He made his assumptions from his knowledge of earlier statements, by Portal in particular, who had freely criticized the Americans until Churchill began taking him too seriously. Arnold, assuming he was still up against the entire British establishment on the issue, had summoned Eaker as the man closest to it and therefore best informed about it.

Arnold may also have been influenced by Eaker's well-known ability as a special pleader. During Eaker's military career, he had taken time out to study both law (at Columbia University) and journalism (at the University of Southern California). He had developed a knack for condensing arguments, and more than ever before in his life he would now be called upon to demonstrate it. He was acquainted with enough of Churchill's associates to know that the Prime Minister did not react well to lengthy presentations.

It was to be three days before Churchill had time to meet Eaker. Meanwhile, the 8th Air Force commander, with the help of Capt. James Parton, the aide he had brought with him, got right to work.[17] As a first step, at Arnold's request, Eaker wrote a two-page report entitled "Why Have U.S. Bombers Not Bombed Germany?" This was a question for which Arnold needed answers not only against the British but also against his critics in the U.S. Navy. He had created "an explosion" at a recent U.S. Chiefs of Staff session by asking for top priority in the build-up of heavy bombers in England.[18] Adm. Ernest King had been openly contemptuous, declaring that it was useless to bomb Germany and that the available heavy bombers should go to the Pacific. Arnold was at a disadvantage in trying to answer such arguments because his English-based planes had not yet ventured inside the German border.

Eaker could give Arnold no new ammunition to fire at the Navy, because there wasn't any. He dutifully listed all the problems Arnold already knew—the submarine pen priority, the loss of the best groups to TORCH, the weather, and the lack of escort fighters, which were just now arriving and would not be ready for action until March. But his men were ready, he said, as soon as weather permitted, and they were eager because they thought it might be easier than what they were doing. The antiaircraft defenses over the submarine pens were tougher than in many parts of Germany, and there were one hundred day fighters protecting the sub-pens but fewer than thirty-five in the Bremen area of north Germany. Before the end of January, he promised, the 8th Air Force would have to its credit at least two or three raids inside Germany.

This prediction assumed that the 8th would not in the meantime have to start retraining its men and reequipping its planes for night missions. Eaker felt that Arnold was "at his wit's end" and had summoned him to Africa as a desperation measure. It wasn't as if Churchill had simply put the question on the agenda for discussion. He had already won Roosevelt's agreement on it. The likelihood that Eaker could talk Churchill out of it seemed slight, but it was worth the try.

Eaker and Parton set themselves up at a table in Arnold's villa and went to work, trying to overcome the distractions of a steady flow of visitors, including such men as Averell Harriman, a special adviser to Roosevelt, and Harold Macmillan, who had just been appointed assistant to Robert Murphy, the American political representative in North Africa. Eaker and Parton organized their arguments against Churchill by putting them down on paper in an outline called "The Case for Day Bombing." Parton had got from Maj. Harris Hull in 8th Bomber Command Intelligence a thick stack of reports that told all about the 8th's first seventeen hundred sorties. From these reports he was able to cull some promising statistics in support of the general points with which Eaker hoped to convince Churchill. It took them several hours to write their paper, and when they were through it came to twenty-three pages in long-hand.

Then Eaker attacked the much more difficult job of boiling it down. After ruthless pruning, there wasn't much room for statistics, but Eaker had produced a memorandum less than a page long, and it made eight major points:

1. Day bombing is more accurate and can destroy obscure but important targets the night bombers can't find.
2. Being more accurate, day bombing is more economical because a small force concentrating its bombs is more effective than a large force scattering its bombs.
3. By bombing the devils around the clock, we can prevent the German defenses from getting any rest.
4. If the R.A.F. works by night and we work by day, we can prevent airdrome and airspace congestion.
5. Our crews are trained for day bombing. There would be a long delay in retraining them.
6. Our planes and equipment are designed for day operations. They would require extensive modification.
7. Day bombing permits the destruction of enemy fighters—one of our prime objectives—by exposing them to the B-17's twelve half-inch guns.
8. We can coordinate day raids with R.A.F. night raids. We can ignite obscure targets by day which the R.A.F. can bomb that night by the light of our fires.

Armed with his one-page brief, Eaker nervously reported to the villa Churchill was occupying, also within the closely guarded, barbed-wire-enclosed Anfa Hotel compound, at 10:00 A.M. on the morning of January 20. It was a lovely house with two-story double windows. When Eaker was admitted to the foyer, he looked out through these windows to a cluster of orange trees in the garden. While he was still gazing at this exotic view and enjoying the warm sunlight that came through the high windows, he became conscious that the British Prime Minister was descending the graceful staircase in an air commodore's uniform. Eaker had heard many times that Churchill liked to wear his Army uniform when he entertained a general and his naval uniform when he was seeing an admiral. It seemed a good omen that he should be wearing an airman's uniform this morning.

Churchill did not wait until he was all the way down the stairs before speaking. As he reached the landing he said, "Young man, General Arnold tells me you are most unhappy that I've suggested to your President that your 8th Air Force discontinue its daylight efforts and join the R.A.F. in night bombing. I want you to know and

187

remember that I am half American. My mother was a U.S. citizen. And the tragic loss of so many of your gallant crews tears my heart. Marshal Harris tells me that his losses average 2 percent while yours are at least double that and sometimes higher."[19]

By this time Churchill had reached the ground floor and was ushering Eaker into a spacious living room. Eaker's statistics did not agree with those Churchill had just quoted; indeed he had figures indicating the exact opposite—2 percent losses for the Americans and 4 percent for the British. But this was no time to argue about that.

"Mr. Prime Minister," Eaker said, "I've learned from a year's service in the United Kingdom that you always listen to both sides of an issue before making a decision. And I've set down here in a memorandum less than a page long the reasons why, in my judgment, it would be most profitable to the war effort if we were to continue our daylight bombing while the R.A.F. continues its night bombing."

Churchill took in hand the piece of paper and sat down on a long couch, motioning for Eaker to sit beside him. He began reading the brief, half to himself, half aloud, mumbling some of the words and enunciating clearly others that seemed to appeal to him. Eaker noticed with satisfaction that when he came to the sentence about bombing the devils around the clock so they would have no rest, he "rolled the words off his tongue as though they were tasty morsels."

After Churchill finished reading, he showed no indication that he was convinced. He still "regretted that so much effort had been put into the daylight bombing," and he still thought the Americans would now be delivering more bombs to Germany if they had begun with night operations. As for the question of accuracy at night, new scientific methods were being developed to take care of that.

Eaker augmented verbally the case he had put on paper by stating it in greater detail. Churchill was impressed by the "powerful earnestness," the "skill and tenacity" with which the American general made his points. He mentioned the immense preparations that had already gone into the build-up of the 8th Air Force in England.

But, Churchill pointed out, this was the beginning of 1943 and the Americans had been in the war more than a year. They hadn't yet thrown a single bomb on Germany. The British had been led to believe a year earlier in Washington that within four or five months American aircraft would be making very heavy deliveries of bombs.

Eaker said it was quite true they had not yet struck their blow. He

188

didn't have to go into the reasons because Churchill already knew them. But the 8th Air Force was now ready and within a month or less would be bombing Germany.

Finally Churchill said to him, "Young man, you have not convinced me you are right, but you have persuaded me that you should have further opportunity to prove your contention. How fortuitous it would be if we could, as you say, 'bomb the devils round the clock.' When I see your President at lunch today, I shall tell him that I withdraw my suggestion that U.S. bombers join the R.A.F. in night bombing, and that I now recommend that our joint effort, day and night bombing, be continued for a time."

When General Eaker reported the result of this meeting to General Arnold, the Air Force commander was encouraged but hardly contented. After commending Eaker for his apparent success, he offered him no opportunity to rest upon it. "Now I suggest," he said, "that you start back to England within the hour and devote your maximum effort to proving our case."

The following day, January 21, the Combined (British-American) Chiefs of Staff issued an order, soon to be known as the Casablanca Directive,[20] which certified that Churchill had kept his word. It defined for the first time with some degree of precision the nature and purpose of the combined aerial offensive from England:

> Your primary object will be the progressive destruction and dislocation of the German military, industrial, and economic system, and the undermining of the morale of the German people to a point where their capacity for armed resistance is fatally weakened.

The directive also listed target priorities—submarine yards, aircraft factories, transportation facilities, oil plants, and so on—and stipulated that the bomber fleets could be called upon at any time for such special purposes as attacking the German Navy or supporting an Allied invasion. But for the 8th Air Force, the most satisfying paragraph in the directive was one that guaranteed it at least a chance to prove itself:

> You should take every opportunity to attack Germany by day, to destroy objectives that are unsuitable for night attack, to sustain

continuous pressure on German morale, to impose heavy losses on the German day fighter force, and to contain German fighter strength away from the Russian and Mediterranean theaters of war.

It was five days before Eaker managed to get back to England. On the 25th, his plane made an emergency landing, due to bad weather, at Clovilly, and he took a train to London.

Two days later, on the 27th, a fleet of sixty-four B-17s and B-24s took off on the first American mission to Germany. Led by Col. Frank Armstrong and his reorganized 306th Group, they followed a North Sea route toward a submarine construction yard at Vegesack, about thirty miles up the estuary of the Weser River. They encountered no opposition on the way, but when they reached Vegesack, the clouds were so thick they couldn't see it. Armstrong chose a secondary target, the nearby port of Wilhelmshaven, which was also veiled by clouds but not completely invisible, and fifty-eight of his bombers dropped their loads upon it, still unhampered by fighters and only lightly disturbed by flak.

The Americans were on their way home when the first German fighters caught up to them. A German lance corporal named Erich Handke, who was in one of these planes—an ME-110—has recorded his reaction to his first sight of the big American bombers: "Suddenly we saw the Boeing Fortress IIs ahead in a great swarm. I confess the sight put me into a bit of a flap, and the others felt the same. We seemed so puny against these four-engined giants. Then we attacked from the beam."[21]

Handke's plane was one of an estimated sixty German fighters that met the Americans that day. They shot down one B-17 and two B-24s—not a prohibitive loss. American gunners claimed twenty-two victories. Even allowing for exaggeration (German figures claimed a loss of only seven fighters that day) the big bombers had made an auspicious debut against the Hitler homeland. It looked almost too easy.

11

A few hours after the Wilhelmshaven mission, Air Chief Marshal Sir Arthur Harris sent a message to General Longfellow at 8th Bomber Command welcoming the Americans to a club the R.A.F. had founded and for which it had been eagerly soliciting new members:

> Greetings and congratulations from [British] Bomber Command to all who took part in the first United States raid on Germany. This well-planned and gallantly executed operation opens a campaign the Germans have long dreaded. To them it is yet another ominous sentence in the writing on the wall. . . . To Bomber Command it is concrete and most welcome proof that we shall no longer be alone in carrying the war to German soil.

There was no irony in Harris's congratulations. Though he had argued for a long time against the day bombing of Germany, he had never joined Sinclair and Portal, or later Churchill, in criticizing the Americans for being so slow to get to it. He remarked to an aide one day that British critics of the Americans had short memories. It had taken the British two years or more, from late 1939 to early 1942, to

191

get their bomber offensive into high gear. Eaker and his first six officers had arrived in England only eleven months before, with nothing but their suitcases. All their men, planes, and equipment then had to be brought from three thousand miles away. The logistic accomplishment alone was worthy of commendation.

Although Harris, operating under similar circumstances, understood the 8th Air Force's problems, General Arnold in Washington was not so easily convinced that Eaker was moving ahead fast enough. In response to Arnold's queries, Eaker had to submit two reports, one entitled "Why There Have Been so Few Missions," and the other, "Why There Have Been so Many Abortive Sorties." In both reports he mentioned the loss of facilities to TORCH and the inclemency of British weather. Ninety percent of the 8th's maintenance capability including the Air Service Command, he pointed out, had been engaged in setting up planes for the African operation, with the result that equipment failures had sharply increased on the remaining planes. And in one mission, 46 percent of the planes had aborted because of paralyzing weather. These planes, after taking off in rain, had to fly through rain more than halfway to their target. By the time they came out of the rain at 22,000 feet, where the temperature was about thirty degrees below zero, their bomb-bay doors were frozen shut and their machine-gun turrets were frozen in fixed positions. They had to abort because they could neither defend themselves nor drop their loads. (This was the February 4 raid aimed at Hamm but redirected at Emden. Of the eighty-six bombers that took off and flew through the rain to Germany that day, only thirty-nine were able to drop their bombs on Emden.)

Eaker concluded his report on the paucity of missions by recalling Arnold's original instructions never to operate so recklessly as to sustain a loss rate that would eliminate or deplete his force. By reassuring Arnold he would never do such a thing, Eaker was reminding him subtly that, since TORCH, the bomber build-up in England and the replacement of losses had been almost suspended.

Eaker was now so concerned about attrition and about diversion of his forces to other theaters that he devised a devilish scheme to counteract the problem. He began systematically to enlist all possible allies in a discreet propaganda campaign to get the 8th Air Force build-up resumed.[1] While his bombers were attacking such places as Hamm, Emden, Bremen, and Wilhelmshaven with gradually increasing losses, he was making phone calls, writing letters, and sending cables in an effort to generate more letters and cables in support of his aim. His strategy was to stimulate correspondence, even among the already convinced, so they would have messages, all with the same theme, to show each other and to use against the unconvinced. The basic theme was that the bomber offensive against Germany was the main business of the American Air Force, and its strength in England must be rapidly augmented for this purpose.

Eaker wrote first to Arnold in Washington (February 26) expressing his concern about the build-up of the 8th Bomber Command—or rather the lack of it:

> The two heavy groups we were supposed to get in February have, as you of course know, been sidetracked to the Twelfth Air Force [in Africa]. We have been told that there will be no shipping in March or April. This makes it appear that we are not to build up an increased force of heavy bombers to be available this spring. . . . There is only one thing that we require here to do a job—the job that will hurt the enemy most, and that is an adequate force. . . .
>
> We have, to date, received but 24 replacement crews and 63 replacement aircraft. We have lost 75 planes and crews in 2,206 sorties. We feel, therefore, obliged to save our force for days when we can deliver maximum effort under favourable conditions, until we can get a larger force, and until the flow of replacements matches expenditure. We never have, and never will, let one of these days pass without operating at maximum effort.

One outcome of the Casablanca conference was the appointment of Lt. Gen. Frank M. Andrews, a highly respected senior Air Force officer, to replace General Eisenhower as commander of all American forces in the European Theater of Operations. Eaker, who had worked under Andrews on several occasions before the war, welcomed him happily to London and began immediately to enlist him in the 8th Air Force build-up campaign. The paper bombardment began February 27 with a letter to Andrews that included an apparently solicited letter from one of Eaker's preenlisted advocates, and, in addition, a ready-made cable that Eaker hoped Andrews would send to General Marshall over his own signature. Eaker's letter said:

Enclosed is a personal letter to me from Brigadier General Frank Armstrong which I commend to your reading. It reflects the very serious depression in morale of our bomber forces, due to the failure to build them up. . . .

I have done a lot of thinking on this situation and I urge that a cable such as the enclosed be sent by you to the War Department. If you agree to send it I should like authority to pass to my units a copy of the cable you send, in order to show them the efforts you are making to support them.

The cable Eaker had provided for Andrews's signature was hardly a modest proposal. It began by pointing out that the only U.S. force which could hope to fight the German war machine in Germany during the coming year was the 8th Air Force:

Its experiment in daylight bombing has been markedly success-ful even with the very small force which has been available. It could be a tremendous factor in the depreciation of the German war machine and German civil morale if built to significant propor-tions, a minimum of three hundred heavy bombers operational at once.

Eaker knew that such a force was out of the question at the moment, but he had better ask for 300 if he hoped to get even 150. His average daily combat strength in February had been 84 planes and 74 crews. And it would surely be better to ask for them over Andrews's signature than over his own.

At the same time, Eaker was enlarging his campaign by enlisting the British. On the last day of the month, Portal sent Arnold a cable that was almost certainly inspired by Eaker:

I told you in my message of 19th February how great an impor-tance I attached to building up our day and night offensive against Germany. This offensive is of the highest strategical importance and is hitting Germany hard at a time when the Russian successes on the eastern front, the hard struggle in the Mediterranean and the constant air fighting in the west have so stretched Germany's resources that the strain on her industrial organization and on the civil population generally is intense. . . . An essential part is played

194

by the 8th Air Force. Their recent attacks have been strikingly successful considering the limited number they can put into the air. My one fear is that their efforts may be curtailed or even brought to a standstill by lack of numbers.

Eaker on March 3 virtually acknowledged his role in Portal's efforts when he wrote him a short note enclosing more ammunition:

In connection with your recent cable to General Arnold, I thought you would be interested to have a copy of a cable I have suggested that General Andrews should send back to General Marshall. I attach it along with a copy of my covering letter to General Andrews.

Portal demonstrated that he had caught the spirit of the campaign by firing some new ammunition right back to Eaker the same day:

I am very pleased indeed to know that you are taking this action. The whole of our experience in the last war as well as in this one goes to show that one of the greatest factors in sustaining the morale of fighting units is the prompt replacement of their losses. Losses which are insignificant in relation to a single operation assume a very different aspect when four or five operations are added together and then no replacements are received.

It is not difficult to envision Eaker and Portal on the phone saying to each other, "I'll write such-and-such to you so you can quote it to so-and-so, and you write such-and-such to me so I can quote it to so-and-so. Then we'll both write to a few other people and enclose our messages to each other so they can quote us to whomever." Eaker's next communication, the same day (March 3), was to Harris, who was also solidly on their side in the matter. After going to more than ordinary lengths in congratulating R.A.F. Bomber Command for the fine work they had done against the Germans in February, Eaker finally got to the meat of his letter:

It is now evident that the only remaining factor yet to be developed to insure the destruction of the enemy is the build-up of an adequate force.

195

Harris, a quick man to pick up a cue, sent Eaker (March 5) exactly what he wanted—a stirring endorsement of the urgent need to augment Eaker's command:

> Our only regret is that the VIIIth Bomber Force, which we know already to be fully equal in quality to the best we can produce, is still too small to take its full share of the attack. Had you the force to operate by day on the same scale as we have done and shall continue to do by night, there would be no hope for the enemy in Europe, who could not long stand against such a weight of combined offensive.
>
> The whimperings of the German propagandists at our opening blows in the campaign of 1943 show that the enemy now strives to win the sympathy of the world in his misfortunes. When the Devil is sick, the Devil a saint would be. This change of tone in itself reveals his fear of what is still to come and increases my conviction that, when you can hit him as hard by day as we can at night, the day of reckoning will set on Hitler's Germany.

The British air marshal's strong sentiments about the need to bomb Germany into complete submission were now so well known that people were beginning to call him "Bomber" Harris, but he didn't mind. He hated Hitler and the Nazi cause so passionately that he felt fully justified in bombing the people who had made Hitler their leader. He was not the least bit self-conscious about it. One day in 1942, when he was hurrying from the Air Ministry in London to his headquarters at High Wycombe, he had been stopped for speeding. Though he had a "priority" sticker on his car, it was attached to the front bumper and the pursuing policeman didn't see it. When the policeman realized whom he had stopped, he decided not to issue a citation, but he did say, "I hope you will be careful, Sir. You might kill somebody." To this, Harris replied, "My dear man, I'm paid to kill people."[2]

On March 4 it began to look as if Eaker's campaign for more planes was about to be answered. A cable from Arnold announced that three heavy-bomb groups (94th, 95th, and 96th) plus one medium group were "being prepared for immediate movement" to England, and that each month thereafter, he hoped, two more heavies and one medium would be sent. Replacement aircraft in March would total

236 B-17s and 48 B-24s. In April it would be 115 B-17s and 14 B-24s. Arnold was doing his best despite the demand for planes in other theaters, the severe shipping bottleneck caused by the U-boats, plus the African campaign, and the continuing efforts by the U.S. Navy to siphon off planes and matériel. But the strain of fighting the Battle of Washington had aggravated Arnold's heart condition, and he had to go to Florida for a rest. From Coral Gables he wrote Eaker a letter (March 15) that illustrated some of the pressures upon him.

He asked Eaker to continue sending him any information he could use to support the Air Force cause, and he expressed some optimism about the possibility of building up Eaker's air fleet. But he also included a caveat:

> As you know, from time to time we have one crisis after another in various war theaters, and I am never sure as to when somebody who cries longer or louder will bring about sufficient pressure to cause diversion from the main effort. That I cannot take care of, although I try my darnedest. . . .
>
> At this writing, [George C.] Kenney from Australia, [Nathan] Twining and [Millard] Harmon from the Solomons, together with various and sundry naval officers from places in the Pacific are here endeavoring to straighten out plans and policies for operations in the Pacific. Each and every one of them is doing his best to get more airplanes for his particular theater. If we can withstand this blast, I think that we are safe for a while at least in assuming that we can continue to build you up.

On the basis of this less-than-absolute assurance, Eaker expanded his plans and stepped up his operations. Ninety-seven bombers (seventy-three B-17s and twenty-four B-24s) returned to the submarine yards at Vegesack March 18 to score the 8th Air Force's greatest victory to date. At the expense of only two bombers, they damaged seven submarines and destroyed about two-thirds of the shipyard that had built them. (These estimates were derived from British reconnaissance photos.) American gunners that day claimed fifty-two German fighters destroyed plus twenty probables and nine damaged. Four days later, in another successful raid against Wilhelmshaven, they claimed twenty-eight more fighters for the loss of three bombers.

197

Such claims of success against German fighters were somewhat embarrassing to Eaker because, compared to R.A.F. claims, they sounded outlandish. Though the R.A.F. bombers were not so well armed and flew at night when it was almost impossible to see German fighters, the discrepancies were so great that the British couldn't believe the Americans were that good, and Eaker was inclined to go partway toward agreeing with the British. He knew that several gunners, shooting at the same fighter and seeing it fall, would all claim it. But aside from instituting the R.A.F. rules for allowing claims and intensifying intelligence questioning after each mission, he was loathe to discount the figures publicly. He believed he would be a poor commander if he said to a man who had just risked his life to reach a target, "I don't believe your report."[3] In speaking to his crews, which he did once a week at one air base or another, he had said on several occasions that he supposed some of them were shooting at the same fighters and therefore, through no fault of theirs, double-claiming some kills. But he didn't know how often this happened, and as long as he was their leader, he wasn't going to let anyone question their veracity. It might also have occurred to him that those high claims must sound good to the folks back home.

Eaker was so pleased with the results of the Vegesack and Wilhelmshaven missions that he went with Harris (March 23) to a war correspondents' luncheon at the Savoy Hotel. Both men were in expansive moods that day. Harris told the newsmen the British and Americans were serenely and completely cooperative with each other. Then in terms that he didn't have to exaggerate, he described how well he and the 8th Air Force commander got on together.

"When General Eaker stays at my home," Harris said, "he kisses my wife the same as I do, and I like it."

(The next day, when Eaker's own wife, Ruth, at her home in Washington, was told by newsmen about this remark, she said, "Good heavens! Is that in the paper?" She knew, of course, about her husband's close friendship with the Harrises. Since wartime conditions had prevented her from accompanying Eaker to England, she was not yet acquainted with Lady Jill Harris, but the two had at least one thing in common: both were beautiful women. A Washington newspaper had recently featured Mrs. Eaker under the heading, "Beauty of the Week.")

During Eaker's first thirteen months in England, he had never held a press conference. He decided to do so. In January 1943, a month after replacing Spaatz as 8th Air Force commander, he and six members of his staff had moved into a lovely Tudor house named Castle Coombe, which his aide, Captain Parton, had been able to procure for them in Kingston Hill, near their Bushy Park headquarters. Parton was a young man with a good eye for the finer things. The house was virtually a mansion, with broad, well-landscaped grounds abutting a golf course. It also had a tennis court. Though it was already well furnished, Parton gave it an extra touch of class by borrowing for its walls a selection of paintings from the Tate Gallery. Here Eaker was able to entertain from time to time such people as the Harrises, Sir Louis Greig who had been equerry to the abdicated King Edward VIII, the Averell Harrimans, Sir John and Lady Dashwood who had been his friends and neighbors at High Wycombe, General Andrews, and American literary figures like Cass Canfield and Robert Sherwood. On March 24, Eaker invited to Castle Coombe the war correspondents who had invited him to lunch the previous day. It was a perfect opportunity to spread the American Air Force gospel.

After describing the successes in the daylight raids against Vegesack and Wilhelmshaven, he announced that U.S. fliers had now shot down 356 German aircraft in 51 missions at a cost of 90 bombers.

"We have come to the end of an experiment," he said, "and the Liberators and Fortresses have proven themselves completely. It is agreed by British and American authorities that the experiment of using our bombers for daylight high-precision attack has succeeded without uneconomical loss. We are now going to have the maximum number of aircraft and crews. Hundreds of United States bombers will be operating from Britain by the middle of this summer."

Eaker entertained Winston Churchill two nights later (March 26) at a Bomber Command dinner in High Wycombe, honoring the Prime Minister. It was a convivial evening attended by Harris, Andrews, and all the 8th Air Force wing, group, and squadron commanders. Churchill, who was in sharp form, delivered a stirring speech of praise for the American air effort, giving the distinct impression that he no longer disapproved of daylight bombing. After dinner he let drop a gentle hint that he wished it would develop more quickly. He proposed that they send a cable to Arnold in Washington which would say: "We are dining together, smoking your cigars, and

199

waiting for more of your heavy bombers. Signed Churchill, Andrews, Harris, Eaker.''

In a letter to Arnold after this dinner, Eaker said, "It was quite evident that he [Churchill] is fully in accord with the day bomber offensive."[4] Here, in fact, was another example of the ease with which Churchill could give misleading impressions of his actual thinking. Unknown to Eaker, the Prime Minister just two weeks earlier (March 13) had sent another minute to Portal that showed he still had heavy doubts about the American policy. Commenting on a note from Air Marshal Arthur Tedder, the British Mediterranean air commander, Churchill wrote to Portal:

> The real question is not whether ''the American heavy bombers can in fact penetrate into Germany by day without prohibitive losses,'' but how often can they do it and what weight of bombs can they discharge for the vast mass of ground personnel and material involved.

Once again Portal had quickly come to the defense of American day bombing. He pointed out to Churchill that it ''is bound to be more accurate and ton for ton will probably do as much industrial damage and kill far more Germans than our average in night raids.'' Churchill was still not convinced. He gave the opposite impression, however, at that 8th Air Force dinner in his honor.

When Eaker mentioned during his optimistic March 24 press conference that ''hundreds of United States bombers will be operating from Britain by the middle of this summer,'' it was fortunate that he hadn't quoted any exact figures. On that very day, Arnold was sending him a letter that hedged on his earlier build-up hopes:

> I sincerely appreciate your problems and your desire for some concrete flow chart. . . . I am also aware of the embarrassment which undoubtedly results in your conferences with Air Chief Marshal Portal on the build-up of your Air Force. However, as you can well realize, I am unable to definitely and finally commit myself to any set of figures or dates at this time. I have had my people compile the following estimated flow. . . . These are figures for you to play with, and to give you some indication of our

line of thinking over here. They cannot and positively must not be used as definite commitments.

Arnold hoped, he said in this letter, that Eaker would have nineteen heavy-bomb groups by June 30, 1943, and thirty-seven groups by December 31. But he was making no promises. To Eaker, the hopes suddenly began to look forlorn because March was now almost gone and the three groups Arnold had said on the 4th were "being prepared for immediate movement to your command" had not yet appeared in England.

As the days passed and the airplanes failed to come, either in new groups or replacements for his older groups, Eaker's blossoming offensive began to wither. He had always believed that the size of the force was the key to daylight bombing—the larger the formation, the less attention the defense could pay to each bomber. As his force slowly dwindled, therefore, through unreplaced operational losses, it became increasingly perilous to send it into Germany, where the defenses were expanding day by day. The Germans might one day manage to concentrate all their fighters in the right place and deliver a crippling blow to his meager fleet. To avert this possibility, he had to suspend his attacks against Germany proper, sending his bombers instead on short, relatively safe missions against Rouen (March 28), Rotterdam (March 31), Paris (April 4), and Antwerp (April 5).

Eaker's frustration at this new and unexpected interruption of his plans soon turned to anger and then to uncharacteristic fury as he saw the effect upon his veteran crews of having to remain on the combat roster without any apparent hope of replacement when their tour was finished. He was now so short of crews he had to extend the twenty-five mission limit, which he had considered inviolable, to thirty missions per man. And he wasn't certain he could hold it there.

The group commanders were beginning to report a growing depression among the crews. The men in Colonel LeMay's 305th Group were "sitting around figuring out what their chances were" to survive their full tours of duty, and they were coming to the conclusion that the chances "weren't very good."[5] It seemed to them that if they lost 4 percent of their planes (and they figured they were actually losing more) on each mission, they would all be shot down within twenty-five missions unless they got some replacements. In every

201

group the crews made similar calculations. There was only one bitter consolation, as the black humorists pointed out. If they were all gone after twenty-five missions, they wouldn't have to fly the extra five for which they had now been scheduled.

At Eaker's headquarters, one of his staff members, engaging in the same kind of arithmetic, remarked to him that at their present rate of loss without replacements, the last B-17 would take off on its last mission within a month.

Eaker's reply to this was, "O.K., I'll be on it."

At the end of the first week in April, with no new bombers yet in sight, his exasperation had grown beyond control. He wrote a blistering indictment to Arnold on "The Position of the 8th Air Force." It was an essay hardly likely to enhance his reputation for tact and diplomacy:

> The current position of the 8th Air Force is not a credit to the American Army. After sixteen months in the war we are not yet able to dispatch more than 123 bombers toward an enemy target. Many of the crews who fly this pitiful number have been on battle duty for eight months. They understand the law of averages. They have seen it work on their friends. . . .
>
> They know that we have been promised replacement crews as often as we have been promised more planes. They have seen the number of planes dwindle until its scarcity has restricted most of our raiding to relatively futile forays on the coast of France.
>
> They have seen our precision bombing improve, in bloody lessons, until they know with confidence what they can do, or could do, if they had enough planes to run the increasing gauntlet of enemy fighters to important targets. As it is, they know that we have not enough. They know that they will have to continue battle duty after the limit of thirty tours lately set. And they know the reason, which is that after eight months in this theater, the 8th Air Force is still an unkept promise.
>
> This is written in no apprehension of trouble with the crews. They are American, and they will pay for the mistakes of their superiors as uncomplainingly as the men of Wake and Bataan did. This is written as a statement of our critical need of planes and crews with which to redeem the promise of the 8th Air Force while there is still time.

The purpose of the 8th Air Force was, and is, to strike the chief Axis enemy in his heart. No other American military or naval force was capable of this at the outset of the war. No other one will be capable of it this year. Nor is any other Allied force except the Bomber Command of the R.A.F. capable of it.

On these two forces alone rest our hopes of bringing the war home to civilian, economic and political Germany. On these two forces alone rest our chances of crippling or destroying the sources of submarines and Panzer divisions. . . .

With every day that the western sky has shown us only the sunset of another hope, the German has strengthened the fortress of Europe. . . .

Some day the Navy and Ground Forces . . . may give us back our planes to pave the way for their well-covered approach to the heart of the enemy.

But neither they nor anyone else can give us back the time with which the German has tightened his stubborn grip on the Aerial Supremacy over Europe. That is the rising price, the daily increasing forfeit we have yet to pay for the unkept promise of the 8th Air Force. . . . It is respectfully requested that the 8th Air Force be given sufficient planes to redeem its unkept promise.[6]

Even if Eaker had achieved no other purpose, he had put on paper an eloquent rationale for the existence of the 8th Air Force. Arnold was sufficiently moved by Eaker's anger to write in return an essay of praise for the men of the 8th. After saying he wished he could send them more planes, he told them they had been pioneers. They had continued the best traditions of the Army and had established "splendid new traditions for the Army Air Forces." They had proven their ability to fend off fighters and drop their bombs with precision. "No bomber attack of the 8th Air Force has ever been turned back by enemy action." The experience they had gained would make it possible to "build rapidly and soundly for the death blow which we surely will deliver the Axis."

It sounded good, but it amounted to nothing more than words. Where were the planes?

In fact, Arnold was as concerned as anyone else about the stunted growth of the 8th Air Force, and he was at work on an elaborate documentary scheme to do something about it. On March 24 he wrote to Portal through Andrews and Eaker a letter that included a report by his operations analysts about strategic targets in Europe. This report, from three thousand miles away, probably contained nothing that Portal hadn't already learned from a British Cabinet agency called the Ministry of Economic Warfare, which had been compiling information about German targets since the war began; but the American report, of itself, was not important. Arnold simply used it as an introduction to what he was about to propose. After commending the report's data to Portal, he wrote:

> In view of the new facts we now have, I believe we should review the bombing priorities set out in paragraph 2 CCS/1/D, approved by the Combined Chiefs of Staff at Casablanca. . . .
>
> Our efforts in the past to build up a large bomber force in the United Kingdom have been disappointing. Bombers for that Theater have too often been regarded as a reservoir from which the demands of other Theaters could be met. As I see it, a definite program of operations from the United Kingdom must be initiated without delay. This is the best answer to a plea for diversions.

The Casablanca Directive, to which Arnold referred, had been helpful in establishing the respectability of daylight bombing, and it had implied some kind of day-night cooperation between the R.A.F. and the A.A.F. It had not, however, stipulated specific programs or methods of cooperation between the British and the Americans, nor did it list specific targets, how or in what order they should be attacked, or by whom.

The vagueness of the Casablanca document didn't bother the British because Harris, at Bomber Command, already knew exactly what he wanted to do; he was already doing it—attacking German industry by bombing its workers in their homes at night. What this meant was the destruction of German cities. It was primarily a matter of deciding which cities contributed most to the German war effort and which were easiest for the R.A.F. to find and hit in the dark.

The American commitment to destroy specific military and industrial facilities, some of which were very small, hard-to-find targets, necessitated much more careful planning. The targets had to be evaluated according to their contribution to the German war effort, then they had to be scouted and photographed by reconnaissance planes. In these endeavors, Eaker had found the British exceedingly helpful. The Ministry of Economic Warfare had worked out detailed studies of potential German targets and was delighted to pass its information on to the Americans because Harris wasn't interested in it. He had argued with some logic that since his planes could bomb only at night, and since until recently they had found it difficult even to locate large cities in the dark, it was silly to hope they would be able to pick out specific military and industrial targets. The M.E.W., finding him unreceptive to their data, passed it on to the 8th Air Force, which accepted it gladly and, after digesting it, chose the likeliest targets for R.A.F. reconnaissance planes to photograph.

By the beginning of 1943, Eaker knew fairly well what he wanted to do as soon as he was able to do it. He had a program in mind. It was clear to the men around him and it was clear to Arnold. There was no need to put it in documentary form until Arnold came up with his scheme. But Arnold hadn't spent forty years in the Army without learning about the power of documents and the uses to which they could be put. The right kind of document, he decided, would give him a heavy weapon in the Battle of Washington, which he seemed, at the moment, to be losing to the Navy. A simple report from Eaker about the needs of the 8th Air Force would not be strong enough to have the required impact in the battle for daylight bombing. He had gone into many a skirmish against Admiral King armed with such reports, and they hadn't even dented King's naval armor. He would have to have a document stately in style, carefully researched, with vivid promises, persuasive arguments, precise statistics, and an impressive title. Better still, it should have international sanction. For this purpose he decided to enlist the British and their prestige in his design. Arnold's March 24 letter to Portal was his opening move. He gave it for hand delivery to a well-instructed member of his staff, Col. C. P. Cabell, who took it to London and, before delivering it, discussed it thoroughly with Andrews, Eaker, and several of Eaker's men.

It was a few days before Cabell reached London and a week before he took the letter to Portal, along with one signed by General Eaker. Eaker's letter introduced Cabell, who was there, he said, to discuss "an idea close to General Arnold's heart."[7] Eaker's letter was more specific than Arnold's about the true purpose of Arnold's initiative:

> General Arnold believes that in order to build up an American Air Force of sufficient size in U.K. he must be armed with two needs: first, a list of the industrial targets in Germany which, if destroyed, will cripple her ability to wage war; and secondly, the size of the air forces required for the accomplishment of this task. If armed with this evidence General Arnold will then be in a position to present it to the Combined Chiefs of Staff and obtain from them, we hope, an agreement and directive which will make the build-up of our air forces in this theater to that size first priority of the U.S.

Portal was receptive because he understood sympathetically Arnold's need for such a document, and because he knew it would not be designed to affect British operations in any substantive way. He assigned one of his men to a committee of American officers whom Andrews and Eaker had selected, and this nominally Anglo-American committee went to work drafting a document they called the Combined Bomber Offensive Plan. They thrashed out the details with the help of Arnold's operations analysts' report, a lot of information from the Ministry of Economic Warfare, and careful attention to Arnold's instruction. As soon as they were finished, they submitted their plan to Eaker, who made some changes, wrote a summary, then got the whole thing approved by Portal, Harris, and Andrews.

This then was the origin of what came to be known as the Combined Bomber Offensive. It was nothing but a document devised to help Arnold get more planes and men for the 8th Air Force. Though it was to have small effect on the major policies of either the R.A.F. or the A.A.F., it did set some much needed standards of procedure and coordination between the two forces. And it codified American target priorities so specifically that such remote places as Schweinfurt and Regensburg became unavoidable and inevitable destinations for American bombers.

The essence of the Combined Bomber Offensive Plan,[8] which eventually became known also as the Eaker Plan, was a commitment to enlarge the 8th Air Force into equal partnership with the R.A.F. in the battle against Germany. Eaker wrote into the text that "300 heavy bombers is the minimum operating force necessary to make deep penetrations," and that "at least 800 airplanes must be in the Theater to dispatch 300 bombers on operations."

Six specific target systems were singled out for bombardment. But to accomplish their destruction, the plan pointed out, the 8th Air Force would need a steady flow of airplanes. The minimum requirements would be 944 heavy bombers in England by July 1, 1943: 1,192 by October 1, 1943; 1,746 by January 1, 1944; and 2,702 by April 1, 1944.

The six major targets listed were submarines, aircraft, ball bearings, oil, synthetic rubber, and military vehicles. The plan promised that with the required number of airplanes, the 8th Air Force could knock out 89 percent of the submarine construction; 43 percent of the German fighter and 65 percent of its bomber production; 76 percent of its ball-bearing manufacture; and 50 percent of its synthetic-rubber capacity. Its oil supplies could be disrupted and its military vehicle supplies seriously depleted.

The plan carefully stated, however, that unless the 8th Air Force could achieve daytime air superiority in the skies over Germany, none of those goals could be accomplished. Eaker himself inserted a strong warning when he wrote: "If the growth of the German fighter strength is not arrested quickly, it may become literally impossible to carry out the destruction planned."

Eaker had been confident in September 1942, after a few missions, that the B-17 could defend itself in the skies over Germany. But soon thereafter he had begun to realize that fighter protection would be urgently needed to hold down losses, and that the farther the fighters could go with the bombers, the smaller the losses would be. It was this realization that had prompted him in October 1942, and again in January 1943, to explore the possibility of having auxiliary fuel tanks made in England for the newly arriving P-47s. In February, having received no satisfactory answer from the British Ministry of Aircraft Production, he had ordered sixty thousand tanks of 200-gallon capacity from the United States.

In his January 16 paper, "Why Have U.S. Bombers Not Bombed Germany?" Eaker had pointed out that "we have no fighters with sufficient range to accompany our bombers into Germany. We have had three groups equipped with such long-range fighters, but before they were trained they were taken from us, assigned to the 12th Air Force, and dispatched to Africa.''

In a February 26 letter to Arnold he said: ''I believe there is no question that our bomber losses will be greatly reduced when our fighters are ready to accompany us. . . . The early receipt of any adequate quantity of long-range tanks will give us the needed range for these P-47s in general support of our bombers all the way to and from the targets.''

On April 5, however, after two types of auxiliary tanks had been tried, the 8th was still without any long-range fighting capability. In a letter to Arnold, Eaker said the P-47 situation had so far proven ''most disappointing.'' He and Brig. Gen. Frank O'D. Hunter, who was in charge of Fighter Command, had expected to have two groups in action by this time, but none had yet seen combat:

> As you know, technical difficulties with the radio and the engine prevented this. . . . [I] believe the P-47 will be all right when these technical difficulties are corrected. I know by your cable which came this morning that you are doing everything possible to expedite the changes in the engine, the correction of the radio difficulty, and the supply of an auxiliary fuel tank which will function at high altitude. These are the three critical factors with this plane.

The radio and engine problems of the P-47 were destined to be corrected quickly enough, but Eaker had a lot of trouble ahead in his effort to develop a long-range fighter by finding a satisfactory auxiliary tank. The tanks tested so far were too difficult to attach and so heavy they limited the P-47's ceiling. Without workable drop tanks, the 8th Air Force would have difficulty achieving the Combined Bomber Offensive's requirement of air superiority over Germany through the defeat of the German fighters.

When the C.B.O. Plan, or the Eaker Plan, was ready for presentation to the American Joint Chiefs of Staff in Washington (which body, it was hoped, would present it to the Combined Chiefs of Staff), Arnold decided that since Eaker had argued so effectively with Churchill in Casablanca, he should come home for a few days and argue with the Joint Chiefs.

Eaker left London April 23 and spent ten days in Washington. As expected, Admiral King objected to the plan when Eaker presented it to the Joint Chiefs. King said it was too firm a commitment to make in light of the current shipping problems. But Marshall was sympathetic to the Air Force, and he prevailed. Arnold's documentary strategy had worked. On May 4, the Joint Chiefs adopted the plan substantially as Eaker had presented it and scheduled it for presentation to the Combined Chiefs of Staff, who were to meet in Washington ten days later. With assurance of support from Portal, the Combined Chiefs were likely to accept it (which they did). Eaker returned to London the day after his success with the Joint Chiefs, expecting large armadas of B-17s to follow him shortly across the Atlantic.

Meanwhile, four new heavy-bomb groups (the 94th, 95th, 96th, and 351st) had reached England in mid-April and were now in transitional training. By mid-May they would be ready for combat, and the 8th Air Force might finally be able, in Eaker's terms, "to redeem its unkept promise."

12

During the months of curtailed operations in the winter and spring of 1943, the men of the 8th Air Force flew practice missions whenever they could get off the ground. They maintained their aircraft, attended ground school, logged "sack time" in their Nissen-hut barracks, read paperback novels, huddled around the coal stoves brooding about the cold English days, sloshed through the thick, sticky mud to their latrines and mess halls, and, every time they got the opportunity, went into the nearest towns to sample British hospitality, which was generous in spirit though materially limited. Wartime English beer seemed weak, and for most of the boys, Scotch whisky was something they heard about but seldom saw.

For those in the 91st Group, the one-street village of Bassingbourn, with a population of about three hundred, offered only one pub, the Hoops. It was a charming, friendly bar in a two-story thatched building, but it provided less excitement than Cambridge, nine miles away, where there were several American Red Cross clubs, the most popular of which was in the Bull, a hotel that dated back to at least 1546. Here an American airman could find coffee, doughnuts, Coke, a hot shower, and sometimes a warm-hearted girl. The aggressiveness of many Americans, plus the gauche remarks they often made about the British way of life, created a lot of awkward moments. And the friendliness of British girls toward the free-spending Yanks produced resentment among the ill-paid British men, many of whom repeated the currently popular remark: "The only thing wrong with the Yanks is that they're overpaid, oversexed, and over here." But even this male British complaint was usually good-humored. There was amazingly little quarreling or fighting.

British forebearance deserved credit for much of the amiability. However naive, uninformed, and rude they might consider the Americans, they were delighted to have them as allies against the Germans. And beneath whatever resentment the British might feel about Yankee brashness, there was also a family sentiment, an unvoiced assumption that Americans were still to some small degree British, that they were unruly colonial relatives, returning when they were most needed, to help protect the mother country whence they had sprung.[1] At the same time, most of the Americans were on good behavior, and their leaders exercised a degree of tact that was some-times amusing. For example, when the 92nd Group at Bovingdon established prophylactic stations in Chesham and Hemel Hempstead, they called them "First Aid Stations" in deference to British sen-sibilities about what was happening between their girls and the Yankee boys.[2] The fact that such stations were needed, however, was a measure of how quickly British-American solidarity was developing.

Early in January, the 92nd had been transferred to Alconbury near Huntingdon, where boredom soon became an exasperating enemy. After being cannibalized as a replacement pool for other groups, the 92nd had only a few B-17s left and little prospect of combat within the immediate future. To keep the men busy, training courses were devised in such subjects as chemical warfare and camouflage, but most of the men had already endured the heavy tedium of such courses before leaving the States. Whenever possible, they got out-side to play baseball, football, or volleyball, but seldom with much enthusiasm because if, as occasionally happened, the sun shone, the ground was usually muddy. U.S.O. entertainers like Bob Hope, Frances Langford, and Adolphe Menjou came once or twice to cheer them up, but only for a few hours. Despite all attempts to bolster morale, disciplinary problems and courts-martial in the 92nd increased month by month.

The group's outlook began to improve in late April, when the four new groups arrived from the States and the air echelon of one of them, the 95th was sent to Alconbury for combat training. Compared to these rookies, the men of the 92nd felt like veterans, as indeed some of them were. Small contingents from their group had flown several missions. Even the men who hadn't seen combat had been in England long enough to learn something about it, and they could at least get a bit of fun out of shouting "You'll be sorry," a traditional Air Force welcome to new boys. The crews of the 92nd helped indoctrinate those of the 95th in combat maintenance requirements, and the few pilots still in the 92nd flew as instructors on the 95th's practice missions. They found the inexperienced rookies so cocky that the hardest thing to teach them was respect for their German enemies. Each new group arriving from America seemed to be imbued with the notion that the war would soon be under control now that they were on the scene. This was undoubtedly a healthier attitude than shivering fear, but it was an attitude the Germans would soon take out of them. When these youngsters began to realize what kind of war they were entering, they would indeed be sorry.

The ground echelon of the 95th, which arrived in Scotland May 11 on the Queen Elizabeth and went directly by truck to Framlingham (another temporary base), absorbed a quicker, more direct lesson in the kind of war they were entering. On their first night at Framlingham the sirens wailed at midnight. Anybody who didn't know enough to jump out of bed immediately and run outside to find the nearest ditch was soon rousted out by a German bomb that hit a mess hall and blew open the doors of several Nissen huts. No one was hurt. From the safety of whatever muddy ditches they could find, the boys of the 95th watched their first dogfight as British Spitfires went after the German bombers.[3]

The air echelon of the 379th Group under Col. Maurice Preston arrived April 24 at Bovingdon, where they remained for a month of training before transferring to Chelveston, then to their permanent base at Kimbolton. For Lt. Edwin Millson, one of the group's four original squadron bombardiers, this was the first opportunity to visit his grandmother.[4] Both of Millson's parents had emigrated from

London to Seattle, where his father was a baker and chef. His grandmother still lived in Hammersmith, but he got only a few chances to see her because Preston put his planes in the air on practice missions as soon as they reached Bovingdon and kept them there, day after day, until his men were exhausted. He wanted them to learn immediately about the complications of flying in England, where they might meet another plane around the corner from any cloud, and where contact navigation was difficult because English towns, if you were fortunate enough to see them through breaks in the clouds, tended to look alike. Landmarks were not easy to distinguish. Preston also wanted his pilots to come to terms with the English weather. It was a new experience for them on takeoff "to start down the runway in sunshine and before clearing the ground to be in the midst of a downpour."[5]

When the air echelon of the 384th Group reached Prestwick, Scotland, May 24, its commander and flight leader, Col. Budd J. Peaslee, was three hours behind some of his planes. His own plane had lost its No. 4 engine four hundred miles out of Newfoundland. A few days earlier on takeoff from Kearney, Nebraska, en route to England, his plane had lost both the No. 4 and the No. 3 engines. After an immediate forced landing, both were repaired, whereupon the No. 4 died a second time between Kearney and Newfoundland. When it died the third time over the Atlantic, he decided to fly on without it. His decision was vindicated when he reached Scotland safely.[6]

Peaslee's was not the only plane in the 384th to develop trouble over the Atlantic. Battlewagon, piloted by Lt. Philip Algar, lost its ball-turret door, possibly because one of the crewmen inadvertently hit the latch; then Battlewagon's No. 3 engine sprang an oil leak, eventually spewing out all of its thirty-seven quarts onto the wing. The plane was landing at Prestwick, however, by the time the last drop leaked away. The engine hadn't stopped running, and it showed no sign of damage.

To Sgt. L. Corwin Miller, one of the waist gunners in Algar's crew, landing in Prestwick was like landing on a golf course. He had never seen grass so green. Miller and two of his buddies, Sgt. John Schimenek and Sgt. Casmir Majewski, as soon as they could clear the base, took a tram ride into the nearby town of Ayr. The first thing they noticed about the people on the tram was that they "didn't speak good

English at all." The three sergeants had nothing but American money, and after making several inquiries to the Scottish girl who was taking fares, they still didn't know how much of it they had to pay. It wasn't that she was uncommunicative. She had a broad smile on her face and seemed to enjoy talking to them, but they couldn't understand a word she said.

Finally, another American soldier on the tram paid their fares for them and the conductress walked away down the aisle, glancing back at them with a gleam in her eye as she whistled "Deep in the Heart of Texas."[7]

The next day, the planes of the 384th flew down to their permanent base at Grafton-Underwood, or Grafton-Undermud as the men were soon calling it. Within a week, Miller, Schimenek, Majewski, and the rest of the gunners were sent for a refresher course to the gunnery training range at Snettisham, up in the Wash. The commanding officer there was a captain so rigidly devoted to discipline that the men decided he was trying to make general in one jump. The accommodations were primitive, and the food was so atrocious that many of the men developed diarrhea. When one man was late for a class because he didn't dare leave the latrine with the others, the commander punished him severely to make an example of him.

Within a day or so, Colonel Peaslee, hearing about the incident, flew up to Snettisham to look into it, and in front of the captain had the punished gunner explain why he had been late for class.

When the gunner finished, the captain said, "That's no excuse."

"That's excuse enough for me," Colonel Peaslee said, whereupon he earned the gratitude of his men forever by loading them into their planes and leading them back to their base.

On one of Peaslee's first trips to London he encountered his first air raid. He was absorbing the wonders of the blackout—the dim silhouettes of people in the gloom, the speed of the taxis with only slits of light to guide them—when he heard the mournful sound of sirens, saw the searchlights crossing the sky, and was startled by the first bomb blast. Glancing around him, he was amazed to see that none of the shadowy figures on the street seemed in any hurry to escape. People were walking calmly into Underground entrances or simply taking shelter beneath sidewalk overhangs to avoid being hit by the falling shrapnel from their own antiaircraft guns. When taxis stopped, passengers nonchalantly took time to pay their fares before

214

walking toward shelter. Watching these Londoners that night, Peaslee felt he was learning something important about the British people. If they could be this calm in the face of falling bombs, then Hitler had been foolish to think he could scare them into surrender, even during the dark days of 1940 to 1941.

General Eaker's excitement at the promised growth of his air force was tempered on his return to England by the news that General Andrews had been killed in a plane crash against an Icelandic mountain. Eaker had felt affection as well as respect for the senior Air Force officer who had replaced Eisenhower as European Theater commander. During Andrews's short time in London, he had given the 8th Air Force his full support. Fortunately for Eaker, his successor, Lt. Gen. Jacob L. Devers, though a grounds-force officer, was very much air-minded and likely to be helpful.

As the new groups finished training and prepared to enter combat, Eaker's outlook expanded. In early May he formed a new combat wing, the Fourth, under command of Brig. Gen. Fred Anderson, who had come to England with the highest possible recommendation of Arnold's Chief of Air Staff, Maj. Gen. George Stratemeyer. "There is not a finer officer in the world," Stratemeyer had said of Anderson. "When and if you get in any kind of a jam and need some good straightforward, fine-thinking advice, don't ever hesitate to call on this fellow. He's got it, Ira."[8] Anderson's new wing was to include the new 94th, 95th, and 96th groups.

On May 13, Eaker was feeling so cheerful about developments that he wrote an almost euphoric letter to General Arnold: "This is a great day for the 8th Air Force," he said. "Our combat crew availability went up in a straight line today from 100 to 215. That is because the five new groups have finished their two weeks' training and are off this afternoon on their first mission."[9] Eaker was full of enthusiasm for these new groups: "They tell me the five group commanders seem to be excellent men, and the groups possess a much higher state of training than did the earlier groups. If these groups prove to be superior in combat to the old ones, it will scarcely be a fair fight!"

The commanders of whom he wrote were Col. John Moore, 94th Group; Col. Alfred Kessler, 95th; Col. Archie Old, Jr., 96th; Col. William Hatcher, Jr., 351st; and Col. Maurice Preston, 379th.

The 94th, 95th, and 96th made their debuts that day against the airfields at St. Omer, a comparatively easy target. The next day (May

14), they and the 351st joined the older groups in the 8th Air Force's biggest operation to date when, for the first time, more than two hundred planes invaded the Continent. Anderson led two of the new groups against German installations at Antwerp while the two others bombed the airfield at Courtrai. The older groups that day took on a tougher assignment, returning to Germany to bomb the shipyards at Kiel.

Though losses were light in these raids, the Germans were now augmenting their western fighter squadrons. Eaker expected much fiercer resistance to his bombers in the near future. In a letter to Maj. Gen. Oliver P. Echols at Matériel Command in Washington (also May 13), he wrote about improvements then being made in the engines and radios of the P-47 fighter plane, which had so far been less than satisfactory in combat. Despite the plane's problems, Eaker wanted as many of them as he could get.[10]

"It seems to me the P-47 situation has worked out all right with one exception," he told Echols. Then he referred once more to a need that was almost as great as his need for the fighters themselves. "That [exception] concerns the early supply of auxiliary fuel tanks to extend the range of our fighters sufficiently to accompany our bombers to their targets and on their return. . . . I still think the picture is not too gloomy with respect to [the P-47]. I would appreciate it, however, if you would figure out how to get us the auxiliary fuel tanks which will maintain pressure at altitude, and get them here in quantity to extend the range."

Another experiment that acknowledged the vulnerability of the B-17 to German fighters was now at the testing phase. Vega Aircraft Corporation, a Lockheed subsidiary, had been busy since the previous August converting thirteen Flying Fortresses into flying battleships called YB-40s. These planes, equipped with heavy armor plate, fourteen machine guns, and a mechanized chin turret, were designed to carry twice as much ammunition as other B-17s but no bombs. Their function would be to accompany the bomber formations and protect them from German fighters.

The concept of the YB-40 had sounded good. But when Eaker put his thirteen "battleships" into action, he found that their developers had forgotten to do some basic thinking. Because of their added weight, they were too slow to keep pace with the bombers they were

216

supposed to protect.[11] After a few frustrating missions, the YB-40s were retired, undefeated but also unappreciated.

Increasingly anxious for help in his campaign to gain long-range fighter support for his bombers, Eaker took advantage of a visit by Robert A. Lovett, Assistant Secretary of War for Air, who arrived in London May 13 to look at what the 8th Air Force was doing. Eaker was ready for Lovett, meeting him at the train when he arrived from Prestwick (the weather prevented flying between Scotland and England that day) and moving him right into his own Castle Coombe home for the duration of his stay. The general had also prepared his staff and his wing and group commanders for the Secretary's arrival.[12] On each base he visited, Lovett was told first by the commanders, then by fighter pilots and bomber crews, one after another, that they had to have long-range fighters. Though many of them spoke about the newly improved P-51, of which they were beginning to hear rumors, their more practical hopes centered on getting suitable auxiliary tanks and other improvements for their P-47s.

When Lovett returned to Washington, he wrote two memoranda to General Arnold (June 18 and 19) setting forth his appraisal of the 8th Air Force and its needs on the basis of what he had seen and what he had been told. These memoranda, which were to have a significant effect on the future development of the air war in Europe, reflected the prevalent attitudes of Eaker and his men in May 1943.

Lovett began his first memo by pointing out that he had visited all the fighter groups and talked to "a large proportion" of the fighter pilots, of which there were now more than one hundred in General Hunter's Fighter Command.[13] They had given Lovett a precise comparison between their P-47s and the FW-190s and ME-109s, which they had begun battling above the Channel and the continental coastal region. The P-47, they said, was "faster than the Focke-Wulf at altitude and in the dive," but it was inferior "in rate of climb, angle of climb, search vision, and simplicity of control." They believed they had an edge on the FW-190 "in firepower and in any combat where they start with an initial height advantage."

At the time of Lovett's visit, the P-47s had experienced very limited contact with the latest (G-model) ME-109, but the pilots were much impressed by it. "The majority of the experienced pilots feel that the 109G has a definite edge on them in all the important fighter

217

characteristics and they will, therefore, have to adjust their tactics accordingly.''

Their suggestions for improving the P-47 included larger propellers to increase climb rate and general performance, water injection boosters for emergency power, a canopy bulge for better rear visibility, more flexible rudder controls, and ''belly tanks with adequate pumps to operate at altitudes of 30,000 feet or over.'' As a result of his visit, Lovett had come to some specific conclusions about the use of fighters in the European Theater:

> It is increasingly apparent that fighter escort will have to be provided for B-17s on as many missions as possible in order particularly to get them through the first wave of the German fighter defense, which is now put up in depth so that the B-17s are forced to run the gauntlet both into the target and out from it. The P-47s can serve as top cover if satisfactory belly tanks are developed for them. The ideal plane, however, now in production is the P-38 for long escort duty. Its two engines are a definite advantage and, strangely enough, its ease of recognition is a definite protection to both B-17s and the escorting fighters themselves.

In time, the two-engines on the Lockheed twin-fuselage P-38 and the large size of the plane were to create problems for it against the smaller but more maneuverable German fighters. Lovett's predictions for it were too optimistic. The last paragraph of his memo, however, contained a seemingly offhand remark that would one day prove to have greater import than anything else he had said:

> High hopes are felt for the P-51 with wing tanks. The 8th Air Force needs from three to five groups of P-38s and some P-51s in order to meet the increasing opposition it is facing and will face on an ascending scale during the balance of this year.

The only miscalculation in Lovett's prophecy was his estimate of the number of P-51s the 8th Air Force would need. In the early summer of 1943, neither he nor anyone else could foresee just how important this airplane, improved by the installation of the Rolls

218

Royce Merlin engine, was destined to become in the air war over Germany.

Lovett's second memo to Arnold (June 19) listed what he found to be the most urgent needs of the 8th Air Force. These included more replacement crews and more forward firing power for the B-17s. The new crews should receive better training in gunnery and in formation flight above 20,000 feet.

"If these urgent needs are promptly met," Lovett told Arnold, "the operational efficiency of the 8th Air Force will, in my opinion, increase by at least 50 percent."[14]

Even such an operational improvement, however, would not suffice to see the 8th Air Force safely through the year. In conclusion, Lovett referred again to the most urgent requirement of all: "There is an immediate need for long-range fighters. This may be met by proper tanks for P-47s, but ultimately P-38s and P-51s will be needed."

It is difficult to measure accurately Arnold's reaction to Lovett's memoranda. In his postwar book, *Global Mission*, Arnold wrote: "It may be said that we could have had the long-range P-51 in Europe rather sooner than we did. That we did not have it sooner was the Air Force's own fault."[15]

Initially this fault lay with the Matériel Division, which was indifferent to the Mustang when the plane was being developed for the British, and then with the Wright Field experts who believed the plumbing of liquid-cooled engines would be too vulnerable to bullets. In the autumn of 1942, both the British and the Americans had conducted tests that established the splendid capabilities of the Merlin Mustang. But by this time the American Air Force fighter budget and most of the available fighter manufacturing facilities in the United States were committed to the P-47 and P-38. (Though the P-38 also had liquid-cooled engines, it was considered less vulnerable than the P-51 because of its two engines. It could survive even if one failed.)

In the early days of the war, Arnold, like Eaker and others, had no doubt underestimated the eventual need for fighters. The success of the first B-17 missions seemed to provide convincing evidence that the plane could take care of itself. But after only two months of combat Eaker had begun asking about auxiliary tanks to extend the range of the few fighters he then had. By the end of 1942, Arnold was aware of the need for long-range escort. He also knew by then about the problems of the P-47 and the potential of the P-51. Could the shortcomings of the P-47 be solved? It seemed likely. And it was now in mass production. It would be ready for combat long before the P-51 could be produced in numbers. The need for fighters of any kind, especially in Europe, was growing so rapidly by spring and summer of 1943 that it might seem foolish to disrupt or diminish P-47 production in favor of a heavy commitment to the P-51. In any case, there is no indication that Lovett's memoranda prompted Arnold to immediate action in that direction.

June of 1943 was a difficult month both for Arnold and Eaker. Arnold had been fighting the Battle of Washington, especially against the Navy, for a year and a half, and it hadn't helped his heart condition. He had been forced into his two-week Florida vacation at the same time Eaker, in renewed operations against the German West Wall defenses, was discovering that the enemy fighter forces on the continent were bigger, tougher, and more clever than they had been in the early months of the year. The war was subjecting both men to pressures they had never before experienced, and for the first time during their long association, their professional relationship began to threaten their personal friendship.

In late April when Eaker was in Washington for the presentation of the Combined Bomber Offensive Plan to the Joint Chiefs of Staff, Arnold had told him he didn't think very highly of some of the key men in his command.[16] Arnold was especially critical of Eaker's bomber commander, Brig. Gen. Newton Longfellow, and the Bomber Command's chief of staff, Col. Charles Bubb.[17] Some of the wing and group commanders disliked Longfellow. He was an officer with estimable abilities, but when things went wrong he so frequently lost his temper that his men referred to him as "the screaming eagle." Eaker, having known Longfellow since they served together in 1919 in the Philippines and then traveled around the world together, admired his abilities and considered him equal to the job of bomber commander.

Arnold seemed to feel that in this instance Eaker's notorious loyalty to his friends was clouding his judgment. Influenced, perhaps, by reports of discontent, Arnold had decided Longfellow was a poor risk as bomber commander and said so. He also believed

Eaker needed better officers in several other command and staff positions, but he didn't press the matter during his conversations with Eaker in Washington.

Shortly after Eaker's return to London in early May, he had realized uneasily that the issue was not settled. At his first meeting with General Devers, the new Theater commander had said to him, "They tell me in Washington you don't have much help over here."[18]

Arnold was obviously the original source of Devers's remark. Eaker, bristling with anger, told Devers it was "a gross slander on some mighty fine officers who had done some very hard work." At the same time, Eaker was well enough acquainted with Arnold's persistence to realize that if he wanted to put the matter at rest, he would have to agree to at least some changes. With Devers's approval, Eaker sent a cable May 13 asking for several new officers, many of them specialists in maintenance and supply, crucial areas of concern both to him and to Arnold.

The fact that the 8th Air Force had so many new airplanes increased its maintenance problems not only because of the greater numbers but also because with the new planes had come largely untried mechanics. A tragic accident at Alconbury on the evening of May 27 demonstrated that rookies on the ground could be as dangerous as rookies in the air. Mechanics of the new 95th Group there were loading and fusing 500-pound bombs for the next day's mission when several of the bombs exploded, one after another, until the area looked as if it had been the target of a German air raid. Nineteen men were killed, twenty seriously injured, and fourteen slightly injured. Four Flying Fortresses were totally destroyed and eleven others damaged.

German fighter resistance was also intensifying as the summer progressed, thus increasing the number of aircraft damaged in combat as well as destroyed and heightening the problem of getting damaged planes back in operation. Robert Lovett noticed that 80 percent of the planes used on missions during his two and one-half weeks in England were damaged to some extent. "The greatest single factor differentiating the 8th Air Force operations from those of other theaters," he declared in one of his memos to Arnold, "is the extremely high proportion of battle damage resulting from combat with the best of the German fighters."[19] Battle damage and repair difficulties were almost as effective as the British weather in keeping the big bombers on the ground. If the maintenance and repair problems could be solved satisfactorily, Arnold might gradually forget his determination to have Longfellow replaced.

Eaker, while reluctant to lose Longfellow, was now becoming almost eager to lose his fighter commander, Brig. Gen. Frank Hunter, whose dismissal Arnold had never suggested. Eaker had developed a truly substantive problem with Hunter. In fact he was having almost as much trouble with his fighter commander as he was with his less-than-adequate P-47 fighter planes. He and Hunter profoundly disagreed about the best use of fighters. Hunter, a World War I fighter pilot and a highly respected tactician, believed the most effective tactic for fighters was to sweep an area and clear out the opposition, thus enabling the bombers to fly through unmolested. Eaker, though once a fighter man himself, was now so much concerned about his bombers that he believed the fighters should accompany them in close formation, above, to each side, and below, in an effort to hold off the Germans en route to and from the target.[20]

Eaker's argument was slightly hampered by the fact that the P-47s available to them lacked the range to penetrate more than a few miles into the continent. But even though this fighter couldn't go all the way with the bombers, he insisted that if Hunter and his pilots would change their policies they could go much farther than they were presently going. The plane's range was supposed to be 300 to 400 miles with the 200-gallon drop-tanks Eaker had got from the States. This range took into account the high use during formation flying, at least twenty minutes for actual combat, and a comfortable reserve if the planes cruised at about 75 percent of maximum power.[21]

In practice, the P-47s with drop tanks had shown a range of only about 170 miles, and Hunter's policy of sweeping an area rather than patroling a corridor was only one factor responsible for this limitation. More important was his understandable fear that if his planes took off overloaded with extra gasoline, they would be too slow to cope with the Germans, and his pilots would be burned up as well as shot down. This consideration had led him at first to oppose the use of any auxiliary tanks. When he eventually agreed they were necessary, he remained unenthusiastic about them. In fact, no one was very enthusiastic about the type of auxiliary tank available at that time. Besides lowering the plane's speed and maneuverability, the tank was difficult to install and didn't work very efficiently at high altitudes. But Eaker was certain that if used cleverly it could be more helpful than it was. He wanted the fighters to climb to maximum ceiling and fly as far as possible on their drop tanks, even avoiding combat if necessary until those tanks were emptied and released.

It was standard operating procedure for Hunter's pilots to drop their heavy belly tanks as soon as they reached ceiling, even though as much as eighty gallons of gasoline remained in them. The pilots were in a hurry to get rid of them because they were also eager to use up, before going into combat, the fuel in another auxiliary tank, which was directly behind their seats. This tank's proximity to the pilot made him uncomfortably aware of being a potential human torch, and the weight of the gasoline there altered the plane's performance unfavorably by shifting the center of gravity.

While a fighter pilot undoubtedly increased his risk to some degree by engaging in combat with the tank behind him full of fuel, the bomber crews were already increasing their risks by flying missions unescorted most of the way. And it was the bombers that were doing the primary, essential job of attacking important enemy installations. What was the purpose of the fighter planes if not to protect them? What good were the fighters when the bombers were getting credit for almost all of the enemy planes shot down? Hunter, concerned about his young pilots, fended off these arguments, insisting that his men wouldn't be able to accomplish what Eaker expected of them until they had more experience.

Because Eaker had no one in England qualified to replace Hunter, he had been slow to resolve this issue.[22] But in early June, faced with the evident build-up of German fighter strength in western Europe, he decided he had to settle the matter. He asked Arnold to send him a new fighter commander and suggested two candidates. One was Maj. Gen. Barney M. Giles, at present an aide to Arnold; the other was Maj. Gen. William Kepner, a tough, able fighter expert.[23]

By the time Eaker sent his unsolicited request for a new fighter commander, more than a month had elapsed since Arnold's suggestion that he find a new bomber commander. Eaker soon received a letter (June 11) not from Arnold but from Giles, who apparently wanted to warn him about Arnold's frame of mind. Arnold had returned from Florida only a few days earlier and, according to Giles, looked in the best of health. "No doubt the badly needed rest did him a great deal of good."[24] As Giles very well knew, however, despite

223

the vacation, Arnold's heart condition was still precarious and his patience was limited. Though Giles didn't mention it in his letter, the 8th Air Force hadn't flown a mission since May 29. This lapse was understandable because the weather had been prohibitive every day, but it didn't improve Arnold's mood. He had spent a lot of his personal energy and ingenuity getting planes for Eaker's organization. With these planes finally arriving in England, he wanted some quick results. Instead, he was getting long weather delays between missions, aggravated maintenance problems, and now, a request for a new fighter commander. In Arnold's opinion, Eaker's greatest need was for a new bomber commander, a man who could get those B-17s in the air despite the weather and despite certain equipment shortages.

In Giles's letter to Eaker, he didn't mention the request for a new fighter commander, even though he himself was one of the men suggested for the job. He wrote instead about what was on Arnold's mind, warning Eaker rather pointedly that the big man was not very happy:

> General Arnold has been much concerned and, as you know, sent you two or three cablegrams reference the small number of heavy bombers reported ready and actually used for combat. I pointed out to him that a large number of your groups were very new and that a number of your combat crews had recently arrived in your theater.
>
> General Arnold believes that you are especially weak in your Chief of Staff and your Bomber Commander.

While Arnold continued to worry about the bomber commander, Eaker was still more concerned about the situation in his fighter command, and he now received help from another source in his quest for a new man. One of Arnold's brightest young aides and a member of his Advisory Council, Col. Emmet "Rosey" O'Donnell, had listened to the Eaker-Hunter debate during a visit to England. Back in Washington, he wrote a memo to Arnold June 12 entitled "Ineffective Fighter Support to Bombardment in the U.K."

The fighters, O'Donnell said, were not doing the bombers much good. The P-47s hadn't yet suffered many losses, but on the other hand, they hadn't shot down many enemy planes. After describing the situation as he found it, he said, "If the P-47 airplane does not actually have the ability to escort on fairly deep penetrations, we have been badly fooled and our planning is extremely faulty. . . . The large number of fighters we have allocated to the U.K. are not paying their way if their participation in the bomber offensive comprises escort across the Channel only. This in effect simply insures the bombers' safe delivery into the hands of the wolves."

O'Donnell attached to this memo a cable that he suggested Arnold send to Eaker. But Arnold was not inclined to take action that day on the fighter-command issue. He was thinking about bombers, and he was convinced that with the number of B-17s now available, 8th Bomber Command should be sending out more planes per mission. The previous day, June 11, 252 Fortresses had hit Wilhelmshaven, but this was the first mission since May 29. It would seem that after a thirteen-day hiatus, a greater number of planes should have been ready to go. From Arnold's viewpoint in Washington, it was hard to accept explanations for all the difficulties developing day by day in England, especially since they were of a size and type never before encountered by an American air combat unit. He was convinced the maintenance problem was basically a personnel problem and that the men under Eaker were to blame.

On the 12th, Arnold fired off to Eaker a cable "further relative to" a previous cable on the "low percentage of airplanes your organization has been able to keep in commission." If Eaker was already having maintenance trouble with his present force, he asked, how much more trouble would he have when he received "the very large additional number of airplanes assigned to your theater within the next few months?" What Eaker needed, he insisted was a "clearcut supply and maintenance plan" and "an air service commander with sufficient initiative, force, and executive ability to carry out this plan."

Within the next three days, Arnold had received an answer from Eaker explaining once more why he could send out only 250 planes in one day, how much work was required to maintain aircraft in combat, how long it took to repair and patch bullet-riddled planes, and how easy it was to run short of combat crews. But Arnold also knew by that time the sorry results of the June 11 Wilhelmshaven raid in which

225

one of the lead planes, hit by flak on the bomb run, almost collided with several others, scattering the formations behind it and thereby also scattering the bombs. And he had time to learn about the disastrous strike against the Kiel submarine yards two days later in which fighter resistance was so strong only sixteen planes managed to bomb the harbor area and twenty-six were lost, some of them because crewmen of the 94th Group, nearing home and convinced there would be no more action, were cleaning their guns when the last wave of German fighters struck. Arnold was not in a good mood as he sat down to write Eaker June 15:

> All reports I have received have admitted that your maintenance over there is not satisfactory and yet you have not taken any steps to recommend removal of those responsible, nor have you attempted to put in men who can do the job.

Arnold realized, he said, that the new planes had to be modified and the damaged planes had to be repaired. He knew it took time to get crews ready for operations, but he didn't know how there could be a shortage of them:

> I do know that we have been sending over quite a few combat crews month after month. I also realize that when you lose a plane over Germany, the crew goes with it, but I cannot accept the fact that when a plane is shot up the whole crew is knocked out. There must be some salvage and from this salvage we should be able to make up crews which can operate.

In a handwritten afterthought, he threatened that if Eaker had no partial crews to build around, if all new crews had to come from the States, then such crews would be sent piecemeal, and no new heavy-bomb groups would come as units from August to December. He did not mention what this policy would do to his own creation, the Combined Bomber Offensive, which was behind schedule because Eaker had received only seven hundred of the nine hundred planes already due him under the original plan. Arnold concluded this letter with a fatherly lecture that could hardly have pleased Eaker or heightened his sense of job security:

226

I am willing to do anything possible to build up your forces but you must play your part. My wire [of the previous day] was sent to you to get you to toughen up—to can these fellows who cannot produce—to put in youngsters who can carry the ball. I will send over Kepner but I cannot let you have Giles. . . . In any event, a definite change seems in order but you have to be tough to handle the situation.

This is a long letter but I am writing it because I want you to come out of this as a real commander. You have performed an excellent job but there are times when you will have to be tough. So be tough . . .

Arnold hoped in closing that Eaker would accept the letter ''in the spirit in which it is written,'' and Eaker might have done so had he been more confident of the spirit in which it was written. But a short time after it arrived, Averell Harriman was in England and told Eaker that Arnold, while not ''inimical'' to him either ''personally or officially,'' was nevertheless critical of some of his methods. Then on June 26, Eaker received a cable from Arnold that seemed to blame him for waiting too long before replacing Hunter as fighter commander. And on June 28, Eaker received a letter from Robert Lovett in Washington that repeated essentially the same things Harriman had said about Arnold's frame of mind.

Eaker, who already had enough trouble coping with his British allies and German enemies, didn't need any more trouble from his old friend Hap Arnold. The next day he wrote Arnold a chilly five-page letter that would either cost him his job or clear the air. It covered all the matters at issue between them, both professional and personal:

Regarding the Bomber Command, Longfellow and Bubb will be relieved July 1st and replaced by [Brig. Gen. Fred L.] Anderson as Commander and Colonel [John A.] Samford as Chief of Staff. . . . I will never agree that there has, until recently, been anybody in this Command better qualified for the Bomber Command, who was available to me to take Longfellow's place. Anderson had to be brought along very fast to be ready by July 1st. . . . This Bomber Command job of ours is a man-killer. It will break any-

227

body down in six months unless he be a very unusual fellow. . . .

Regarding the Fighter Commander, Hunter was definitely the only man I had for that job. I believe Kepner will make a good man in Fighter Command but I cannot put him into the job without some experience and indoctrination in this theater. I have talked the whole situation over with Hunter and he understands the position thoroughly. . . . He still insists that it was absolutely necessary, having new men and a new plane, to break them in gradually. I thought, along with Tooey [Spaatz], that the situation was so critical for fighter support for our bombardment effort that we should have taken more of a chance with our fighters, and I have continually urged Hunter to greater boldness in this regard. I must admit, however, that Hunter's system is now paying results. His fighter pilots have high morale; they are enthusiastic about supporting the bombers and they have complete confidence. . . . The principal handicap, of course, to full and thorough support of the bombers has been the lack of long-range [fuel] tanks. . . .

Regarding the Air Service Commander . . . I agree fully that it is very important to get Hugh Knerr here as soon as possible. The arrival in recent times of more than 15,000 Air Service Command personnel, including depot groups and station complements, will greatly improve this situation.

Col. Hugh Knerr was a maintenance and matériel expert who had recently visited England to figure out how damaged aircraft might be repaired more quickly. His idea—to send mobile repair units to the planes instead of shipping the planes to a depot—was so simple but so brilliantly practical that Eaker had asked Arnold to send Knerr back permanently.

With the addition of Anderson, Kepner, and Knerr, the 8th Air Force command structure would undoubtedly be strengthened. But how long would Eaker himself be around to direct this new team? Reflecting on his recent relations with Arnold and on Arnold's well-known penchant for shaking up the men under him, Eaker could well ask himself that question. He decided he had better, in effect, ask it of Arnold:

Averell Harriman talked to me the day after his return about his two conferences with you. His conversations, plus your own recent letters, lead me to make the following comment quite frankly and after careful consideration.

Regarding our personal relation, I have always felt the closest bond of friendship between us as two individuals. I have never thought that you placed quite the confidence in me officially as an officer, as you did as a friend. I sometimes thought that you were tough on me officially in order to make certain that nobody had a feeling that I got the positions I held through our personal friendship, and to make doubly sure that you did not allow that friendship to influence you unduly toward me officially.

. . . I shall always accept gladly and in the proper spirit, any advice, counsel or criticism from you. I do not feel, however, that my past service which has come under your observation indicates that I am a horse which needs to be ridden with spurs. I think you know that I will do my best, not only for you but because I realize the importance in this War and to our Air Force of the job I have to do here. Naturally, I am working pretty hard and under considerable strain. . . . We have been through a very dark period and we are not entirely out of the wood yet, but I think we will make the grade in one of the toughest spots imaginable if I can maintain your confidence and backing.

A week later Arnold sent Eaker what might be called a vote of confidence. In a July 7 letter, he was at great pains to point out the high regard in which he held the 8th Air Force commander:

I want you to get this firmly in your mind that had I not had confidence in you—confidence in your ability, I would never have built you up for the job that you now have. I give you full credit for having the inherent ability—the knowledge and judgment that goes with the command that you now hold. That being the case, I see no reason in the world for any fears or suspicion as to our relationship entering your mind. But you must know me well enough by this time to know that I am very outspoken. I say what I think and do what I think best, so when you hear these rumors, comments, criticisms, or what-have-you, always remember that if there is anything serious you will be the first one to hear of it and it will come from me direct.[25]

229

On casual reading this sounded like a forthright statement, but what exactly did it mean? It didn't actually say Eaker's position was secure. It simply reaffirmed their close personal relationship and promised that if he were ever to be dismissed, he would hear it from Arnold first. In other words, Arnold was still his friend, but their friendship would not save him if he failed to deliver.

13

Eaker's B-17s encountered one of the most dreaded hazards of precision bombing June 28 when a diversionary force of more than fifty planes flew to Brussels to bomb the German fighter facilities at the airfield there while the main force was hitting the harbor at St. Nazaire. The Brussels mission was delicate because the airfield was on the edge of the city. The danger of bombing a populated area was acute. American crews had been warned that they were inviting courts-martial anytime they dropped a bomb on French, Belgian, or Dutch civilians. The best approach to the airfield was over the city, however, because it was known that there were fewer antiaircraft batteries along that route. The Germans did not waste antiaircraft artillery defending the populations of occupied cities, especially since they were aware of the Allied policy to leave such cities alone.

Realizing it was the safest route, Gen. Robert Williams, commander of the First Bombardment Wing, had expressly directed the three groups to fly over Brussels on the way to the airfield.[1]

As they moved through the clear blue skies above the city, the B-17s encountered no flak, no opposition of any kind since the German fighters stationed at the field were apparently many miles away, attacking the St. Nazaire force. With Col. Budd Peaslee and his 384th Group in the lead and two other groups in a column of formations behind, the Fortresses flew directly across the center of Brussels on their bomb run. The bomb-bay doors of all the planes were open. The bombardiers in every plane had taken control and were carefully checking their bomb-sights, ready to release their loads the moment the lead bombardier in each group released his load.

Just ahead now, in one of Brussels' better residential districts, was a beautiful rectangular green park surrounded by fine homes. The 384th Group passed this park and Colonel Peaslee, in the lead plane, was looking back at it when he noticed a terrible mistake in progress. One of the two groups behind his had released all of its bombs, presumably on the signal of that group's lead bombardier. The park and the houses at its edge suddenly exploded "in a mighty series of bomb bursts." Peaslee's bombardier shouted over the interphone, "My God! Someone has bombed the city!"

While smoke and flames arose from the stricken area, the B-17s continued on to the airfield where the 384th dropped its bombs as did the one other group that hadn't already done so. When the three groups reached home, Peaslee didn't yet know which of the other two had committed the unspeakable offense or who was responsible for it. He didn't even want to know who had done it, but General Williams wanted to know. Two days later, all the commanders and the key men (pilots, bombardiers, and navigators) of the lead crews were summoned to his headquarters at Brompton. The gray-haired general looked stern as he entered the room where these men were assembled. With his one good eye, he glanced at them sharply. A critique of the St. Nazaire mission came first, then it was time to talk about Brussels.

A young major stood up and came to the rostrum, his face pale and his fists clenched. Addressing General Williams and staff, he said, "Gentlemen, our part of this mission was flown as planned until, on the bomb run, our bombs were released prematurely and we bombed the city. My bombardier will tell you how it happened."

A slight, blond first lieutenant who looked barely twenty years old stepped forward and explained the dreadful mistake as best he could. All of his switches had been on as they should have been. To check his drift, he had sighted on the park at the center of the city. Then he had looked up from his instruments toward the airfield target ahead. Suddenly he felt the lift that accompanies a bomb release, and when he looked down, he saw his bombs falling. Then he saw the bombs of his whole group, also falling.

"I was panic stricken," he said. "It was like a bad dream, but I could not wake up. I wanted to die. It's still a bad dream and I still can't wake up."

When General Williams arose from his chair he said, "Gentlemen, you are all aware of the seriousness of what has happened." He reminded them of how often they had been cautioned against dropping bombs on friendly people in occupied cities. He pointed out that the principals in this case were liable and courts-martial appeared warranted. He also pointed out that he himself felt some responsibility because he had directed the task force to avoid flak by flying over the city. But that did not make the matter less serious. It was so serious, he said, that it had been investigated by a higher command "through agents in Belgium and other intelligence sources." He paused, and his audience listened as if awaiting a verdict.

"Gentlemen," he said, "we find the results are not so bad as had at first been feared. We are informed that the German occupation command considered the park area and the better-class adjoining residences an excellent locale for the billeting of troops. The entire circumference of the park was used for this purpose. We are informed there were 1,200 casualties among these forces and only a few Belgians were injured or killed. Across the Channel this accident is being called a remarkable exhibition of American precision bombing. Such are the fortunes of war. This meeting and the incident are now closed."

The "fortunes of war" were seldom this generous to the men of the 8th Air Force. Their task was rigorous and becoming more so. The loss rate for the first six months of 1943 offered an ominous hint of the troubles the 8th could expect. From the beginning of January to the end of June, an average of 6.6 percent of its attacking heavy bombers were shot down, and 35.5 percent were damaged to some degree. For the first four and a half months of the 8th's operations over Europe, August through December of 1942, the average had been 4 percent lost and 34 percent damaged. The Germans were now showing how much more aggressively they would defend their fatherland than France and the Low Countries.

When General Eaker studied these loss trends, he realized his predicament. First of all, even though he now had fifteen heavy groups under his command, he was running short of bombers. And General Arnold in Washington didn't seem to realize it. Arnold, in his June 15 letter, had stated flatly that the 8th then had "a total of 851 B-17s and B-24s." This figure was apparently reached by subtracting the number of planes reported lost from the number he had sent to England. It did not measure with any accuracy the number disabled by serious damage. Actually only 275 heavy bombers were operational July 4, when they hit Le Mans, Nantes, and La Palisse after a five-day weather lull.

Combat was not the only threat to the strength of the 8th. Its growth had been slowed by the two-hundred-plane lag in delivery of bombers promised (or at least projected) under the terms of the Combined Bomber Offensive Plan. None of its four groups "temporarily" diverted to Africa had been returned. And now talk in high circles suggested diverting several B-17 groups to an operation against the German navy. Eaker fervently petitioned Arnold to resist such a move.

The increasing losses and shortage of planes heightened Eaker's realization of the dire need for long-range fighters. Though the 200-gallon American drop tank had proven less than satisfactory on the P-47, he entertained hopes for a 110-gallon British paper tank that had been tested satisfactorily on the Spitfire. The British had agreed to give him 1,500 of these tanks by mid-July. But an extra 110 gallons would hardly be enough fuel to make the P-47 a long-range fighter.

At the same time, Robert Lovett, in response to requests made when he was in England, promised to send some new American belly tanks with pumps that would make them work even above 30,000 feet.[2] But these were 75-gallon and 150-gallon tanks. If and when they arrived, they would also be too small. For the immediate future, if the Flying Fortresses were to continue going very deep into Germany, they would have to go alone. Since German fighter strength in northwest Europe had grown from 270 to more than 500 in the three months between April and July,[3] the big American bombers would be in for some very rough afternoons. It was quite possible that, before the end of summer, the losses could become prohibitive.

Eaker, realizing now how vulnerable unescorted B-17s could be against mass attacks by Germany's best fighter squadrons, knew that he had to send the bombers anyway. The war would not wait until conditions were favorable for him. He and Arnold and dozens of other American Air Force spokesmen had promised on countless occasions that if they had enough heavy bombers, they would be able to destroy great numbers of important German targets in daylight attacks. Though Eaker did not yet have as many bombers as he had stipulated in the Combined Bomber Offensive Plan, he had nevertheless a sizable force. And he couldn't let those bombers sit on the ground while German industry was turning out more warplanes, more oil, more synthetic rubber, more vehicles, more ball bearings.

The British were still skeptical about the basic U.S. Air Force strategy of daylight bombing, and so were many Americans in high places. If this strategy was not viable, why were all these American planes taking up so much British airspace and airfield space. If they weren't useful against the Germans, why weren't they in the Pacific, helping the Navy defeat Japan? The daylight strategy had to be proven, and it had to be proven this summer. Winston Churchill wasn't likely to wait much longer for proof that it would work, and neither was Franklin Roosevelt, nor General Arnold, nor the U.S. Navy, which had a very legitimate claim to Air Force planes if the Air Force was not prepared to use them.

Eaker had promised an offensive and he had to deliver it. With or without long-range fighter support, 8th Air Force bombers had to plunge deeper and deeper into Germany in an effort to wipe out Hitler's war-making capability. But it would be costly. Eaker knew that, as he said in his June 29 letter to Arnold:

One of my principal worries now is that our official supporters in the highest levels, and our supporting public, may not be able to stand our losses in combat. I want you to know that we can stand them and that we are doing everything possible here to keep them at the minimum. I hope you can keep everybody in line there so that we can go through with this battle, which is a necessary prelude to any future effort against the Germans on the continent. . . . It is perfectly evident now that the Germans admit that our daylight bombing against their industry is the principal threat, and they are marshaling their strongest and best defenses to cope with it. We may as well frankly admit that it is going to be a bloody battle.

235

Eaker had based his estimate of German reaction on the ever-increasing fighter resistance against his bombers and on intelligence reports of the German fighter build-up in northwest Europe. After the war, German sources indicated that their fighter strength in France and the Low Countries had increased from 270 in April 1943 to 630 by the end of July.[4] Eaker may have been premature in his assertion to Arnold that the Germans now considered the 8th Air Force "the principal threat." But there was no doubt that the Germans were deeply impressed by the U.S. heavy bombers.

In mid-July, Eaker made one more effort to counter the German build-up. Another of Arnold's envoys, Gen. Delos C. Emmons, came to England to inspect the 8th Air Force, and Eaker told him exactly what he most needed. Emmons then sent a cable to Washington making several suggestions, with special attention to the fighter situation:

> German fighters are not being interfered with to much extent by [U.S] fighters in close and area support and are operating with near maximum effectiveness. One of the best ways to support our bombardment in this theater is to attack German fighters while they are taking off, refueling, and landing. Our fighters are not now bombing and strafing hostile airdromes because of the shortage of fighters and the unsuitability of the P-47 for this type of work. Recommend that the P-51 with Merlin engine be supplied this theater in the proportion recommended by Eaker for this and other purposes.[5]

Arnold was now fully aware of the capability of the Merlin-powered Mustang. He put in his first order for P-51s to be sent to England. But the order was for only 181 of them, and they would not be delivered until late autumn.

Eighth Air Force planners, meanwhile, had begun in late June to work out the details of the long-contemplated mission against the crucially important ball-bearing factories at Schweinfurt. British planners at the Ministry of Economic Warfare (M.E.W.) had marked Schweinfurt as a prime candidate for attack since the brutally successful German raid, early in the war, against a ball-bearing plant at Chelmsford, thirty miles northeast of London.[6] The Germans had hit a plant that specialized in bearings for aircraft production, causing enough damage to delay the flow of Spitfire fighters and Lancaster bombers. They created a ball-bearing shortage in England that was overcome only after a large purchase from the United States. The M.E.W. believed that if the partial destruction of one ball-bearing factory could hurt England that much, the destruction of the five plants at Schweinfurt could be catastrophic for the Germans, since those plants made up to two-thirds of Germany's ball and roller bearings.

When Air Marshal Harris and his Bomber Command associates belittled this idea, insisting that their bombers at night wouldn't be able even to locate a town of fifty thousand people deep in Bavaria, the M.E.W. planners had turned eagerly to the day-bombing Americans, among whom they had found all the enthusiasm lacking at Harris's headquarters. From then on, Eaker and his target-selection specialist, Col. Richard D. Hughes (a British-born American citizen) had been eagerly awaiting the day when a Schweinfurt mission would be practicable.

In Washington, General Arnold became almost euphoric about the possibilities. In a March 25, 1943, letter to Harry Hopkins at the White House, Arnold said, ". . . it is considered that a stoppage, or a marked curtailment, of the production of ball bearings would probably wreck all German industry." Arnold was getting his enthusiasm not only from Eaker directly but from his own Operations Analysts' group, which had also been indoctrinated by the M.E.W.

The M.E.W. had prepared, in 1942, a "Bombers' Baedeker," which contained all the information available about every potential target in Germany and the whole of occupied Europe. Through intelligence sources as well as aerial reconnaissance photography, they kept their status files up to date on all the important targets, placing special emphasis on what they called "bottlenecks"—industries upon which all other industries depended. Oil was one of these and communcations was another, but both of these industries were diffuse. And in the case of oil, the principal facilities were in southeastern Europe, far beyond the range of airplanes based in England. Of all the "bottleneck" industries, the ball bearing was considered the best target for destruction because the bulk of it was concentrated in one place, Schweinfurt, where the techniques of mass-producing balls and bearings had been invented.

The status of Schweinfurt as a potential target was therefore under constant review. In November 1942, M.E.W. estimated that 52 percent of Germany's current ball-bearing production came from the factories there. Postwar German sources indicate that this estimate was low and that Schweinfurt was producing closer to 65 percent, including most of the highly specialized precision bearings that were indispensable to the war effort.[7] But even the 52 percent assessment made Schweinfurt an apparently irresistible target.

It was a source of constant frustration to M.E.W. experts, however, that Harris found Schweinfurt so easily resistible. When he argued that his bombers wouldn't be able to find it at night, they suggested that British agents on the ground might plant portable radio transmitters that would lead the bombers to it. Harris also found this suggestion impractical and resistible.

M.E.W. did, however, have some friends at the Air Ministry. Portal, who had been deputized at Casablanca as the final authority on target priorities both for the R.A.F. and the A.A.F., fully appreciated the value of M.E.W. assessments. Though he couldn't prevail upon the fiercely independent Harris to make much use of them, he did encourage the Americans to do so. It was Portal, in his target-selecting capacity, who issued the official order for the Schweinfurt attack, although that order was prearranged with Eaker, who was also eager to undertake the mission. Eaker's enthusiasm was indicated by his plan to go on it personally, a plan that was abandoned only when the European Theater commander, General Devers, expressly ordered him not to go.

The most ardent M.E.W. supporter at the Air Ministry was Air Commodore Sidney O. Bufton, Director of Bomber Operations on the Air Staff. It was ironic that a man with such a title should have been almost without influence at Bomber Command, but Bufton, as an advocate of selective strategic targets, was anathema to Harris, who didn't even want Bufton visiting the bomber squadrons or trying to influence them with his views about strategic bombing.

Bufton's ideas were welcomed, however, by such American intelligence officers as Col. Richard Hughes and Col. Harris Hull. Bufton took an active part in preparing the 8th Air Force for its thrust against Schweinfurt, which was scheduled to take place on the first day of favorable weather after July 17. Together with the M.E.W., his office provided 8th Bomber Command with all the information necessary to prepare special maps and build plaster mock-ups of the target area. And on July 15, he made one more attempt to commit British Bomber Command to a follow-up night attack against Schweinfurt a few hours after the American day attack. Surely the British bombers would be able to find the place after the Americans set it afire. But Harris was still not interested. His mind was on another very important target—the German secret-weapon research laboratory and factory at Peenemünde on the Baltic. He said later, ''I knew very well that the Germans were preparing all sorts of secret weapons against England, and that these would give us a very bad time indeed unless we could get the enemy down first and destroy his industries.''[8]

Among these destroyable industries, Harris did not include the ball-bearing factories at Schweinfurt. He referred to most of the so-called ''bottleneck'' industries as ''panacea targets'' and spoke contemptuously of the hope that the destruction of any one industry, however essential, would paralyze Germany. He didn't believe in attacking ''panacea targets'' because he didn't believe there were such things. He was convinced the Germans had stockpiled indispensable supplies and that the target experts had gone ''completely mad'' in their enthusiasm for bombing the ball-bearing plants at Schweinfurt. But while he expressed this feeling to the men around him, he did not dwell on it with General Eaker. Harris knew that Eaker was irrevocably committed to bombing just such targets as Schweinfurt.

The planning for Schweinfurt was in progress when Eaker realized that a more immediate necessity had arisen. The German aircraft industry had expanded its capacity and was turning out so many fighter planes that it posed an almost prohibitive threat to his bombers. The B-17s would have little hope of success against targets like Schweinfurt unless they first managed to pinch off the supply of the fighters that were giving them so much trouble.

Intelligence reports indicated that two factories were then producing 48 percent of all Germany's fighters—the Messerschmitt assembly plant at Regensburg and the Focke-Wulf plant at Wiener Neustadt in Austria, thirty miles south of Vienna. Unfortunately, both of these plants were far from England. Regensburg might be just barely within the range of the B-17, but Wiener Neustadt, at a distance of more than seven hundred miles, was far outside. The Austrian plant was not, however, outside the range of the heavy bombers, mostly

B-24s, that had been taken from the 8th Air Force and were now in Africa under the command of Eaker's friend, General Spaatz. Eaker decided that with the help of Spaatz, he might be able to do something right away about those two worrisome fighter factories.

After working out a plan, he sent a copy of it July 18 to General Arnold, with a covering letter that explained its urgency:

> The Germans are struggling mightily and squirming to beat hell to figure some way of stopping our bombers. They have tried air bombing from fighters, long-range cannon fire, head-on attacks and rocket-equipped fighters. None of these systems has yet been tried in sufficient force or with sufficient skill and accuracy to be alarming. I am convinced, however, that there is grave danger that some one of these systems may eventually be tried in such force and with such good equipment and highly trained crews as to increase greatly the cost of our bombing.

To counteract this danger he had two suggestions. First, he wanted Arnold to test all the new German methods of attack at a special Air Force proving ground and develop the best possible measures against them. Secondly, and more immediately, he wanted permission to go ahead with his plan of attack against the two huge fighter factories. In the hope of winning approval, he again dropped some big, reliable names into the letter:

> Portal feels that this has a much higher priority than the oil attacks, and General Devers and I do also. Nothing we can do is as important as destroying German aviation. It will be absolutely impossible to execute a successful invasion next year unless we break up the German Air Force.

Eaker on the following day, July 19, wrote a letter to Spaatz outlining his plan of attack against the two factories and asking for Spaatz's cooperation:

> I believe the best way for us to do this is for us to take on one and you the other, each wiping out the one closest to him. This will take a lot of coordination. If either makes his attack first, it will make a tremendous difference in the defenses that the other will have to

240

engage. We have here complete target data on each of these. My proposal is, therefore, that I send two officers, one especially qualified on the Intelligence side and the other on the Operations side, for conferences with you and your staff to work out the joint plan for doing this job.

As an afterthought, Eaker also asked Spaatz to send back "as soon as possible our three Liberator (B-24) groups now with you." He hadn't yet forgotten the four groups taken from him for the African invasion (including also one B-17 group), but his request for their return was pro forma. He must have realized by now that he would have to go to Africa if he ever wanted to see them again. The Regensburg-Wiener Neustadt operation was, at least, a way of getting some good out of those lost groups. When Spaatz approved the joint project, Col. Curtis LeMay flew to North Africa and the Regensburg-to-North Africa shuttle mission went into the planning phase. August 7 was the date set for it.

On July 24, the 8th Bomber Command began the offensive that led to Schweinfurt. Since July 4, the B-17 groups had been almost totally defeated by the weather. Germany was cloudy for the entire month. A July 10 thrust at Villacoublay was wasted when a blanket of clouds moved in at the wrong moment to shield the target. On Bastille Day, July 14, the bombers reminded France that the Americans were coming when they hit Paris and Amiens airfields effectively, but this was not a very strong reminder to Germany. With a promising weather forecast on July 17, a record 332 B-17s (including two new groups, the 385th and 388th, which were making their debuts) took off for Hamburg. But the weather closed in before they arrived, and the mission achieved only minor results.

Tired of waiting for the skies to clear over Germany, General Anderson, on the 24th, sent 324 Fortresses against harbor installations and German factories in occupied Norway. The mission was an outstanding success, closing for three and a half months to come a large factory at Heroya that made nitrate for gunpowder. Because the Germans had not expected a strike against Norway, only one B-17 was lost, and it managed to land in neutral Sweden. This raid began what soon came to be known in the 8th as "Blitz Week."

The Forts returned to Germany the next day to hit Kiel, Hamburg, and Warnemünde. This time the Germans were ready. Nineteen bombers were lost, and clouds limited the accuracy of the bombing. The clouds were even heavier on the 26th, completely frustrating more than 200 of the planes that took off. But 92 others attacked a rubber factory at Hanover with such accuracy that 21 direct hits were recorded and smoke arose to a height of 22,000 feet. Unpromising weather gave the crews a rest on the 27th. The following day 302 B-17s went after aircraft factories in Kassel and Oschersleben. Clouds held the First Wing to limited success at Kassel, but the Fourth Wing, led by Col. Fred Castle, one of Eaker's original six staff officers and now commander of the 94th Group, had better luck against a Focke-Wulf plant at Oschersleben. After bad weather scattered the Wing's formations, Castle found that he had behind him only his own group plus a few planes from the 96th. Moving persistently forward, they managed to find a break in the clouds just as they approached the target, and their bombs caused a month's production loss—possibly 50 FW-190s. Fifteen B-17s failed to return home that day.

On the 29th, the Forts returned to Warnemünde and Kiel (where they dropped 200 tons of bombs and three quarters of a million propaganda leaflets over the shipyards), and on the 30th, it was Kassel. This time only 186 B-17s took off, and 12 did not return. The weather was clear the next day, but the 8th Air Force was quiet. After six missions in seven days, 100 planes were gone and 1,000 men were either dead, missing, or wounded. Eaker had not underestimated the price he would have to pay for this offensive. The survivors needed a rest.

An indication of how badly the men needed a rest can be found in the fact that about seventy-five of them suffered emotional breakdowns during July 1943. Fear was the basic cause. Nearly all crew members suffered some degree of fear at one or more stages before, during, or after a mission. But fear was only one of several horrendous problems the bomber crews encountered.[9]

Almost as hazardous was the need to avoid flak by flying at high altitudes where the air was as frigid as it was thin. The B-17 was not a pressurized airplane. There was no such thing at that time. At 20,000 feet, the men had to use oxygen masks. Nor could the plane be heated when several of its guns had to be fired through open windows. The result was that for every three men wounded in combat, four were disabled by frostbite. Flight surgeons estimated that more than half of

242

all crewmen suffered "some degree of anoxia" (ill effects from lack of oxygen) during their combat tours.

The A-8-B oxygen masks used in the B-17s, the best masks then available, tended to freeze when used above 20,000 feet. Ice would form in the bag, then in the tube between bag and mask, causing complete stoppage. Inexperienced crewmen were sometimes slow to realize what was happening. Anoxia casualties were highest among men on their first five missions. Sometimes also the plane's entire oxygen system would fail because of battle damage or mechanical malfunction. If such failure happened during an attack by enemy fighters, it might be safer to fly on with whatever oxygen was still available in "bottles" than to leave the relative safety of the formation and descend alone to a lower altitude.

In some crews, one member was assigned to make regular oxygen checks by calling everyone on the interphone. If a man didn't answer, someone near him was sent to make sure he was conscious and breathing properly.

The dangers of anoxia, however, did not match the awesome misery created by air temperatures of thirty to fifty degrees below zero. One flight surgeon who sometimes went to the flight line to watch the returning planes come in would sigh with relief when he saw that none of them were firing "wounded aboard" flares only to watch with horror later as his dispensary became "jammed with men with frozen hands, feet, faces." When the flight surgeons investigated the most common causes of frostbite, they found a variety of factors. Dampness was one of the worst. "Men who walked through the rain to their aircraft; who slept in heated suits; who played sweaty games in their flying clothes, were wet when they took off. They were casualties when they came back." Ball-turret gunners, who might get no opportunity to leave their turrets during protracted periods of combat and would therefore succumb finally to the necessity of urinating where they sat, sometimes returned to England with frozen backs, buttocks, and thighs.

The heavy, leather sheep-lined flying suits were cumbersome and not warm enough to keep crewmen comfortable. But no more than two or three key men in each crew could wear electric suits. Engineers had determined that the plane's generators couldn't safely handle a heavier load. And those who wore electric suits wished they hadn't when the wires burned out (sometimes through lack of proper

243

care) after a few missions. The electric gloves that many gunners wore were especially annoying. They were hooked to electric boots by a single wire, and if one glove or boot went dead, so did the whole assembly. When a doctor asked one man why his right hand was frozen, he said it was because "my Goddam left boot burned out." When a gun jammed in such low temperatures, the gunner would have to remove his heavy gloves to work on it. Then he would have to work fast because the metal, even if overheated from firing, soon became cold enough to freeze his fingers on touch.

Shortage of oxygen, besides being a menace in itself, also made a man more susceptible to frostbite. In one B-17, a flak fragment shattered the plexiglass nose and perforated the oxygen mask of the navigator without, however, injuring him. Unaware of his danger, he soon lost consciousness, a fact that was not discovered until an hour or so later when the plane reached home base. Six weeks later, this man's hands, feet, ears, and nose had to be amputated, and his frozen eyeballs had fallen out of their sockets. Flight surgeons had become accustomed to seeing men come in with hands and feet that were white at first, "became red and swollen in a few hours, purple and macerated in a few days, then black and dry." One man who suffered a head wound on a mission, was saved from death by a quick-thinking buddy who gave him rapid first aid. But his buddy either didn't think about his hands or had no way to keep them warm. They were so badly frozen by the time the plane returned home that they had to be amputated.

The physical miseries caused by the cold and lack of oxygen were only small factors, however, in creating emotional disorders among the crews. While the men might gripe about physical conditions, they could endure them and, after gaining experience, could counteract them. But fear of combat was a factor that few men ever completely overcame. For some of them it was an ordeal with which they never learned to cope. And it included a new kind of horror, never before experienced by men in battle: the horror of confinement. A ground soldier, no longer able to endure the carnage, could at least turn and run, whatever the consequences might be. In a bomber under attack at 20,000 feet, there was no place to run. At the end of "Blitz Week" (July 24 to 30), 80 percent of the 8th Air Force squadron and group surgeons mentioned in special reports to headquarters that their men had developed "undue fatigue" as a result of the six missions in seven days. This "undue fatigue" was, of course, a manifestation of fear.

Psychiatrists found that most men went through three phases in handling their fears during a tour of combat duty. New arrivals in England, insecure and defensive, covered their apprehension by acting "either overly self-assured or particularly diffident, usually the former." They were either "loud and continuous" or "mouse-quiet." They either sought advice excessively or refused to take advice. They drank more than usual and, above all, they denied that they were afraid or that they would ever be afraid. Many of them were contemptuous when they heard experienced men speak of their fears. (The veterans often launched cruel psychological attacks upon this overconfidence among the rookies. The older men in the barracks would take delight in describing what a 20-mm. shell could do to a man's brains, or what his feet would look like a few days after they were frozen. When new men went to their first briefing, veterans would tell them to be sure and shut the door because they wouldn't be coming back. And it was a special pleasure for the veterans to go through a new arrival's belongings and ask him which items he would bequeath them when he was shot down.)

After four or five missions, most new men began to lose their defensive mechanisms. Having experienced combat, they "spoke of the change in themselves and shamefacedly deprecated their former 'cocky' attitude." Now they talked about their fears, and some of them could talk about nothing else, "feeling quite hopeless about their chances of survival."

After about ten missions, most men, aware now that they could deal with their fears, passed into a third phase, which was likely to continue to the end of their combat duty. They were now "effective, careful fighting men, quiet and cool on the ground and in the air." But they were paying a heavy emotional price: "They were drained of most feelings other than those having to do with combat. No values existed other than those meaningful in combat."

Among the majority of men, the greatest tension occurred between briefing and takeoff, especially if the weather was bad and they had to await a decision about whether the mission was on or off. Surprisingly, while the men were sweating out these decisions, most of them preferred to go rather than stay. They would rather face the German guns than return to their barracks with nothing accomplished. This

245

observation by the psychiatrists confirmed a belief held by General Eaker that canceled missions were more damaging to morale than difficult missions. Canceled missions delayed the completion of a man's tour of duty and his return to the States.

After takeoff and the entry to enemy territory, tensions usually decreased and many men were almost relaxed during actual combat, perhaps because they were too busy to think about what they were doing. These same men might suffer violently from "the shakes" after the mission, when they began to think about things that almost happened to them. There were also a few men, a very few, who were never conscious of fear. Such men, psychiatrists decided, were not without fear but were able to convert it into aggression.

A small minority tended to freeze at the height of combat, forgetting their assignments and giving way to nausea, tremors, or diarrhea. One copilot, after seeing his pilot killed, put his arms over his eyes and ignored the controls. A gunner, on the wing of a plane ditched in the Channel, leaped into water covered with flaming gasoline when he could have scrambled over to the other side of the fuselage where there was no fire on the water. But the kind of man who experienced his emotional breakdown in action was rare. Most of the breakdowns came gradually, after an accumulation of difficult experiences or a period of brooding apprehension.

One first lieutenant, a pilot who "broke down" during "Blitz Week," had flown sixteen missions before succumbing to the pressure. His first, to Lorient April 16, had been a rough introduction to combat. Two of his engines were shot out and he had a difficult time getting home, but he made it without injuries to any of his crew. The next day he went to Bremen, where the Germans put a lot of holes in his ship, but again he brought it home safely. Most of his missions were rough. He went to Bremen twice and Kiel twice, as well as Lorient, St. Nazaire, and Wilhelmshaven. But he seemed to hold up well until his fifteenth, to Paris July 14, when he again lost two engines and again managed to bring his plane home. He now became aware of his nervousness and tried to do something about it. He spent a week at a luxurious rest home the 8th Air Force had opened for tired crews, a place called Stanbridge Earls on a large estate near the south coast. The week there made him feel so much better that he returned to combat.

His sixteenth and last mission was the July 24th raid against

Norway. After a seven-hour flight over water, his was the first plane to bomb the target. The trip back that day was uneventful for most of the planes but not for his. While his copilot was flying, fighters attacked, and his gunners shot down two of them, one of which had come in from the front and barely missed a head-on collision. During this attack his navigator was wounded so badly that the bombardier had to hold the man's head for five hours to keep him from bleeding to death. One 20-mm. shell knocked out the hydraulic system and another blew the plane's tail to pieces. A bullet punctured the fuel tank and sprayed gasoline over the underside of the fuselage. Despite all this misfortune, the pilot once again brought his plane home. But his nerves were so frazzled it would be dangerous to send him out again. The flight surgeon could only ground him, rest him, and hope he would recover. In such cases, the recovery rate was fairly high.

The prospects were not so bright for a second lieutenant copilot who had grown up as a typical all-American boy. Raised in Illinois, he had been a high-school football player who liked people and took a job in a soda fountain so he "could talk to everyone." He was a good flier and during his training liked to fly until, toward the end of transition school, he became acutely aware that he was on his way to combat. Having heard rumors about high casualty rates, he rapidly lost his enthusiasm for the glamorous life of an Air Force pilot. As his alarm increased, he requested transfer to noncombat flying. The Air Force did not look sympathetically upon such requests from men it had just spent $50,000 to train as combat pilots. He was sent to England as a frightened copilot who was destined to become more so.

On his first mission he was appalled when he saw how tight the formations were. He had never flown that close to another plane, and he didn't intend to do so. Looking up at the open bomb-bay doors of a B-17 just above and just ahead, he became convinced he was about to be bombed. He grabbed the control away from the pilot and swerved so violently that their plane fell out of formation.

The pilot was amazingly cool about this erratic behavior. After resuming control and attaching the plane to another group, he patiently explained how important it was to fly tight formations in combat. The copilot's reaction to that opinion was to get drunk as soon as they returned home and stay drunk as long as possible. But drinking didn't help. Ten days later, on his second mission, he was sober enough to observe that the fools around him were still flying too close together. He made such a scene about this that his pilot again had trouble managing the aircraft. When the copilot announced after this mission that he didn't want to fly any more of them, none of his fellow crew members tried to talk him into it. Neither did the flight surgeon. The copilot was sent to the Central Medical Board for evaluation.

A second lieutenant navigator had flown four missions before reporting to his flight surgeon that he had "lost his nerve." The first mission, which was routine and uneventful, hadn't bothered him. On the second, his plane was hit by flak and lost two engines. Another crew member, wounded by flak in the neck and shoulder, apparently panicked and bailed out. The navigator, tempted to do likewise, sat down instead, shocked, stunned, and stupefied. Five minutes later he looked out the window just in time to see another B-17 go down in flames. The reality of the scene was so much more hideous than his previous conception of combat that he couldn't adjust himself to it. His plane returned to base without further damage, however, and he prepared to continue his tour of duty.

A week later, as the time approached for his next mission, he developed a "sense of dread" and "sick feelings" in his stomach. He got drunk and found some relaxation in it. When his crew took off again, he was with them. Even though this mission was called back after an uneventful hour or so above the clouds, it filled him with "a tremendous sense of dread." He tried one more; it too was aborted but still left him feeling like "a mechanical man." He could no longer stand the sound of airplane engines or any other noise connected with flying. He hoped for bad weather. After a week of this, he decided he was cracking up and sought medical help. As soon as the flight surgeon grounded him, all of his symptoms disappeared.

A technical sergeant who was a tail gunner developed a horror of flying as a result of an experience before he was introduced to combat. Shortly after arriving in England, his crew was on a practice mission at 26,000 feet when one man passed out from lack of oxygen. The pilot, anxious about the man, impulsively dived to a safer altitude, but when he tried to pull the rapidly accelerating bomber out of the dive, its control cables snapped, its right wing fell off, and the fuselage caught fire. One of the bomb-bay doors broke away, flew rearward and sliced off the entire tail section. The tail gunner, uninjured but stuck in the tail section, plunged earthward with it, end over end.

Unable to smash his way through the rear plexiglass bubble, he attacked the metal fuselage skin with his feet. He finally managed to get his body through but his shoulders became wedged. Then in some way that he could never explain, he broke free, opened his parachute just before reaching the ground, and landed without injury in the middle of a British antiaircraft installation.

The plane had crashed only a hundred yards away, and when he reached it, he could see his fellow crew members (presumably all dead except one other man who had parachuted) burning inside. With the help of British soldiers, the tail gunner tried to pull out one of the bodies, but they were forced back by a new burst of flame.

That night in a British barracks the tail gunner lay sweating, shaking, and sleepless. Next morning, when his commanding officer arrived and they inspected the wreckage, he saw the charred remains of his crew. Thereafter, he slept poorly and dreamed of plane crashes. He had to force himself to get into an airplane. Whistling and whining noises reminded him of the sound of the tail section hurtling toward the ground. Enclosed spaces heightened his anxiety. Yet in spite of all this, he embarked with another crew on his tour of missions. He didn't want to be considered "yellow" or a "quitter."

On one mission, his plane was badly battered by flak. It came home from another on two engines with holes in one wing and the fuselage. On this mission, which he flew as a waist gunner, some control wires broke loose and wound around his neck, while chunks of canvas covered his head and got into his mouth. He had a sudden urge to bail out but overcame it and stayed at his post. On another, flying again as a tail gunner, he saw his tracer bullets explode the oxygen bottles in an FW-190 that had closed to within fifty feet of him. The German fighter burst into flame, and as he watched the pilot go down inside it, he thought again about himself in that plunging tail section.

Eventually, other crew members noticed his worsening condition, and he was sent to the Central Medical Board though he had never asked for relief from flying duty. To one of the doctors he was finally able to admit that he never wanted to get into an airplane again. The doctor granted his wish.

Taking into account the ever-increasing ferocity of the air battles over the continent, nervous breakdowns among U.S. fliers were not surprising. Yet less than 2 percent of the crew members on active duty at the time had such breakdowns.[10] The rest of the men flew their missions, absorbed their punishment, griped about conditions, but at the same time found some pleasure in their lives.

The men of the 91st at Bassingbourn were, in one respect, the envy of all the others. The permanent R.A.F. base on which they resided was luxurious in comparison to other bases. When Lt. Ted Winslow reached England as a replacement in June, he and his crew requested they be sent to the 91st because he had been told Bassingbourn was "the country club of the 8th Air Force."[11] They got their wish and were not disappointed. The only Nissen huts at Bassingbourn were briefing rooms and storage buildings. The barracks were solid, substantial R.A.F. dormitories. Winslow, who was assigned to the senior officers' mess, found himself bunking in a handsomely furnished room with a wash stand, mirror, white sheets, bedspreads, and, best of all, an orderly to keep the place clean.

The first time Winslow went to London, he got an immediately favorable impression of the British. As he came out of the Underground station at Piccadilly, he saw some British officers and asked them to recommend a cafe. One of them said, "Come along with us, old chap," and they took him to an excellent restaurant in Leicester Square.

For the enlisted men, Bassingbourn was slightly less luxurious but better than they had expected. Sgt. Douglas Gibson, a clerk in the 401st Squadron orderly room, ate well because he lived in the same barracks as the squadron cooks, who took special care of themselves and their friends.[12] But Gibson felt the ordinary mess hall food was poor, for which he blamed the mess officers. He knew the cooks could do better. The mess officers didn't seem to care how well the enlisted men ate, perhaps because they themselves ate quite well at the officers' mess.

Gibson's job was to fill out the statements of effects for all members of lost crews. Under an officer's supervision, he had to go through the personal property of every missing man, as soon as it was determined that his plane would not return, and make a list of every item—socks, 6 ea.; shirts, 4 ea.; mirror, 1 ea.; photographs, 3 ea.;

letters, 13 ea.;—on a yellow pad, later to be typed in septuplicate and sent with the man's belongings to a special depot, pending confirmation of his death or of his capture by the Germans. The final disposition of the letters and photographs was a matter requiring tact and discretion. A man's widow might not want to receive, among his effects, nude pin-up pictures or letters from other women.

Air Force policy was to remove a man's property from his barracks the same day he was declared missing so that his buddies wouldn't brood any more than necessary over his loss. July had been a busy month for Gibson. His was not a pleasant assignment, but he could hardly complain when he thought about what these aircrew members had to endure. On his days off he went to nearby Cambridge, wandered through the university buildings, or punted on the Cam River. He liked the British, but he had "no truck" with English girls. In this respect, he was different from many of the men of the 91st.[13]

Miss Audrea Howden, a beautiful twenty-year-old English nurse from Wakefield who worked at the Fairfield Evacuation Hospital near Bassingbourn, found that her entire life changed when the men of the 91st arrived. Until then, the nurses at Fairfield, which was in a wooded countryside, had very little social activity. Most of them had lost their boyfriends to the services. Miss Howden's fiancé had been killed. Her first contact with the Yanks did not seem promising. When they arrived at the base, many of them had suffered food poisoning on the ship that brought them, and she was assigned to nurse a forty-bed ward full of them. They were not sick enough to resist commenting on her charms and suggesting several things they would like to have her do with them. It seemed to her also that most of them had unpronounceable names, and those who had pronounceable names were pronouncing them wrong. The peculiarity of American names and their pronunciation soon became a source of amusement to all the nurses at Fairfield.

Miss Howden and her friends quickly decided, nevertheless, that these American men were like "a gift from God," not only because they turned out to be quite entertaining but also because they had excessive quantities of food at their disposal, and they were as generous as they were hopeful. When they took a girl on a date, they would bring her "a carload of food from the PX." With food so scarce in England, this consideration was not to be ignored. The

251

Fairfield nurses began organizing dances and sending blanket invitations to Bassingbourn. The boys came by the truckload with canned goods and chocolate and great expectations.

The more attractive girls, like Miss Howden, soon had a selection of eager men inviting them to pubs or to "dinner houses" like the Green Lantern in Baldock. Her first date was with a major who took her to London, but before long she realized officers were not necessarily the best boyfriends. The G.I.s had a knack of beating the Army system. They had sources of supply the officers could never tap, and they often showed up driving jeeps or cars while the officers had to walk. Miss Howden liked the enlisted men. Eventually she married one.

When the 95th Group moved in June from Framlingham to the tiny town of Horham six miles northwest, it was a boon to Basel Rodwell, the village blacksmith there. The first thing an American airman tried to buy when he arrived at a base was a bicycle. Except for those who knew how to wangle jeeps or trucks, the bike was the most dependable transportation available. But bikes were in such demand they weren't always available. Rodwell had a shop where he not only sold bicycles; he also repaired them.[14] And since most of the Americans didn't take good care of their bikes, his services were in great demand. He soon found such favor with the men of the 95th that they would sneak him onto the base and into the line at the mess hall.

One night Rodwell had a momentary scare. While he was eating with his new friends in the mess hall, some officers came in to make a surprise inspection. The men around Rodwell quickly locked him in the ice-cream refrigerator. When the inspection was finished and they hurried to the refrigerator to let him out before he began to freeze, they found to their surprise that he was in no hurry to come out. Rodwell loved ice cream.

There was never a shortage of girls around the American bases. Rodwell was astonished at the number of girls who showed up in Horham after the Yanks arrived. On Sundays, or on the nights when the men staged dances in one of the hangars, young women came from miles around.

The same was true at Thorpe Abbots, five miles north of Horham, where the new 100th Group had arrived June 9.[15] Harry Chenery, a ferret keeper there, gazed with wonder upon the parade of girls, with their fashionably short skirts and high heels, walking past his house on the way to the air base.

Mrs. Daphne Redgrave, who lived across the street from the Chenerys, near the top of the lane leading to the base, had been tending an eight-year-old boy named Jimmy Sowter when the first American planes landed. It was about five o'clock on a warm, summery afternoon. Though bewildered by the noise of the B-17s coming in one after another at half-minute intervals, she took little Jimmy up the lane with her to watch them land. Mrs. Redgrave soon got to know several of the airmen and liked them. Then she developed the habit of counting the planes as they took off in the morning and counting them again as they returned from their missions in the afternoon. On some days, she noticed, a lot of them didn't return.

To the men of the 100th, the girls around Thorpe Abbots, and in the Norfolk area, were not glamorous—"seamed cotton stockings, mended dresses, cheap ribbons in their hair"—but they were girls and they were available.[16] Besides those who came to the base for dances (they seemed to have "a flair for jitterbugging"), there were others to be found at places like the Samson and Hercules at Norwich or at a hundred places in London. (If you wore wings you were "halfway home with a girl" the minute you met her.) But it was difficult to get to London and difficult to cope with the place when you got there. Lt. Ernest Warsaw decided he must be a jinx to London because the city was bombed every time he went there.[17] And besides the shortage of food, there was the shortage of hotel rooms. The reason so few were available, it seemed to Warsaw, was that those American officers who had them held onto them, and most of them were probably "guys who didn't fly." Among the fliers, there was a natural hostility toward ground officers because they didn't have to "risk their asses" on missions. And even when they did, it seemed to some of the fliers that they chose the easy ones.

Major Gale "Buck" Cleven, commander of the 100th Group's 350th Squadron, felt he could always tell when the next day's mission was going to be rough.[18] Nobody came to see him, and he couldn't get anyone on the telephone. But if the base was full of staff cars and officers from wing headquarters were all over the place, he could sense that they'd be hitting the coast of France on a milk run.

The men the American fliers admired most were their R.A.F.

counterparts. The Yanks especially admired them for being able to find their way to German targets in the dark and for flying poorly armed, lightly built planes like the Lancaster, which the Americans considered "flimsy kites" compared to their heavy Fortresses. The R.A.F. fliers, on the other hand, admired the Yanks for invading the continent in daylight, when the Germans could so easily find and attack them.

The Americans did sense some "snobbishness" in the British fliers, who tended to be condescending to the Yanks, perhaps because they had been in the war longer and thought they knew more about it. The Americans believed that the condescension grew out of the British class system. Most of the pilot officers were from the "establishment." Pilots who were not from good schools or good families were usually sergeants, and many Americans thought this arrangement was a reflection of caste, which in British minds might also apply to them as "colonials." The Americans noticed, however, that British officers and nonofficers alike shared a comradeship of the air, which they quickly extended to the American fliers.

There was an almost carefree attitude among the British that astonished some Americans. Cleven, a man so dedicated to fighting the war that he was willing to fly seven days a week, thought the British were taking the war lightly because on such trivial occasions as bank holidays, they "just shut it down." While the impatient Americans were "working seven days a week," the English were "living a little each day." They were "spreading a little life in amongst the chaos and strife" because they knew the war would still be there tomorrow. Cleven admired them for it.

The American fliers, especially in the 100th Group where casualties were alarmingly high, did not seem as light-hearted as the British. With the missions becoming tougher and the tension increasing, more and more of the men ignored the available girls and stopped going into town on their free nights. Most of them were becoming convinced they had no chance of surviving twenty-five or thirty missions. Although they were fatalistic about it, they were also bitter. Many of them drank too much. Fistfights often broke out at the 100th Group's officers' club. Getting drunk and attacking a superior officer was a popular way to spend an evening. But insubordination was usually overlooked because everyone understood what caused it. One of the big continuing issues was the lack of long-range fighter escort

254

for the B-17s. The colonels and majors kept promising that with the arrival of auxiliary tanks, the P-47s would soon be going all the way with the bombers. But as the weeks passed without the development of a satisfactory tank, the fighters kept turning for home just when they were most needed, and the bomber crews became more cynical every day.

At Molesworth, the men of the 303rd were getting to know their new commander, Col. Kermit Stevens, and he was getting to know them.[19] He had taken over the group at the worst possible time, July 19, just before "Blitz Week." He had led the 303rd on three of the six missions that week—to Hamburg, Norway, and Kassel. When he wasn't preaching his "tight formation" gospel to his men, he had one other strong piece of advice.

"Don't look at the flak coming up at you," he told them, "and don't look into the muzzles of their guns."

On his first mission, to Huls as an observer June 22, Stevens had almost made himself a laughingstock. Standing between the pilot and copilot during a fighter attack, he had occasion for the first time to look down the cannon barrel of an FW-190 coming in from the front. When the cannon fired, he instinctively ducked his head, as if he were actually quick enough to dodge a shell. At that moment he was twice-blessed. First, the shell missed the plane; second, no one in the crew saw him duck his head. He would never have lived it down. He still felt foolish about it, but he also remembered the horror of staring straight into the mouth of a firing cannon. As a mental-health measure, he advised his men against it.

In the historic pre-Norman town of Kimbolton (where King Harold II kept a hunting lodge until he lost the Battle of Hastings, and all of England with it, to William the Conqueror in 1066), a teacher at the local boys' school had found a new way to help his students develop a sense of history.[20] When the B-17s of the 379th Group took off in the morning, it was usually so early that only a small percentage of townspeople were up to watch them go. But when they returned, it was midafternoon, and everyone wanted to watch them land, see how many gaps the formations had, how many planes were limping home with dead engines or with ripped wings and fuselages.

Kyffin Owen, like the other teachers at Kimbolton School, found it difficult to hold the students' attention after they heard in the distance the first sounds of the returning planes. A few boys would glance toward the windows, then, as the sounds grew louder, all of them would look that way out of the corners of their eyes. Finally, though they might still pretend they were listening to Owen's history lecture, he would notice that he had lost all of them.

One day, when the planes were in the traffic pattern approaching their base up the hill from Kimbolton, Owen had decided it was pointless to try to compete. "Get up and go to the windows," he said to his students. "Why should we be talking about history down here when they're making it up there."

The long-planned Schweinfurt mission, now scheduled for August 10, was threatened once more at the end of July when Arnold informed Eaker of a plan to take away four more of his heavy-bomb groups.[21] Gen. Douglas MacArthur was preparing a new offensive in New Guinea, for which his air commander, Gen. George Kenney, was urgently demanding more Flying Fortresses. The groups in England were the only ones that could be sent on short notice. Besides being needed for the New Guinea offensive, four experienced groups from the big league in Europe, where they had been facing the Germans, would significantly elevate the quality of the MacArthur air force. So it was said, anyway, perhaps to soothe Eaker by flattering him about the skill of his men. But this new development did not put him in a mood to be soothed.

In distress again at the prospect of being stripped of his planes just as he launched an offensive, he called upon his British friends for help once more. Portal immediately wired a protest to Washington and at the same time sent a letter to General Devers, for circulation, praising the work of the 8th Air Force during "Blitz Week."[22] A few days later, Portal flew to Washington for a Combined Chiefs of Staff meeting, at which time Eaker and Anderson stimulated a wire to him from Harris on that old familiar theme, the horrors of diversion:

> . . . I am certain that given average weather and concentration on the main job we can push Germany over by bombing this year. But to do so we must keep diversions cut to the bone. On every front but this one the United States and ourselves now regard it as reasonable, as well as necessary, that we should vastly outnumber our opponents locally in the air. . . . But here we and the U.S. 8th Bomber Command still remain as residuary legatees in air resources while charged with the execution of the first, most difficult

and most strenuous item of inter-Allied strategy. United States are still making no adequate effort to implement their agreed bomber reinforcement of 8th Bomber Command. . . . I hope you will do your utmost to make them keep their allocations to 8th Bomber Command up to plan and to make up present leeway. I have found the best approach to leading Americans here to be an expression of astonishment that, while boasting of complete air supremacy everywhere else, they continually leave their 8th Bomber Command in this prime theater always far below planned strength . . . and hopelessly outnumbered. Outnumbered is a true and, to these people, a startling expression. . . . Eaker and Anderson wish particularly to get these facts put over at this juncture.[23]

Eaker had learned long ago that the best way to get concessions from his superiors in Washington was through the British, but how many times could he get away with that ploy? On August 16, he learned that he had gotten away with it once again. Portal, in a telegram to Harris through the War Cabinet Offices, disclosed that he had averted the new crisis:

Please inform Harris that the question of expediting reinforcements to 8th Bomber Command, and particularly of avoiding further diversions and restoring the three groups loaned to North Africa, was brought up by me at the C.C.O.S. meeting today. My attitude, which was largely based on his telegram, met with general approval of British and American Chiefs of Staff, and Harris can rest assured that existence of opportunity for decisive victory in the Battle of Germany during the next three months is fully appreciated, and that Arnold will continue to do his utmost to build up and sustain the 8th Air Force.

Portal had won a significant concession. But by tying it to Harris's argument, he had brought into play the question of whether Harris and Eaker could actually deliver on the Harris promise to "push Germany over by bombing this year." Eaker felt the pressure to help Harris keep this promise and, in the process, prove once and for all the worth of a concept in which, ironically, Harris still did not believe—the American daylight precision bombing strategy.

To this end Schweinfurt was undoubtedly the ideal target and

257

Eaker's men were ready to attack it, but once again the weather thwarted them. On the night of August 9, the groups were alerted; on the morning of August 10, the mission was postponed.

The weather was also delaying the projected double mission against the Regensburg ME-109 factory from England and the Wiener Neustadt FW-190 factory from Africa. This combined thrust, scheduled for August 7, had been postponed each day. As the weather in England continued bad, General Spaatz in Africa decided to wait no longer. On August 13, he sent his heavy bombers, including the three B-24 groups he had borrowed from Eaker, against the Wiener Neustadt factory.

With the combined thrust from Africa and England thus eliminated, 8th Air Force planners began to work on a different kind of combined thrust—a shuttle mission to Regensburg and then to Africa, which would draw off the German fighters while a larger force attacked Schweinfurt. Thus the Regensburg-Schweinfurt plan replaced the Regensburg-Wiener Neustadt plan. And when on August 16, the meteorologists forecast sunny skies over central Germany the next day, the teletypes began to chatter in orderly rooms at all the East Anglia bases. The Regensburg-Schweinfurt mission of August 17, 1943, was begun, the mission that poured enormous devastation on the Messerschmitt factory and the vital ball-bearing plants; but it was so costly to the 8th Air Force that it left still undecided the wisdom and practicality of the daylight bombing policy.

14

By the time General Eaker got back to England August 23 after assessing the damage to Colonel LeMay's Fourth Bombardment Wing in Africa, he had a fairly full picture of how much the Schweinfurt-Regensburg mission had cost the 8th Air Force. On the Schweinfurt operation alone, 36 Flying Fortresses were shot down and 27 so badly mauled they would never fly again, constituting an actual loss of 63 aircraft. Another 95 were damaged to some degree. On the Regensburg operation the toll would be much higher than he had realized because maintenance facilities were lacking in North Africa. For LeMay's mission against Bordeaux en route home to England (August 24), he had only 60 airworthy planes. He had to leave another 60 in Africa because he couldn't get them repaired. Though some of these might later be salvaged, they must now be considered lost, bringing the Regensburg toll to 84 aircraft (plus 3 more on the Bordeaux raid). This raised the aircraft toll for the entire Schweinfurt-Regensburg mission to 147. And more than 550 of the crewmen in those planes were either killed or captured.

The pressing questions were whether the results at Schweinfurt and Regensburg justified this great expense, and whether such enormous losses could be sustained even if the results were excellent. Reconnaissance photos showed that the Regensburg results were perhaps even better than excellent. The British were astonished by the bombing accuracy of LeMay's task force. Vice Chief of Air Staff Slessor, in a report to Portal, called it "outstandingly successful. Probably the best concentration on target yet seen."[1]

The photos showed that nearly all the craters were within the Messerschmitt factory. All six main workshops were destroyed or badly damaged; also damaged were the final assembly shop, the gun-testing range, a large new shop, a boiler house, main store and workshops, plus several other facilities. A hangar was more than half destroyed, and thirty-seven aircraft—presumably ME-109s just off the assembly line—seemed to have been damaged by bomb blasts.

At Schweinfurt, where the target included five factories and was therefore less concentrated, the results were more difficult to interpret. Photos taken directly after the attack were virtually useless because the area was still obscured by smoke and fire. Subsequent photos showed that General Williams's task force had scored eighty direct hits on the two largest factories, Kugelfischer and VKF. And the mission report said bombing results were very good:

Considerable damage was inflicted on a number of buildings of the Kugelfischer Works (ball bearings), Fichtel & Sachs (aircraft components) and the Vereingte Kugellager Fabriken (ball bearings) Works I and II. Communications, including the main railway station, also suffered very heavy damage as well as a number of residential areas. . . . At the Kugelfischer Works the power house, a single-story machine shop, a multi-story machine shop and a large group of office buildings and stores received hits. At the Fichtel & Sachs plant at least two bombs burst directly on a single-story machine shop, with three more on adjoining buildings. Direct hits were scored on two machine shops of the Works II plant of the V.K.F., and other buildings received blast damage. At Works I of the V.K.F., part of the manufacturing buildings were destroyed.

This report and the aerial photos were, however, inconclusive. The organization of ball-bearing factories was complicated, and the de-

260

struction of one building or group of machines might or might not interrupt production in another group. Many buildings in the three-square mile area were undamaged. Were these more or less important than the ones that were hit? The statement that the main railway station was heavily damaged (actually it was destroyed) might sound good in the report, but the station was not part of the target. The fact that it and several residential areas were hit meant that a significant number of bombs had missed their mark.

Damage to the Schweinfurt factories had undoubtedly been severe. But Eaker was unable to say how severe it was or what effect it would have on ball-bearing production. His information left too many questions unanswered. He was not privy to the German reports from the scene that had thrown Albert Speer into such alarm. Hence the German authorities, knowing in detail the results of the attack, considered it a much greater American success than did the Americans. If Eaker and other Allied authorities had known then what Speer disclosed later—that the August 17 attack had caused an immediate drop of 34 percent in Schweinfurt ball-bearing production—they might have prevailed upon British Bomber Command to follow up the American daylight raid immediately with a series of night attacks, which would no doubt be less costly. But Eaker could make no positive assertions about the Schweinfurt results, especially since Williams said he was "not satisfied with our bombing accuracy although there was considerable damage to the ball-bearing plants."

Eaker in an August 27 letter to Robert Lovett praised the Regensburg results without mentioning Schweinfurt. However much damage had been done at Schweinfurt, he obviously did not believe it had been enough. In answers to the congratulations he had received for the double mission from such people as Sir Archibald Sinclair, Air Marshal Sir Trafford Leigh-Mallory, and Air Marshal Sir Douglas C.S. Evill, he carefully avoided boasting about the 8th Bomber Command's accomplishments at either Schweinfurt or Regensburg. He wrote instead about the help the R.A.F. had given the 8th Air Force since its "feeble beginnings" and about "the little success we have had to date," while thanking the British for their cooperation and promising to press forward with them to greater accomplishments. In his letter to Sinclair he said, "We in the 8th Air Force take the greatest pride in the fact that we are just now beginning to join up

261

with the Royal Air Force and really be of some help.''[2] These were not the words of a man basking in victory. Even though Eaker had expected heavy losses, he was capable of grief when they occurred and of shock when they were as extensive as those of August 17. His immediate assessment of his most ambitious operation to date could hardly bring him much comfort. Shaken by his losses, he didn't even have the satisfaction of realizing his victory. Only the Germans were aware of that.

One of Eaker's heaviest concerns, expressed to his staff members, was that he and the 8th Air Force might lose support in Washington as a result of the August 17 losses. Though his information about the bombing results that day was still far from complete, he knew enough to be convinced that the Germans had suffered grievously. Despite the cost, therefore, he retained his faith in daylight bombing, but he feared that other people might now waver. General Arnold had been quick to express strong public support, issuing a statement that said, ''The American idea—high altitude precision bombing—has come through a period of doubt and experimentation to triumphant vindication.'' Arnold, of course, had to support Eaker publicly. But how would he react privately when he learned the full price of the August 17 operation? General Anderson sent him the preliminary reports, and Eaker, on his return to England, sent Arnold all the briefing and debriefing data.

Eaker was soon relieved to learn there would be ''no upbraiding'' from the Air Force Chief.[3] Arnold perhaps regretted the loss as much as Eaker and Anderson, but he showed no indication of discouragement. On the contrary, since new B-17s were now arriving in England at a steady if not abundant pace, he expected Eaker and Anderson to press on with their offensive as if nothing untoward had happened.

Eaker appreciated Arnold's support but was taken aback by his expectations. After losing 147 planes and 55 crews in one day, the 8th Air Force would have to retrench temporarily until it could regain its strength. General Williams's postoperation report illustrated the sorry condition into which it had fallen. There had been ''a noticeable sag in combat crew morale,'' he said, because ''crews had expected to be given some extra liberty privileges after maintaining such a long period of alert for this particular mission,'' and also because crews, having been led to expect that the R.A.F. would follow their day effort with a night attack on Schweinfurt, were disappointed to learn that the R.A.F. had bombed Peenemünde instead on the night of the 17th. They "felt they had been let down," Williams observed, "after their bloody fight to pave the way." But however much the men might gripe, they would fly again when they were commanded to do so. To get their planes into the air would require more than a command. "Four groups of this Air Division were so decimated by losses during this week," Williams reported, "that a total of only six combat boxes [15-18 planes per box] can be flown until suitable replacements are made operational."

Not until August 27, ten days after Schweinfurt, could the 8th Bomber Command launch another mission, and it was one of the shortest of the war, to Calais, where the Germans were building concrete bunkers for the V-rockets they planned to launch against England. On August 31, September 2, and September 3, the big bombers went to the Paris area, where they were relatively safe. On the 6th, when 338 of them, many manned by rookie crews, set out for Stuttgart, they were belabored by a combination of bad weather, inexperience, and German fighters. In one of the most dismal and unproductive missions of the war, another 45 aircraft went down. It looked as if the 8th would have to be content for a while to find more targets in France.

Eaker, in the meantime, had renewed his quest for long-range fighters to accompany the bombers, and Arnold, in late August, had promised to send him some P-38s with extra tanks and some P-51Bs with Merlin engines. In an August 30 letter, Eaker thanked Arnold for the promise, but it was not yet clear when the desperately needed fighters would arrive. Arnold himself arrived in England September 1 to see what was happening, and Eaker quickly called his attention to the fighter problem. Two days later, Arnold, from London, sent a cable to General Marshall in Washington reflecting Eaker's urgent plea: "Operations over Germany conducted here during the past several weeks indicate definitely that we must provide long-range fighters to accompany daylight bombardment missions."

Arnold followed this with another cable to Marshall in an effort to prevent diversion of more fighters from England to Africa. Eisenhower had requested additional fighters, and the tone of

Arnold's cable suggests that he may have agreed, before leaving Washington, to send them. After talking with Eaker and Devers in London, he decided it wasn't such a good idea:

> Believe it would be a great mistake to divert P-38s from U.K. to North Africa at this time. The battle for complete destruction of German Air Force is approaching most critical stage. 8th Air Force must be built up rapidly—more rapidly than planned—to administer a knockout blow while they are groping for any respite they can get.
>
> All information here indicates that the North African Air Force has a greater numerical strength than the entire German Air Force. The N.A.A.F. is at least five times as strong as the German Air Force which opposes them. I realize the desire of Eisenhower to get as many airplanes as possible but strongly recommend that the answer to his request for P-38s be "No," repeat "no."

Devers and Eaker concur.

Eisenhower needed as many aircraft as he could get because on September 3 his forces invaded Italy. Eaker questioned the military usefulness of the Italian campaign, which he saw as another diversion from the primary task of invading the continent from England, and he said so to Arnold as well as others in his efforts to get more planes for his 8th Air Force. This attitude was not likely to increase Eaker's popularity with Eisenhower, but the vigor and persistence with which he expressed it did influence Arnold during the first three days of his visit. One of Eaker's problems with Arnold was distance. When he had him at hand, he could quickly convince him of his needs and difficulties. But he couldn't be certain what the Air Force Chief might do when he was again three thousand miles away in Washington, under the equally persuasive influence of other commanders with needs as urgent as Eaker's. Arnold spent nine days in England and left with the impression that, aside from the disastrously muddled September 6 mission against Stuttgart and despite the desperate need for more bombers and fighters, the 8th Air Force was doing a good job.[4] He was especially impressed by something Portal confided to him. Either the R.A.F. radio monitoring section or the Ultra people had intercepted a message in which Hermann Goering told his fighter pilots that "the Fortresses must be destroyed, regardless of everything else.'' The message also said the German fighters must stop attacking the straggling Fortresses and apply their efforts instead, under pain of court-martial, against the formations, which had to be prevented at all costs from reaching their targets. This was exactly the kind of news Arnold wanted to hear. It meant to him that his B-17s were in fact hurting Germany as grievously as Eaker had claimed.

Portal and Slessor also spoke to Arnold about the Schweinfurt mission and its importance, which they, unlike Harris, had never doubted. After visiting with them, Arnold told Eaker the British still felt a great concern about the ball-bearing situation. They considered it one of the highest American priorities.[5]

"I know you'll get at it," Arnold said to Eaker, "as soon as the weather permits."

More impatient than ever, Arnold could not be satisfied unless his bombers were hitting Germany every day. Even though he knew why such a schedule was impossible, he had difficulty accepting the limitations. Now that Eaker was hurting the Germans, he must not let them rest. He must hit them harder and harder, send out more planes, and bomb more German targets every day. It was an order Eaker would be happy to obey as soon as he could, but for the present, with his forces depleted by "Blitz Week," the Regensburg-Schweinfurt mission, and the unfortunate Stuttgart mission, he would have to limit his Bomber Command to short strikes.

Eaker now received through intelligence sources further confirmation of his belief that the Fortresses were hurting Germany. He was told that 30 new fighters had just been added to the German force at Frankfurt, placing 755 single-engine fighters plus 680 twin-engine fighters in the western defense corridors.[6] These 1,435 planes, he was informed, were 65 percent of the total German fighter strength. If the figures were accurate, they did indeed indicate the Fortresses were hurting the Germans. They also suggested that the Germans were preparing to hurt the Fortresses, perhaps prohibitively unless the Americans stormed the defenses in sufficiently large numbers. Eaker, maintaining the principle that his force must never be allowed to dwindle, that it must always be a growing force, chose for the moment a prudent course.

On September 7, one flight of B-17s hit Watten in France while another hit Brussels. On the 9th, 15th, 16th, 23rd, and 26th, they hit more French targets, some in support of a mock invasion operation code-named STARKEY. Even if the 8th had been ready during this period to return to Germany, the weather would have prevented it. September, which meteorologists had expected to be the clearest month of the year over Germany, turned out to be the worst. But the number of Fortresses was rising again, and the skies had to clear sometime soon. Perhaps October would be sunnier.

While awaiting improved weather, Eaker had to contend once more with the impatience of Arnold, who was back in Washington wondering why the 8th was flying so few sorties after he had sent it so many planes. Eaker could do no more than explain the conditions and repeat the same old story about bad weather and damaged aircraft. That was not what Arnold wanted to hear. He wanted action. On September 27 the Fortresses returned to Germany, 305 of them this time, in the hope of bombing the port of Emden through an almost complete cloud cover with the aid of a newly developed British radar device called H2S. The results were indifferent, and for five days thereafter the 8th flew no missions. On October 2, when an even larger force returned to Emden in another attempt to use H2S, the results were worse. If these two experiments were indicative, radar bombing would never replace visual contact bombing.

During all this time, Schweinfurt was ever present in Eaker's mind. Exactly how good a job had his men done there in August? Neither the British nor American experts could answer this question accurately, and perhaps for this reason, doubts were rising in many minds about how effective the Fortresses had really been against the ball-bearing plants on that epic raid. Had they done as much damage as the 8th Air Force claimed? Some people in the R.A.F. were skeptical. Reactions from Washington had been reserved. Each week since August 17, reconnaissance planes had returned to photograph the stricken factories, and each week Eaker, Anderson, and their staffs studied the pictures, listened to the expert analyses, read the reports, asked questions about the buildings still standing, and even more anxious questions about the buildings that had been knocked apart but were now, with astonishing dispatch, being put back together again. What people said about German efficiency was obviously true. When they wanted to do something in a hurry they were phenomenally quick. The speed with which they were rebuilding the Schweinfurt plants raised the question of how soon they would be back at full production.

266

But even more significant, the speed of rebuilding demonstrated to Eaker what a well-chosen target Schweinfurt had been. It seemed to him that if the ball-bearing plants were that important to the Germans, they could not be allowed to resume operation unmolested, despite the awesome cost of bombing them. It would be nice to wait until the long-range fighters arrived to escort the bombers, or at least until satisfactory drop tanks had been developed for the P-47s. It would be nice to wait until they had a thousand bombers with which to overwhelm the German fighters. But he had too often been accused by Arnold of delaying operations even when he had been moving as fast as his resources would allow.

With Anderson, Williams, LeMay, and the group commanders, Eaker discussed options. They were getting more fighters now, but these were mostly P-47s, and no one had yet developed a drop-tank that would lengthen their range significantly. These fighters still could not escort the bombers more than a few miles inside Germany. The new B-17s that were arriving had chin turrets and greater forward-firing capacity to cope with the now general German policy of attacking from the front. But the added firepower of the latest bombers would hardly balance the fact, also disclosed by reconnaissance photos, that the Germans were placing more and more fighters in corridors that led directly to Schweinfurt. In studying the locations of fighter bases on a map, Eaker and Anderson realized to their amazement toward the end of September that it would be easier for their bombers to go to Berlin than to Schweinfurt. That told them all they had to know about the importance of the little town that was Germany's ball-bearing center. But the one vital question still had not been answered positively: how much production loss had the August 17 mission caused? And how much damage could they hope to do to the machines that made ball bearings? They got a convincing answer when the intelligence agencies reported about German efforts to get ball bearings from every corner of Europe.[7] From France and Italy they could virtually confiscate whatever was available. But even this quantity was not enough. Germany was urgently demanding more ball bearings from neutral Sweden, one of Europe's top producers. The Germans would accept nothing less than the entire Swedish output.

It was apparent now that the August 17 raid had produced the desired result. After only one attack against Schweinfurt, the enemy was scrounging for ball bearings just as England had been forced to do after one German attack against Chelmsford. Here was proof enough that another raid would be worth the cost. There could be no doubt now. The 8th Air Force would have to return to Schweinfurt. And as quickly as possible, before all the August damage could be repaired.

In most of the bomb groups, morale improved as new crews and planes arrived. But the mood of the men was increasingly thoughtful and somber. They knew too much for comfort about their future. The veterans had not forgotten Schweinfurt, and they had told the rookies all about it. As the dark gloomy days of September passed and the men spent most of their time on the ground, listening to briefings for missions destined to be scrubbed or flying short, easy milk runs to France, they had too much time to brood about their prospects. The Germans were ready for them now and they knew it. The B-17 crewmen were aware of the fighter build-up along the corridors toward their likely targets, and they were also aware that every cloudy day, every day they had to wait before returning to Germany, gave the Messerschmitt and Focke-Wulf factories twenty-four more hours to turn out more fighters.

In the 381st Group at Ridgewell, which had lost more planes (eleven) at Schweinfurt than any other, the men had not yet recovered from the shock. The group surgeon had noticed an immediate drop in the morale of the crews on the night of August 17, after their return from Schweinfurt, ''as soon as stories were compared and total losses realized.''[8]

Even the commander of the 381st, Col. Joseph Nazzaro, who had not flown that mission, was ''visibly affected'' by it. He told the surgeon he was more tired that night than when he himself had flown long missions. Looking at Nazzaro, the surgeon could believe it. He had noticed in the colonel ''the personal feeling for his men that is sometimes lacking in commanders.'' But there was very little Nazzaro could do to relieve the ominous mood of his men. Their lives were on the line, and he had no way to distract them from that awesome realization.

On the morning of September 17, a captain in command of one of the squadrons in the 381st went to the medical section and announced that he did not wish to go on that day's mission.[9] He had flown seven missions including Schweinfurt, which was his fifth, and he told the doctors that since Schweinfurt he had been experiencing "ideas of homicide and suicide." He was introspective and downcast. He had not been sleeping well. He spoke softly. He said that he had "no desire whatsoever to get near a B-17" again and that he was "not equal to going" on that day's mission. He felt that "the odds [were] overwhelmingly against the individual in raids over German territory."

The doctors who talked to him could not decide whether he was concerned only for his own personal safety or whether he was worried about the responsibility of leading other men into combat. They reminded him of his role as one of the group's leaders and pointed out that other men looked to him for direction and guidance. They said if he refused to fly it would have "a disastrous effect upon the squadron and very likely upon the group as a whole."

Despite continuing reluctance, the captain finally agreed to attend the briefing for that day's mission. When Colonel Nazzaro was informed of the man's precarious condition, he had a talk with him. The captain agreed to go on that day's mission. The weather intervened, however; the mission was scrubbed. Nazzaro, determined to save the man from a personal failure that could affect his self-image for the rest of his life, took him as his own copilot on the next two missions he flew. On each of them, the captain performed satisfactorily. It began to look as if he might gradually come to terms with his fears, like most of the other men of the 381st.

In the 384th Group at Grafton-Underwood, many men after returning from Schweinfurt, where they lost five planes, had made clear that it was one place they never again wanted to see. But as time passed, they seemed to mellow somewhat. Colonel Peaslee, the 384th commander until September 6 when he became a deputy wing commander, assumed after the August mission that they would have to go back.[10] He had noticed that the 8th Air Force always went back to important targets. It was, however, an observation he didn't emphasize among his men.

During the September doldrums, the crewmen seemed to recover their spirits. In the barracks, they filled the hours writing letters, teasing the rookies, or singing songs. The veterans would check out the shoe sizes of the new men and tell them to keep their spare pairs shined because no one would want to inherit them if they were scuffed. They sang a song about something of which they weren't

269

getting much around the tiny town of Grafton-Underwood. It was a parody on one of the top tunes in the 1943 Hit Parade, "Praise the Lord and Pass the Ammunition":

Praise the Lord, she gave me her permission,
Praise the Lord, now look at her condition.
Praise the Lord, I knew the right position
And she fell for me . . .

They also sang a self-deprecating parody of the Air Force anthem, "Into the Air, Army Airmen," based on a popular children's radio program:

Into the air, Junior Birdman,
Into the air, Birdman true.
Into the air, Junior Birdman,
Get your ass into the blue . . .

Sgt. Corwin Miller, the waist gunner in Lt. Philip Algar's crew who was wounded on the August 17 raid, had now begun a slow recovery at a general hospital in Nottingham.[11] The ingenuity of the 384th Group Surgeon, Maj. Henry Stroud, in pumping Miller's own blood out of his lungs back into his arteries had saved the gunner's life. But only by the narrowest of margins. Miller was not yet aware of the innovative procedure that had snatched him from death. While Dr. Stroud was working on him, Miller had awakened once to find himself punctured by what looked like a field of needles. He had said, "Doc, if you had any more needles, I guess you'd use 'em on me." Then he had lapsed again into a coma from which he didn't awake until the next day. It was twelve more days before he was able to eat anything, and it would be several months before he was fully recovered. But none of his buddies felt sorry for him when they came to visit him. Some of them even envied him. He had been awarded a Silver Star citation, and he wouldn't have to fly any more missions.

At Kimbolton, the men of the 379th Group were getting acquainted with the town pub, the Jones, where they could get drunk on the wartime British beer if they had stomach capacity for a lot of it. Many a man, "mild-and-bittered up" after an evening at the Jones, would find himself bottoms-up in a hedgerow when he tried to ride his

270

bicycle up the narrow, black-dark lanes to the base. Sometimes there were dances at the Red Cross Aero Club, but most of the crewmen were in no mood to dance. Most of them would hang around their barracks, listening to Glenn Miller, Dinah Shore, Betty Hutton, Bing Crosby, or the skinny kid, Frank Sinatra, on the Armed Forces Network. They often listened to Lord Haw Haw, with his precise British diction, delivering the "news" on the German propaganda network. Haw Haw was startlingly accurate in his little items about activities of the American bomb groups, but few of these items were of any importance. They were designed simply to make the Americans think there were enemy spies around them, and perhaps there were. But if so, they were wasting a lot of time on trivia. As for Lord Haw Haw's major stories about the war, and especially about the air war, they were not very convincing to men who were taking part in it.

The barracks at Kimbolton were never warm enough, because there wasn't enough coal for the stoves, a circumstance that gave rise to raids on the coal bins of other barracks. Capt. Derwyn Robb of the 379th found that he was usually chilled, but the damp British cold was no more discomforting to him than were the air-raid alarms.[12] It seemed to him that the minute he got his "sack warmed" and was on the verge of sleep he would hear the sirens start their "eerie screeching in the distance." As the German bombers came closer, "succeeding towns would set theirs to wailing until our own blasted you awake." The loudspeaker would then announce, "Air raid warning red!" which was merely an alert to make certain all blackout curtains were closed. If the Germans kept approaching, the next announcement would be "Air raid warning purple!" which was an order to take shelter. To do so, a man had to get up, get dressed, and go out in the cold. Most of the veterans didn't bother. Having lived through German gunfire at point-blank range on mission after mission, they couldn't get very excited about German bombs dropped in the dark from 10,000 feet. Some of the men didn't even seem to care. They expected to die anyway, and they were fatalists about it. What difference did it make whether it happened in their planes or in their sacks?

Capt. William Smith of the 351st Group at Polebrook had completed twenty-four missions by the end of September and was sweating out his last one.[13] As the weather socked in again after the September 27 Emden mission, he became more nervous and impatient by the hour. He wanted to get that twenty-fifth mission in and be done with it. Yet he dreaded it more than any of the others. He could envision the hideous fate of surviving twenty-four missions, including such horrors as Schweinfurt, and then going down on the last one.

He was brooding about this possibility when a teletype message came to Polebrook from 8th Air Force headquarters ordering Capt. William R. Smith, 0790727, to report immediately to General Eaker at Bushy Park. Smith hadn't seen the commanding general since flying him to Africa after the Schweinfurt-Regensburg raid. But Smith and his entire crew had received, on August 26, a commendation from Eaker for that flight, conveying his appreciation of their hard work and his admiration of their "superior qualities."

When Smith reached Bushy Park and walked into Eaker's office, the general (now wearing the three stars of a lieutenant general since his September 13 promotion) looked up and smiled. "You thought I'd forgotten about you," he said, "didn't you?"

Smith said, "Well, sir, I didn't know there was any reason for you to remember me. Are you going on another trip?"

"No, but I've had someone keeping track of your tour. You're just about finished, aren't you?"

"Yes sir. One more mission."

"Are you anxious to get home?"

"Well, sir, I'm a bachelor. I don't have any family to worry about, but I had figured on going home to get into B-29s."

"Would you object to postponing that a few months?" Eaker asked. "I'd like you to set up a plane and crew with you as my pilot."

Smith could scarcely believe his good fortune. There was no better and safer duty for a pilot than flying a general. He mumbled something about being honored. Then he said, "I'm not in that much hurry to get home."

Eaker, dismissing him, said, "Fine. Go out and tell General Chauncey about our conversation."

When Smith approached the chief of staff's desk, Chauncey asked, "Well, how did it go?"

"I guess I'm it," Smith said.

"All right, get on up to Polebrook, pack your things, and come back down. We'll have a billet for you."

Smith enjoyed another moment of elation before remembering that he still had something else hanging over his head. "But sir," he said, "I've got one more mission to go."

"Oh forget that."

Smith realized he would be happy to forget it. He hated missions as much as any man, but he thought about all the other men in his group who would have to finish theirs, and he wondered how they would feel if he didn't do the same. "That's a great temptation, sir," he said to Chauncey, "and I'm no hero. But may I think about it over lunch?"

When Smith returned to Chauncey after lunch he said, "Sir, I came over here to finish a tour, and I don't want to have to explain to people the rest of my life why I didn't finish it. I may regret it, but I've got to fly that last mission."

Chauncey laughed and sent him on his way. Smith's last mission was the October 2 Emden raid. He was so nervous when he took off he could just manage to hold the controls steady. But fortunately for him, the port of Emden was such a short run that the P-47s could accompany the bombers all the way. The 351st Group was virtually unmolested, and for Smith, that last mission was "a piece of cake." The next day he reported to Eaker's headquarters.

The men of the "Bloody 100th" Group, so named because of its atrocious loss rate, had little cause for laughter, especially after the August 17 mission in which they lost nine planes. Life looked so unpromising that many of them began to treat it as a joke. If they took it seriously, it became unbearable. When the ragged remnants of the 100th reached Africa from Regensburg August 17, the survivors were so badly shot up only a few could fly the return mission against Bordeaux. Most flew instead across North Africa and out over the Atlantic to reach England. One pilot, Lt. Owen D. "Cowboy" Roane, had "requisitioned" a donkey in Africa and brought it home on his plane. Entering the traffic pattern at Thorpe Abbots, he radioed to the tower: "Stand by, I'm coming in with a frozen ass."

Col. Neil Harding, the 100th Group commander, was a former football star and a convivial man who kept in shape at the officers' club bar. He liked to give the impression that he didn't take anything seriously. One night at the club he laughingly strummed a base fiddle while his men engaged in a brawl with some uninvited visitors from the neighboring 95th Group at Horham. A favorite pastime at the club when the officers weren't drinking or brawling, and sometimes when they were, was indoor bicycle racing around the lounge. In the barracks, the men tried to relieve their combat pressure by pulling outrageous gags on each other and composing songs with titles like "Your Rear is like a Stovepipe, Nellie Darling" and "I'm in the Nude for Love." The latter gave rise to another: "I'm not in the Nude for Love, I'm Selling This Thing for Money."[14]

A sergeant named Walter Grenier became famous in the 100th although he belonged to it for only a few hours. Arriving as a replacement the morning of September 6, he was at table in the mess hall when he was told to fill in for a sick crew member on the Stuttgart mission that day. The plane he flew was shot down, but Grenier was never forgotten. He was always referred to thereafter as "The Man Who Came to Dinner."

Two other members of the 100th, Sgts. George Janos and Frank Dannella, bailed out over Germany that same day and were marched through the streets of Frankfurt with fifty other prisoners while angry crowds shouted at them in English, "Son of bitch Roosevelt children!" When Janos and Dannella reached prison camp, the German officer who interrogated them already knew their group and squadron numbers as well as their names. He smiled and said, "How is Thorpe Abbots?"

Lt. Ernest Warsaw of the 100th, who had been shot down August 17 and had thrown away his dog tags to prevent the Gestapo from learning he was Jewish, was now in Prisoner of War Camp Stalag 3, about twenty miles from Breslau, Poland.[15] Warsaw, navigator of the crippled B-17 that had fired on approaching German fighters after its wheels were down, had undergone some interesting experiences on his odyssey across Germany to the camp. After one day with the Gestapo, he had been handed over to a Luftwaffe sergeant and two privates who were to escort him to his destination. Because there was no other transportation available, they had to travel from Aachen to Cologne by streetcars, seven of them, transferring from one to another; and Warsaw was conscious every moment of how conspicuous they were—three well-dressed German soldiers with one ragged, disheveled American in a flying suit that had "the ass shot away." They took a "Cook's tour" of Cologne, which was a "huge mass of rubble" as a result of R.A.F. raids. Bodies were still strewn on the streets, and the city seemed in a state of paralysis. Warsaw's escorts, who were polite and friendly, told him Cologne had been in ruins for several months.

After twelve hours of streetcar travel, the Germans brought him to the Cologne airport, which was also a fighter base, and put him in a cell. Here Warsaw let his captors know he spoke German, a fact that fascinated them so much they took him to the officers' mess and then to the control tower. He was a novelty. Most of the fighter pilots had never before seen an American flier except through their gun-sights. And none of them had ever met one with whom they could converse in their own language.

One day while Warsaw was still held at Cologne, a German captain, a flier wearing an Iron Cross and several other medals, came in drunk to see "the American flier who speaks German." Though apparently friendly with Warsaw, he was angry at "some son of a bitch" who had "shot me down after his plane surrendered."

As the captain loudly described the B-17 that had put its wheels down and then opened fire with all its guns, Warsaw began to wonder uncomfortably if the man was talking about his plane. He recalled that as he looked out of his navigator's window before bailing out, he had been vaguely aware that for some reason the bomber's wheels were down. Though he hadn't given it much thought at the time, it occurred to him now that the wheels were probably down when he and the rest of the crew fired on the German fighters sliding in as if to fly formation with them.

The captain bellowed indignantly about the hoodlums who had violated the unwritten airmen's code by firing with their wheels down. What kind of people were they? Gangsters, nothing more or less. Warsaw remained discreetly silent as the outraged German flier continued his tirade.

Finally the man's anger spent itself. He subsided, looked at Warsaw in his cell, smiled, and offered him a cigarette. "Never mind," he said, "all men who fly are comrades." and after a final handshake, walked away.

Warsaw could breathe more easily. He had not been found out. But that was not the last he would hear about the "gangsters" who fired their guns after putting their wheels down. When he finally reached Stalag 3 after a long, arduous journey through war-torn Germany, and other American prisoners learned he was from the 100th Group, they would say to him, "Oh yeah, the Bloody One Hundredth. You're the guys who keep firing after your wheels are down." He never told any of them how right they were.

Morale was slightly higher in the 96th Group at Snetterton Heath than in some others, partly because the group's losses had been relatively low, and partly because of the leadership of Col. Archie Old, who was the group's commander until September 6, when he became a wing commander. Old was the kind of commander who ate with the enlisted men almost as often as he did with the officers. He kept a fighter plane on the base that he flew as an observer when the group practiced formations. He would cruise above a formation and if it began to straggle, dive right down through it, "chewing ass" on his radio until the bombers tightened up again. When Old went to wing, Col. Robert L. Travis took over a well-disciplined group.

The 96th, like other groups, was receiving a slow but steady stream of replacements. One replacement crew that arrived in September was headed by Lt. Robert H. Bolick, pilot, and Lt. Edward F. Downs, copilot. Bolick was a flier with such natural skills that Downs had developed a strong admiration for him even before they left the States. It seemed to Downs that Bolick handled a plane as if it were his right arm.[16] When they flew across the Atlantic and reached Scotland, they found it completely covered by clouds. They were able to contact the Prestwick tower by radio, but they couldn't understand what the Scottish traffic controller was saying. Bolick decided to go down through the clouds and make a blind instrument approach. Though he didn't come out of the overcast until he was under five hundred feet, he found the runway and landed easily. Then he learned what the man in the tower had been saying: "Go elsewhere. The field is closed."

While Bolick and Downs were still at the Bovingdon Replacement Depot, before being assigned to the 96th, they and their bombardier, Lt. Harold Edelstein, got some free time and went to London. It was a rainy, blacked-out night, and they were standing in almost total darkness under a Piccadilly awning when Downs felt a hand on his shoulder. Was he about to be robbed? He turned but could see absolutely nothing behind him. Then he smelled perfume. A girl's voice said, "Would you like to come home and sleep with me, lieutenant?" She had touched his shoulder to ascertain his rank from his insignia. At the same time, another girl was doing likewise with

Bolick. It was their first encounter with the easy ladies of Piccadilly and they were titillated, but they were not accustomed to choosing girls sight unseen. They declined with thanks.

When Bolick's crew reached Snetterton Heath after going through transition training and being assigned to the 96th, most of his men had never heard of Schweinfurt. They had been in Grand Island, Nebraska, when the costly August 17 mission took place. They soon heard about Schweinfurt from the older crews, but it didn't make a strong impression. On October 2 they flew their first mission to Emden, and that frightened them sufficiently. Though it was not considered a difficult mission, they thought it was rough enough. Still rookies, they couldn't yet imagine the kind of experiences in store for them.

Staff Sgt. Leo Rand, a big, persuasive-looking gunner and former steelworker from Youngstown, Ohio, who joined the 94th Group at Bury St. Edmunds as a member of a replacement crew in early October, was less reserved than Bolick and Downs around British women. He learned quickly that the kind of girl he might meet at Piccadilly considered all Americans rich. He had been told by an Englishman he met that when the Canadians came, the British "was gettin' a piece of ass for a shilling." But the Canadians "gave 'em two shillings. And when the God damned Yanks came over, they didn't know where to stop. They were liable to give 'em a few pounds."

That was not Rand's style. He preferred to meet nice girls in pubs, and he found them very approachable. Some of the British men might resent the way the Americans dressed and the way they flashed their money, but the girls didn't. And as for the men, Rand didn't have any trouble. Not many men enjoy making trouble for steelworkers from Youngstown.

The 94th had bounced back after finding itself in a sorry condition after the June 13 mission to Keil. That was the day nine of its planes were shot down in the Channel on the way back because the gunners, thinking they would see no more Germans, were cleaning their weapons when a squadron of JU-88s arrived. A week later, General Eaker had decided the group needed a new commander and had sent one of his original six staff members, Col. Frederick Castle, who had been nagging him for a chance to be airborne rather than chairborne. The group did not welcome Castle when he arrived. Many of the men were cynical, not only about their chances of survival but also about the prospect of being commanded by a desk officer. Before the end of July, Castle had turned that feeling around by personally leading the 94th, plus thirteen planes from the 388th, on a mission against a Focke-Wulf fighter plant at Oschersleben. The clouds were so heavy no other groups could even find the target, but Castle's planes broke through a small opening and bombed so effectively that reconnaissance photos indicated a whole month's production, perhaps fifty FW-190s, had been lost. Thereupon, life had become easier for Castle at Bury St. Edmunds. He had won a lot of respect, and the 94th Group records were steadily improving.

Lt. Ted Winslow, the 91st Group bombardier who had been shot down in Belgium August 17 and had broken his leg parachuting into a beet field, was still at large in early October, protected by members of the Belgian underground.[17] The day after he landed, a doctor had come to the farm where he was hidden and had set his leg. Whenever the farmer heard motorcycle sounds, indicating the German police might be coming, his two daughters jumped into bed with Winslow, one on each side, tenting up the covers to make it look as if they were the only ones in the bed.

After three days Winslow had been taken to another house, then another in the town of Flobecque. The man there, fearing Winslow might be a German posing as an American, asked him where he was from in the United States. Winslow said Springfield, Massachusetts. What was the population there? Winslow wasn't sure, but he had better come close because the man was looking it up in an atlas. Winslow said, "About 100,000." It was close enough to satisfy the man. (He must have had an old atlas. The 1940 population of Springfield was actually 148,000.)

Eventually Winslow was moved to a house in Wannebecq, where he still remained. His leg was healed now. He could move if he wished, but where would he go? Belgium was full of German secret police, looking for downed American fliers and the people who were hiding them.

Winslow's old buddies in the 91st Group at Bassingbourn, who had led the August 17 mission against Schweinfurt and had lost ten planes including Winslow's in the process, were very much aware of the possibility that they might have to go back there, and they didn't like the idea. Schweinfurt still stood out as the supreme symbol of horror in the entire 8th Air Force. Even new men who had arrived since August shuddered at the thought of it once they heard the stories. Lt. Bruce D. Moore, a navigator, had joined the 91st a few days after Schweinfurt to learn that several good friends from training days had died that day. Another friend who had survived it, Lt. Charles Hudson, a bombardier, had described the mission to Moore, making him wonder if there weren't some way he could get into another business.

After Moore's first four missions, between late August and early October, he was even less enthusiastic about the occupation he had chosen. On each mission, at least one man in his plane had been wounded and at least one engine had been shot out. The plane had been on fire once, and Moore had once blacked out from lack of oxygen. Yet no one claimed any of these missions was as tough as Schweinfurt.

With the numerical strength of the 8th Air Force building up once more since Schweinfurt, the bombers were beginning to invade Germany again. It was only the short run to Emden so far, on September 27 and October 2. Emden wasn't so bad. The P-47s could now go that far even with the puny drop-tanks they were carrying. But the B-17s couldn't spend the rest of the war hitting Emden. Every man in his right mind knew they would soon be going deeper into Germany. Would they have to go back to Schweinfurt? Moore, like most of the men in the 91st and like most of the men in the 8th Bomber Command, was afraid they would, but he preferred not to think about it.

On October 3, forecasters indicated the weather would be good over western Germany the next day. General Anderson at 8th Bomber Command had 361 heavy bombers (B-17s and B-24s) waiting for this word. On the morning of the 4th, the B-24s, 35 of them, took off on a diversion flight while 326 B-17s headed straight for Frankfurt, with more P-47s than ever before escorting them, at least as far as Aachen. Fighter opposition was strong, but the Forts hit several targets in Frankfurt. Only 12 bombers were lost. The new, remotely controlled chin turrets performed effectively against frontal attacks. Gunners claimed the destruction of 56 German fighters.

Even if General Anderson discounted this figure to a reasonable extent, he had to be pleased. His loss was light, the offensive was on again, and the weather outlook for October was promising.

It was four days later, on the 8th, however, before the Fortresses could fly again. This time 30 were shot down in a two-pronged attack on Bremen. Despite the loss, 352 heavy bombers were able to take off the next morning to hit Gdynia naval yards as well as aircraft factories at Marienburg and Anklam. The Germans were caught by surprise at Marienburg, which was so far east they didn't realize it had to be defended, and the bombing there was so precise that Sir Charles Portal, after seeing the photos, wrote a glowing report to Prime Minister Churchill:

> This is about the best high altitude bombing we have seen in this war. You asked yesterday whether they could put their bombs into the area of St. James' Park. As a matter of interest, I have attached to the photograph a tracing of St. James' Park on the same scale, from which you will see that almost all the bombs went into the area.
>
> Only one building of the factory is not destroyed, and that one is damaged. It was a magnificent attack.[18]

At the same time, the results over Anklam were less spectacular, and the B-24s that flew to Gdynia missed their target completely. Twenty-eight heavy bombers were lost on the 9th.

Münster was the target of 274 Fortresses on the 10th. Despite heavy flak and attacks by an estimated 200 fighters, the B-17s dropped their bombs on the city. However, 30 of them went down. The 8th had lost 88 bombers in three days, but not without hurting the German fighter force. B-17 gunners claimed 177 enemy fighters at Münster. Though this figure was undoubtedly too optimistic, it did indicate that the fighter toll was heavy. Perhaps the German defenses had been softened sufficiently. The time had come to look toward Schweinfurt once more.

A prompting in that direction came from Washington on the 11th, in a congratulatory cable from Arnold to Eaker:

> The employment of larger bombing forces on successive days is encouraging proof that you are putting an increasing proportion of

your bombers where they will hurt the enemy. Good work. As you turn your effort away from ship-building cities and toward crippling the sources of the still-growing German fighter forces the air war is clearly moving toward our supremacy in the air. Carry on.

The same day brought congratulations also from Churchill, who said in his message, "I am confident that with the ever-growing power of the 8th Air Force, striking alternate blows with the Royal Air Force Bomber Command, we shall together inexorably beat the life out of the industrial Germany and thus hasten the day of final victory." At the same time, Eaker was informed that King George VI had made him a Knight Commander of the Most Excellent Order of the British Empire.

By the 12th, Anderson's staff at Bomber Command had completed the new Schweinfurt plan. It needed only final approval before execution. Eaker traveled to Anderson's headquarters at High Wycombe (now in underground bunkers like those of the R.A.F. Bomber Command) for a briefing on the operation. He listened while Anderson and staff outlined the details.[19] There would be no division of forces this time as there had been in August. All available bombers would go to Schweinfurt in the 8th Air Force's greatest show of strength. How many planes were ready? More than four hundred. Were the crews ready? They had been resting for two days. Was there anything else to decide? Nothing. It was settled then, Eaker and Anderson agreed. On the first clear day, the Fortresses would return to Schweinfurt, the most hazardous target in Europe.

15

The air was cold and foggy as the seventeen crews of the 381st Group assembled in their briefing hut at 7:00 A.M. the morning of October 14. The question among most of the men was not where they would be going today but whether they would be going at all. The fog did not look as if it would ever lift. But this being England, any kind of weather change was possible.

As soon as the men were settled in their chairs, a briefing officer began pulling back the curtain that covered the map on the front wall.[1] He pulled and pulled, exposing, moment by moment, more and more of Belgium, then Germany, more and more of the string that plotted the route they were supposed to take that day—Clacton, Antwerp, Aachen, Bonn, Frankfurt, Bad Kissingen, and finally, the end of the string, Schweinfurt.

At the briefing officer's first mention of the word "Schweinfurt," a hush fell over the men. They hadn't forgotten the eleven B-17s the group had lost there in August. A medical officer standing by at the briefing observed that the crews seemed to be completely shocked. He also noticed that as the briefing continued, nothing was said about the number of fighters they were likely to encounter. After the briefing, the doctor went from crew to crew, checking equipment, making sure everyone had sandwiches and coffee. Most of the men didn't seem to care about such small matters. They were deeply frightened, and to the doctor it was "obvious that many doubted they would return."

When he asked one briefing officer why nothing had been said about fighters, he was told that the omission was intentional. There was little point in reminding the men that the entire German fighter force in the west was stationed within eighty-five miles of their course. Most of the crewmen already knew it. If not, they would find out soon enough.

One fairly prominent member of the 381st Group would not be going today. The captain who had tried to resign from flying as a result of his experiences on the first Schweinfurt mission had now finally managed to do so.[2] Though Colonel Nazzaro, the 381st commander, had talked the fear-stricken officer into flying two more missions since then, the captain had reported once more to the medical section just the day before, October 13, and had reiterated his announcement that he had "no desire to continue flying." This time he was sent to the Central Medical Board for reclassification. Anyone familiar with his case could hardly help wondering if he was clairvoyant. How did he know yesterday that the group would be going back to Schweinfurt today?

At the briefing of the 96th Group in Snetterton Heath, Col. Archie Old felt a special determination as he listened to the intelligence officers outline the mission plans, describe the route, and estimate the opposition.[3] The fact that Old's plane had been forced to abort on the August 17 mission increased his resolve to see Schweinfurt today. The August mission was the only one on which he had ever aborted.

If this background hadn't provided enough incentive, today Old also had the heavy responsibility of leading an entire task force. During a recent Bomber Command reorganization, the former First and Fourth Combat Bombardment Wings had been expanded and redesignated as the First and Third Air Divisions, each composed of three newly created combat bombardment wings. Old, who had been 96th Group commander, was now in charge of the 45th Combat Bombardment Wing, which was to spearhead the Third Division against Schweinfurt. He would command from the copilot's seat of the division's lead plane unless Curt LeMay showed up at the last

283

minute to bump him out of the job, as LeMay had done August 17. Since LeMay was now a brigadier general and commander of the Third Division, he should no longer be flying missions, but no one could predict what that man might or might not do at any time. Old's crew today would be the same one which carried LeMay in August.

Lts. Robert Bolick and Edward Downs had arrived for this same 96th Group briefing without any inkling of their destination, and they did not react immediately when the map curtain was drawn back and Schweinfurt was revealed as the day's target.[4] Bolick and Downs were still relative newcomers, preparing for their sixth mission. While they had heard about Schweinfurt, they hadn't given it much thought. They realized the place was special, however, when groans arose from the men around them, and they were even more deeply impressed when the briefing officer read a message to all groups from General Anderson at Bomber Command:

> This air operation today is the most important air operation yet conducted in this war. The target must be destroyed. It is of vital importance to the enemy. Your friends and comrades that have been lost and that will be lost today are depending on you. Their sacrifice must not be in vain. Good luck, good shooting, and good bombing.

The briefing officer at the 96th spoke honestly and openly about the hazards of the task in front of them. He made no attempt to gloss over how rough the mission would be. But could it be any worse than the Bremen and Münster raids of the previous week, each of which had cost thirty planes? The older men seemed to think so, especially for their group, which would be leading the entire second task force today.

Sgt. Phillip R. Taylor, a waist gunner in Capt. Beryl Dalton's 91st Group crew, was ready for a tough mission (it would be his tenth) when he reported for the briefing at Bassingbourn, but neither he nor any of his buddies was ready for Schweinfurt.[5] An immediate silence fell upon the room when the target was announced. These men remembered the ten crews they had lost in the August raid. Taylor suddenly considered himself dead, and he found that the men around him felt the same way. After the briefing, the entire crew went back to their barracks and put on their best Class A uniforms—wool olive-drab pants and shirts—beneath their flying suits. They decided they did not want to be captured or killed in the nondescript fatigue clothing they wore on most missions.

Maj. William E. "Pop" Dolan, the 384th Group intelligence officer who conducted the briefing at Grafton-Underwood, began by telling the men: "You're in the big league now. You're not in the bush leagues any more." After describing the ball-bearing factories and referring to the August attack against them, he concluded, "You're going to have to get them this time or you'll go back again."

Capt. Philip Algar, who had flown the first Schweinfurt mission and would be piloting the 384th's lead plane today (with Maj. George W. Harris, the group leader, as copilot), decided he was "in for a really bad time."[6] What bothered him most was his realization that the P-47s could escort them for only a pitifully short distance.

Capt. Edwin Millson of the 379th Group, a veteran of twelve missions, had been awakened about 3:30 A.M. by the charge-of-quarters and told he was expected at the operations building.[7] As he walked along the dark streets of the Kimbolton base, he felt an "odd excitement" in wondering what the target would be. As one of the group's lead bombardiers, he had been making a special study of Schweinfurt for several weeks, but he didn't know he was going there until he walked into Operations. Capt. Joseph G. Wall, a lead navigator, looked up from a map on which he was plotting a flight plan.

"You sure picked a nice one for your thirteenth," he said to Millson. They were both scheduled to fly with that day's group leader, Lt. Col. Louis W. Rohr.

The so-called "Bloody One Hundredth" Group had been living up to its name so appallingly during the previous week that it seemed in danger of extinction. At Bremen October 8 it had lost eight of its fifteen Fortresses; at Münster two days later it had lost twelve of thirteen. These disasters had so badly depleted the group that its commander, Col. Neil Harding, had gone to 8th Air Force headquarters to ask that all his surviving men be allowed to rest for a few days.[8]

From the staff officers with whom he talked there, Harding had received a severe dressing down and a suggestion that he change his training methods "so that your boys can learn to fly the B-17." Then their losses might not be so heavy.

Harding in return had suggested angrily that "You junior officers might need to learn, but not my boys.'' He had then returned to Thorpe Abbots to get the remnants of his group ready for the next mission, which was today's trip to Schweinfurt. This time the 100th could muster only eight airworthy planes, not enough to fly as a unit. Four were assigned to the 95th Group; the other four to the 390th.

S. Sgt. Leo Rand of the 94th Group would be flying his first mission today. He had trained for it by playing blackjack in the barracks until the early-morning hours.[9] He had won so many pounds, shillings, and pence that when the game was finished, one of his opponents had said jokingly, ''I hope you go down tomorrow.''

At the briefing, when Rand saw how the other men reacted to the Schweinfurt announcement, he began to think there was at least some small likelihood of it. He couldn't figure out why they were so worried. Did they get this excited before every mission?

''It's bad,'' one of the men near him said when the map curtain went up, and several others repeated, ''It's bad, bad, bad.''

''What's so bad?'' Rand wanted to know. He realized he was a ''greenhorn,'' but even though he had never been on a mission, he couldn't imagine its being as bad as they pretended. Yet their concern worried him a little. He wanted to survive, and he wanted to make a showing for himself. So he looked around and, picking out some of the old-timers in the group, began asking them questions he had never before thought to ask. They were glad to describe for him what it was like to fly a really tough mission. They told him all about the first Schweinfurt raid. And Sergeant Rand was suddenly struck by the realization that today he would be gambling not just for money but for his life.

Col. Budd Peaslee, now deputy commander of the 40th Combat Bombardment Wing and air commander of the First Division today, almost missed the briefing of the 92nd Group, with which he was to fly, because his driver became dismally lost in the fog on the way to Podington, fifty miles north of London, where the 92nd was now based.[10] But Peaslee did arrive in time for the group rollcall and the unveiling of the map.

''It's Schweinfurt,'' said the briefing officer, a neatly uniformed major.

As a buzz of excited chatter filled the room, one voice rose above the others: ''Sonofabitch! And this is my last mission.''

Peaslee thought to himself, it might well be.

The major, after explaining the importance of the ball-bearing plants and the reason they had to revisit them, assured the men that flak would be light along their route, except over the Ruhr and at Schweinfurt, where the Germans had installed three hundred 88-mm. guns with excellent crews as a result of the August raid. "You new crews—don't panic and try to dodge," he warned. "And you'll leave yourself wide open to get picked off if you straggle." He also cautioned the tail gunners to "keep a sharp watch for twin-engine ME-210s sneaking up vapor trails to blast you." The older B-17s still left thick white wakes behind them at high altitudes.

When the major finished, another officer showed films of Schweinfurt, its factories, and several landmarks on the way to it. The group navigator explained the route, and the meteorologist gave an uncertain weather forecast. Visibility was now only a quarter of a mile, but it should increase to one mile by takeoff time. At 2,000 feet, he said, they would break out of the overcast. The continent was expected to be clear, and by the time they returned, southern England should be fairly clear.

Colonel Peaslee then stood up. He told them to fly their formations as if it were "a Presidential review," to conserve their ammunition, to fill the hole quickly if another plane dropped out, and to keep their guns loaded until landing. He reminded them of the nine B-17s of the 94th Group that were shot down in June over the Channel while their crews were cleaning their guns. And he concluded with a joke about today's bombs scattering so many millions of steel balls around Schweinfurt that the Germans there would soon be skittering and pratfalling as if they were on rollerskates. The men laughed and Peaslee sat down. There was nothing to do now but wait for the ceiling to rise. It began to look as if the weather in England would not stop them. The fog was already clearing.

At the underground Bomber Command headquarters in High Wycombe, Gen. Fred Anderson and staff waited for the last report they would need before ordering the planes to go—the continental weather report. High over Germany, above fighter range, a British Mosquito weather plane was now cruising. About 9:00 A.M., its pilot announced over his radio transmitter, "The continent is clear."

This word, monitored in England, was soon passed to Anderson. He announced calmly, "The mission is on."

Takeoff at all bases began shortly after 10:00 A.M. Most of the

287

planes were in the clouds within a half-hour, but they did not rise above the clouds as quickly as the weathermen had predicted. The overcast was gloomy and solid, not just to 2,000 but to 6,000 feet and more, a circumstance that delayed assembly and forced lead planes to circle for two hours, firing signal flares to shepherd their followers into formation.[11] A total of 377 heavy bombers were now in the air over England, including 163 B-17s of the First Division, 154 B-17s of the Third Division, and 60 B-24s of the smaller Second Division. While this force included about 60 fewer aircraft than Anderson had hoped to send, it was still sizable. It was destined to diminish quickly, however, when only 24 of the B-24s could find one another at their rendezvous location. Rather than send such a pitifully small contingent to a target as dangerous as Schweinfurt, Bomber Command sent the B-24s on a diversion raid up the North Sea to the Frisian Islands.

Meanwhile, mechanical failures were diminishing the two B-17 forces so that when it was time to fly eastward toward the Channel, the First Division had 149 planes in the air, and the Third Division, 142. But even then, not all of these planes were where they belonged. The 381st Group, which was supposed to take the low position in the First Division's 1st Combat Bombardment Wing, had suffered an aggravating delay in assembly because its planes did not break out of the overcast above Ridgewell until they reached 10,000 feet. When their group leader, Maj. George Shackley, finally got them together and led them to the wing assembly point, he found the 92nd and 306th Groups there, but he was looking for the 91st and 351st. Shackley contacted the 91st Group leader and arranged a rendezvous over Orfordness. His planes lacked the speed to make this rendezvous, however, and the three groups assigned to the 1st CBW did not get together until they reached mid-Channel. By that time they had acquired another lost group.

Colonel Peaslee, in the lead plane of his 40th Combat Bombardment Wing had assembled the entire 92nd Group behind him, and the 306th Group was sliding into the high position on his right when he began to wonder why he hadn't yet seen the 305th Group, which was supposed to be on his left wing.

"Where the hell is our low group?" he asked his tail gunner on the interphone. "Can you see a loose group anywhere?"

This "gunner" was actually the crew's regular copilot, whom

288

Peaslee had displaced and who was acting as his rearward observer. "No, sir," he said. He did not see any unattached groups.

They were now at 20,000 feet and approaching the Channel coast. After one final circle to tighten the entire First Division formation, the task force would be moving eastward across the water toward the continent. But Peaslee could not lead the force with only two groups in his wing. The lead group was required to have three groups for maximum defensive firepower because the Germans in recent weeks had been concentrating on frontal attacks against leading elements. As the division began its final circle, Peaslee ordered the bombardier to fire a signal flare every twenty seconds in the hope of attracting the errant 305th, but even as he gave the order, he felt it was futile. While he could see in the distance the two other wings of the First Division, he could not see any single groups. After finishing the circle, he gave the order to his pilot, Capt. James K. McLaughlin, to set a course for the continent. "Maybe they're waiting for us over the Channel," he said hopefully.

At the English coastline the clouds ended abruptly, revealing the blue Channel waters below and the dark-green continent ahead but no loose B-17 group searching for its wing. Peaslee had to decide quickly what to do. On the radio he called the leader of the 1st CBW, Lt. Col. Theodore Milton in the high position to the right.

"I'm short one group," Peaslee said. "You will take over the lead. I'll fly high on you, and I'll retain air command from that position."[12]

While Peaslee's 40th Combat Bombardment Wing was executing a slow 360-degree turn to let Milton's 1st Wing move forward, Peaslee at last located his missing 305th Group. It was attached to the 1st CBW as the low group.

The 305th had taken off six minutes late, and after completing assembly over Chelveston, had been unable to find the two other groups of the 40th CBW, the 92nd and 306th. Maj. C.G.Y. Normand, the 305th leader, had led his seventeen aircraft to Daventry, then to Spalding without finding the rest of the wing. He had tried but failed to contact Peaslee by radio. He did however encounter the 1st CBW, and by this time was so desperate for company he slipped into its low position, which was open because the 381st Group had not yet caught up to it. This meant that when Major Shackley's 381st finally did catch up in mid-Channel, its assigned low position was already occupied. Shackley found room for his sixteen planes next to the 351st Group in the high position. This move probably saved the lives of many of Shackley's men.

The arrival of a fourth group for his 1st CBW offered some comfort to Colonel Milton and the men of the 91st Group because they had been able to muster only eleven planes that day and four of them had already aborted.[13] The 91st was just seven planes strong when Peaslee ordered it to take the lead, and the veterans in those seven planes were suddenly reinforced in their memory of August 17. The 91st had been the lead group that day, also, as the wreckage of ten of its planes along today's route would testify.

Capt. David Williams, lead navigator for the entire task force August 17, found himself in the same position today since he was in Colonel Milton's plane as the 91st Group navigator. Thinking back as he looked ahead, Williams had only one thing for which to be thankful: at least he knew the way to Schweinfurt. He would never be able to forget it.[14]

The Third Division, led by two units of the exceptionally well-stocked 96th Group, with Colonel Old in command, was fortunate enough to escape the assembly problems of the First Division. Adopting a course parallel to that of the First but ten miles south, the Third crossed the English coastline at 12:25, only five minutes behind schedule. Old, concerned about even this small delay, radioed Ground Control that he might be late for his rendezvous with the 56th Fighter Group's P-47s at Sas-Van-Gent.

On its route across the Channel, the Third Division encountered a cloud bank at 21,000 feet and for a short time lost one high squadron after its leader was forced to abort; but this squadron soon got back into position, and the entire division was ready for action, with crews at their stations and machine guns tested by short bursts, when, at 1:05 P.M.., it met the forty-eight Thunderbolts that would escort it as far as possible.

Because the First Division was ten minutes late, its escort, fifty Thunderbolts from the 353rd Fighter Group, overtook it in mid-Channel. Both task forces now had an escort, but not for very long. The P-47s were still using a belly tank that didn't work very well and had a capacity of only seventy-five gallons. They would be able to fly no further than the Aachen area, which was exactly where the B-17s had lost their escorts on the August 17 mission.

At General Eaker's 8th Air Force headquarters in Bushy Park, he could do nothing but sit stewing in his office as his bombers invaded Germany.[15] Once again he had found himself sending them out on a dangerous mission, this time probably the most dangerous of the war, with inadequate fighter support. He was getting tired of it. For a whole year he had been trying to get auxiliary tanks that would significantly lengthen the range of his fighters, but he still didn't have a tank that was both large enough and properly designed. Washington was partly responsible. The American tanks he had received were unsatisfactory, and too little effort had been applied to develop better ones. At the same time, Eaker also blamed the British. Their Ministry of Aircraft Production had promised to supply him a tank that was fairly satisfactory, but it had not delivered it. He had already remonstrated on the subject with Sir Wilfred Freeman, the director of M.A.P. Today he decided to try another tack. While waiting for news about the Schweinfurt mission, he wrote an uncharacteristically snappish letter to Sir Charles Portal, one of the most cooperative of his British associates:

> I think there is no question but that our mission last Sunday [to Münster] cost at least twenty heavy bombers which could have been saved had we had an ample supply of 108-gal. droppable fuel tanks. These tanks had been promised us by the Ministry of Aircraft Production in ample quantity as early as last month. M.A.P. has not been able to make good the promised deliveries. I have just received a cable from General Arnold which indicates that these long-range tanks cannot be supplied from the United States before December 1. If we can at once obtain an accelerated supply from M.A.P. it definitely would save a minimum of fifty long-range bombers, in my opinion, between now and the arrival of the U.S. produced tanks.

It was surprising that Eaker should call upon Portal in this matter since the M.A.P., while under Air Ministry jurisdiction, was outside Portal's control. But Eaker's exasperation had apparently reached its limits. Portal would at least be sympathetic. It was not so surprising that Eaker should choose this day to write him, when almost three hundred unescorted Flying Fortresses were on the way to Germany's best-protected target. Eaker knew they were about to catch hell.

In Germany, the Central Defense Headquarters' monitoring service had picked up signs of heavy air activity over England before 11:00 A.M. Whenever a flight of planes took off from East Anglia airfields and reached a height of five hundred feet, the monitoring service would broadcast the report, "Assembly has begun in England."[16] The Twelfth Air Corps in Zeist and other western air-defense installations had been notified immediately, and more than a score of fighter bases, with four hundred to five hundred planes standing by, had been alerted. At 12:20, when the American force began crossing the English coast, the Germans already knew its size and direction. The one thing they didn't yet know was its final destination. By 12:50, when the First Division crossed the Dutch coast, German planes from such bases as Antwerp and Abbeville were in the air to meet them.

Over the Walcheren Islands, twenty of these planes, all ME-109s, attacked, at 32,000 feet, the fifty P-47s of the U.S. 353rd Fighter Group under the command of Maj. Glenn E. Duncan. The second battle of Schweinfurt had now begun. These first German planes ignored the American bombers and concentrated on the fighters in an apparent attempt to break up the escort and send it home immediately rather than wait until its short range forced it to go home. This attempt failed. After a series of dogfights above the bombers, the ME-109s had managed to knock down only one P-47. The American pilots claimed ten Germans. Many of these were undoubtedly duplicates, but the Thunderbolts had proven that they would not be driven away until they ran short of gas.

Some of the early German pilots in the air were not so quick to attack. Lt. Heinz Knoke and his eleven ME-109s of the Fifth Squadron, *11 Gruppe Jagdgeschwader 2*, out of Jever, approached the First Division over Antwerp. But because the Fortresses were still accompanied by fighters and because Knoke's planes were carrying wing rockets that restricted their speed, he merely followed the American armada without getting too close.[17] He could afford to be patient. He knew the fighter escort would have to turn back near Aachen.

As the big bombers cruised across Belgium at 150 miles an hour with the protective fighters overhead, there were so few German planes around them that they looked as if they were on a milk-run mission. But one person on the ground below could tell this was not so. Lt. Ted Winslow, still at large since Aug. 17 and still being hidden by the Belgian Resistance in a house at Wannebecq, heard the unmistakable drone of B-17 engines from the northwest and looked out the dining-room window at the approaching armada.[18] Where was it going? Though he didn't know, he could tell by its size that it was on a major mission. Was it returning to Schweinfurt? This was the route to Schweinfurt, but it was also the route to several other important German targets. The B-17s, to keep the Germans in suspense as long as possible, almost always took an indirect route to their destination. Winslow couldn't even guess where they might be going today. He knew only that if they continued on their present route, they were in for trouble. He had traveled that way himself, and he sympathized with the men in the planes. Many of them would not come back. Yet as he watched those Fortresses, a shiver of thrills went through him. They were a beautiful sight, moving through the clear sky in solid formations, with P-47s cruising above them and long white vapor trails spreading out behind them.

16

It was shortly after 1:00 P.M. when the P-47s, now low on fuel, had to abandon the B-17s of the First Division between Aachen and Düren. Moments later the German fighters moved in like snarling beasts released from their cages. The sky around the bombers filled up with ME-109s, FW-190s, ME-110s, ME-210s, JU-88s, and even Stuka dive bombers. They had all been hovering at a safe distance, waiting to pounce.

The fifteen planes of the 305th Group apparently presented the most inviting target, perhaps because they were in the vulnerable low position on the left wing of the 1st CBW. Against the 305th, the German fighters attacked in groups of three to seven from every direction and using every known tactic. They came in such numbers and from so many angles that they were in danger of colliding, not only with the B-17s but also with each other. The twin-engine ME-110s and ME-210s lobbed rockets into the formation, emptying their entire arsenals before retiring. The Stukas climbed safely above the Fortresses and dropped time-fused bombs among them. The ME-109s and FW-190s sped in from front and rear, firing 20-mm. cannons, rockets, and machine guns.

The 305th Group gunners, overwhelmed by the unprecedented number of German planes at which to shoot, forgot everything they had been told about conserving ammunition. Future moments would have to take care of themselves. The moment of peril was now. More enemies than they had ever seen were upon them, and their only possible response was to spend more bullets than they had ever before fired.

So many German planes were in the air that even with this concentration on the 305th, the other groups were not neglected. There were enough enemy fighters for everybody today. The small, seven-plane contingent of 91st Group Fortresses, which led the First Division was "getting the hell shot out of" it when Lt. Bruce Moore, navigator in Lt. Henry G. Evers's crew, was nudged by the bombardier who was manning one of the forward guns.[1] He motioned toward Moore's metal, bowl-shaped compass cover and Moore handed it to him. Quickly he unzipped his leather flying suit and emptied himself into the bowl.

At that moment, someone shouted over the interphone, "Fighter at twelve o'clock level!"

The bombardier turned back to Moore, handed him the bowl full of urine, then began firing his machine gun at the German fighter coming at them from straight ahead.

When the fighter dived to avoid collision, the bombardier, his lower face covered by his gas mask, glanced back at Moore with laughter in his eyes. Moore, after resisting the temptation to dump the contents of the compass cover on his head, also began to laugh and laid the cover down near their escape hatch, where it soon tipped over. The urine spilled and almost immediately froze around the door joints. If they were forced to bail out today, they would have to find another exit.

Colonel Milton, commanding the 1st CBW from the lead plane of the 91st, sat helplessly in the copilot's seat, looking out at as fierce a fighter attack as he had ever seen. He had been on many previous missions, but mostly with the 351st Group from which he had transferred a few weeks earlier to become the 91st executive officer. A 1940 West Point graduate and son of an Army colonel, he had risen quickly despite his youth and was already under consideration as a group commander. Only by "gathering up bits and pieces" had he been able to muster even the seven planes in his depleted group this

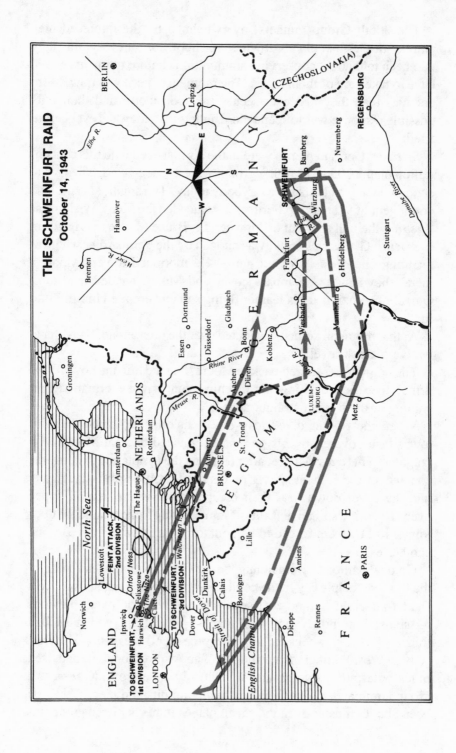

THE SCHWEINFURT RAID
October 14, 1943

morning. He hadn't dreamed of leading the division, but when Peaslee had ordered him to the front, he had not hesitated. Looking for something positive to distract him from the swarms of buzzing fighters, he glanced up at the sun and thought to himself: "At last, we've got perfect weather. Too good a day to go home without accomplishing something." But beneath this rationalization, he was beginning to wonder if he would be going home at all.

For several minutes after the P-47s departed, Colonel Peaslee, commanding the First Division and 40th CBW from the lead plane of the 92nd Group, watched the skies around him fill up with German fighters and wondered in dread when they would make their moves. Then, as he stared straight ahead, he saw a series of flashes that he recognized as the reports of 20-mm. cannon. A moment later, enemy planes were rushing toward his formation at closing speeds of more than five hundred miles an hour. As they veered right, left, or downward at the last possible second, he wondered how so many of them, approaching head-on, could avoid collision. Maybe the B-17s deserved some credit for this performance because they made no attempt to dodge. If they were to do so, they might dodge into the fighters' paths rather than away from them.

After the shock of the first attack, Peaslee talked by interphone to the copilot, who was his rear gunner, and learned that no planes had fallen although two were smoking and one seemed to be drifting back. The attacks resumed, and Peaslee's ears were assaulted by almost constant machine-gun fire. On the radio he chewed out his men for wasting ammunition with such long bursts. He reminded them they had hundreds of miles yet to go—if they were lucky. This German attack, he decided, was the finest he had ever seen, exceedingly well coordinated. The timing and technique were masterly.

While these thoughts raced through his head, he got a new report from the rear: "B-17 going down in flames. No parachutes yet."

They were over Düren, and this was the first Fortress to go. Its No. 3 and No. 4 engines were afire. As it fell, nine parachutes eventually appeared.

At the same time, more news came from the rear: "We have two aircraft lagging badly—back about three hundred yards."

Before Peaslee had time to react to this report, the pilot of his plane, Captain McLaughlin, directed Peaslee's attention ahead, below, and to the left. A bomber in another group, probably the 305th,

297

had just been hit by a rocket. The plane's right wing folded upward; the fuselage opened "like an eggshell," and a man with one arm torn away fell out to begin hurtling earthward. For a moment, Peaslee could see the pilot, still at the controls; then the entire plane burst into flames and dropped out of sight below the left wing of Peaslee's plane.

Peaslee noticed that, while the attacks were becoming even more intense, his gunners had stopped shouting out reports about them. It was pointless to talk about "bogies" here or "bogies" there when the "bogies" were everywhere. The interphones fell silent. The battle was becoming too desperate to talk about.

The entire First Division was now under constant siege by about two hundred German planes. The FW-190s and ME-109s plunged out of the sun to attack from ten o'clock to two o'clock level—alone, in pairs, in line abreast, and in line astern, sometimes as many as six or seven at once, though usually in smaller groups. Lt. Edwin Millson, firing his bombardier's gun from the 379th lead plane, dreaded these concerted attacks by larger groups because he feared they might indicate a change of tactics by all the German fighters. Millson felt the B-17 formations could survive if the Germans kept hitting "in oneseys and twoseys," but that if they were to make all their attacks in organized squadron strength, they might succeed in breaking up the armada.

The single-engine fighters, coming from the front, would fire their cannons and machine guns all at once, then break off into half-rolls or sudden dives within a few yards of collision points. Some of them, just before attacking, would engage in mock dogfights with each other to create the impression that they themselves were under attack by P-47s.

The twin-engine fighters came in mostly from the rear, between five o'clock and seven o'clock level, to a range of fifteen hundred or a thousand yards, whereupon they would lob their shells or rockets into the formations.

Some of the single-engine fighters also carried rockets. These included Lt. Heinz Knoke's squadron of eleven ME-109s, which had been following the B-17s since they passed over Antwerp. Ready now to attack, Knoke, with his comrades behind him, closed in on the First Division from the rear. Before he had a chance to fire either of his rockets, a Fortress gunner hit the underside of his left wing, ripping a great hole in it and shooting away the rocket rack attached to it. Knoke, controlling his suddenly unbalanced plane with difficulty and fearful that his left wing might snap off at any moment, nevertheless continued to move in on the bombers, determined to lead his squadron's attack even though he now had only one rocket to fire.

Avoiding any sharp turns that might snap off his damaged wing by putting too much stress on the main spar, Knoke maneuvered his ME-109 into the best position he could achieve and fired his right rocket. It passed harmlessly through the bomber formation, hitting nothing. The ten fighters behind him fired theirs. On explosion, the rockets looked four times as big as flak bursts. Red flares appeared first, followed by dense black smoke. Each rocket burst exposed clusters of smaller shells that would explode a few seconds later. If a rocket were to penetrate a bomber, it would then distribute its shrapnel fragments in all directions—enough of them for every man in the crew.

Of the twenty-one rockets fired by Knoke's squadron, nineteen were wasted on the air, but two scored direct hits. The two stricken B-17s, probably from the 40th CBW, exploded and plunged earthward in fragments.

Lieutenant Knoke, unable to lead his squadron's follow-up cannon assault, broke away and landed carefully at a fighter base near Bonn, where he learned that the main spar of his left wing was indeed broken and his plane was out of action. He had to stand by while other fighters landed, refueled, rearmed, and took off again to rejoin the battle, which was moving quickly eastward.

One ME-109 dropped a bomb into the 351st and 381st formation, but it exploded harmlessly, too far away. Several of the twenty-five B-17s in this formation had been hit, yet none had gone down or fallen back. In the most severely mauled groups, the 305th, 92nd, and 379th, one B-17 after another had begun to smoke, or had lost engines, burst into flames, fallen backward or downward. Bouquets of white American parachutes floated toward earth, sometimes with one or two yellow German chutes among them, like buttercups among daisies. The ground to the rear, along the flight path, was dotted with flames from crashed aircraft, both American and German. And there was no sign of let-up in the German attack. As soon as one group of fighters ran out of ammunition and fuel, another would arrive to replace it.

Captain McLaughlin, watching the carnage around him, turned to Peaslee and said, "Colonel, I don't think we're going to make it."

The air commander looked at his pilot and nodded. Though equally pessimistic, he didn't want to admit it.

The Third Division, running on schedule now about thirty minutes behind the First, came under attack even before losing its fighter escort. Over Aachen, the forty-eight Thunderbolts of the 56th Fighter Group, led by Maj. David C. Schilling, counted forty-four enemy aircraft around the bombers and engaged as many of them as they could catch. The P-47s claimed three kills (two twin-engine and one single-engine) before abandoning the B-17s to their fate. As the American fighters turned for home, their pilots saw two Fortresses of the Third Division already going down in flames, probably from flak. They could see four parachutes emerge from one of them but none from the other.

Major Schilling noticed one other thing about the Third Division before leaving it. The bombers seemed to be "flying in excellent line abreast formation." Colonel Old, in command of the Third, was also pleased with its formation. The 4th and 13th CBWs were only about two hundred yards behind his 45th CBW, even though they would have been within reasonable distance if they had been two miles behind. The leading 96A Group sustained its first severe attack near Eupen. Its first plane went down a few minutes later, with six chutes emerging.

In general, however, the attacks against the Third Division on the way to Schweinfurt were less severe than those against the First, which had drawn the bulk of the German fighters by arriving earlier. Fewer than one hundred enemy aircraft took part in the initial skirmishes with the Third Division.

At Neubiberg fighter base near Munich, Group Two of the famous Molders Wing had been alerted shortly after 1:00 P.M. and had been ordered a few minutes later to fly its ME-109s to Weisbaden-Erbenheim. Among the pilots, a rumor circulated that an American armada had just left England via Belgium. To veterans like Lt. Hans Langer this "news" may have sounded routine. The group was often sent on short hops from here to there, just to be in position if the American bombers moved too far eastward, as they had done August 17. Today's flight didn't even excite brand-new 2nd Lt. Gunther

Stedtfeld, who had only recently joined the Molders Wing and had not yet seen a moment of combat.[2]

Stedtfeld, a Dortmund University student when the war began in 1939, had volunteered immediately for the Luftwaffe, hoping to achieve his boyhood dream of becoming a flier. Though he soon realized this ambition, he was not destined to see combat for another three years, because he was assigned to a flying school in Berlin as an instructor. He enjoyed a comfortable life as an instructor, spending much of his free time with a college girlfriend who was now a medical student in Berlin and whom he eventually married. But he was not content as an instructor. Every six months he had petitioned for transfer to one of the fighting units. Every six months he had been refused until the summer of 1943, when a general who was a relative interceded for him. Three days later he was sent to a fighters' training center, and he now found himself the youngest second lieutenant in the Molders Wing, but still without a taste of battle.

Before taking off today, Stedtfeld packed a small bag with tooth brush, cigarets, a clean shirt, and so on, supposing he would fly to Weisbaden, spend the night there, and fly back to Neubiberg in the morning. Flying on the right wing of Capt. Gunther Rubell, commander of his Fifth Squadron, he took off from Neubiberg with thoughts of a pleasant evening in Weisbaden. Wing Commander Major Karl Rammelt led the three squadrons (thirty-three planes) of the Second Group out of the cloudy weather around Munich into the bright sunshine farther north, and the pilots had already dropped their wheels to land at Erbenheim when the tower there radioed an urgent message to Rammelt.

"Do not land! Do not land! Group Leader, assemble your squadrons and proceed toward Koblenz. Fortresses have just crossed the border at 23,000 feet."

The possibility that he might at last see action hit Stedtfeld "like an electric shock," and his excitement grew as he and his comrades pushed their throttles forward to gain altitude. Were they actually going to meet the Americans at last? Several times during the previous month or so they had taken off to chase the Fortresses, but not since August 17, before Stedtfeld joined his group, had the big bombers come far enough east for Munich-based fighters to catch them. Something different was happening today, however. The

301

number of German squadrons in the air around Stedtfeld, bombers as well as fighters, all moving north, told him that Central Defense Command was expecting a deep penetration.

The feelings that surged through him included little or no fear because his anticipation was blocking it out. For more than four years he had been looking forward to combat, and for more than a month he had been impatiently expecting it. Today he was convinced that "something very big" lay ahead.

Over the radio came another order. All units were to change to the same frequency. When they did, they heard the cool voice of an air commander (perhaps a general, though Stedtfeld could not identify him) who was cruising above the battle telling at least a dozen squadrons where to go, how to position themselves, when to attack.

Near Koblenz, within sight of the Rhine River, flying at 23,000 feet and still climbing, Stedtfeld and the other pilots in the Fifth Squadron got their first glimpse of B-17s when one of them exploded several miles ahead. Moments later he saw his first "big box of Forts flying close together," and a few minutes after that his squadron was flying directly parallel to them, side by side though at a safe distance, in compliance with a radio order to gain more altitude before attacking. As Stedtfeld passed the Fortresses and rose above them, he saw other units attacking them. From a cruising position a few thousand feet higher and less than a mile behind, where his squadron and several others formed a line astern awaiting their turn, he watched Fortresses burst into flames and parachutes appear as ME-109s darted in and out of the boxes. When black puffs of flak began exploding near the bombers, he noticed they were now approaching Frankfurt. He felt as if he were sitting in a theater, watching a movie about an air battle.

Even after the order came for his squadron to attack, Stedtfeld felt no fear. Still flying on Captain Rubell's right wing, he dived toward the rear of the bombers, contemplating not their guns but their beauty. He admired the lines of their gigantic tails and their silvery aluminum fuselages shimmering in the sunlight. Closing fast on those gigantic tails, Stedtfeld saw Rubell's cannon and machine guns begin to spit. He pushed his buttons, and his own guns fired. But the bomber at which he was aiming showed no sign of being hit. The one Rubell attacked now had two engines in flame, and the captain was pulling away, apparently confident of his success. Stedtfeld stopped firing and moved closer to take better aim. Until now he had seen no gunfire from his bomber, and as he pulled within 150 feet of it he could see why. The tail guns were hanging downward uselessly and there was a large hole in the tail assembly. His aim had not been so wild after all. He must have hit the rear gunner. But if so, he asked himself, "Why the hell doesn't the bird react?"

Slipping to the left, he fired again at the wing section between the two engines. He was so close it was "impossible to miss." The wing exploded; the plane rolled left and disappeared straight down.

In his elation, Stedtfeld shouted to himself, "I made it! I made it!" But he now found himself flying between two other American bombers. In his haste to get himself "out of this mess," he rolled leftward and became aware for the first time of heavy gunfire coming at him from all directions. He heard a drumlike noise behind him, and his stick went dead. An explosion right in front of his face blew away the glass bubble above his head. For a moment he knew panic. Then, acting reflexively as a result of long training, he unfastened his safety belt, bailed out, and pulled his rip cord. Since he had never jumped before, he waited for several seconds with increasing anxiety for something to happen, more and more convinced that his chute was not going to open. Finally it did so, painfully snapping his legs and shoulders.

As the noise of the battle above him receded, giving way to a peaceful and absolute silence, Stedtfeld began to feel he was safe at last. But when he looked downward, he feared there was something wrong with his vision. He saw two burning planes below, but they were blurry. Finally he realized his eyes were covered with blood from a wound in his face. A piece of metal was sticking out of this wound, and another was sticking out of his right hand. He landed in a treetop and had to be helped to earth by a group of farmers who rushed him to a hospital. After the metal had been extracted from his face and hand and he had been "anesthetized" by a few cognacs, Lieutenant Stedtfeld began to realize what a busy introduction to combat he had just experienced. In his first battle he had shot down his first B-17, had been shot down himself, had received his first wound, and had made his first parachute jump. It was, he decided, an occasion to celebrate. He drank more cognac while his face and hand were being bandaged.

Lt. Hans Langer of the Molders Wing Squadron Four approached the day's battle with some knowledge of what to expect since he had been a combat pilot for a year and a half and had shot down two B-17s in the August 17 defense of Schweinfurt.[3] When his squadron came upon the B-17s October 14, he was convinced they were again on their way to Schweinfurt. He was somewhat surprised, however, because he knew how many bombers the Americans had lost in August. He had been pleasantly aware of the 8th Air Force hiatus since then, and he was certain it had been caused by the heavy losses that day. It seemed to him that he and his comrades on August 17 had proven their control of the air over Germany. The Americans could hardly afford to repeat such losses. Yet here they were again, so they would have to be dealt with again.

Langer and his companions, unlike Stedtfeld's squadron, attacked from the front, one plane after another in a line astern, because they had discovered the dangers of a frontal attack from a line abreast formation. If two fighters flying parallel routes happened to zero in on the same bomber, they might converge and hit each other. They might also bank into each other in their last-second roll or dive to avoid collision. Langer's squadron therefore met the bombers one after another as the American armada approached its Initial Point near Würzburg. But after several passes, Langer could still not claim a kill. While he was convinced he had inflicted damage, none of the Fortresses at which he fired had gone down, or even slowed down. It was as if he hadn't scored a hit. Meanwhile, his own plane had been hit twice, in the fuselage and in one wing. He was out of ammunition and low on fuel. Forced to land, he did so with a heavy heart because he was leaving what had to be the fiercest air battle of all time and he would not be able to rejoin it. His plane was about to fall out from under him just when he needed it most. Even though great clusters of American bombers had gone down, greater clusters were still coming. Despite the heroic efforts of more German fighters than had ever before accepted an enemy challenge, the air was still full of Fortresses, and he could do nothing about it. He and his comrades had failed to stop them. Schweinfurt would soon be punished again for this failure.

Lt. David Williams, lead-plane navigator to Schweinfurt in August and lead-plane navigator again today, proved that his precision had not been accidental on that earlier occasion by bringing the First Division, or what was left of it, to its predetermined Initial Point west of Würzburg exactly on schedule at 2:34 P.M. Colonel Milton, being new in the 91st Group, didn't know Williams very well, but he now developed a deep appreciation of the slender young man who had been named Group Navigator only five weeks earlier. Despite the heaviest fighter attacks any American task force had ever suffered, attacks that had already knocked more than thirty bombers out of the First Division formations, Williams had brought the division to the starting point of its bomb run on the appointed minute. The ball-bearing factories at Schweinfurt lay open to them in the hazy sunshine, fifteen miles ahead.

The rest of the way, however, would not be easy. The defenders of Schweinfurt, the crews manning the town's three hundred 88-mm. antiaircraft batteries, were no doubt ready. Worse than that, the German fighters were still pressing their attacks even though their pilots had to be aware that they were now entering their own flak zone.

On Milton's left, the 305th Group was pushing bravely forward under command of Major Normand though twelve of its fifteen planes had already fallen and only three remained in formation. After looking at this pitiful remnant, Milton picked up his microphone and asked Normand if the 305th would like to pull in and make its bomb run with the 91st.

Normand answered proudly, "No, sir. The 305th will make its own bomb run."

On Milton's right wing, the combined 351st and 381st formation was in "excellent" condition. Though most of its planes were full of holes, only one or two had fallen. Milton's own 91st Group, despite the drubbing it had taken, was still intact though only seven planes strong.

Colonel Peaslee's 40th CBW had been badly hurt by the time it turned onto the bomb run. During this turn he made a hasty count of the planes behind him and found only eight left in his 92nd Group plus six in the 306th. Over the radio he invited those six planes to close in on the 92nd. Captain Schoolfield didn't answer, but his pathetic remnant soon sidled up to Peaslee's pathetic remnant.

The 41st CBW on Peaslee's left was, up to now at least, in better condition than either of the two other combat bombardment wings. Only a few holes were noticeable in its formations. When the leading 379th reached the Initial Point at 2:37 P.M., Colonel Rohr, the group leader, turned over the controls to Lieutenant Millson, the bombardier, who began immediately to look ahead for his aiming points. He found that the target area was identical to the photos of it he had studied. After opening the bomb-bay doors and checking his switches "for the umpteenth time," Millson bent over his Norden bomb-sight and began to check the drift for which he would have to compensate. He tried to put from his mind the fighters that were still harassing the formation, but it wasn't easy. Never on any previous mission had he experienced so many and such determined assaults.

Up ahead, the leading 91st was still sustaining vicious attacks on its bomb run. Just seven miles from Schweinfurt, cannon shells from a fighter silenced one engine in a Fortress piloted by Lt. Harold R. Christensen. When copilot Lt. Stuart Mendelsohn tried to feather the dead propeller, nothing happened. It continued to windmill with its blades fighting the air currents, creating drag and drastically slowing the aircraft. Christensen pushed the throttles full forward on the three other engines. He was determined to stay with the formation at least until he could drop his bombs. But he knew that unless he could get that propeller feathered, he would soon have to fall behind and face the fury of the German fighters alone.

By the time the 91st reached Schweinfurt at 2:39 P.M., flak was filling the sky around it and smoke was rising from some of the pots below, but nothing obscured the ball-bearing factories, which—despite their rapid reconstruction—still showed signs of damage from the August raid. As Lt. Samuel Slayton, the lead bombardier, released his bombs, everyone in the crew tried to follow their downward path, and when they exploded, a cheer filled the plane. They were right on target. But no one in the crew was in the mood for a lot of cheering. They were soon occupied once more by the fighters around them and the problem of getting home. Colonel Milton, for one, didn't think they would make it if the attacks continued, but he kept his fears to himself.

The three remaining planes in the 305th Group, still under attack by fighters, followed grimly behind the 91st, but as they approached the target, Lt. John Pellegrini, the lead bombardier, expressed dissatisfaction with their position. Convinced they were slightly off target, he suggested they go around and make a new approach. Normand, aware that if they took time to do so they would be separated from the rest of the 1st CBW, told Pellegrini to do the best he could. As a result, the three planes of the 305th dropped their bombs on the center of the city.

By this time these three planes, besieged without relief for an hour and forty-five minutes, had spent all but a few rounds of their ammunition. For one of them it wouldn't matter. Within minutes after leaving Schweinfurt, the group's thirteenth victim fell back, then drifted aimlessly toward earth like an exhausted bird. Now there were only two bombers left in the 305th. On the way to the posttarget rally point west of Nuremberg, they quickly attached themselves to the 91st.

As Colonel Peaslee approached the target in the lead plane of the 92nd Group, he could see Schweinfurt "rapidly going to hell" under the impact of the bomb strings the 1st CBW had unloaded upon it. Flak was coming up to greet the 40th CBW, but it was inaccurate. Picking up his microphone, Peaslee said to the bombardiers in the planes behind him, "Let's make it good. We've come a long way for this."

His plane, controlled now by the bombardier, moved relentlessly toward the ball-bearing plants even though fighters were assaulting it "from all directions." Peaslee had expected the fighters to break off when the flak began, but they kept coming. He had never encountered braver men than these German pilots.

Despite fighters and flak, the bomb run of the 40th was quite satisfactory. Peaslee was pleased as pilot McLaughlin, once more in control of the plane, banked to the right in the direction of the rally point. On the radio, Peaslee sent a two-word message back to England: "Primary bombed."

When the 379th Group brought the 41st CBW to the target, smoke was rising but lead-plane bombardier Millson had no difficulty seeing the factories. His approach was precisely as he wanted it. At the very moment he released his bombs, a burst of flak hit the side of the plane, its shrapnel sounding like hailstones on a tin roof.

"Bombs away!" Millson shouted. "Let's get the hell out of here!"

As they turned from the target, fifteen FW-190s dropped out of the sun "in an unannounced attack." Millson heard the sharp crack of a bursting 20-mm. shell behind him. He whirled around, half expecting to find that the navigator, Capt. Joe Wall, had been hit, but Wall, with a grin on his face, was pointing to a pile of tattered shreds on the

307

floor. It was Millson's parachute, which had taken the full impact of the bursting shell. No more than a ruined remnant now, it couldn't possibly save his life if he had to bail out. On the other hand, it had already saved his life, and Wall's also, by absorbing the shell explosion.

Another Fortress in the 379th was less fortunate than Millson's when the FW-190s attacked. An overly daring German pilot misjudged his frontal approach and collided with the bomber. The 550-mile-an-hour combined speed of the two planes coming together was so great that they both immediately disintegrated.

After the First Division had dropped its bombs and cleared the target, the German attacks diminished (though they did not end) and the men in the surviving planes began to look around at the damage. Lt. Richard Wolf of the 384th Group, Capt. Philip Algar's copilot who was acting as tail gunner on this mission, had developed a new respect for the men who regularly rode in the rear. He was doing so today because the group leader, Maj. George Harris, had replaced him in the copilot's seat. During the course of the almost continuous action, Wolf had seen more shells and bullets fired at him from the rear than he had ever seen from the front. One 20-mm. shell had blown the plane's tail wheel out from under him. If this shell had been aimed a foot higher, it would have taken him too. Hereafter he would gladly sit in the copilot's seat and leave the tail gunning to the tail gunner.

When Lt. Henry Evers of the 91st Group asked his crew members to check in and let him know if they were all right, he got no answer from his tail gunner, Sgt. Douglas Gibson, the nineteen-year-old "baby of the group." Lt. Bruce Moore, the navigator, went aft to investigate, carrying an oxygen bottle, and found Gibson unconscious from shock and loss of blood. He had taken a 20-mm. shell against the armor plate between his knees, receiving a severe wound in one leg. Moore dragged him forward to the radio compartment and tried to administer morphine, but it was so cold in the airplane that each time he melted a Syrette in the palm of his gloved hand, it would freeze again before he could get it into Gibson's arm. Finally, on the fourth attempt, Moore was able to inject the drug, and the wounded man lapsed into sleep.

Most attacks against the First Division came now from the rear. Though they were less frequent, they were as ferocious as ever. The

303rd Group, which had not previously lost a plane, lost its first. In the 91st Group, Lt. Harold Christensen, still struggling to stay in formation with one propeller windmilling and the three others at top speed to compensate for its drag, was beginning to accept the fact that he couldn't keep pace with his companions. Gradually he fell back, but he was not alone for long. The Germans soon found him, pumping bullets into his fuselage and wounding his ball-turret gunner, S. Sgt. Walter Molzon. After announcing on the interphone that he had been hit, Molzon walked forward, had the bombardier dress the wound, then returned to his gun. Christensen and his crew were not yet ready to surrender.

At 3:00 P.M. the First Division reached its rally point and reassembled its depleted ranks. Its bombs had created so much havoc in Schweinfurt that the crew members, now twenty miles away, could still see the smoke and flames rising there. But as one after another of their planes fell, they were not certain they had inflicted as much damage as they had suffered.

Less than an hour earlier, Schweinfurt had been enjoying the loveliest day of the entire autumn. The trees were in every color from yellow to purple to red.[4] Dahlias and asters were still blooming. Lorries were bringing in the grape harvest from surrounding vineyards. Boats floated lazily on the Main River. The streets were full of people, especially around the vegetable market in the town square. The scene was idyllically peaceful. Yet many Schweinfurters were nagged by a continuing worry they could not put from their minds. The expression, ''Schweinfurt weather,'' was making its way into local usage. People had noticed that the American bombers attacked only on clear, sunny days, like the day in August when they had come to Schweinfurt. This realization was almost enough to make everyone pray for clouds. On nice days they would look up at the sky and say, uncomfortably, ''Schweinfurt weather.'' Today was just that kind of day. The sky was cloudless, the air crisp, and the visibility almost unlimited.

Shortly after 2:00 P.M., the sirens began to screech. People looked anxiously toward the southwest but saw nothing. Was it a false alarm? There had been several. It was almost two months since that August attack, and some people had begun to think the Americans might never come back. Though the German newspapers had neglected to mention Schweinfurt after the August raid, they had at least mentioned the presence of enemy bombers over southern Germany and had announced that fifty-one of them [sic] had been shot down. Surely the Americans could not afford such losses. No doubt that was why they had not returned in the last two months. Yet the sirens continued to wail. Were those gangsters actually coming again? Many people were righteously indignant at the very thought of enemy attacks. It was inhuman to drop bombs on civilians, to murder people by the tens of thousands, and to destroy whole cities the way Hamburg had been destroyed. News reports about Hamburg had been very vague, yet descriptions of the devastation there had spread by word of mouth, and most German city dwellers now felt the anger and frustration that arises from vulnerability. Parachuting enemy airmen were fortunate if they came down among policemen or soldiers because many civilians were eager to vent their rage against these killers from the sky. The average German was too furious about the destruction of his own cities to think about the populations of Polish, Czech, Russian, Rumanian, Yugoslav, Greek, Norwegian, French, Belgian, Dutch, and English cities whom German fliers had bombed. It was enough to know that innocent Germans, many of them women and children, were being killed by these terrorists.

When the sirens continued, the people of Schweinfurt began to believe them and moved toward the shelters. At the ball-bearing factories, now back to almost full production as a result of the two-month respite, the workers moved unhurriedly toward the underground bunkers, some of which had been built for them since August. Still they saw no approaching bombers.

At VKF Plant II, an artisan named Heinrich Weichsel went into a bunker, then ran back to his work bench because he had "a funny feeling." Gathering up his precious measuring tools, he took them with him. As he again approached the still-open door of the shelter he could see clusters of silver dots in the distant air to the southwest. The flak batteries in the southern hills began to fire. Shortly after Weichsel entered the shelter, its door closed and he noticed in the dim light that many of the men around him were becoming pale, perhaps from fear. He sat down next to a young woman and tried to make himself comfortable. At least he had chosen VKF's best bunker. While the concrete was only twenty inches thick, it had the added advantage of being under a ramp. It should be safe enough.

310

At Kugelfischer, Wilhelm Stenger had remained at his desk in the administration building for some time after the alarm began. He was still one of the managers of the ball factory, part of which had been removed since August to the new Eltmann facility. Another executive, a friend of Stenger's, called him from the command shelter directly under the administration building.

"Where are you?" he said. "You'd better come down here. We expect something today."

Stenger had work to do. "I'll stay here," he said. "It's just another alert."

"Listen," his friend said, "I want you to look out at the sky."

Stenger glanced out the window. It was Schweinfurt weather. He couldn't deny that.

"This time it's likely to happen," his friend said.

Stenger was finally persuaded. Even as he went down the stairs of the building toward the basement shelter, he heard no sound of airplanes outside, but he guessed it was sensible to play it safe. Two minutes after he entered the command shelter, the first bombs fell on the building and exploded in front of the reinforced shelter door. With the blast came the sound of glass breaking on the upper floors. A fire extinguisher fell from the trembling wall, spreading foam throughout the chamber. But the wall held.

Leo Wehner, the antiaircraft commander at Kugelfischer, had moved his gun post to the roof of a sturdy building in the center of the plant. Forewarned of the approaching planes, he and his men were ready for them, but his guns were not. Wehner still had nothing better to shoot than the same 20-mm. cannon, which could not send shells even half as high as the bombers. Since the Americans obviously weren't going to descend to seven thousand or eight thousand feet, it seemed pointless and needlessly dangerous for Wehner to keep his men at these useless guns. But he had been told to do so, and he did what he was told, even though the bombing was much more accurate and fearsome this time than it had been in August. In addition to the high explosives, the enemy today was dropping many more fire bombs. Those of his men who had been in service and had seen action were not noticeably frightened by the bombardment, which soon filled the air around them. Some of the other men, however, began to tremble and shake. One bomb, exploding nearby, picked up a huge metal rail and flung it toward the gun emplacement. All but one of his men were able to get out of the way. The rail hit this man on the upper leg, injuring him so severely that within twenty-four hours he would be dead from loss of blood.

In the VKF Plant II shelter, the young woman sitting next to Heinrich Weichsel leaped into his arms when the first bomb fell. She clutched him so tightly he couldn't move. Another bomb exploded moments later and "a terrible detonation took everyone's breath away." The top of the bunker had suffered a direct hit. As the chamber filled with dust, people panicked and began to scream. Finally the dust settled and it became evident that the walls had held. But the ceiling had cracked and the concussion had been strong enough to kill six workers.

More bombs were falling on the factories than in August and fewer on the city, but there was a concentration of explosions near the central market and several apartment buildings were soon aflame. Some of the people rushed out of the shelters and back to their homes to remove furniture or other valuables. When new waves of bombers approached, these gamblers would drop what they were carrying and scurry for cover. Some of them found safety; others did not. As the bombs continued to explode, several people fell wounded or dead in the streets. Firemen tried to prevent the spread of flames from building to building. Soldiers and teenaged Hitler Youth members helped them. But as wave after wave of Flying Fortresses passed over, dropping their bombs despite the German fighters that harassed them, Schweinfurt's smoke and fire increased. The damage grew.

17

In the 94th Group toward the rear of the Third Division, Sgt. Leo Rand, on his first mission, was firing his left waist gun and thinking how wrong the briefing officers had been that morning. The route with the least flak? Bunch of shit. Least fighters? Another bunch of shit. P-47 escort? A crock of it. The only escort he had seen was squadron after squadron of German fighters, from the coast all the way to the Initial Point, which the 94th was now approaching. During his less than two hours of combat, Rand had already fired so many bullets he was up to his ankles in empty shells, and he had been fired upon through his big, square waist window, by ''a whole shitpotful'' of German planes.

A few miles southwest of Würzburg, an ME-109 came at his Fortress from the left rear and Rand began shooting at it. His first burst hit the engine, which quickly died though the damage to it was not apparent. Rand was still firing when the German pilot flipped open his canopy and bailed out. His parachute opened prematurely, just as he cleared his disabled fighter, but before Rand had stopped firing. Another burst from his machine gun raked across the man's torso, cutting him in half with the perforating power of perhaps twenty-five bullets. Stricken with horror, Rand watched the parachute descend, its gruesomely truncated burden dangling beneath it. Wasn't there an international law against shooting a man in a parachute? He'd have to confess it when he got home. And even though it was accidental, he'd probably be court-martialed for it. Such thoughts were still going through Sergeant Rand's head when more German fighters moved in to attack. Gripping his gun, he resumed firing. He'd have plenty of time later to worry about being court-martialed.

At the front of the Third Division, the lead plane of the 45th CBW, carrying Col. Archie Old, the task-force commander, was now on its bomb run. Looking straight ahead, Old could easily see the target, which was ''pretty well smoked up'' from previous bombings. The last of the First Division planes had just finished their runs and were banking to the right away from Schweinfurt.

The Germans were now throwing up flak in barrages, which, as Old had long since discovered, ''scared hell out of you,'' though it was ''supposedly not too dangerous.'' At 23,000 feet, the altitude his B-17 was flying, few planes were ever hit by flak, but today, his became one of those few. Just as the plane was approaching the target, under the control of the bombardier, Capt. James L. Latham, an antiaircraft shell exploded against the nose of the plane, driving a piece of shrapnel into Latham's belly and knocking him off his stool.

Maj. Robert Hodson, one of two navigators with Old today, was standing next to Latham when he was hit. A tough campaigner who didn't believe the group's bombs should be wasted just because a bombardier had been wounded, Hodson picked Latham up off the floor and put him back on his stool. After a quick pat on the back he said to the bewildered bombardier, ''Now hit that target, you son of a bitch.''

Latham, probably in shock and not yet fully aware of his wound, bent over his bomb-sight and took aim. When his bombs fell it was obvious that he was not quite as accurate as usual. Of his ten 500-pounders, half landed on the factories, the other half on the adjacent railway yards.

With part of its nose blown off and its bombardier wounded, Old's Fortress turned away from the target into the path of 160 FW-190s and ME-109s, which attacked the lead group in waves of 10 and 20. Only one of the planes in Old's 96A formation had gone down so far, and two in the 96B formation on his right wing, but the prospects for the homeward journey didn't look good. The bulk of the German fighters, which had been concentrating on the First Division, now turned their attention to the Third. And at the same time, barrages of flak continued to jolt the planes as they flew over the hills north of the city.

Another heavy blast hit the front of Old's Fortress while it was still in its gradual turn from the target. Once again shrapnel flew through the navigator's and bombardier's station. This time a fragment hit Major Hodson and killed him instantly. The Fortress shook and shuddered under the impact of the explosion but did not fall off course.

Group after group followed Old and the 96th, dumping their deadly cargo into the witch's brew below. The smoke was so heavy that it became the target, since it was impossible to make out the landmarks beneath it. After the last bomber group passed over, the fighters chased it north and Schweinfurt's torment was apparently at an end. Then one more B-17 appeared out of the southern sky, flying on three engines, and approached the target alone. A 94th Group plane, which had been part of the 96B Group formation, it was flown by Lt. Silas Nettles of Montgomery, Alabama, and it was bidding now to become the last of all the bombers to hit Schweinfurt that day.

This plane reached the target as a lonely straggler because a German fighter had gotten to it near the Initial Point. Unable either to keep pace with the formation or to maintain altitude with one of its engines gone, it had fallen back and downward until it was alone. Though Nettles might have been forgiven for jettisoning his bombs and heading immediately for home, he was determined to fulfill his mission. Plodding slowly forward, he finally reached the target area after all the other B-17s had dropped their bombs and retired. Even the German fighters had deserted Schweinfurt now, to follow and harass the Third Division formations en route to their rally point. And the antiaircraft crews on the ground were apparently so surprised to see this lone, low-flying straggler they couldn't find the range for it. The bombing opportunity was ideal except for one problem: the target was so shrouded in smoke that Nettles's bombardier, Lt. E. O. Jones, could only drop his bombs into the maelstrom and hope they would hit something worthy of attention. As soon as Jones called out, "Bombs away," Nettles turned for home, realizing that if he was to get there, he would have to do it alone. He now had a runaway propeller on the engine that had been hit, and there was little chance he could catch the formation.

Nettles's navigator, Lt. Robert E. O'Hearn, plotted the best course for him, then watched helplessly and with growing depression as the damaged bomber struggled westward. O'Hearn's melancholy was not relieved when he saw in the distance another straggler. It was already under attack, and within minutes it was on its way down. The runaway engine on Nettles's plane soon began to smoke. The Third Division formations moved farther and farther into the distance. Then the Focke-Wulfs arrived, as everyone had expected, four of them, attacking from the rear.

At this moment, Nettles's top-turret gunner ran out of oxygen. As he stooped down to pick up a spare bottle, a 20-mm. shell hit his turret and knocked out one of his two guns. The copilot, Lt. Jerry LeFors, coming back to see what had happened, noticed that the gunner was now idle but didn't know why.

"What the hell do you think you're doing?" LeFors demanded. "Get back to those guns."

The gunner climbed back into the wrecked turret, where he would have lost his life three minutes earlier if he hadn't run out of oxygen, and began firing his one undamaged gun. Three FW-190s came at him. The first two he missed, but on the third he scored a direct hit.

By this time, however, the fighters had knocked out another of the B-17's engines and had started a fire in the third. The plane was about to expire. Nettles ordered the crew to prepare to abandon, then he rang the bail-out bell.

Everyone except the two pilots had jumped, and the plane was on automatic pilot when they decided they would exit through the still-open bomb-bay doors. Since neither man wanted to go first, they agreed to close their eyes and go together after counting to three. At the count, Nettles did jump but LeFors did not. When he opened his eyes, he found Nettles dangling from the bomb bay, his chute harness caught on one of the racks. The copilot finally freed the pilot, and the two men, like the rest of the crew, were soon floating earthward toward captivity in a German prison camp.

With the Third Division absorbing heavier attacks on the way home, its planes were dropping out at a more rapid rate. A 95th Group Fortress fell near the rally point after its pilot, with wheels down, waved goodbye to his companions. Ten chutes appeared. Ten minutes later a Fortress from the 96A Group dived earthward and managed to crash land with FW-190s still firing at it. Three minutes after that, another from the 96th went down a few miles south of Würzburg. At the same time, the 390th Group, which had not lost a plane, now lost its first. And also at the same time, 3:24 P.M., the 94th lost another. During this one minute, three B-17s had fallen out of the division.

About twenty-five miles ahead of the Third Division, the First was enjoying a relatively calm flight toward France with only a few fighters pestering it. These fighters did bring down one more 384th Group Fortress, however, within the German border about sixty-five miles east of Metz. S. Sgt. Peter Seniawsky, a waist gunner on this plane, landed by parachute in a field, and when five German farmers came looking for him with shotguns, he managed to hide from them in a ditch. German soldiers then arrived to look for him. He managed, by crawling through weeds and high grass, to avoid them also. But for how long could he do so? And what was the point of even trying? Weren't they certain to catch him eventually? Seniawsky didn't think so. The 384th Group Intelligence officer, Maj. William E. "Pop" Dolan, himself a flier in the Lafayette Escadrille during World War I, had told the crew members that if they were shot down and had a chance to escape, it was their duty to do so. Though Dolan might not think that a predicament like Seniawsky's present one offered much of a "chance to escape," Seniawsky had taken him seriously and did not intend to surrender. At nightfall, he would figure out the most direct route to France and start walking.

At the German airbase near Bonn, Lt. Heinz Knoke was still chafing because his plane had been damaged in an engagement with the Fortresses on their way to Schweinfurt. Now that they were on their way back, he decided that despite the broken spar in the left wing of his ME-109, he would go up and take another crack at them.

Over the protest of an inspector, Knoke got his plane refueled and rearmed, then took off with a group of younger pilots who accepted his command. At 22,000 feet they met a formation of B-17s, and Knoke sent the other fighters in, one by one, to attack. Aware of his own plane's problems, he himself picked on a straggler that was limping along to the left and below the formation. When he opened fire from five hundred feet behind, the straggler's gunners replied with a vicious salvo. Bullets flew past Knoke on all sides. He couldn't avoid them, because with a broken wing he dared not take evasive action. When he closed to three hundred feet, the American gunners got his range. They put several bullets in his engine and fuselage. But he also hit the Fortress, which burst into flames and fell off to the left.

Knoke had now attracted the attention of other Fortresses. They began peppering him with bullets. Flames erupted in his engine, and smoke filled his cockpit. He opened his window and cut the ignition. The flames subsided. He dived to 12,000, then 10,000 feet, and tried the engine again. It started, and he decided he might yet make it back to Bonn. But the smoke and fumes returned. He dived to 5,000, then 3,000 feet, and found a level field. Ready to land in it, he tried to start his engine once more. This time his propeller froze rigid. Just above the treetops now, he had no choice left. Putting the plane down in a small open space, he hoped for the best. Chunks of dirt flew up around him. Fence posts snapped as he went through them. He bounced and hit the ground again. He was just beginning to lose speed when a dike loomed up ahead of him. Unable to avoid it, he sped straight into it, bracing himself to await the worst. After a crunching crash there was silence. He looked around and discovered he was still alive. Unfastening the seat belt, he leaped out of the plane and examined himself. He was undamaged except for a cut on his right arm. As for the plane, nothing was left intact except the tail wheel.

When the Third Division approached the Aachen area, where it was supposed to rendezvous with its homeward fighter escort, there were no P-47s in sight. They had all been grounded by more bad weather in England—an unhappy omen for the returning bombers. Instead of American fighters, more barrages of German flak greeted the lead plane of Colonel Old. Having been hit twice by flak today, his plane was not likely to be hit again. The odds against being hit even once by flak were fairly heavy. German fighters accounted for the great majority of B-17 casualties. To take three serious flak bursts on the same mission would almost indicate some kind of fatal attraction for it. Yet this was what awaited Old and his crew as they neared Aachen. A heavy barrage knocked out two of their engines (No. 2 and No. 3) at the same time. The plane dropped out of formation and lost two hundred feet in a matter of moments, before Maj. Tom Kenny, the pilot, could regain control of it. Old feathered one engine while the stand-by copilot feathered the other. As they lost altitude and gradually fell back, they could see the formation pull away, above and ahead. At 10,000 feet, after throwing out everything but their guns, they were able to maintain altitude on two engines. Fighters closed in to attack. As the bullets flew, the situation looked hopeless. Some crew members suggested on the interphone that the time had come to bail out.

"Hell no," Old announced. "We're going back to England."

They were now approaching clusters of puffy, cumulus clouds. Kenny flew into the first one he could reach. The fighters lost them. When they flew out the other side, the fighters found them again, but before the fighters could do them any more damage, Kenny was disappearing into another cloud. If the Germans were determined to shoot them down, they would have to play hide-and-seek to do it.

Lt. Harold Christensen's 91st Group Fortress was now hedgehopping its way across France on three engines, having escaped the German fighters by dodging into a convenient bank of clouds. Just above treetop level it was relatively safe from the high-altitude ME-109s and FW-190s but perilously vulnerable to ground fire. Skimming over the crest of a hill, Christensen found himself heading toward a city in a valley ahead. Cities meant flak. He veered away but not in time. A shell exploded against the side of the plane, and a fragment from it tore a jagged hole in his arm.

Since the plane was approaching more guns and another hill, Christensen, with a fountain of blood spurting from his arm, insisted on remaining at the controls until he was convinced they were out of immediate danger. Then, after his copilot, Lt. Stuart Mendelsohn took over, he collapsed. The bombardier and navigator applied a tourniquet, bandaged him and administered morphine. Though he looked as if he would be all right, his blood loss had been too great. He had saved his plane and his crew, but by the following morning Lieutenant Christensen would be dead.

Between Rheims and Soissons more than two hundred of the fighters that had attacked the bombers on the way to Schweinfurt were waiting to meet them again on the way back. The 96th Group absorbed the brunt of their attack. At 4:35 P.M., one of its planes went down and seven chutes emerged. A few minutes later, another fell after six chutes appeared. At the same time, a 20-mm. shell exploded in the cockpit of the Fortress flown by Lt. Robert Bolick and Lt. Edward Downs.[1]

Though Bolick was the pilot, he had taken the copilot's seat a few minutes earlier to relieve Downs, who had been doing most of the flying. Because their plane was on the left side of the 96A Group formation, it was easier to manage from the right-hand copilot's seat, which was closer to the plane on whose wing they were flying. Downs had just bent over to adjust a trim tab when the explosion occurred. He blacked out for perhaps a minute or more. When he regained consciousness, he saw that Bolick, his body blown open by the blast, had fallen forward onto the control column, putting the plane into a dive. The rest of the formation was now far above and to the left.

Since Downs himself was aware of multiple wounds on his right side, he had to reach across with his left hand to pull Bolick off the control column. The mortally wounded pilot regained consciousness, sat up, and tried to take hold of the controls. When he realized he could not do so, he patted the yoke as an indication that Downs should take over. Then he slumped in his seat.

Downs, noticing clouds below, brought the plane out of its dive just above them, ready to descend into them if more fighters appeared. Lt. Miles McFann, the navigator, and Lt. Harold Edelstein, the bombardier, both of whom had hurried to the cockpit after the explosion, removed the dying Bolick from the copilot's seat. Downs, who was becoming weak from his wounds, asked McFann where they were, and the navigator showed him on a map their approximate position.

"Get in the copilot's seat," Downs said, "and fly a heading of 270 degrees."

Downs now had time to assess his own wounds. His right arm was ripped from elbow to shoulder. His head, his right side, and his right leg were also gashed. Because he was in great pain, Edelstein wanted to administer morphine, but Downs refused it because he didn't dare pass out. He was the only pilot in the plane.

Remembering that he had an apple in his flight jacket, he asked the engineer, S. Sgt. John Rourke, who was slightly wounded in the backside, to find it and feed it to him. Though the apple was covered with blood, Downs chewed it slowly, bite after bite, and found that it helped him remain conscious.

Someone noticed that the No. 1 engine was out. Rourke feathered it. The No. 3 engine was losing power. Downs told Rourke to watch it. McFann, in spite of these difficulties, was keeping the aircraft in level flight. Whenever he needed advice or instruction, Downs would let him know what to do, either with a nod, a word, or a gesture. But as they came upon dense clouds near the French coast, McFann realized he didn't know exactly where he was. And now they learned that their radio was also out.

A discussion ensued over what they would do when and if they reached England. Could Downs land the plane? In his condition it seemed doubtful. Should they bail out? Everyone agreed this was unthinkable because they had two wounded men aboard as well as Bolick's body. McFann, then, would have to land the plane with Downs's help and advice. But while McFann had flown a plane straight and level a few times, he had never landed one.

All of this planning would be academic unless they could get through the clouds, find out where they were, and locate an English airfield. It looked as if England was again completely overcast. McFann flew until he and Downs agreed they must have reached it, even though they could see no land through the thick cloud cover. Then Downs told McFann to begin flying a triangular course, twenty seconds per leg. If someone in British radar noticed them, he would know they were in distress and send up Spitfires to lead them down through the clouds.

Fortunately the system worked. In due time a pair of Spitfires popped up through the clouds and signaled them to follow. During the descent, Downs had to take over because the clouds required instrument flight. With his good left hand on the yoke and good left foot on the rudder pedal he could manage the gentle moves that were necessary since McFann was handling the throttles. But would the injured copilot have the strength to land the plane?

Their Spitfire escort led them out of the overcast at 2,000 feet and directly to Ford Field, a fighter base in Sussex. Edelstein, standing between Downs and McFann, called out the air speeds as they descended toward the runway. Over the treetops they dropped to 120, 110, then 105 miles per hour. Downs could feel the plane shudder as if about to stall and crash. He needed more gas and he needed it quickly, but he failed in his attempt to convey this need to McFann, whose hand was on the throttles. Finally, despite his pain, Downs

321

raised his wounded right arm and pushed McFann's hand forward. The three operating engines roared, the plane cleared the trees, and Downs dumped the nose slightly to pick up more air speed. As the big bomber settled toward the ground and McFann brought the throttles all the way back, Downs tried to pull the yoke toward his belly for a tail-low landing, but he didn't have the strength. McFann, sensing what he wanted to do, did it for him, and the B-17 hit the ground, roughly but safely.

A 94th Group Fortress flown by Lt. Joseph Brennan had lost two engines after several encounters with fighters and flak, but it was still flying proudly as it approached the English Channel just above treetop level. Then one more in a series of flak bursts hit it and knocked out its third engine. Could a B-17 with full crew fly on one engine? Brennan and his men were determined to find out. To help it fly on two engines they had discarded everything in it that was unattached. Now, to help it fly on one, they detached and jettisoned every fixture they could pull loose. With its single motor at full throttle, the straining plane crossed the continental coast and skimmed the Channel waves as its radio operator, T. Sgt. Willard Wetzel, broadcast an alert to the British air-sea rescue service that they might need help. In mid-Channel, the crew could make out the English shore ahead despite the gloomy weather. They might yet get there. Five miles from land they were still flying. But now the plane had nothing left. Before its demise, it gave Brennan just enough time to warn his men. As it settled toward the waves, he was able to get its tail low and head high so it would die proudly and at the same time let them down safely. When it hit the water, Brennan and his entire crew scrambled into life rafts to await rescue.

The weather that greeted the returning Fortresses over England was an appropriate finale to all the other miseries they had suffered that day. The clouds were so thick that scores of planes landed at whatever fields they could find. And five of them, after struggling to get home, couldn't land at all. One 92nd Group plane crashed at Alden Maston. One from the 303rd crashed near Riseley. Three from the 284th went down over England, one near Blatherwycke, one near Corby, and the third right over home base at Grafton-Underwood. Fortunately, the crews of all these planes were able to bail out.

When Colonel Peaslee landed at Podington in the lead plane of the 92nd Group, only eleven planes were left in his formation. He was greeted by Col. Howard "Slim" Turner, commander of the 40th CBW, who asked him, "Where's the rest of the group?"

"You've just watched the group land," Peaslee said. "All that's left of it."

Of the twenty-one B-17s that had taken off from Podington that morning, four had aborted and six had been shot down. But several other groups had been hit just as hard or harder. The 305th had lost thirteen; the 306th, ten; the 96th, seven; the 379th, 384th, and 94th, each six.

Col. Archie Old and his crew couldn't make it to the 96th Group base at Snetterton Heath, but they did make it back to England. After the German fighters got tired of chasing them in and out of clouds, Major Kenny, the pilot, had nursed the plane across the Channel on two engines at 125 miles an hour "with the nose up." Their navigation had been perfect. They hit the shore at Beachy Head, flew up the Thames estuary, and landed at Gravesend.

When the returning 379th reached Kimbolton at 6:30 P.M., Col. Maurice Preston, the group commander, was waiting.[2] Having flown the August 17 mission, he knew what to expect. One look at Colonel Rohr, who had led the group today, told Preston that the man had been through something. Besides the six planes lost, there were several others that would never fly again. Although Rohr was very much in control, Preston could see he was unusually nervous.

"In my opinion," Rohr said simply, "this was an extremely rough mission."

His bombardier, Lieutenant Millson, fell to his knees in thanksgiving as soon as he got out of the plane. But as his fear receded, a certain excitement returned. After he had been debriefed by intelligence officers, Millson hurried to the photo lab. He wanted to see the strike photos, which had been sent for immediate development. Capt. Ted Rohr, the group photo-interpreter, was examining the wet prints when he arrived.

"You hit it," Captain Rohr said. "Brother, you plastered hell out of that place."

When the 94th Group landed at Bury St. Edmunds, Sgt. Leo Rand, having completed his first mission, turned to his fellow waist gunner, Sgt. Donald McCabe, and said, "How did I do, Mac?"

"You live through that," McCabe said, "you'll live through anything."

"I guess so," Rand said. "Today I found out for the first time that farts could have lumps in 'em."

Rand had no trouble relaxing after the excitement of the mission, but one thing still disturbed him deeply, and he decided to get it off his chest at the interrogation. He walked up to the "full-bird colonel" who was in charge of debriefing and said, "Sir, I guess this is the end of me."

The colonel said, "What do you mean, sergeant?"

"I know it's gonna be reported," Rand said, "so I may as well tell you. I killed a guy in a parachute."

The colonel listened while Rand described the whole incident. "You didn't do it on purpose, did you?"

Rand assured him it was an accident.

The colonel put an arm on his shoulder. "That's all right, Sarge. Don't worry about it."

As copilot Edward Downs and navigator Miles McFann brought their battered 96th Group Fortress to a stop at Ford Field near Chichester, a British ambulance was on the spot waiting to assist them. Downs, despite his wounds, said, "I can make it," when the attendants asked if he needed help. They therefore removed first the body of the pilot, Lieutenant Bolick, since it was blocking the catwalk from the cockpit to the rear.

The moment Downs stood up his parachute harness fell off his back. A piece of shrapnel had severed both straps. His oxygen mask had also been shredded by one of the fragments that hit his head. Blood was dripping from his face and from his whole right side. He was splattered from head to foot with Bolick's blood. Making his way toward the rear, he passed one of the waist gunners, S. Sgt. Theodore Bergstrom, the youngest man in the crew. The color faded from Bergstrom's face as he stared at the ghastly sight of the wounded copilot. Had this bloody mess been flying the airplane?

As soon as the British ambulance men got a look at Downs, they paid no more attention to his insistence that he could proceed under his own power. They placed him on a stretcher and hurried him to the field hospital, where the shrapnel was removed from various parts of his body. The other members of his crew were to be commended in person the next day by Winston Churchill, who happened to be at the R.A.F. fighter base on an inspection tour and noticed their shell-riddled plane. But Downs would know nothing about that until much later. His condition was so serious he was quickly transferred to a British civilian hospital where he began a painful recovery that would take more than six months.

The 8th Air Force's second mission to Schweinfurt was now completed. Of the 291 planes dispatched on the morning of October 14, 227 had survived mechanical difficulties and German guns to attack the target. Sixty Flying Fortresses and the 600 men they carried would not be coming home tonight. Among the 231 that did reach England, 142 were damaged. Once again the Germans had failed to turn back the American daylight bombers. The B-17s had accomplished their mission against Hitler's most zealously defended target. They had dropped over 500 tons of bombs on the ball-bearing plants. But the cost had been the highest the American Air Force had been forced to pay in its entire history. Many people were certain to ask whether the damage at Schweinfurt had been sufficient to justify this cost.

To the people on the ground at Schweinfurt it was evident immediately that the Americans had done much more damage this time than in August. The center of town was still burning and Mayor Ludwig Posl was already aware that the death toll would be in the hundreds. (Actually the total was 276 dead—106 men, 66 women, 26 children, and 78 foreign workers—but these figures had not yet been determined.) Posl, besides disposing of the dead and seeking medical care for the injured, had to organize rescue squads to help free hundreds of other people trapped in shelters by falling debris.

About sixty high-explosive bombs aimed at the factories had fallen on the city, as well as countless incendiaries. Many fires were still burning unchecked and were likely to continue to do so until long after nightfall because the firemen were too busy to get to them.

Despite this number of errant bombs—actually a small percentage of the approximately fifteen hundred that were dropped—the damage to the factories themselves was much greater and more concentrated than the damage to the community. American bombardiers, because of steadily improving techniques, were much more accurate now than two months earlier. In addition, the American tacticians, learning from their previous mistake, had sharply increased their ratio of incendiaries with the result that huge fires were raging in all five of the target factories. Kugelfischer had taken at least fifty-three direct hits, and all but one of its main buildings were damaged. When Wilhelm Stenger came out of the command shelter after the bombers had gone, he found that a phosphorous fire bomb had ignited a petroleum tank in front of the factory's highest building (five stories), and the flames had leaped to the building itself. The company's outmatched fire brigade was battling both blazes with no help because the city firemen were more than busy in town. As workers emerged from the shelters, they wandered back and forth in bewilderment, realizing they should do something but not knowing what.

At Fichtel & Sachs, a smaller plant, fifteen or more direct hits had spread destruction from wall to wall and had virtually obliterated three large shops. Even at Deutsche Star Kugelhalter, which suffered the least, the main works building was shattered by a bomb blast within its very center. Another bomb destroyed a warehouse. At VKF Werke I, all the westerly buildings including the powerhouse were on their way to total destruction by fire, and four buildings to the east were damaged by explosives.

At VKF Werke II, all buildings were damaged and seven were more than half destroyed. When Heinrich Weichsel emerged from his bunker there, he found the most serious fires in the ball plants, where the oil in and around the machines had ignited. These machines were now useless. While assessing the damages, Weichsel thought he heard a voice. It turned out to be a gasping man. A bomb had lifted a heavy press and pinned two men beneath it. One had been crushed to death but the other had taken only part of the weight and was still alive. Weichsel summoned the medics, who freed him and carried him away.

Weichsel now walked through the factory in a daze. Some of the fires were still unattended. The desolation was so general it was impossible even to know where to begin attacking it. He didn't want to look at any more of it. Passing the remains of one building, he glanced through a hole into the basement. A bomb had apparently fallen neatly down the elevator shaft and exploded at the bottom, where several women workers were huddled for shelter. Their twisted bodies were mixed with the debris.

Weichsel left the plant and ran to his home on the outskirts of town, hurrying past more dead bodies in the streets. He found his house untouched, his wife and children unhurt. Together they stood and looked down on Schweinfurt. Clouds of smoke still covered it.

*   *   *

At the hospital near Frankfurt where Lt. Gunther Stedtfeld's face and hand wounds had been dressed, he was feeling mellow from the cognac with which the doctors had plied him.[3] He had unwound sufficiently from the excitement of his first battle to realize he should call his unit headquarters at Neubiberg and let his superiors know what had happened to him.

To the men around his bedside he was such a hero that one of them volunteered to make the call for him. The controller at Neubiberg was happy to learn that Stedtfeld was alive and not badly hurt. Otherwise the controller was already aware of everything that had happened to him. His success in shooting down his first B-17 had been observed, and he had received credit for it. The demise of his own plane and his parachute jump had also been reported. For the Molders Wing it had been an exciting day, although an expensive one. The controller said that of the sixty ME-109s that had taken off from Neubiberg-Munich, only one had returned undamaged. Not all of the others had been shot down, but many had landed at other fields or crash-landed. He didn't yet know exactly how many of the sixty had gone down, but it was apparently a significant number because many of Stedtfeld's comrades, like himself, had reported making parachute jumps. Despite the airplane losses, the controller at Neubiberg was in a mood of elation because none of the Molders pilots had been killed, and they had received credit for shooting down twelve American bombers. The feeling among the pilots was that they had scored a great victory.

As for Stedtfeld himself, he was eager to get out of his hospital bed, return to Neubiberg, and get back in action again. Now that he was actually in the war, he wanted to hurry up and win it. The doctors who had treated him promised to put him on a train for Munich as soon as he was in shape to travel.

Albert Speer and several other people were in conference with Adolf Hitler at his Rastenburg headquarters when Hitler's adjutant, Julius Schaub, entered the room to interrupt.[4]

"The Reichsmarshal [Goering] urgently wishes to speak to you," Schaub said to Hitler. "This time he has pleasant news."

Hitler left the room to take the call and when he returned Speer could see he was "in good spirits." The Americans had again tried a daylight attack on Schweinfurt, he said, but the battle had ended with

327

a great victory for the German defenses. The countryside was strewn with the remains of American bombers.

Speer, aware that this information had come from Goering and familiar with the Reichsmarshal's habit of exaggerating victories while he ignored defeats, decided he had better find out for himself what had happened at Schweinfurt. In the two months since the August attack Speer had not succeeded in doing very much to ward off the dangers of further attacks. The factory dispersal plan had remained nothing more than a plan. Despite numerous discussions, the only accomplishment had been to order more new machines and to start building a few small component factories in towns around Schweinfurt. While the afflicted factories were being patched up, he had been forced to call on the German Army and Air Force to relinquish for war-production uses all the ball bearings they had in storage. These reserves had lasted until early September, long before the factories at Schweinfurt had returned to anything approximating full-scale production. At that time, output was still so sparse that ball bearings were delivered each day, as soon as they came off the line, from the factories to the waiting assembly plants. Sometimes the desperate assembly plants sent men with knapsacks to pick up however many bearings the factories had ready. Attempts were made to increase the ball-bearing purchases from Sweden and Switzerland, but these countries, which were already sending Germany more bearings than they pretended, were willing to increase the volume only minimally, even under extreme German pressure, because they feared they might lose their neutral status in the eyes of the Allies. During those days, Speer and his associates anxiously wondered "how soon the enemy would realize that he could paralyze the production of thousands of armament plants merely by destroying five or six relatively small targets."

Speer did not know that Gen. Ira Eaker at 8th Air Force headquarters in England was of the same mind but had been able to do nothing about it until he had restored the crew and aircraft losses he had suffered at Schweinfurt in August. In late September and early October, as new planes and men were strengthening the American force, the bombed-out Schweinfurt factories were also gradually returning to approximately full production. The bearing crisis ended. The days passed and the Americans failed to renew their attack. Speer was reinforced in his original hunch that the August attack had been

328

an isolated incident, that it was not part of a concerted American program to destroy the German ball-bearing industry. Just as he had suspected, the Americans apparently didn't realize the vital importance of Schweinfurt and therefore might not have any plans to attack it again.

Under this assumption, Speer gradually laid aside his concern about ball bearings as other pressing problems demanded his attention. On October 11, for instance, three days before the second attack, he and his staff conducted a lengthy discussion about putting aircraft factories underground. Nothing was said about doing likewise with the ball-bearing factories. The subject of ball bearings was not mentioned.

When Hitler relayed Goering's announcement that Schweinfurt had been hit again, Speer sensed immediately that his original hunch had been wrong. The Americans apparently knew what they were trying to do after all. But had they managed to do it? On that question he didn't trust Goering, who hated to tell Hitler bad news, and whose primary concern in any case was not production loss but Luftwaffe performance. Speer would agree that it was desirable to knock down American bombers, but on August 17, when sixty of them had been knocked down, more than three hundred others had survived to plaster both Schweinfurt and Regensburg. How many had gotten through to Schweinfurt today? That was a more important question than how many were strewn across the German countryside.

Speer was so uneasy he asked Hitler to recess the armaments meeting, then hurried to a telephone with one of his aides to call his contacts in Schweinfurt. As Speer stood by, the aide tried and failed. He was told that all communications to the stricken city had been shattered. Because the call was being made from Hitler's headquarters by a man as important as Albert Speer, the operators could hardly be accused of a half-hearted effort, yet they were unsuccessful in all their attempts to reach the town or any of the ball-bearing plants. This news by itself was chilling. Finally Speer's aide turned to the police, who maintained an auxiliary communications system. They were able to put him through to a man who said he was a foreman in one of the factories. The story he told took much of the luster from Goering's story. All the factories, he said, had been hard hit. The oil baths had caused serious fires in the machine shops. The damage was ''far worse than after the first attack.''

Speer, deeply worried now, returned to the conference room to find Hitler still basking in the good news from Goering. Speer could see Hitler's happiness reflected in the brilliance of his eyes. The brilliance faded when Speer told him what the Schweinfurt foreman had said. His disappointment was immediately evident, but he made no effort to question this new information. He obviously trusted Speer. The war-production minister had always found it easy to influence him, to alter his thinking. But if he were to believe Speer, could he still believe Goering? As Hitler digested the apparently conflicting reports, Speer could see, perhaps with some satisfaction since he was not a Goering enthusiast, that the Führer was beginning to doubt the story of the glorious victory for the German defenses. Finally Hitler's doubts came to the surface. "There must be a thorough check by a neutral committee," he said. "I want to find out the exact number of American planes on the ground."

18

When the October 14 losses were tallied, Gen. Ira Eaker once again, as in August, knew the extent of his defeat but could only make an educated guess at the extent of his victory. He and Gen. Fred Anderson stayed up at Bomber Command headquarters almost the entire night of the 14th/15th, talking to task-force leaders, reading the crew interrogation reports, and, in the early morning, studying the strike photos taken at Schweinfurt.[1] After compiling all the information they could get, they hopefully judged that the three largest ball-bearing factories had been destroyed, and that of the three hundred fighters the Germans sent up in more than seven hundred sorties, ninety-nine had been shot down, plus thirty more probables.

The two men were aware, of course, that these were no more than informed estimates. The attack had obviously been very costly to the enemy, but only the Germans could know exactly how costly. Eaker and Anderson had been in the bombing business long enough to realize that strike photos could be misleading due to smoke over the target, and that bomber crews could not avoid duplicating fighter claims when several gunners were firing at the same plane. Under these considerations Eaker might have preferred to make no appraisals until he had much more information, but he was oppressed by the compelling fact that of 291 Flying Fortresses dispatched to Germany, 60 had failed to return. This loss rate—19 percent—was one that no air force could afford. Such a loss demanded immediate explanation.

If the Germans had actually lost 99 fighters out of 300, as Eaker and Anderson believed after making adjustments for duplicate claims, that would be a 33 percent loss, which would be much more expensive to the Luftwaffe than the 60-plane loss was to the 8th Air Force. The Germans were no longer able to replace aircraft at the same rate as the Americans. (On the 14th, the day of the Schweinfurt mission, 93 new American crews arrived in England. During October, Eaker was expecting 250 to 300 replacement aircraft plus crews.) And if the attack had actually damaged the ball-bearing factories as extensively as the photos indicated, then the loss of 60 Fortresses, though awesome, was not too high a price to pay. But since none of these assumptions could be proved, would other people believe them? Already the U.S. newspapers would be announcing in huge headlines that 60 Flying Fortresses had been lost at Schweinfurt, a little German town which meant nothing to most Americans. In the early hours of the morning General Arnold had sent Eaker a personal cable indicating some alarm in Washington at such a heavy loss.

"It appears from my viewpoint," Arnold wrote, "that the German Air Force is on the verge of collapse. . . . We must not (repeat) not miss any symptoms of impending German air collapse. . . . Can you add any substantiated evidence of collapse?"

In light of the performance of the German Air Force on the previous day, this cable looked like nothing more than a frantic plea from Arnold for Eaker to send him all possible ammunition with which to counter expected attacks in the Battle of Washington. The message could hardly surprise Eaker. It was obvious that there would be a strong reaction any time he lost sixty planes in one day, and it was equally obvious that he had no time to waste before justifying this loss. On the morning of the 15th, he sent both a radiogram and a letter to Arnold.

"Yesterday the Hun sprang his trap," Eaker said in the radiogram. "He fully revealed his countermeasure to our daylight bombing." After describing the great air battle and its outcome, the aircraft losses on both sides as well as the apparent damage to the factories, he was careful to reassure Arnold that "this does not represent disaster." The 8th Air Force was ready to answer the enemy's challenge. But there were three things Arnold could do to help. He could rush the replacement bombers and crews. He could send large supplies of 110-gallon and 150-gallon drop tanks. And as soon as possible he could send more fighters, especially long-range P-38s and Mustangs. "We must show the enemy we can replace our losses," Eaker concluded. "He knows he cannot replace his. We must continue the battle with unrelenting fury. This we shall do. There is no discouragement here. We are convinced that when the totals are struck, yesterday's losses will be far outweighed by the value of the enemy matériel destroyed."

The very fact that Eaker felt obliged to say there was "no discouragement here" seemed to indicate he thought there might be some in Washington. He was sensitive to the importance of arming Arnold against it. The letter with which he immediately followed his radiogram had the obvious purpose of shoring up Arnold's support and staving off criticism:

I have, within the past half-hour, seen the first strike photos of yesterday's attack on Schweinfurt, and I shall be surprised if it is not classed as one of the best bombing efforts yet. Unless the strike photos are very deceiving, we shall find that the three ball-bearing factories at Schweinfurt are out of business for a long, long time. . . .

I received an hour ago your personal cable to me regarding the German Air Force. I see exactly what is in your mind. I feel there is much evidence pointing in the direction you are inquiring. Yesterday's effort was not, as might at first appear, contrary thereto. I class it pretty much as the last final struggles of a monster in his death throes. There is not the slightest question but that we now have our teeth in the Hun Air Force's neck.

Before concluding, he again pleaded with Arnold to help him put more bite into those teeth. "Nothing is more critical to our big battle here than the early arrival of P-38s and P-51s, and particularly the earliest possible delivery of three to five thousand 100- and 150-

333

gallon auxiliary droppable tanks for fighters.'' Eaker's plea to lengthen the range of his fighters in one way or another had been a recurring feature of his correspondence with Arnold for several months. Now it had become a desperate prayer.

In Washington on the 15th, President Roosevelt replied to a press conference question about the staggering losses at Schweinfurt with his usual political delicacy but without his usual clarity. He said the 8th Air Force could not afford to lose sixty bombers every day; then he hastened to add it was not losing that many. He noted that Germany's apparent loss of one hundred fighters did not involve as great a crew loss as when sixty bombers went down, besides which fighter planes could be produced much faster than bombers. But he concluded, on the credit side, that an important German war plant, or plants, had been put out of action. He didn't sound as if he were thoroughly convinced of any of this. Roosevelt was at all times an astute politician. If he was going to praise any operation that had cost the mothers of America six hundred of their sons (whether killed or taken prisoner), he would want to know more about it than he could possibly learn within one day after it, and he would want to make some judgment about probable public reaction to it. The President's disjointed press conference remarks were less than reassuring. He left the impression that he was not necessarily persuaded the Schweinfurt results had been worth the cost.

General Arnold, perhaps disappointed by Roosevelt's reaction, hastened into print with a statement of his own about Schweinfurt.[2] No one could accuse him that day of withholding support for Eaker. After explaining the importance of ball-bearing factories and the difficulty of reaching them so deep inside Germany, his statement tried to convey the enormous scope and success of the operation:

> This attack on Schweinfurt was not merely a spectacular air raid. It was an engagement between large armies—a major campaign. In a period of a few hours we invaded German-held Europe to a depth of 500 miles, sacked and crippled one of her most vital enterprises.
>
> We did it in daylight and we did it with precision, aiming our explosives with the care and accuracy of a marksman firing a rifle at a bull's-eye.
>
> We moved in on a city of 50,000 people and destroyed the part

334

of it that contributes to the enemy's ability to wage war against us. When that part of it was a heap of twisted girders, smoking ruin and pulverized machinery, we handed it back, completely useless, to the Germans. Ball bearings cannot now pour from this ruin, and no moving machinery will operate without ball bearings.

It was a politically motivated statement. Arnold's political instincts were usually very sharp. To some of his associates it seemed that he was as skillful a politician as he was a general. One reason he had been so successful in building the Air Force was that he never lost sight of the fact that the money came from the American people. To those who worked under him he might be irascible at times, but to the people and their Congressmen he was always "Happy" Arnold, a smiling, white-haired, fatherly man whom any mother might reasonably trust as her son's commander. Arnold undoubtedly realized that in the public mind the loss of sixty U.S. planes with six hundred American boys would make a deeper impression than the destruction of five German ball-bearing factories. Many Americans had never even seen a ball bearing. It was not easy to dramatize the importance of such a product, but he apparently felt he had to do so. An element of doubt had arisen. Even the R.A.F., during four years of war, had never lost sixty planes on one mission. Arnold could sense the doubt because he felt some of it himself. Like any military commander he was reconciled to losses, yet he wondered how long the 8th Air Force could sustain losses like this.[3] It worried him, but he didn't dare show it.

Three days later (October 18), Arnold felt obliged to conduct a news conference to assure the public that the Schweinfurt mission had been worth the cost. This time his remarks were not quite so shrewdly conceived. He said that on such an operation high losses were to be expected and he gave the impression that even a 25 percent loss ratio might be acceptable. Since the number of attacking B-17s had not been announced, some reporters naturally concluded that this 25-percent figure applied to the Schweinfurt raid, thus making it seem to have cost even more than the actual 19 percent. He also suggested that the Germans might have been forewarned of the attack, a supposition that had been rumored but was apparently without foundation. (Monitored German radio conversations between pilots and ground control, even up to the time the American

335

planes were approaching Frankfurt, indicated an expectation that Frankfurt would be the target.) Arnold then concluded his press conference with an overoptimistic remark. "Now," he said, "we have got Schweinfurt." These words might haunt him if his men ever had to return there.

When Eaker and Anderson read in the British papers what Arnold had said, they were both disturbed. On October 19 Eaker gently remonstrated with him in what may have been an imprudent letter to write to his commander. There was nothing in the enemy reaction, he said, that would indicate previous warning. And as for the 25-percent loss figure, he thought it might be well to remember that "our overall losses are still below 5 percent. From the standpoint of maintaining crew morale, I am anxious that our crews do not feel that their leaders anticipate enormous losses."

Eaker and Anderson were clearly displeased by Arnold's statements, but whatever damage his remarks may have done was uncorrectible. As the days passed after the second Schweinfurt mission and there was no announcement of new missions, people began to wonder if the 8th Air Force losses had been even worse than Eaker had admitted. Why was nothing happening? Was the 8th reduced to impotence? Dispatches from England blamed continuing bad weather for the inactivity, but not everyone was convinced. Finally on October 20 the B-17s attacked the metal factories at Düren, just east of Aachen within P-47 escort range. Were they now afraid to go any deeper into Germany without an escort? The American public and many powerful people in Washington began raising questions. Had the daylight-bombing concept failed? Which side had been the real winner October 14? If, as Arnold suggested, a security leak had enabled the Germans to predict and counter an 8th Air Force operation, what was being done about it? And how did anyone know for certain that the B-17s had done as much damage at Schweinfurt as Eaker had claimed? Unfortunately for Eaker, there was no absolute proof. Subsequent reconnaissance photos had confirmed the great damage to the factory buildings, but pictures taken from high altitude could not show how much vital machinery had been destroyed, how much the German war effort had been hurt. Only the Germans knew.

On October 23, at a German airbase near Deelen, Holland, Hermann Goering assembled the day-fighter pilots of the Third Division in the auditorium for a lecture.[4] Standing before them, tightly corsetted into his carefully tailored uniform, the fat, hard-faced Reichsmarshal looked stern. He wanted to talk to them again, he said, about the failure of Germany's day fighters. They had failed because "they were not clear about certain things and because they were also tired and somewhat cowardly." He wanted these men to know he was not pleased. He had thought that after he had brought the majority of Germany's fighers back from the fronts to use in home defense, the day attacks of the enemy would soon be ended. He had thought his fighters would have a feast shooting down enemy bombers, but he had been wrong.

"The German people have suffered immensely under the terror of enemy bombers, day and night," he said. "The people can understand that it is difficult to fight at night. But they cannot understand why, in the daytime, our fighters do not fight as they should."

He had received many letters from German people describing the activities of the fighters during the attack on Schweinfurt, and these people did not find them aggressive enough. "In a word, the population is very embittered about the action of the day fighters, and they are right. The good name of our air force has been damaged very much by the fighters, not only with the people but also with the Führer. And most of all with the enemy. He scorns you, and he shows it by attacking in daytime, in clear weather."

It was particularly galling to Goering that these enemy bombers flew, not over the Baltic Sea or over neutral countries "but right over the middle of Germany, under everyone's nose." And this they did because they had no respect for the German fighters.

"On that day," he declared, "it was almost impossible for me to endure the scorn of the enemy [and the fact] that he flew so impertinently all the way across Germany . . . without having been destroyed."

Even taking Goering's histrionic tendencies into account, the severity of this scolding indicated that he was now deeply disturbed at the Schweinfurt result. No doubt he was unfair in blaming the fighter pilots. According to their commander, General Galland, they had flown 800 sorties that day. They had not destroyed the 139 American

337

aircraft the German press claimed, but they had shot down more four-engine bombers than had ever before been destroyed in a single engagement. (Galland also said that only 35 German fighters had been lost, a figure much smaller than the Americans had claimed, and surprisingly small in light of the Neubiberg controller's disclosure to Lt. Gunther Stedtfeld that only one of the 60 planes which flew from there had returned undamaged. Even after the war it was impossible to determine any official count of German fighters lost that day. Some Americans who took part in the battle still believe an accurate count would be closer to 100 than to 35. General Eaker in a recent conversation asked pointedly why there were no German planes left to resist the Normandy invasion if the habitually small German loss claims were accurate.)

Goering's criticism of his fighter pilots, despite their unquestionable courage and resourcefulness, probably grew out of his own frustration at being unable to stop the daylight bombing. He had assured Hitler a year earlier that German industry had little to fear from American daylight attacks. This prophecy embarrassed him now. The Americans were not only bombing important factories; they were doing so with increasing accuracy. Field Marshal Milch, after the October 9 Marienburg attack, had said to Goering: "The Americans certainly know their business. At Marienburg not one bomb hit the town—every one landed on the target area."[5] At Schweinfurt they had been only slightly less accurate despite the unprecedented harassment by Goering's fighters and flak—the greatest air defense any bombing force had ever faced.

It is possible that Hitler, after learning from Speer what had actually happened at Schweinfurt, had blamed Goering for it. The Reichsmarshal liked to pass along any blame that came his way. In any case it was evident that Goering no longer considered the colossal air battle of October 14 a German victory.

On that subject he was now in agreement with Albert Speer, who often disagreed with him. Speer's aides, together with the factory managers, had carefully compiled the results of the American bombing and had concluded that the October 14 attack had destroyed 60 percent of Schweinfurt's total production capacity, based on a comparison with the undisrupted July output. As expected, the incendiaries had been most devastating. A member of Speer's staff told him: "Where only explosive bombs went off, there is only a hole and the machines are full of dirt. They can be repaired. But where there was fire, that was the end of the machines because the shafts burned out." And in this raid, fires had been general throughout all the factories.

Speer was so alarmed at the proportions of the ball-bearing crisis that he flew to Schweinfurt October 18 to see the damage for himself, and afterward, on that same day, he conducted a meeting at Nuremberg to determine what could be done about it.[6] First he appointed his "most vigorous associate," Dr. Philip Kessler, as special commissioner for ball-bearing production. Then with Kessler he worked out methods to reduce the transit time from factory to assembly plant and set in motion the development of a porcelain substitute for metal bearings in nonprecision machinery. But more important, Speer and Kessler pushed the immediate reconstruction of the stricken factories and at the same time made serious plans to begin the industry dispersal about which they had been talking since the August Schweinfurt attack. This time they would have to go through with the dispersal despite the temporary disruption it would cause and despite the reluctance of the gauleiters to welcome potential target factories into their communities. Speer had already told Hitler that "fresh attacks on the ball-bearing industry will bring production to a standstill."

"You're the one who must settle it," Hitler had said; and Speer was convinced he must settle it quickly because the Americans had now found the best technique to use against ball-bearing machinery. The B-17s would almost certainly return soon with more of their fire bombs. And for the next several months, even if dispersal plans proved effective, the industry would continue to be woefully vulnerable.

Speer had now seen enough bombing of Germany to reach some dismal conclusions about it—conclusions he was to disclose after the war to Allied intelligence officers.[7] He believed that the American daylight attacks on key industrial targets were even more dangerous to Germany than the British night attacks on the cities. He was convinced that strategic bombing alone might be enough to force a German surrender if the bombing were concentrated on the chemical industry, the electric power stations, or the ball-bearing plants.

339

Concentration on the ball-bearing industry, for instance, would render Germany defenseless within four months if all the ball-bearing factories (at Schweinfurt, Erkner, Steyr, and Cannstatt) were attacked at the same time, if these attacks were renewed at two-week intervals, and if reconstruction attempts were met by a pair of heavy attacks every two months.

What Speer did not know was that despite the success of the October 14 attack, General Eaker couldn't possibly repeat it within two weeks. The sixty bombers he had lost that day, added to the eighty-eight he had lost in the previous week's operations, were a prohibitive depletion of his force. And it was evident now, not only to Eaker but even to his superiors in Washington, that his bombers had to have fighter escorts all the way to their targets. During October, bomber replacements were arriving so quickly that by the end of the month, Eaker and Anderson were capable of sending out five hundred at a time. Yet it was not until November 3 that the next mission was launched. While the weather could be blamed for day-to-day postponements, it was not primarily responsible for the curtailment of operations after the second Schweinfurt mission. The need for long-range fighters was now fully acknowledged. The B-17s would not go deep into Germany again until they could be escorted all the way.

When more than five hundred Fortresses took off for Wilhelmshaven November 3, they were accompanied by P-38s, which at least had the virtue of being able to go that far, even though they were a poor match for ME-109s and FW-190s. On this day they wouldn't meet many German fighters, because Wilhelmshaven was known to be covered by a thick cloud layer. The purpose of the mission was to try once more the new British radar device, H2S, which might make it practical to bomb through clouds. The Wilhelmshaven harbor was an ideal target on which to test H2S because radar could pick up land-water boundaries precisely and make an identifiably shaped harbor easy to find. The bombing at Wilhelmshaven that day was fairly accurate under the circumstances though not up to the standards the B-17 groups had gradually established. Expectations of a weak fighter defense were well founded, however; the bombers were virtually unchallenged by the Luftwaffe, and the P-38 received only a cursory test as an 8th Air Force bomber escort. But it had already been tested sufficiently in Mediterranean action to reveal its limitations. Eaker said its first appearances with the 8th were "encouraging"; but he knew it was not the ultimate weapon, the fighter plane that would solve his primary problem.

Fortunately, Eaker could now look forward to something much better. His year-old prayer for a long-range escort was about to be answered. General Arnold, as a result of the Schweinfurt losses, had promised him on October 16 "the majority of U.S. allocated Mustang production" as well as one-third of the P-38 production. And on October 30, Arnold decreed that all Mustangs, as well as all of the longer-range models of the P-38, were to be assigned to Europe. It was the greatest news Eaker had received since his arrival in England. There was no longer any doubt, thanks to exhaustive tests, that the Merlin-powered Mustang was faster and more maneuverable at all altitudes than either the FW-190 or the ME-109. In addition, the Mustang had a range of more than six hundred miles. It could take the bombers anyplace in Germany and bring them back.

When Eaker learned (October 30) that he would soon be getting all the Mustangs he needed, he immediately cabled his appreciation to Arnold: "We need them badly. We can accommodate them all. And I guarantee you they will be fully employed. Their primary task will always be to accompany and protect our bombers."

In late October, an exciting rumor had begun circulating among 8th Air Force fighter pilots. Someone had seen a new Merlin-powered Mustang with U.S. Air Force markings at the Greenham Common Air Service Command base in Berkshire. Every American fighter pilot was now aware of what the Merlin-Mustang could do, and everyone wanted to fly the plane. Did the sudden appearance of this one mean that others were coming to replace the P-47s?

On November 4, a new fighter group, the 354th, which had been bound for the Mediterranean but was detached to the 8th as a result of Arnold's decision, arrived at Greenham Common. Most of these men, fresh out of training, had never flown anything "hotter" than the Bell P-39, a pretty little fighter that was used for training because it had proved inadequate for front-line duty. The young pilots of the 354th expected to be put into P-47s when they arrived in England. It was with happy astonishment that they learned that they were going to fly the P-51B. The 354th would soon make its debut as the first Mustang group in the European theater. After a month of transition training, it would begin the "primary task" Eaker had already assigned it: "to accompany and protect our bombers."

While these 8th Air Force rookies were learning to handle their new planes, an 8th Air Force veteran, who had been at large in German-held Europe since he was shot down October 14, was making his way slowly toward Spain. S. Sgt. Peter Seniawsky of the 384th Bomb Group, having parachuted into Germany sixty-five miles east of Metz, was now in France.[8] He had traveled south through Dijon, Lyons, and Avignon to Narbonne, sometimes walking, sometimes taking trains, helped along by knowing Frenchmen or by conscripted Polish farmworkers, whose language he had learned from his own parents in New York.

At Narbonne, a French conductor helped him catch a train for Perpignan, about thirty miles above the Spanish border. Arriving at Perpignan about midnight, he slept in the station until dawn, then walked south into the Pyrenees, trying to avoid German patrols. At dusk he reached the crest of a ridge and saw a town far across a valley. From a hermit with whom he had talked, he knew the town was in Spain. After crawling down the mountain, keeping away from even the roughest trails to avoid being seen, he finally reached the valley and began to walk across it. Before he had gone very far, two Spanish soldiers stopped him, searched him, and found that he was wearing an electric flying suit beneath the outer clothing he had picked up in France. Unable to deny his identity, he told them he was an American flier fleeing from the Germans, but because of the friendship between Adolf Hitler and Spanish dictator Francisco Franco, he wasn't confident that this admission would do him any good. The soldiers took him to a local jail where he was questioned before being moved to another jail a few miles away in Figueras. There he sat in a cell for more than a week, wondering what would happen to him. He was beginning to think he might be there for the rest of the war, or perhaps forever, when he was delighted to learn one day that the U.S. consul had arrived from Barcelona. However much Franco might like Hitler, he was reluctant to offend the American and British allies, who were now beginning to look as if they would win the war.

Sergeant Seniawsky was soon on his way to Gibralter, then back to England, where, on the first day of December, he was destined to amaze everyone in the 384th by walking into group headquarters at Grafton-Underwood.

As mid-November approached, almost three months after the first Schweinfurt-Regensburg mission, two of the American fliers shot down August 17 were still at large in Belgium. Lt. Edward Winslow, joined now by another uncaptured member of his crew, Sgt. Gerold Tucker, was still hiding out under the protection of the Belgian Resistance in a house at Ath. On November 13 the two men were to be moved to another hideout in Brussels.

An attractive girl whom they hadn't met before escorted them from Ath to Brussels by train. At the station, she led them calmly past the guard and left them standing among German soldiers while she went to a phone booth and made a call. From there she took them by streetcar to a residential section where they were to meet two men who would take them to their new hideout. They got off the streetcar near a large church. It seemed to Winslow that the girl was becoming nervous. They walked around the church but saw no one. Evidently worried, the girl made another phone call, after which she announced that the men were on their way.

She took Winslow and Tucker behind the church. Soon they heard footsteps and the girl said, "Here they are now."

The men were in civilian clothes. She introduced them and said to one of them, "The lieutenant speaks French."

This man turned to Winslow and said, "Oh. I suppose you speak English, too."

Winslow and Tucker laughed, acknowledging the joke. The girl said goodbye and was walking away when two men in German uniforms appeared. They approached the two Americans, spoke to them in German, then, without ceremony, backed them up against a wall while the two "escorts" watched. The four men marched Winslow and Tucker off to St. Giles Prison. The girl, supposedly a member of the "Armée Blanche," had betrayed them to the Gestapo.

In mid-November, the 354th Fighter Group moved from Greenham Common to Boxted, near the English Channel about fifty miles northeast of London, and continued its transition training in P-51s, which were arriving by ship, a few at a time. As soon as they had all of their twenty-four planes, the rookies of the 354th began intensive training under Lt. Col. Donald Blakeslee, at that time the

8th Air Force's most experienced fighter pilot. On December 1, Blakeslee decided the new men were ready for a little action. He led them in their sleek and shiny Mustangs across the Channel to Calais and the Belgian coast, just far enough to give the Germans a good look at them. The German antiaircraft gunners got too good a look at some of them, perforating their bottoms with flak but doing no serious damage. On December 5 they accompanied the bombers for the first time in a shallow penetration of France, and on the 11th they made their first trip to Germany, escorting the bombers to Emden. A few German fighters appeared in the distance but did not engage them. Five days later, on the 16th, after their first combat, with ME-109s and JU-88s, the Mustangs claimed their first victory. Their young pilots still had a lot to learn, and the plane itself still had a few bugs to be eliminated, but day by day its performance was becoming more impressive.

As additional Mustangs arrived, the veteran P-47 pilots would begin flying them. Swarms of them would soon be surrounding the bombers, and the Germans would have a long time to wait if they continued to hold back until this escort ran short of gas and turned for home. The P-51s would not turn for home until the bombers were ready to do so. And if the German fighters decided to attack the bombers anyway, they were not likely to enjoy the experience with the quick and well-armed Mustangs on their tails. The air war over Europe was about to undergo a decisive change, and the Germans, when they saw the Mustang, began to sense it. Hermann Goering, after his capture in 1945, admitted to Gen. Carl Spaatz that when he saw the first P-51 over Germany, he feared that the war was decided.

General Eaker could now see an increasingly triumphant future in store for his 8th Air Force. He had brought the 8th Bomber Command to England when it consisted of only himself and his six-man staff, without headquarters, without aircraft, without bombs, guns, or even paper clips. As 8th Air Force commander he had built it into a mighty force that could now send out more than five hundred aircraft on a single mission, and within a few months would be able to send out a thousand. (In mid-December he had 720 bombers at his disposal.) He had seen it through the two greatest air battles in American history. And now, with the help of the P-51, he would see it through to the day of complete victory over Nazi Germany.

These were Eaker's happy prospects when, on December 18, he

received an astounding cablegram from General Arnold in Washington:

It has been decided that an American will take over command of the Allied Air Force in the Mediterranean. . . . As a result of your long period of successful operations and the exceptional results of your endeavors as Commander of the Air Force in England, you have been recommended for this position. Other changes which have been set up tentatively are as follows: Spaatz to command the United States Strategic Air Force in Europe. [Lt. Gen. James] Doolittle to command 8th Air Force.

Eaker could scarcely believe that this communication meant what it said. The 8th Air Force was to be taken away from him just as it finally reached the strength toward which he had been building it for almost two years. His astonishment turned to anger. He believed his old friend "Hap" Arnold had let him down. They had often differed in the last two years. Arnold had frequently been impatient with him, but Arnold could be impatient with anyone. After each of the Schweinfurt missions, he had been supportive in his communications and in his public statements. Did Arnold nevertheless harbor secret reservations about those costly operations? In spite of the kind words in his cablegram, was he dissatisfied with Eaker's management of the 8th Air Force? Or were there other, as yet unexplained, reasons for transferring him?

On the 19th, after Eaker recovered from his shock, he decided not to surrender without a struggle. He vigorously protested his removal in a cable to Arnold, which he first wrote by hand to make sure it was worded strongly enough:

Believe war interest best served by my retention command 8th Air Force: otherwise experience this theater for nearly two years wasted. If I am to be allowed any personal preference, having started with the Eighth and seen it organized for major task in this theater it would be heart-breaking to leave just before climax. If my services satisfactory to seniors, request I be allowed to retain command 8th Air Force.

Not content with bombarding Arnold alone, Eaker then fired off similar salvoes of protest to General Eisenhower, who was about to be named Supreme Allied Commander in Europe, and to General Spaatz, who would, in effect, be replacing Eaker in England. Eaker even protested to General Devers, the present European Theater commander, who immediately cabled Arnold in Eaker's behalf. (Devers was the man Eisenhower would be replacing, but, ironically, Devers didn't yet know that and would not learn it until a week later when he read it in the December 29 London *Times*.)

Arnold, on December 20, answered Devers in a cable that politely invited him to mind his own business: "For retaining Eaker in command of the 8th Air Force, all the reasons that you have given are those that have been advanced as reasons why he should go down and be commander of the Allied Mediterranean Air Forces." On the 21st, Arnold sent an even firmer answer to Eaker's protest:

. . . The dictates of world-wide air operations necessitate major changes being made. This affects you personally, and while from your point of view it is unfortunate that you cannot, repeat, not stay and retain command of the organization that you have so carefully and successfully built up, the broader viewpoint of the world-wide war effort indicates the necessity for a change. I extend to you my heartfelt thanks for the splendid cooperation and loyalty that you have given me thus far and for the wonderful success of your organization, but I cannot, repeat, not see my way clear to make any change in the decisions already reached.

On Christmas Eve, Eaker decided the matter was so firmly settled it could not be unsettled. He wrote a short, curt cable to Arnold that read: "Orders received. Will be carried out promptly Jan. one." There was nothing left for him to do in England now but to make arrangements for his move, then say goodbye to the men of the 8th and to his British friends.

Eaker's transfer was not, in fact, a reflection on the job he had done as commander of the 8th Air Force. Arnold, whom he immediately blamed for the transfer, probably had little or nothing to do with it. When General Eisenhower was told by General Marshall that he would be returning to London as Supreme Allied Commander, it was natural that he should think about taking with him men who had worked under him in the Mediterranean, men whose skills he had closely observed. Among these men were Spaatz and Doolittle.

Eisenhower confidante Harry C. Butcher records that while the general was eating breakfast December 29, 1943, he received a message from Marshall about reassignments of commanders. The message was that Eisenhower was to get "everything you wanted."[9] Spaatz and Doolittle were included in what he wanted.

Eaker's British friends were so sympathetic they scheduled a farewell dinner in his honor for New Year's Eve. That afternoon at 6:00 P.M., a messenger on motorcycle came to his house with a note which said that a "Colonel Holt" would like to see him on his way to his new assignment. Who was Colonel Holt? Eaker had never heard of him, but after talking to Sir Charles Portal, he decided he would stop and see the man on his way to the Mediterranean.

More than two hundred people came to the R.A.F.'s farewell dinner at the headquarters in Bushy Park. Portal and Harris were the hosts. The senior members of the 8th Air Force staff had also been invited. At least fifteen people made brief talks. The next day, Air Chief Marshal Harris and Lady Harris, Eaker's first firm friends in England, came to see him off at the Bovingdon Air Base. Harris, still uncertain why the American general was being transferred, felt some concern that Eaker might think their differences of opinion about bombing policy were a factor in his removal.[10] He did not mention this to Eaker, however, when they said goodbye in one of the hangars. An R.A.F. guard of honor was standing at attention as he boarded his plane—a Flying Fortress that had been fitted out for him.

Capt. William Smith, now his pilot, had the engines running. Smith, who had fallen in love with a beautiful Red Cross girl in England, was no less reluctant than Eaker to go to Africa. As the plane took off, Eaker sat silently among the staff members accompanying him. Alone with his thoughts, he said very little to anyone on the entire trip. Still bitterly disappointed by his transfer, he could not overcome his feeling that the Mediterranean was a secondary theater and that he was taking over a secondary command.

When his plane landed in Casablanca, Eaker went immediately to see "Colonel Holt." He found himself entering a familiar villa, the one he had visited the previous January during the Casablanca conference.[11] "Colonel Holt" was the secret pseudonym for Winston Churchill when he traveled. He was in Africa now recovering from a bout of pneumonia. Eaker found him in the same two-story living room where they had argued about the American daylight-bombing

347

policy. Just as on that previous occasion, the sun was shining through the tall glass windows and the trees in the garden outside were laden with oranges.

Churchill said to him:

I can understand your disappointment, young man, at having to leave the 8th Air Force just when it's achieving its maximum effect in the war effort. But as for your new assignment, I want to remind you that we're entrusting to you two of our favorite British units, the Balkan Air Force and the Desert Air Force. If we didn't have great faith in you we wouldn't put them under your charge. You'll also have the R.A.F. Coastal Command, the French air forces, and your own very considerable Twelfth and Fifteenth Air Forces. All in all it will be a much larger command, with more responsibilities, than you had in the United Kingdom.

Eaker had not thought of his new job in such terms. He appreciated the Prime Minister's kind observations. They talked for a half-hour, and then the general prepared to leave.

Churchill had one parting remark. Reminding Eaker of their previous meeting here, he said: "This gives me an occasion to tell you that your representations to me at that time have been more than verified. Around-the-clock bombing is now achieving the results you predicted."

It was an acknowledgment that meant much to Eaker. He thanked the Prime Minister and returned to his plane for the rest of the journey to his new command. He felt better now.

Notes

CHAPTER 1

1. Maj. Gen. Ira C. Eaker to Lt. Gen. Henry H. Arnold, Apr. 5, 1943. Eaker to Maj. Gen. Oliver P. Echols, May 13, 1943.
2. *Mission With LeMay*, p. 293. Also, author's interview with Gen. Curtis LeMay, Ret., Dec. 7, 1973.
3. 8th Air Force Fighter Command Narrative of Operations, Aug. 17, 1943.
4. Author's interviews with Col. Beirne Lay, Jr., Ret., Dec. 30, 1974; also, "The Great Regensberg Raid," by Col. Beirne Lay, Jr. in *Battle*, a *Saturday Evening Post* anthology, p. 105 et seq.
5. 8 F.C. Narrative of Operations, Aug. 17, 1943.
6. *The Fifty-Sixth Fighter Group in World War II*, p. 15.
7. Galland, Ballantine edition, pp. 184-85; also, Jablonski, *Double Strike*, pp. 51-52.
8. Sir Archibald Sinclair to Asst. Chief of Air Staff, Air Marshal Sir John Slessor, Sept. 25, 1942.
9. Chief of Air Staff Air Chief Marshal Sir Charles Portal to Sinclair, Sept. 27, 1942.
10. Prime Minister Winston Churchill, "Note on Air Policy," Oct. 22, 1942.
11. Eaker directive, "Participation in Combat Missions," Aug. 8, 1942.
12. Author's interview with Lt. Gen. Ira C. Eaker, Ret., Apr. 24, 1975.
13. Author's interview with Ernest Warsaw, Feb. 4, 1975.
14. Secret Report No. 33, Belgian Ministry of National Defense (in exile), Nov. 17, 1943.
15. 390th Group Operations and Casualty Report, Aug. 17, 1943.
16. Author's interview with Dr. Gale Cleven, Jan. 26, 1975.
17. Secret Report, Sept. 5, 1943, 8th Bomber Command to 8th Air Force Headquarters, re: Mission 84, Schweinfurt and Regensberg. This report has been corrected to conform with the 390th Group's Operations and Casualty Report of Aug. 17, which shows that two of its planes were lost before reaching the target.
18. 8 BC Operations Report, Aug. 17, 1943.

19. R.A.F. Interpretation Reports K-1671, Aug. 21, 1943; K-S112, Sept. 9, 1943; K-S124, Oct. 20, 1943; and K-S407, Feb. 3, 1944.

CHAPTER 2

1. Brig. Gen. Fred Anderson's report to Eaker on operations of Aug. 17, 1943.
2. Author's interview with Maj. Gen. Robert Williams, Ret., Sept. 29, 1975.
3. In operation these limits were often ignored. Col. Lay recalls that on the Regensburg mission, the B-17s took off with more than 30 tons.
4. Author's interview and correspondence with Col. David M. Williams, Ret., Dec., 1974.
5. Author's interview with Maj. Edward P. Winslow, Ret., Feb. 20, 1975.
6. Author's interview with Col. William R. Smith, Ret., Apr. 25, 1975.
7. Author's interview with Col. Kermit D. Stevens, Ret., Feb. 24, 1975.
8. Author's interview with Gen. Maurice A. Preston, Ret., Apr. 2, 1975.
9. Author's interview with Lt. Col. Joseph Brown, Ret., Feb. 24, 1975.
10. Author's interview with Capt. Philip M. Algar, Ret., Feb. 21, 1975.
11. Author's interview with L. Corwin Miller, Feb. 24, 1975, and with John F. Schimenek, Oct. 2, 1975.
12. Anderson Report to Eaker on operation of Aug. 17, 1943.
13. Eaker interview, Apr. 24, 1975.
14. The Combined Bomber Offensive Plan, also called the Eaker Plan, issued Apr. 12, 1943.
15. Bekker, p. 320.
16. Galland, p. 154.
17. Author's interview, Oct. 3, 1975, with Hans L. Bringmann, who now lives in Wichita, Kans.
18. Galland, pp. 154-55.
19. Combined U.S.-British intelligence report of an interview with an unnamed German Air Force colonel, captured Jan. 1, 1945. Prisoner had been a fighter wing commander.
20. Author's interview, Feb. 14, 1975, with Hans Langer, who now lives in Long Beach, Calif.

CHAPTER 3

1. Author's interview with Maj. Gen. Stanley Wray, Ret., Feb. 8, 1975.
2. 384th Group Leader's narrative from a report by Maj. W. E. Dolan, Intelligence Officer, Aug. 19, 1943.
3. Miller interview, Feb. 24, 1975.
4. Interviews with Miller (above), Algar, Feb. 21, 1975; and Schimenek, Oct. 2, 1975.
5. 92nd Group Operations Report for Aug. 17, 1943.
6. 381st Group Operations Report for Aug. 17, 1943.
7. Col. Williams interview, Sept. 21, 1975.
8. Gen. Williams interview, Sept. 29, 1975.
9. 8FC Narrative of Operations, Aug. 17, 1943.
10. Smith interview, Apr. 25, 1975.
11. Bringmann interview, Oct. 3, 1975.

12. 381st Group Narrative of Operations, Aug. 17, 1943.
13. Author's interview with Delmar Kaech, Feb. 8, 1975.
14. Intelligence report of interview with German colonel, captured Jan. 1, 1945.
15. 91st Group Supplemental Report, Aug. 17 mission, to First Bombardment Wing, re: Aircraft 043. Report dated Aug. 18, 1943.
16. Winslow interview, Feb. 20, 1975; also his article, "Schweinfurt Raid," in 91st Group Memorial Association newsletter, *The Ragged Irregular*, July, 1973.
17. "Fortresses en Belgique," an article in Brussels *Le Soir*, Aug. 17, 1973.
18. 384th Group Bombardier's report, mission of Aug. 17, 1943.
19. Preston interview, Apr. 2, 1975.
20. *A Narrative of the 379th Bombardment Group*. (Pages unnumbered.)
21. Stevens interview, Feb. 24, 1975.
22. 303rd Group Operations Report, Aug. 17, 1943.
23. "Bombem auf Schweinfurt" (The Bombing of Schweinfurt), a report to the German government, undated, by Wilhelm Weger, leader of Schweinfurt's Air Defense in 1943.
24. Author's interview with Leo Wehner in Schweinfurt, May 7, 1975.
25. Author's interview with Dipl. Ing. Georg Schafer, Jr. in Schweinfurt, May 7 and 8, 1975.

CHAPTER 4

1. 92nd Group Operations Report dated Aug. 18, 1943.
2. Statements by Lt. James D. Judy and Lt. Roger W. Layn to 91st Group Adjutant, Aug. 18, 1943.
3. Langer interview, Feb. 14, 1975.
4. 8FC Narrative of Operations, Aug. 17, 1943.
5. *The Incredible 305th*, pp. 80-81.
6. 306th Group Intelligence Report, Aug. 17, 1943.
7. Secret Report from Belgian Underground to British Intelligence, Sept. 27, 1943.
8. Winslow interview, Feb. 20, 1975.
9. Warsaw interview, Feb. 4, 1975.
10. 8FC Narrative of Operations, Aug. 17, 1943.
11. Algar, Miller and Schimenek interviews.
12. 91st Group Report on Aircraft 043; also, group operations report, Aug. 17, 1943.
13. 381st Group Operations Report, Aug. 17, 1943.
14. Statement by T/Sgt. Earl Cherry to 91st Group Adjutant, Aug. 18, 1943.
15. Gen. Williams interview, Sept. 29, 1975.
16. Anderson's report to Eaker on operations of Aug. 17, 1943.
17. This calculation by the author is based on a "B-17s in Distress" report of the 306th Bomb Group, plus other crash reports. The 306th report covers 17 of the fallen planes. No exact figures of personnel deaths are available.
18. *Mission with LeMay*, p. 290.
19. Lay interview, Dec. 30, 1974.
20. Eaker interview, Apr. 24, 1975.
21. Author's interviews with Albert Speer in Heidelberg, Sept. 18, 1974, and May 5, 1975.
22. Irving, *The Rise and Fall of the Luftwaffe*, p. 235; also, Bekker, p. 314.

351

23. Author's interview with Wilhelm Stenger in Schweinfurt, May 8, 1975.
24. Speer interview, May 5, 1975.

CHAPTER 5

1. Smith interview, Apr. 25, 1975.
2. The diaries of Gen. Eaker and Gen. Spaatz indicate that Eaker arrived in Africa Aug. 17. But to some extent these diaries were compiled by staff secretaries, and sometimes several days after the fact. There is no doubt that Eaker left England for Africa Aug. 18. His pilot, Smith, had flown the Schweinfurt mission and vividly remembers that the Africa flight began the next day. Smith also has a letter of commendation from Eaker which dates the flight on Aug. 18.
3. Eaker interview, Apr. 24, 1975.

CHAPTER 6

1. The following account of the journey of Eaker and staff to England was compiled from interviews with Eaker, Apr. 8, 1975; Col. Lay, Dec. 30, 1974; and Brig. Gen. Harris Hull, Ret., Oct. 30, 1974.
2. Eaker diary, Feb. 21, 1942.
3. Memorandum, Maj. Gen. Carl Spaatz to Arnold (early January, 1942, but undated), "Organization of the U.S. Forces in the British Isles."
4. Eaker diary, Feb. 22, 1942.
5. Author's interviews with Marshal of the Royal Air Force Sir Arthur Harris at Goring on Thames, Oct. 3, 1974, and May 31, 1975.
6. Eaker interview, Apr. 8, 1975.
7. Eaker diary, Feb. 24, 25, 1942.
8. Portal interior memorandum, Jan. 23, 1942.
9. Harris to Portal, Jan. 29, 1942.
10. Eaker interview, Apr. 9, 1975.

CHAPTER 7

1. Harris interview, Oct. 3, 1974.
2. Harris, *Bomber Offensive*, p. 72.
3. Eaker interview, Apr. 8, 1975.
4. *Aerospace Historian*, Dec., 1974; an article by Gen. Laurence F. Kuter, Ret., "The General vs. the Establishment."
5. The details of Arnold's visit to England, May 26-30, 1942, were compiled from several sources; the diary of Col. Lay who acted as Arnold's recording secretary during many meetings; Eaker interviews on Apr. 8, 9, and 18, 1975; and Arnold's *Global Mission*, pp. 310-18.
6. Arnold, p. 312.
7. Eaker interview, Apr. 8, 1975.

CHAPTER 8

1. Andrews, *The Air Marshals*, p. 175.
2. Eaker interview, Apr. 9, 1975.

3. Eaker diary, Aug. 1, 1942; also Eaker interview, Apr. 18, 1975.
4. Eaker interview, Apr. 18, 1975.
5. Author's interview with Ben Lyon, Feb. 4, 1975.
6. *London Times*, Aug. 17, 1942.
7. Author's interview with R.A.F. Group Capt. Dudley Saward, Ret., May 29, 1975.
8. The description of this raid came primarily from Eaker's report to Spaatz on the operation of Aug. 17, 1942; from the Eaker diary of that date, and from the Eaker interview of Apr. 9, 1975.
9. The 8th Air Force Combat Operations Reports were the basic sources of information about these and other missions described or mentioned in this book. But many other sources were also used.

CHAPTER 9

1. Eaker diary, Aug. 29, 30, 1942.
2. Eaker interview, Apr. 18, 1975.
3. *First Over Germany*, the Story of the 306th Bomb Group. Unpaged.
4. Author's interview with Kyffin Owen at Kimbolton, June 12, 1975.
5. LeMay interview, Dec. 7, 1973; also, LeMay, p. 224 et seq.
6. Harris interview, May 31, 1975.
7. Butcher, p. 114.
8. Eaker memo to Spaatz entitled: "Night Bombing," Oct. 8, 1942.
9. Eaker interview, Apr. 18, 1975.

CHAPTER 10

1. Interpolation from Eaker's Casablanca paper entitled: "The Case for Day Bombing," written Jan. 16, 1943.
2. Freeman, p. 25.
3. Based on interviews with Eaker and Lay, plus a letter, Eaker to Spaatz, Aug. 25, 1942.
4. Eaker interview, Apr. 9, 1975.
5. Harris interview, May 31, 1975.
6. Churchill to Hopkins, Oct. 16, 1942.
7. Verrier, p. 171.
8. Eaker to Arnold, Dec. 6, 1942.
9. Eaker to James Roueche, Mar. 5, 1975.
10. Churchill to Sinclair, Jan. 4, 1943.
11. Portal to Churchill, Nov. 7, 1942.
12. Sinclair to Churchill, Jan. 9, 1943.
13. Sinclair to Churchill, Jan. 12, 1943.
14. Eaker to Arnold, Jan. 11, 1943.
15. Eaker diary, Jan. 14, 1943. Also, Eaker to Arnold, Jan. 11, 1943, and author's conversations with Eaker.
16. The conversations in Casablanca between Arnold and Eaker were reconstructed from the author's interviews with Eaker; from Arnold, pp. 392-99; and from Eaker's article in *Aerospace Historian*, Sept., 1972, entitled: "Some Memories of Winston Churchill." Eaker made stenographic records of his Casablanca talks.

17. Author's interviews with James Parton, Apr. 24, 1975, and with Eaker; also, Eaker's paper, "Why Have U.S. Bombers Not Bombed Germany?" written in Casablanca Jan. 16, 1943.
18. Slessor to Portal, Nov. 20, 1942.
19. This conversation between Churchill and Eaker was reconstructed from interviews with Eaker, from his Sept., 1972 article in *Aerospace Historian*, and from Churchill's "Hinge of Fate," pp. 678-79.
20. Combined Chiefs of Staff directive, "The Bomber Offensive from the United Kingdom," Jan. 21, 1943.
21. Bekker, pp. 301-2.

CHAPTER 11

1. Eaker interview, Apr. 18, 1975.
2. Harris interview, May 31, 1975.
3. Eaker interview, Apr. 18, 1975.
4. Eaker to Arnold, Apr. 5, 1943.
5. LeMay, p. 278. Gen. LeMay, in his memoirs, recalls this situation as having arisen in early March, 1943. Several crew members have confirmed to the author the accuracy of his recollections, except that they place the time in early April, 1943.
6. This memo, entitled "The Position of the Eighth Air Force," was unsigned and undated. Gen. Eaker has disclosed to the author that he wrote it. The approximate date was Apr. 7, 1943.
7. Eaker to Portal, Apr. 2, 1943.
8. The C.B.O. Plan was approved by the Combined Chiefs of Staff May 4, 1943.

CHAPTER 12

1. Author's conversations with R.A.F. Squadron Leader Edwin R. Cuff, Ret., April, 1976.
2. *The Route as Briefed*, p. 25.
3. *The 95th Bombardment Group* (H)—pages unnumbered.
4. Author's interview with Col. Edwin Millson, Ret., Feb. 23, 1975.
5. *A Narrative of the 379th Bombardment Group* (H)—pages unnumbered.
6. *Heritage of Valor*, pp. 40-53; also, author's interviews with Col. Budd J. Peaslee, Ret., Dec. 1, 1974, and Feb. 19, 1975.
7. Miller interview, Feb. 24, 1975.
8. Maj. Gen. George Stratemeyer to Eaker, Feb. 7, 1943.
9. Eaker to Arnold, May 13, 1943.
10. Eaker to Echols, May 13, 1943.
11. Eaker to Arnold, June 29, 1943.
12. Eaker interview, Apr. 24, 1975.
13. Robert Lovett to Arnold, June 18, 1943.
14. Lovett to Arnold, June 19, 1943.
15. Arnold, p. 376.
16. Eaker to Arnold, May 13, 1943.
17. Maj. Gen. Barney M. Giles to Eaker, June 11, 1943.
18. Eaker to Arnold, May 13, 1943.
19. Lovett to Arnold, June 18, 1943.

20. Eaker interviews Apr. 9, 1975, and Apr. 18, 1975.
21. Col. Emmett O'Donnell to Arnold, June 12, 1943.
22. Eaker to Arnold, June 29, 1943.
23. Arnold to Eaker, June 15, 1943.
24. Giles to Eaker, June 11, 1943.
25. Arnold to Eaker, July 7, 1943.

CHAPTER 13

1. Peaslee, pp. 155-64; also, Peaslee interview, May 18, 1976.
2. Lovett to Eaker, July 1, 1943.
3. Eaker to Arnold, July 18, 1943.
4. Freeman, p. 54.
5. Maj. Gen. Delos C. Emmons to Arnold, July 6, 1943.
6. Author's interview with William Wister Haines, Jan. 13, 1975.
7. Schafer interview, May 7, 1975.
8. Harris, p. 75.
9. The following descriptions of medical and psychological aspects of combat flying in the 8th Air Force come partly from recollections of the fliers, but primarily from the secret report entitled: *Psychiatric Experiences of the Eighth Air Force, First Year of Combat,* and from the book *Medical Support in a Combat Air Force.*
10. An interpolation from charts and statistics in *Medical Support in a Combat Air Force.*
11. Winslow interview, Feb. 20, 1975.
12. Author's interview with Douglas Gibson, Feb. 8, 1975.
13. Author's interview with Mrs. Audrea Howden Clapp, Feb. 8, 1975.
14. Author's interview with Basel Rodwell in Horham, June 12, 1975.
15. This description of Thorpe Abbots at the time comes from Mr. and Mrs. Harry Chenery and Mrs. Daphne Redgrave, who still live there, and were interviewed there June 11, 1975.
16. *Story of the Century,* pp. 1-4.
17. Warsaw interview, Feb. 4, 1975.
18. Cleven interview, Jan. 26, 1975.
19. Stevens interview, Feb. 24, 1975.
20. Owen interview, June 12, 1975.
21. Eaker interview, Apr. 24, 1975.
22. Eaker to Portal, Aug. 2, 1943.
23. Harris to Portal, Aug. 12, 1943.

CHAPTER 14

1. Slessor to Portal, Aug. 18, 1943.
2. Eaker to Sinclair, Aug. 24, 1943.
3. Eaker interview, Apr. 24, 1975.
4. Arnold, p. 451.
5. Author's conversation with Eaker, May 27, 1976.
6. Eaker to Lovett, Sept. 16, 1943.

7. Eaker interview, Apr. 24, 1975; and conversation, May 27, 1976.
8. 381st Group Surgeon's Report on the operation of Aug. 17, 1943.
9. 381st Group Daily Operations Report, Sept. 17, 1943; also, conversation with Gen. Joseph J. Nazzaro, Ret., May 25, 1976.
10. Peaslee interviews Dec. 1, 1974, Feb. 19, 1975, and May 18, 1976.
11. Miller interview, Feb. 24, 1975.
12. *A Narrative of the 379th Bombardment Group*. Unpaged.
13. Smith interview, Apr. 25, 1975.
14. *Story of the Century*, p. 10 et seq.
15. Warsaw interview, Feb. 4, 1975.
16. Author's interview with Edward F. Downs, Apr. 6, 1975.
17. Winslow interview, Feb. 20, 1975; also, his article, "Schweinfurt Raid," in the *Ragged Irregular*, July, 1973.
18. Portal to Churchill, Oct. 12, 1943.
19. Conversation with Eaker, May 27, 1976.

CHAPTER 15

1. 381st Group Operations Report, Oct. 14, 1943.
2. 381st Group Operations Report, Oct. 13, 1943.
3. Author's interview with Lt. Gen. Archie Old Jr., Ret., June 2, 1976.
4. Downs interview, Apr. 6, 1975.
5. Author's interview with Philip R. Taylor, Feb. 8, 1975.
6. Algar interview, Feb. 24, 1975.
7. Millson interview, Feb. 23, 1975.
8. *Story of the Century*, p. 29
9. Rand interview, Feb. 20, 1975.
10. Peaslee interview, Feb. 19, 1975; also, Peaslee, p. 187 et seq.
11. The operations reports of the 8th Bomber Command and of the individual groups, as well as the many interviews with participants, formed the basis of the following account of the Oct. 14, 1943 mission against Schweinfurt.
12. Col. Peaslee recalls S-turning to delay so the 1st C.B.W. could take the lead. His memory, so accurate in most instances, may be slightly amiss in this small detail. Both the Operations Report and the Leader's Report of the 306th Group on Peaslee's right refer to a 360 degree turn. Gen. Theodore Milton, Ret., leader of the 1st C.B.W. that day, also recalls the circle move by the 40th C.B.W.
13. Author's interview with Gen. Theodore Milton, Ret., June 3, 1976.
14. Col. Williams interview, Sept. 21, 1975.
15. Eaker interview, Apr. 24, 1975.
16. Bekker, p. 320; also, a British intelligence report (Oct. 19, 1943) on German reaction to the Schweinfurt mission.
17. Bekker, p. 317; also, Knoke's *I Flew for the Fuhrer*. One highly respected and usually accurate authority on the Schweinfurt raids has concluded that Knoke's engagement with Schweinfurt-bound B-17s took place Aug. 17. But Knoke's observation that the Americans were "again" attacking Schweinfurt shows that he was taking part in the Oct. 14 defense.
18. Winslow interview, Feb. 20, 1975.

CHAPTER 16

1. Author's interview with Bruce Moore, Feb. 8, 1975.
2. Author's correspondence with Dr. Med. Gunther Stedtfeld between Sept. 27, 1975, and Apr. 12, 1976.
3. Langer interview, Feb. 14, 1975.
4. The following account of the air raid as it affected Schweinfurt and the ball-bearing factories was compiled from the May, 1975 interviews with Georg Schafer Jr., Leo Wehner, Wilhelm Stenger and Franz Goger, plus shorter talks with more than a dozen other Schweinfurt residents. Also useful were accounts in the book *Schweinfurt Sollte Sterben* (Schweinfurt Must Be Destroyed) by Ludwig Wiener; and from the Cologne Neue Illustrierte and Schweinfurter Zeitung, Oct. 16, 1943.

CHAPTER 17

1. Downs interview, Apr. 6, 1975; also phone conversations with Lt. Col. Miles McFann, Ret., in January, 1975.
2. Preston interview, Apr. 2, 1975.
3. Stedtfeld to author, Nov. 22, 1975.
4. Speer interview, May 5, 1975; also, *Inside the Third Reich*, p. 372.

CHAPTER 18

1. Eaker to Arnold, Oct. 15, 1943.
2. *New York Times*, Oct. 16, 1943; p. 6.
3. Arnold, p. 395.
4. German document from the Milch Papers entitled: "Speech of the Reichsmarshal, Oct. 23, 1943."
5. Irving, *The Rise and Fall of The Luftwaffe*, pp. 246-47.
6. Speer interviews; also, Chronicle of the Speer Ministry, Oct. 18, 1943. (From Speer's personal typescript of his office diary.)
7. American post-war intelligence document entitled: "Defeat," Jan., 1946. It includes an interrogation of Speer which took place July 11, 1945.
8. Peaslee, pp. 228-42.
9. Butcher, p. 397.
10. Harris interview, May 31, 1975.
11. Eaker interview, Apr. 24, 1975.

Sources

INTERVIEWS WITH PARTICIPANTS

(Much of the detailed information in the story came from interviews with participants, verified by official correspondence, personal papers, current eye-witness accounts, secret memoranda, diaries, intelligence reports, mission reports, logs, directives, narratives of operations, raid assessment reports, and so on. The following is a list with dates of the author's interviews with participants—most of them in person and on tape, though a few by telephone or correspondence.)

Algar, Philip M., Feb. 21, 1975.
Bringmann, Hans L., Oct. 3, 1975.
Brown, Lt. Col. Joseph, Ret., Feb. 24, 1975.
Chenery, Mr. and Mrs. Harry, June 12, 1975.
Clapp, Mrs. Robert Howden, Feb. 8, 1975.
Cleven, Dr. Gale, Jan. 26, 1975.
Devers, Gen. Jacob, Ret., Apr. 25, 1975.
Downs, Edward F., Apr. 6, 1975.
Eaker, Lt. Gen. Ira C., Ret., Sept. 24, 1973; Sept. 9, Oct. 29, 1974; Apr. 8, 9, 18, 24, 1975; May 27, 1976; plus correspondence.
Frankland, Dr. Noble, Oct. 4, 1974.
Galland, Gen. Adolf, correspondence, Apr., 1975.
Gibson, Douglas, Feb. 8, 1975.
Goger, Franz, May 7, 1975.
Haines, William Wister, Jan. 13, 1975.
Harris, Marshal of the Royal Air Force Sir Arthur T., Oct. 3, 1974, and May 31, 1975.
Haslam, Group Capt. E. B., Oct. 2, 1974.
Hudson, Charles S., Feb. 8, 1975.
Hull, Brig. Gen. Harris, Ret., Oct. 30, 1974; Apr. 13 and 19, 1975.

Hutchins, Mrs. Jeannette, June 11, 1975.
Kaech, Delmar, Feb. 8, 1975.
Kono, Richard E., Jan. 23, 1975.
Langer, Hans J., Feb. 8 and 14, 1975.
Lay, Col. Beirne Jr., Ret., Dec. 30, 1974, and Jan. 6,1975.
LeMay, Gen. Curtis E., Ret., Dec. 7, 1973.
Lyon, Ben, Feb. 4 and 8, 1975.
Miller, L. Corwin, Feb. 24, 1975.
Millson, Col. Edwin H., Ret., Feb. 23, 1975.
Milton, Gen. Theodore R., Ret., June 3, 1976.
Moore, Bruce D., Feb. 8, 1975.
Nazzaro, Gen. Joseph J., Ret., May 25, 1976.
Old, Lt. Gen. Archie Jr., Ret., June 2, 1976.
Owen, Kyffin, June 12, 1976.
Parton, James, Apr. 24, 1975.
Peaslee, Col. Budd, Ret., Dec. 1, 1974; Feb. 19, 1975; and
    May 18, 1976.
Phillips, Mark, June 5, 1975.
Preston, Gen. Maurice A., Ret., Apr. 2, 1975.
Rand, Leo, Feb. 20, 1975.
Redgrave, Mrs. Daphne, June 12, 1975.
Rodwell, Basel Thomas, June 12, 1975.
Rubell, Dr. Gunther, correspondence, Apr.-May, 1976.
Saward, Group Capt. Dudley, Sept. 30, 1974, and May 29,
    1975.
Schafer, Dipl. Ing. Georg, May 6, 1975.
Schimenek, John F., Oct. 2, 1975.
Smith, Col. William R., Apr. 25, 1975.
Speer, Albert, Sept. 18, 1974, and May 5, 1975.
Spoll, Mr. & Mrs. David, June 12, 1975.
Stedtfeld, Dr. Med. Gunther, correspondence, Sept., 1975, to
    Apr., 1976.
Stenger, Wilhelm, May 6, 1975.
Stevens, Col. Kermit D., Ret., Feb. 24, 1975.
Taylor, Phillip R., Feb. 8, 1975.
Thomson, Mrs. Frances, June 11, 1975.
Warsaw, Ernest E., Feb. 4, 1975.
Wehner, Leo, May 7, 1975.
Williams, Col. David M., Ret., Dec. 6, 1975, and Sept. 21,
    1975.
Williams, Maj. Gen. Robert B., Sept. 29, 1975.
Winslow, Maj. Edward P., Ret., Feb. 20, 1975.
Wray, Maj. Gen. Stanley, Ret., Feb. 8, 1975.

PAPERS AND CORRESPONDENCE

Letters and Memoranda of Generals Henry H. Arnold, Ira C. Eaker and Carl
Spaatz, plus the diary of Gen. Spaatz, in the Library of Congress, Manuscript
Dept.

359

Diary of Gen. Ira C. Eaker, Feb. 4, 1942, to Oct. 15, 1943, provided by Gen. Eaker.

Diary of then Capt. Beirne Lay, Jr., Jan. 31, 1942, to Jan. 22, 1943, provided by Col. Lay.

Selected correspondence and secret memoranda between British Prime Minister Winston Churchill and his air advisors, 1941-43. Also, correspondence between Churchill, President Franklin D. Roosevelt and Harry Hopkins, 1942-43. Public Record Office, London.

Chief of Air Staff (Sir Charles Portal) Papers. Public Record Office, London.

Combined Chiefs of Staff Papers and Chiefs of Staff Papers. Public Record Office, London.

R.A.F. Bomber Command records. Public Record Office, London.

Director of Plans Papers. Public Record Office, London.

Chronik der Dienstellan des Reichs Ministers. Albert Speer, 1943. (Chronicle of the Speer Ministry.) Bundes Archiv, Koblenz, and Imperial War Museum, London. Also, selected portions of Speer's typescript of his diary were provided by him to the author.

Papers of and concerning Gen. Erhard Milch, with an incomplete but comprehensive guide compiled by David Irving. Imperial War Museum, London.

Casablanca notes of Gen. Ira C. Eaker, January, 1943, in the handwriting of his aide, then Capt. James Parton.

Transcript of a post-war interview (undated) between Gen. Eaker and Group Capt. Dudley Saward re: the development of the Eighth Air Force. Provided to the author by Gen. Eaker.

RECORDS AND REPORTS

8th Air Force Bomber Command and Fighter Command Narratives of Operations, 1942-43. National Records Center, Suitland, Md.

Operations and Mission Reports, at the National Records Center, including Narratives and Intelligence interrogations of the following heavy bombardment groups:

91	306
92	351
94	379
95	381
96	384
100	385
303	388
305	390

U.S. Strategic Bombing Survey. German anti-friction bearings industry, equipment division, Jan., 1945; brief study of the effects of aerial bombing on Berlin . . . Schweinfurt . . . Studies Report 8, 1945.

Combined Bomber Offensive Plan, issued by Combined Chiefs of Staff, Apr. 12, 1943.

Target Priorities of the 8th Air Force. A confidential report prepared by then Col. Harris Hull, 8th Air Force Headquarters, May 15, 1945. Provided by Gen. Hull.

Mission diary of then Lt. David M. Williams, Apr. 17, to Nov. 7, 1943. Also, Williams' navigation log, Aug. 17, 1943. Provided by Col. Williams.

Minutes of 8th Air Force, Third Bombardment Division, Commanders' Meeting, Oct. 15, 1943. National Archives.

Impact, Oct., 1943. (A confidential periodical issued by the Assistant Chief of Air Staff, Intelligence, Washington.) "Shuttle Across Alps," p. 19. Provided by Gen. Hull.

Impact, Nov., 1943. "Schweinfurt—Crippling Blow Dealt Despite Losses," p. 19. Provided by Gen. Hull.

R.A.F. and British Air Ministry Interpretation Reports and internal memoranda on 8th Air Force missions of Aug. 17 and Oct. 14, 1943. Public Record Office, London.

British Intelligence Reports: Schweinfurt ball-bearing industry, 1943. Public Record Office, London.

British Ministry of Home Security, Raid Assessment Reports. Public Record Office, London.

The Bomber's Baedeker. A guide to suggested German targets, compiled and kept current by the British Ministry of Economic Warfare.

British Bombing Survey. Unit reports on German cities. Imperial War Museum, London.

Belgian Ministry of National Defense (in exile). Secret Report No. 33, Nov. 17, 1943. Imperial War Museum, London.

"Bomben Auf Schweinfurt" (The Bombing of Schweinfurt). A report to the German government, undated, by Wilhelm Weger, leader of Schweinfurt's Air Defense in 1943. Provided by Kugelfischer Georg Schafer & Co., Schweinfurt.

U.S. Intelligence Report of an interview with an unnamed German Air Force colonel, captured Jan. 1, 1945. Public Record Office, London.

U.S. War Dept. Handbook on German Military Forces, Mar. 15, 1945.

"Defeat." Opinions of defeated German military men about the role of Allied air power in World War II. Headquarters, Army Air Forces, Jan., 1946.

BOOKS

8th Air Force Unit Histories

Bove, Arthur P. *First Over Germany*. (306th Bombardment Group), Newsfoto Pub. Co., San Angelo, Texas, 1946.

Callahan, John F., editor. *One Hundredth Bombardment Group*. John F. Callahan Assoc., New York, 1947.

Davis, Albert H. II and associates, editors. *The Fifty-Sixth Fighter Group in World War II*. Infantry Journal Press, Washington, 1948.

Freeny, Sgt. William A., editor. *The First 300*. (303rd B.G.) Pub. by 303rd Bombardment Group, London. No date.

Hall, Grover C. *1,000 Destroyed*. (4th Fighter Group), Morgan Aviation Books, Dallas, 1946.

Henderson, Capt. David B. *The 95th Bombardment Group*. A.H. Pugh, Cincinnati, 1945.

The History of the 388th Bomb Group. (No publisher or publication date listed.)

Milliken, Maj. Albert E., editor. *The Story of the 390th Bombardment Group*. Eilert Printing Co., New York, 1947.

Morrison, Wilbur H. *The Incredible 305th*. Duell, Sloan and Pearce, New York, 1962.

Nillson, John R. *The Story of the Century*. (100th B.G.) (publisher not listed). 1946.

Owens, Walter E. *As Briefed*. (384th B.G.) (Publisher and date of publication not listed.)

Robb, Capt. Derwyn D. *A Narrative of the 379th Bombardment Group*. Newsfoto Pub. Co., San Angelo, Texas. (Publication date not listed.)

Sheridan, Jack W. *They Never Had It So Good*. (350th Squadron of 100th B.G.) Stark-Raith Printing Co., San Francisco, 1946.

Sloan, John S. *The Route as Briefed*. (92nd B.G.) Argno Press, Cleveland, 1946.

OTHER BOOKS

Allen, Wing Commander H.R. *The Legacy of Lord Trenchard*. Cassell, London, 1972.

Andrews, Allen. *The Air Marshals*. Morrow, New York, 1970.

Arnold, H.H., and Eaker, Ira C. *Army Flyer*. Harper, New York, 1942.

Arnold, H.H. *Global Mission*. Harper, New York, 1949.

Baumbach, Werner. *The Life and Death of the Luftwaffe*. Coward McCann, New York, 1949.

Bekker, Cajus. *The Luftwaffe War Diaries*. Macdonald, London, 1966.

Butcher, Harry C. *Three Years with Eisenhower*. Heinemann, London, 1946.

Caidin, Martin. *Black Thursday*. Dutton, New York, 1960.

———. *Flying Forts*. Ballantine, New York, 1969.

Craven, W.E., and Cate, J.L. *The Army Air Forces in World War II*. University of Chicago Press, 1948, 1949, 1951.

Eisenhower, Dwight D. *Crusade in Europe*. Doubleday, Garden City, 1948.

———. *The Papers of . . .* Johns Hopkins Press, Baltimore, 1970.

Frankland, Dr. Noble. *The Bombing Offensive Against Germany*. Faber & Faber, London, 1965.

———. *Bomber Offensive*. Ballantine, London, 1969.

Freeman, Roger A. *The Mighty Eighth*. Doubleday, Garden City, 1970.

Galland, Gen. Adolf. *The First and the Last*. Holt, New York, 1954.

Goldberg, Alfred. *History of the United States Air Force, 1907-1957*. Van Nostrand, New York, 1957.

Green, Dennis W. *Augsberg Eagle—Story of the ME-109*. Macdonald, London, 1971.

Gurney, Maj. Gene, editor. *Great Air Battles*. Bramhall House, New York, 1963.

Gutermann, Hubert. *Alt Schweinfurt*. (Old Schweinfurt.) Druck und Verlag, Schweinfurt, 1972.

Jablonski, Edward. *Airwar—Tragic Victories*. Doubleday, Garden City, 1971.

———. *Flying Fortress*. Doubleday, Garden City, 1965.

———. *Double Strike*. Doubleday, Garden City, 1974.

Harris, Marshal of the Royal Air Force, Sir Arthur T. *Bomber Offensive*. Collins, London, 1947.

Hastings, Maj. Donald and Assoc. *Psychiatric Experiences of the Eighth Air*

Force, First Year of Combat. Prepared for Army Air Forces Air Surgeon. Josiah Macy Jr. Foundation, New York, 1944.

Hess, William. *B-17 Flying Fortress*. Ballantine, New York, 1974.

————. *P-51 Bomber Escort*. Ballantine, New York, 1971.

Huie, William Bradford. *The Fight for Air Power*. L.B. Fischer, New York, 1942.

Irving, David. *The Rise and Fall of the Luftwaffe*. Little, Brown, Boston, 1973.

Kahn, David. *The Code-Breakers*. Macmillan, New York, 1967.

King, Fleet Admiral Ernest J., and Whitehill, Cmdr. Walter Muir. *Fleet Admiral King—A Naval Record*. Norton, New York, 1952.

Knoke, Heinz. *I Flew for the Fuhrer*. (Translated by John Ewing.) Holt, Rinehart and Winston, New York, 1954.

Lay, Beirne Jr., and Bartlett, Sy. *Twelve O'Clock High*. Ballantine, New York, 1965.

Lee, Asher. *Goering Air Leader*. Duckworth, London, 1972.

LeMay, Gen. Curtis E., and Kantor, MacKinlay. *Mission With LeMay*. Doubleday, Garden City, 1965.

Life Magazine editors. *Target Germany*. Simon and Schuster, New York, 1943.

Link, Mae and Coleman, Hubert A. *Medical Support of the Army Air Forces in World War II*. Pub. by Government Printing Office, Washington, for Office of the Surgeon General. 1955.

Lyall, Gavin. *The War in the Air*. Arrow, London, 1971.

Masterman, J.C. *The Double-Cross System*. Yale University Press, New Haven and London, 1972.

Maximilians, J. *Luftkrieg Gegen Kugellager*. (Airwar Against Ball-bearings.) A dissertation at the University of Wurzburg, 1974.

Milward, Alan S. *The German Economy at War*. Athlone Press, University of London, 1965.

Peaslee, Budd. *Heritage of Valor*. Lippincott, Philadelphia, 1964.

Revie, Alastair. *The Bomber Command*. Ballantine, New York, 1971.

Saturday Evening Post editors. *Battle: True Stories of Combat in World War II*. Doubleday/Curtis, Garden City, 1965.

Saundby, Air Marshal Sir Robert. *Air Bombardment Development*. Chatto & Windus, London, 1961.

Saunders, Hilary St. George. *Royal Air Force, 1943-1945*. HMSO, London, 1954.

Slessor, Sir John. *The Central Blue*. Cassell, London, 1956.

South, Oron P. *Medical Support in a Combat Air Force*. (A study of medical leadership in World War II.) Research Studies Institute, Air University, Maxwell Air Force Base, Alabama, 1956.

Speer, Albert. *Inside the Third Reich*. Macmillan, New York, 1970.

————. *Spandau, the Secret Diaries*. Macmillan, New York, 1976.

Sunderman, Maj. James F. *World War II in the Air*. Franklin Watts, New York, 1963.

Sweetman, John. *Schweinfurt—Disaster in the Skies*. Ballantine, New York, 1971.

Tedder, Air Chief Marshal Sir Arthur. *With Prejudice—The War Memoirs*. Little, Brown, Boston, 1966.

Ulanoff, Stanley M., editor. *Bombs Away*. (Sixty-Nine Stories of Strategic Air Power from World War I to the Present.) Doubleday, Garden City, 1971.

Verrier, Anthony. *The Bomber Offensive*. Batsford, London, 1968.

Webster, Sir Charles, and Frankland, Dr. Noble. *The Strategic Air Offensive Against Germany, 1939-45*. Four Vol. HMSO, London, 1961.

Wiener, Ludwig. *Schweinfurt Solte Staben*. (Schweinfurt Must Be Destroyed.) Verlag Neues Forum, Schweinfurt, 1961.

Wilmot, Chester. *The Struggle for Europe*. Collins, London, 1952.

Winterbotham, F.W. *The Ultra Secret*. Harper & Row, New York, 1974.

Wright, Maj. David G., M.C., editor. *Observations on Combat Flying Personnel*. Published for the Office of the Air Surgeon by Josiah Macy Jr. Foundation, New York, 1945.

PERIODICALS

Aerospace Historian
  "Conversations on the Air War," by Ray L. Bowers, June, 1974.
  "The General vs. The Establishment," by Gen. Laurence F. Kuter, Ret., Dec. 1974.
  "Some Memories of Winston Churchill," by Ira C. Eaker, Sept., 1972.

Air Force Magazine. "Beneath the Rubble of Schweinfurt," by Capt. Eric Friedheim, June, 1945.

Colliers. "Mission Completed." June 21, 1947.

Combat Crew Magazine. "Salute to the 379th," by G. Francis Farrell, July, 1974.

The Journal of Navigation. "Navigation and War," by R.V. Jones, Jan., 1975.

Le Soir, Brussels. "Fortresses en Belgique." Aug. 17, 1973.

New York Times Magazine. "The Team that Harries Hitler," by Raymond Daniell, June 6, 1943.

Ragged Irregular. "Schweinfurt Raid; Hiding Out in Belgium," by Maj. Edward P. Winslow, Ret., July, 1973.

Royal Air Force Quarterly. "The American Bombing Effort," Sept., 1943.

Time. "Victory in the Air," Aug. 30, 1943.

True. "The World's Greatest Air Battle." May, 1960.

U.S. Air Services. "Eaker, Man with a Plan," by Beirne Lay Jr., May, 1947.

NEWSPAPERS

Air Force Times.
London Times.
Neue Illustriete, Cologne.
New York Times.
Schweinfurter Zeitung.
Washington Post.

Index

Aachen, 6, 17, 45, 48, 64, 65, 69, 274, 336
Abel, Lt. Dunstan T., 21
Alconbury base, 150, 211, 221
Algar, Lt. Philip, 31, 41, 43, 48–49, 55, 70, 71, 213, 270, 285, 308
Allen, Lt. Lewis, 63
Allied Air Force in the Mediterranean, 345–46
American Air Force Test Facility, 179
American 15th Light Bomber (A-20) Squadron, 135
American Red Cross, 210, 271
Anderson, Brig. Gen. Fred L., 13, 23, 24, 32–33, 41, 160, 215, 227, 241, 256, 262, 266, 267, 279, 280, 284, 287, 331–32, 336, 340
Andrews, Lt. Gen. Frank M., 193, 195, 204, 205, 215
Anklam, aircraft factories at, 280
Anoxia casualties, 243–44
Antwerp, 6, 41, 43, 46, 50, 70, 201, 292
Arcaro, Lt. Anthony, 50, 51
Armstrong, Lt. Col. Frank, 93, 117, 136, 137, 139, 142, 177, 190, 194
Arnold, Gen. Henry H., 10, 12, 33–34, 93, 95, 96, 101, 102–3, 106, 112, 114, 120, 123–24, 125, 126–27, 129–30, 132, 133, 137, 139, 148, 151, 160, 180, 183–85, 186, 187, 189, 192–94, 195, 199, 202, 203, 208, 217, 219, 220, 222–30, 234, 235, 236, 240, 256, 262–66, 280–81, 291, 332–36, 341, 345–46
Astor, Lady Nancy, 160

Baggs, Lt. Joseph W., 56
Baldwin, Air Vice Marshal J. E. A., 95
Balkan Air Force, 348
Bartlett, Maj. Sy, 178
Bassingbourn base, 24–32, 76, 160, 210, 278
Beasley, Maj. Peter, 93
Beckett, Maj. Thomas P., 41, 55
Bednall, Colin, 146
Beebe, Col. Eugene, 183
Belgian underground, 17, 278, 293, 343
Bell P-39 fighter/trainer, 341
Bergstrom, S. Sgt. Theodore, 324
Blakeslee, Lt. Col. Donald, 45, 343
Blatherwycke base, 322
"Blitz Week" raid, 241, 244, 246, 255, 256, 265
Bloody 100th Group, 273, 276, 285
Boeing Aircraft Company, 25, 111, 127, 190

Boeing Model 299, 25
Bolick, Lt. Robert H., 276, 284, 320, 324
Bolte, Brig. Gen. Charles L., 107–8
"Bombers' Baedeker," 237
Bordeaux raids, 88, 259
Bovingdon Air Base, 85–86, 148, 211, 212, 276, 347
Boxted base, 343
Bremen, 186, 192, 246, 280, 284
Brennan, Lt. Joseph, 322
Brenner Pass, 21
Bringmann, Sgt. Hans, 37, 47
British Air-Sea Rescue Service, 72–73
British Ministry of Aircraft Production, 180, 207
Brompton headquarters, 232
Brown, Capt. Joseph, 30–31, 57
Brussels, 66, 231, 232, 265
B-17 Flying Fortress bombers, 1–4, 7, 8, 10, 11, 18, 25, 26, 32, 34, 37, 40, 41, 43, 46, 47–48, 49, 51–52, 55, 59, 63, 66, 70, 71, 75, 80, 84, 88, 97, 102, 104, 110–11, 112, 117, 123–27, 135, 142, 143–67, 178, 180, 190, 197, 207–9, 211, 216, 221, 224, 231, 234, 262, 267, 274, 279–89, 293–304, 314, 316, 318, 322–27, 332, 335, 339
    crew morale problems, 242–55, 268–70
B-17E bomber, 25
B-17F bomber, 25
B-24 Liberator bombers, 150, 163, 166, 172, 190, 197, 234, 240, 241, 258, 279, 280, 288
BT-13 trainer, 32
Bubb, Col. Charles, 220, 227
Bufton, Air Commodore Sidney O., 238
Burtonwood depot, 149
Bury St. Edmunds base, 277, 323
Bushy Park headquarters, 9–10, 132, 153, 199, 272, 291, 347
Butcher, Harry C., 347

Cabell, Col. C. P., 205
Calais, V-rocket bunkers at, 263
Canfield, Cass, 199
Cannstatt, ball-bearing factory at, 79, 340
Casablanca Conference, 183, 193, 208, 238
Casablanca Directive, 182, 204
"Case for Day Bombing, The" (Eaker and Parton), 186
Castle, Col. Frederick, 6, 93, 117, 242, 277
Catherine of Aragon, 159
Celentano, Lt. Frank, 70
Central Defense Command (Germany), 302
Central Defense Headquarters (Germany), 292
Central Medical Board, 248, 249, 283
Central Planning (Germany), 79
C-47 transport planes, 150
Chaney, Maj. Gen. James, 95, 96, 100, 105, 106, 108, 117, 129
Chauncey, Gen., 272
Chelmsford, ball-bearing factory at, 236, 268
Chelveston base, 102, 148, 212
Chenery, Harry, 252
Cherry, T. Sgt. Earl, 63, 73
Christensen, Lt. Harold R., 306, 309, 319
Churchill, Winston, 10, 91, 96, 118, 120, 123, 125–29, 163–65, 166–69, 170–75, 179, 181–85, 187–90, 191–92, 199–200, 208, 235, 280, 324, 347–48
Ciganek, Sgt. Victor, 69
Clark, Maj. Gen. Mark, 130
Cleven, Maj. Gale "Buck," 8, 18, 19, 253, 254
Cologne, 13, 129, 274
Combined Bomber Offensive Plan, 206, 208, 220, 226, 234, 235
Combined Chiefs of Staff, 189, 204, 206, 208, 256
Cooper, Gary, 27
Corby base, 322
Cowart, Lt. William, 93, 107, 117
Crosby, Bing, 27, 271

Dalton, Capt. Beryl, 284
Dame Satan (bomber), 29, 44, 53, 66, 69
Dannella, Sgt. Frank, 274
Darrow, Flight Officer George R., 72
Dashwood, Sir John and Lady, 199
David, Col. William B., 13
Daylight precision bombing raids, 10, 25, 40, 89, 97, 103–4, 111–13, 182–208, 235, 334–35, 339
  British acceptance of, 191–208, 235
DeCoster, Lt. Edward, 63
Deelen (Holland) base, 336
DeGaulle, Charles, 121
Desert Air Force, 348
Deutsche Star Kugelhalter Werke, 58, 326
Devers, Lt. Gen. Jacob L., 12, 215, 221, 238, 240, 256, 264, 346
Dieppe, British commando landings at, 144
DiMaggio, Joe, 27
Dionne quintuplets, 27
Dolan, Maj. William E. "Pop," 285, 317
Doolittle, Lt. Gen. James, 87, 345–46
Dornberger, Gen. Walter, 81
Douglas DC-3, 94, 150
Douhet, Gen. Guilio, 134
Downs, Lt. Edward F., 276, 284, 320–22, 324
Duncan, Col. Claude, 136
Duncan, Maj. Glenn E., 292
Düren, 45, 297, 336

Eaker, Brig. Gen. Ira C., 3–5, 9–10, 11, 24, 33–35, 78, 85–90, 92–103, 104–5, 106, 111–47, 148–58, 161–62, 163, 165, 166, 170, 177–78, 179–81, 183–84, 185, 187–89, 190, 192–209, 215, 216, 219–21, 222, 223–28, 229–30, 231, 234–36, 238, 240–41, 242, 246, 256–58, 259–61, 262, 263, 264–67, 272, 277, 280–

281, 291, 328–29, 331–34, 336, 340, 344–48
Eaker, Ruth, 198
Eaker Plan, see Combined Bomber Offensive Plan
Echols, Maj. Gen. Oliver P., 216
Edelstein, Lt. Harold, 276, 320–21
Edward VIII, King, 199
8th Air Force, see U.S. 8th Air Force
Eisenhower, Gen. Dwight D., 125, 130, 132, 135, 137, 144, 151, 161, 166, 177, 193, 215, 263–64, 345
El Alamein, 38
11 Gruppe Jagdgeschwader 2, 292
Eltmann, town of, 81
Emden, port of, 192, 266, 271, 273, 277, 279, 344
Emmons, Gen. Delos C., 236
Erkner, ball-bearing factories at, 79, 340
Eupen, 6, 46, 47, 64, 300
Evers, Lt. Henry G., 295, 308
Evill, Air Marshal Douglas C. S., 124, 261

Fairfield Evacuation Hospital, 251
Fichtel & Sachs Werke, 58, 260, 326
Fischer, Friedrich, 58
Fives-Lille steel plant, 163
Flying Fortress, see B-17 Flying Fortress bombers
Focke-Wulf factory, 80, 239
Focke-Wulf 190 fighters, 1, 6, 8, 13, 15, 36, 37, 43, 46, 47, 50, 53, 62, 65, 70, 144, 147, 150, 163, 166, 178, 217, 242, 249, 255, 258, 278, 294, 298, 307, 314, 316, 319, 340
Ford Field base, 324
Fort Bliss, 92
Framlingham base, 212, 252
Franco, Francisco, 342
Frankfurt, 38, 48, 50, 63, 64
Freeman, Air Marshal Sir Wilfred R., 128, 291
Fritsche, Hans, 61

Gable, Clark, 85
Galland, Gen. Adolf, 36, 337
Gdynia naval yards, 280
George VI, King, 281
Gerhart, Col. John K., 5
German Air Force (G.A.F.), *see* Luftwaffe
German Homeland Defense, 35–36, 51
German West Wall, 220
Gerow, S. Sgt. Francis, 42
Gestapo, 69, 274, 343
Gibson, Sgt. Douglas, 250, 308
Giles, Maj. Gen. Barney M., 223, 227
Global Mission (Arnold), 219
Goering, Hermann, 9, 80, 264–65, 327–30, 337–38, 344
Grable, Betty, 27
Grafton-Underwood base, 70, 71, 76, 159, 160, 214, 269, 285, 322, 343
Gravesend base, 323
Greenham Common Air Service Command base, 341–43
Greig, Sir Louis, 199
Grenier, Sgt. Walter, 274
Griffith, Maj. James J., 43
Gross, Col. William M., 32, 41, 62

Hamburg, 36, 79, 169, 241, 255
Handke, Corp. Erich, 190
Hanover, rubber factory at, 242
Harding, Col. Neil B., 5, 273, 285
Hargis, Lt. Jack, 53, 66, 67
Harmon, Millard, 197
Harold II, King, 255
Harriman, Averell, 186, 199, 227, 228
Harris, Air Chief Marshal Sir Arthur, 10, 96, 98, 101–3, 104–11, 112–14, 115–17, 119–20, 125, 129, 134, 136, 138, 141, 144, 161, 168, 170–71, 172, 179, 188, 191, 195, 199, 204, 206, 237–38, 256, 257, 265, 347
Harris, Maj. George W., 285, 308
Harris, Lady Jill, 101, 120, 136, 161, 198, 347

Hastings, Battle of, 255
Hatcher, Col. William A., Jr., 85, 215
Haw Haw, Lord, 271
Hayworth, Rita, 27
Heidelberg, 18
Heinkel Aircraft Company, 38
Henry VIII, King, 159
Heroya, gunpowder factory at, 241
Herstal, Belgium, 44, 47
High Wycombe headquarters, 9, 23, 100, 161, 196, 199, 281, 287
Hitler, Adolf, 27, 36, 38, 77, 80–83, 89, 94, 96, 98, 101, 103, 110, 122, 125, 137, 142, 173, 180, 190, 196, 215, 235, 325, 327, 329, 330, 337–39, 342
Hitler Youth, 312
Hobby, Col. Oveta Culp, 129
Hodges, Brig. Gen. James, 86
Hodson, Maj. Robert, 314
Hong Kong, Japanese capture of, 91
Hope, Bob, 211
Hopkins, Harry, 120, 165, 167, 171, 179, 237
Horham, town of, 252, 273
Howden, Audrea, 251, 252
Hoyt, Lt. Elton "Pete," 57, 76
H2S (radar device), 266, 340
Hudson, Lt. Charles, 279
Hughes, Col. Richard D., 86, 237, 238
Hull, Col. Harris, 93, 117, 186, 238
Hunter, Brig. Gen. Frank O'D., 208, 217, 222, 228
Hutton, Betty, 271

"Ineffective Fighter Support to Bombardment in the U.K." (O'Donnell memo), 224
"Into the Air, Army Airmen" (anthem), 270
Italian campaign, 264

Jacobs, Flight Officer Randy, 76
Janos, Sgt. George, 274
Jeschonnek, Gen. Hans, 80
Jones, Lt. E. O., 315

Judy, Lt. James D., 63–64, 73–74
Judy, Sgt. Leland, 54
Junkers-88 fighter/bombers, 15, 21, 86, 94, 277, 294, 344

Kaech, Sgt. Delmar, 51
Kassel aircraft factories, 242, 255
Kegelman, Capt. Charles C., 135
Kenney, Gen. George C., 160, 197, 256
Kenny, Maj. Thomas F., 2, 154, 323
Kepner, Maj. Gen. William, 223, 227, 228
Kessler, Col. Alfred, 215
Kessler, Dr. Philip, 339
Kiel, 216, 226, 241, 246, 277
Kimbolton base, 29, 76, 102, 159, 212, 255, 270, 285, 323
Kimbolton Boys' School, 159, 255–56
Kindelberger, James H. "Dutch," 179
King, Adm. Ernest J., 10, 185, 205, 209
Knerr, Hugh, 228
Knoke, Lt. Heinz, 292, 298, 318
Knox, Capt. Robert, 13
Koontz, Flight Officer Glenn H., 46
Kugelfischer & Company, 57, 81, 260, 311–12, 325

La Palisse raid, 234
Lafayette Escadrille, 317
Lancaster bombers, 118, 124, 146, 155, 171, 180, 237
Langer, Lt. Hans, 37–38, 51, 52, 64, 300, 303
Langford, Frances, 211
Latham, Capt. James L., 314
Lay, Lt. Col. Beirne, Jr., 5–6, 8, 17, 20, 93, 117, 178
Layn, Lt. Roger W., 63, 73
Le Mans raid, 234
LeFors, Lt. Jerry, 316
Leigh-Mallory, Air Marshal Sir Trafford, 261
LeMay, Col. Curtis E., 3–4, 12, 17, 20–21, 30, 35, 76, 77–78, 86, 88, 90, 159, 160, 176, 177, 201, 241, 259, 267, 283
Liberator, see B-24 Liberator bombers
Lockhart, Lt. Eugene M., 53, 71
London Daily Mail, 146
London Times, 140, 180, 346
Longfellow, Col. Newton, 138, 177–78, 220, 227
Lorient missions, 176, 246
Lovett, Robert A., 217, 218, 220, 227, 234, 261
Luftwaffe, 9, 36, 37–39, 80, 121, 184, 263–65, 274, 301, 326–28, 329, 332, 336–38
Lyon, Ben, 138

MacArthur, Gen. Douglas, 91, 93, 256
McCabe, Sgt. Donald, 323
McClanahan, Lt. James, 42
McCollom, Maj. Loren G., 4–6
McCord, Lt. Lawrence, 57
McElwain, Lt. R. F., 57
McFann, Lt. Miles, 320–21, 324
McKay, S. Sgt. Kenneth, 42, 55
McKeegan, Lt. Rothery, 65
McLaughlin, Capt. James K., 289, 297–300
Macmillan, Harold, 186
Majewski, Sgt. Casmir, 213, 214
Manston, British Air-Sea Rescue Station at, 72
Marienburg, aircraft factories at, 280, 338
Marshall, Gen. George C., 120–22, 124, 125, 130, 137, 151, 193, 195, 209, 263, 346
Martin, Lt. Richard, 66
Masefield, Peter, 140, 180
Matériel Command, 216, 219
Mendelsohn, Lt. Stuart, 306, 319
Menjou, Adolphe, 211
Messerschmitt-109 fighter/bomber, 1, 7, 8, 13, 17, 36, 37, 38, 43, 46, 47, 50, 52, 62, 163, 178, 179, 217, 258, 292, 294, 298–300, 302, 314, 318, 327, 340, 344

Messerschmitt-110 fighter/bomber,
13, 15, 21, 36, 37, 46, 47, 62,
65, 70, 94, 190, 294
Messerschmitt-210 fighter/bomber,
46, 62, 65, 287, 294
Michaud, Sgt. H. K., 51
Middleton, Drew, 134
Milch, Field Marshal Erhard, 80,
338
Miller, Glenn, 270
Miller, S. Sgt. L. Corwin, 31, 42–
43, 48, 55, 70, 71, 213, 214,
270
Millson, Capt. Edwin, 212, 285,
298, 306–8, 323
Milton, Lt. Col. Theodore, 289–
90, 295, 305
Ministry of Aircraft Production,
291
Ministry of Economic Warfare,
205, 206, 236–38
Mitchell, Maj. Kirk, 57
Mitchell, Col. William "Billy," 133
Molders Wing (Luftwaffe), 300,
303, 327
Molesworth base, 29, 102, 135,
159, 255
Molzon, S. Sgt. Walter, 309
Montreuil, 66–68
Montzen, 17
Moore, Lt. Bruce D., 279, 295, 308
Moore, Col. John, 215
Mosquito weather plane, 287
Munger, Lt. William, 44
Münster raid, 280, 284
Murphy, Robert, 186
Murphy, Lt. Thomas E., 8

Nantes raid, 234
Nazzaro, Col. Joseph, 268, 283
Nettles, Lt. Silas, 315–16
Neubiberg, 37, 51, 300, 327
New York Mirror, 163
New York Times, The, 164
Nicolescu, Lt. George, 46
Norden bomb-sight, 26, 27, 57,
104, 112, 306
Normand, Maj. C. G. Y., 289, 305
Norstad, Col. Lauris, 77, 87

North African Air Force
(N.A.A.F.), 264–65
North African invasion, see Opera-
tion Torch
North American Aviation Com-
pany, 178
Nuremberg, 339

O'Donnell, Col. Emmet "Rosey,"
224
O'Hearn, Lt. Robert E., 316
Old, Col. Archie, Jr., 215, 276,
283, 290, 300, 314, 318, 323
Operation Torch, 137, 151, 167–69,
183, 186, 192
Oschersleben, Focke-Wulf plant at,
242, 278
Overacker, Col. Charles B. "Chip,"
158, 177
Owen, Kyffin, 159, 255–56

Parton, Capt. James, 185, 199
Paulsen, Sgt. Walter, 69
Peaslee, Col. Budd J., 213, 214–15,
232, 269, 286, 288–90, 297–
98, 300, 305–7, 322
Peck, Air Vice Marshal R. H., 111
Peenemünde, 80, 239, 263
Pellegrini, Lt. John, 306
Pershing, Gen. John J., 113
P-51 Mustang fighters, 167, 178–
80, 217, 218, 219, 220, 236,
263, 300, 333, 341–42, 344
P-47 Thunderbolt bombers, 3–7,
45–46, 64, 65, 70, 178, 179–
80, 207–8, 216, 217, 219,
220–25, 234, 236, 255, 267,
273, 279, 285, 290–92, 297–
98, 300, 318, 336, 341, 344
Philippines, 91, 133, 138, 220
Pinetree (command headquarters),
23, 32, 161
Podington base, 286, 322
Polebrook base, 29, 84, 102, 135,
136, 140, 142, 144, 271, 272
Pompetti, Flight Officer Pete E., 46
Portal, Air Chief Marshal Sir
Charles, 10, 100, 102, 111,
120, 123, 125, 129, 138, 141,
155–58, 163–64, 167–68, 169,

171–72, 173, 174, 179, 181–83, 184, 185, 191, 194–95, 200, 204, 205, 209, 238, 240, 256–57, 260, 264, 280, 291, 347
"Position of the 8th Air Force, The" (Eaker), 202
Posl, Ludwig, 325
"Praise the Lord and Pass the Ammunition," 270
Preston, Col. Maurice A., 29–30, 31, 49, 56, 212, 215
Prestwick base, 213, 217
Price, Maj. J. C., 65
Prince of Wales (warship), 91
Prisoner of War Camp Stalag 3, 274
Provisional Medical Field Service School, 139
P-38 bombers, 38, 218, 263, 333, 340–41

Question Mark (airplane), 92
Question Mark endurance flight, 133

Radar box defense system (Germany), 118
Rammelt, Maj. Karl, 301
Rand, S. Sgt. Leo, 277, 286, 313–14, 323–24
Raper, Maj. William S., 33, 56
Rastenburg (German headquarters), 82, 327
Redgrave, Daphne, 253
Republic Aviation Company, 178
Repulse (warship), 91
Reuters News Agency, 163
Ridgewell base, 268
Riseley base, 322
Roane, Lt. Owen D. "Cowboy," 273
Robb, Capt. Derwyn, 271
Roberts, Maj. Eugene, 46
Rodwell, Basel, 252
Rohr, Lt. Col. Louis W., 285, 305
Rohr, Capt. Ted, 323
Romilly sur Seine, 176
Roosevelt, Elliott, 87
Roosevelt, Franklin D., 27, 87, 120,

121, 123, 152, 165, 168, 171, 174, 184, 186, 235, 274, 334
Rotterdam mission, 201
Rouen, 141, 144, 150, 176, 201
Roundup (code name), 137
Rourke, S. Sgt. John, 320
Royal Air Force (R.A.F.), 10, 40–41, 69–70, 95, 96–97, 101, 103, 104, 105, 106, 108, 110–14, 115–21, 123, 125, 129, 134, 137, 146, 149, 153, 158–59, 160, 166, 168, 171, 176, 179–82, 184, 187, 191, 195, 203, 204, 206, 238, 250, 253, 254, 261–65, 266, 274, 280–81, 324, 335, 347
   8th Air Force and, 146–67
   night raids, 102–5, 110–13, 119, 144–63
R.A.F. Bomber Command, 97, 100, 105, 117
R.A.F. Coastal Command, 348
Royal Flying Corps, 97
Royal Scots Fusiliers, 153
Rubell, Capt. Gunther, 301–2
Russell, Jane, 27

St. Nazaire, 177, 231, 232, 246
St. Omer Airfield, 215
St. Paul's Cathedral, 98
Samford, Col. John A., 227
Sargent, Capt. Roland L., 44, 48, 62
Saundby, Air Vice Marshal Robert, 111, 112
Saward, Group Capt. Dudley, 141
Schafer, Georg, 58, 61, 81
Schaub, Julius, 327
Schilling, Maj. David C., 300
Schimenek, S. Sgt. John F., 31, 42, 48, 55, 70, 213, 214
Schoolfield, Capt., 305
Schweinfurt mission:
   Allied political reactions, 334–36
   casualties, 62, 66, 233, 259, 323–25, 336
   destruction of German war industries, 21, 58–61, 86–88, 260, 266–68, 325–30, 331–35

Luftwaffe losses, 329–30, 331–32

military reaction to, 259–81

planning of, 231–58

second raid, 282–340

success of, 334–40

Searchlight belt (Germany), 118

Seniawsky, S. Sgt. Peter, 317, 342

Shackley, Maj. George, 288

Sheeler, Capt. Donald, 28

Sherwin, Lt. Robert, 53

Sherwood, Robert, 199

Ship Building Commission (Germany), 78

Shore, Dinah, 271

Short Statistical Report on War Production (1945), 82

Sinatra, Frank, 271

Sinclair, Sir Archibald, 153–57, 158, 168–71, 174, 180, 181, 183, 191, 261

Singapore, Japanese capture of, 91

Slayton, Lt. Samuel, 54, 306

Slessor, Air Marshal John, 153–56, 157, 158, 168, 174, 184, 260, 265

Smith, Sgt. Norman, 18, 20

Smith, Capt. William R., 29, 46–47, 84, 85, 87, 89, 271–73, 347

Smuts, Ian Christian, 110

Snetterton Heath base, 276, 283, 323

Snettisham, gunnery training range at, 214

Sotteville raid, 142–43

Sowter, Jimmy, 253

Spaatz, Lt. Gen. Carl, 77, 87, 93, 95, 103, 106, 124, 132–34, 135, 136, 137–38, 141, 144, 148–49, 151, 153, 158, 161, 165, 166, 170, 171, 172, 177, 178, 181, 199, 228, 240, 241, 258, 344

Speer, Albert, 78–80, 81, 82–83, 86, 261, 327–30, 338–40

Sperry Company, 93

Spitfire escort airplanes, 41, 43, 45, 70, 72, 117, 142, 144, 162, 178, 179, 212, 234, 321

Starkey (mock invasion operation), 266

Stedtfeld, 2nd Lt. Gunther, 300–303, 304, 327, 338

Stendal base, 36

Stenger, Wilhelm, 81, 311, 326

Stevens, Col. Kermit D., 29, 57, 255

Stewart, Lt. J. D., 44, 48

Steyr, ball-bearing factories at, 79, 340

Stone, Lt. Col. James F., 46

Stratemeyer, Maj. Gen. George, 215

Stroud, Maj. Henry, 71, 270

Stuka bombers, 294

Stuttgart, 263, 264, 274

Taylor, Sgt. Phillip R., 284

Tedder, Air Marshal Arthur, 200

Thorpe Abbots base, 14, 252, 273, 286

Thunderbolt bombers, see P-47 Thunderbolt bombers

Thurleigh base, 102, 158, 177

Timberlake, Col. Edward J., Jr., 150

Tobin, Lt. Edwin, 16, 69

Torch (code-name), see Operation Torch

Towers, Rear Adm. John H., 125, 127

Travis, Col. Robert, 276

Trenchard, Gen. Sir Hugh, 134

Tucker, Sgt. Gerold, 69, 343

Tucker, Sgt. Star A., 29, 127

Tunis, 76, 87

Turner, Col. Howard M. "Slim," 32–33, 56, 62, 323

Twelve O'clock High (Lay and Bartlett), 178

Twining, Nathan, 197

2 Gruppe Jagdgeschwader 51, 37, 51, 64

2 Gruppe Nachtjagdgeschwader, 36, 47

Tyson, Lt. S. W., 17

U-boat warfare (1942), 165

Ultra, 180–81, 264

U.S. 8th Air Force:
airplane shortages, 34–35
Bomber Command, 91–114, 115–31
Casablanca Directive and, 189, 204
casualties, 62–63, 66, 233, 259, 323, 335–36
crew training, 210–30
daylight precision bombing raids, 10, 25, 40–41, 89, 97, 102–5, 111–13, 182–91, 192–209, 235, 334, 339
difficulties with the British, 148–75
early bombing missions and, 132–47
England-Africa shuttle, 77–83, 84–90
flying formations, 5, 176–77
long-range fighter escorts, 341–45
missions and operations with R.A.F. 176–90
morale problems, 242–55, 268–70
R.A.F. night raids and, 103–5, 110–13, 119, 144–47, 148–63
second Schweinfurt raid, 282–340
See also names of planes

Vandevanter, Col. Elliott, 6
Vega Aircraft Corporation, 216
Vegesack, submarine yards at, 190, 199
Vereingte Kugellager Fabrik (VKF), 58, 260, 310–12, 326
Versailles Treaty, 98
Vogelsand Airport, 47
V-rockets, 263

Wall, Capt. Joseph G., 285, 307
Wallace, Col. James H., 159
Wannebecq, town of, 69
Warnemünde raid, 241, 242
Warsaw, Lt. Ernest, 13, 16, 69, 253, 274
Watten raid, 265
Weger, Wilhelm, 59

Wehner, Leo, 59, 60, 311
Weichsel, Heinrich, 310–12, 326
Weitzenfeld, Capt. Richard, 74, 75
Wetzel, T. Sgt. Willard, 322
"Why Have U.S. Bombers Not Bombed Germany?" (Eaker), 185, 207
"Why There Have Been so Few Missions" (Eaker), 192
"Why There Have Been so Many Abortive Sorties" (Eaker), 192
Widewing (code-name), 33, 132
Wiener-Neustadt, 80, 239
Wilhelm I, Kaiser, 92
Wilhelmshaven, port of, 190, 192, 199, 225, 246, 340
William the Conqueror, 255
Williams, Capt. David, 28, 44, 54, 290, 304
Williams, Brig. Gen. Robert B., 24, 25, 31, 32, 45, 54, 58, 62, 74–75, 89, 231, 232–33, 262, 267
Winant, John G., 128
Winslow, Lt. Edward P. "Ted," 28, 44, 53, 66–68, 69, 278, 293, 343
Winterbotham, Group Capt. Frederick W., 180, 181
Wittan, Col. Edgar, 13
Woensdrecht, 6
Wolf, Lt. Richard V., 43, 308
Women's Auxiliary Air Force (England), 108, 129
Woodbury, Lt. Clive, 72
Wray, Col. Stanley, 41, 159–60
Wright Field, 219
Wurzbach, Lt. Col. Clemens L., 32, 45, 54
Würzburg, 305
Wycombe Abbey, 106, 108, 117, 122, 129

YB-40 fighters, 216
Yorkshire Evening Post, 163

Zeeland, islands of, 4
Zeist, Holland, 35
Zemke, Col. Hubert, 6, 64, 65
Zuppke, Bob, 30